Ride the Airwaves with ALFA & ZULU

Preparation for the Novice

and

No-Code Technician

Amateur Radio License Examinations

by

John Abbott, K6YB

ABTRONIX
POB 220066
Newhall, CA 91322 U.S.A.
(805) 222-7384
(805) 222-7385 (FAX)

Ride the Airwaves with ALFA & ZULU
by John Abbott, K6YB

Preparation for the Novice and No-Code Technician
Amateur Radio License Examinations

ABTRONIX
POB 220066
Newhall, CA 91322 U.S.A.

All rights reserved. No part of this book may be reproduced or transmitted in any form or by any means, electronic or mechanical, including photocopying, recording, or by any information storage and retrevial system without written permission from the publisher, *ABTRONIX*, except for the inclusion of brief quotations in a review.

Copyright © 1992, 1993, 1996 John Abbott
Copyright © 1996 *ABTRONIX*

First Printing 1993
Second Printing 1995, revised
Third Printing 1996, completely revised

Limit of Liability/Disclosure of Warranty: The author and publisher have used their best efforts in preparing this book. *ABTRONIX* and the author make no representation or warranties with respect to the accuracy or completeness of the contents of this book and specifically disclaim any implied warranties of use for any particular purpose, and shall in no event be liable for any damage, including, but not limited to special, incidental, consequential, or other damages.

Warning - Disclaimer: This book is designed to provide information in regard to the subject matter covered. It is sold with the understanding that the publisher and author are not engaged in rendering technical professional services. The purpose of this manual is to educate and entertain. The author and *ABTRONIX* shall have neither liability nor responsibility to any person or entity with respect to any loss or damage caused, or alleged to be caused, directly or indirectly, by the informaiton contained in this book. **If you do not wish to be bound by the above, you may return this book to the publisher for a full refund.**

Acknowledgement: The Space Shuttle, International Space Station, Moon Rover, MIR Space station, and Hubble Telescope drawings, were adapted from material provided by the National Aeronautics and Space Administration (NASA) Teacher Resource Center, Jet Propulsion Laboratories (JPL) Educational Outreach, Pasadena, California, 91109.

ISBN 0-9651088-0-5 $14.95

WHAT IS HAM RADIO?

Ham radio is a fun hobby! It allows people all over the world to communicate *continuously* with each other, and is available to anyone, anywhere, who has obtained an amateur radio license. You will always find a friend to talk to!

Ham Radio becomes a part of you, as you are now KZ6XYZ, or whatever call sign is issued to you by the Federal Communications Commission. Whether you are 8 or 88, doesn't matter when you are on the air! Those who obtain their licenses will have the "ham experience" for the rest of their lives, and may be able to provide communications to help people during emergencies. Ham Radio can bring you many advantages, and lead to a career in science or communications.

Ham Radio will give you:

1) <u>The ability to talk over a microphone to *anyone*</u>. Once this ability is acquired, public speaking becomes a natural. Never again will you suffer "stage fright", or feel ill at ease when speaking. You will be able to "think as you talk"!

2) <u>A knowledge of the Morse code</u>. Morse code was the first method of radio communications, and was the beginning of today's digital communications. Persons who are physically unable to use either a "mouse" or a key board, can use Morse code to operate computers! Morse code uses the least amount of radio spectrum, can "get through" when voice cannot, and permits contact between people with different languages. Contact with deep space satellites is maintained using very slow speed digital signals, similar to Morse code. If we contact another civilization in space, it will probably be by the use of slow speed digital communications!

3) <u>A knowledge of geography</u>. Ham Radio crosses all borders and time zones. You will talk to people worldwide and become aware of "Universal Time", measured in Greenwich, England. When a station is contacted, it can be located on a map of the U.S.A. or world, and you and the ham at the other end can share interesting details about your locations.

4) <u>A beginning technical knowledge of radio, electronics, and an application of mathematics</u>. Ham Radio requires a knowledge of basic mathematics. You will see how electrical currents flow in a circuit, begin to understand how a radio wave travels around the earth, learn that all phenomenon in the universe are related to some form of electromagnetic wave, such as the light and heat from the stars, planets, and the sun. You will experience the sun's effect on radio waves, caused by eruptions on the sun called "sunspots". *MOST OF ALL YOU WILL HAVE FUN!*

73 (Best Regards!)

K6YB

How To Use This Book For Self Study

"Ride the Airwaves with ALFA & ZULU" was written to simplify the experience of studying for the Novice and No-Code Technician amateur radio licenses.

The No-Code Technician examination substitutes 25 technical questions for the 5 word-per-minute code test of the 30 question Novice examination, for a total of 55 questions. The two licenses are very different: The No-Code Technician license gives full amateur operating privileges on very high and ultra high frequencies (VHF & UHF), but no privileges on high frequencies (HF); The Novice license provides limited operating privileges on HF, VHF, and UHF wavelengths. Of course you can take the Novice code test <u>and</u> the No-Code Technican theory examination, for combined operating privileges as a Technician Plus!

Decide which license you wish to obtain, and refer to the Table of Contents for the topics you will need to study. The Novice license requires theory <u>Element 2 (*page 3*)</u>, and <u>Morse code Element 1A (*page 145*)</u>, and permits Morse code operation on 80 (3.675 to 3.725 MHz), 40 (7.1 to 7.15 MHz), and 15 (21.1 to 21.2 MHz) meters, and Morse code, voice, and data operation on 10 (28.1 to 28.5 MHz), 1.25 (222 to 225 MHz), and 0.23 (1270 to 1295 MHz) meters. The No-Code Technician license requires theory <u>Element 2 and Element 3A (*page 151*)</u>, but not Morse code Element 1A, and grants full amateur privileges on 6 (50 to 54 MHz) meters and above, including the Novice 1.25 and 0.23 meter (23 centimeter) bands. For reference, AM broadcast radio is 0.54 to 1.7 MHz (HF), and FM broadcast radio is 88 to 108 MHz (VHF). See the Novice and Technician Ham Bands chart on *page xii*.

The primary object of this book is to provide you with the minimum amount of information required to pass the Novice and No-Code Technician examinations. A detailed technical explanation of many of the subjects tends to confuse and discourage many potential new amateurs. The rule is "KISS" - Keep It Short & Simple! Additional information is available elsewhere, when you are ready to go further. The following organizations publish many excellent technical books, have computer examination software available, and provide free material for beginners:

1) The American Radio Relay League (Examinaiton Location Information, ARRL Publications & Code Tapes), 225 Main St., Newington, CT 06111 (800-326-3942)

2) W5YI Group Inc. (Examination Location Information, IBM Test Software, & Code Tapes), P.O. Box 565101, Dallas, TX 75356 (800-669-9594)

3) Kawa Records (The Rhythm of the Code Tapes), POB 319-RF, Weymouth, MA 02188 (617-331-1826)

4) Media Mentors Inc (Publications & "Spacecode" Tapes), POB 131646, Staten Island, NY, 10313-0006 (718-983-1416)

5) Coyne Co. (MacIntosh Test Software), P.O. Box 2000-200, Mission Viejo, CA 92692

Taking The Examination

After studying this book, you will reach the point where you are familiar with all of the questions, and are ready for the Element 2 and 3A "written" examinations. You can test yourself by making up your own tests, as described on page 240. If you have also been learning the Morse code, and can receive the 26 letters of the alphabet, the 10 numbers 0 through 9, and the 7 punctuation (and operation) symbols, at 5 words per minute (WPM), you are also ready for the Element 1A "code" examination.

You can create your own written examinations by using the method on page 240. However, if you have a computer available, you can purchase IBM compatible softwave from the ARRL or W5YI Group Inc., or Macintosh software from the Coyne Co., which will allow you to take sample written examinations on the computer. If not, you can purchase published sample copies of the written examination from W5YI. Software is also available for taking the code examination, or you can purchase a new 5 WPM code tape that you are unfamiliar with.

Examinations are given in all major communities throughout the United States, and are usually sponsored by local radio clubs. You can also call the ARRL (800-927-7583) or W5YI Group Inc.(800-669-9594), to determine where a nearby examination point is located, and the dates on which the examinations will be given.

Element 2 is the first examination that you will take. Every amateur applicant must pass this examination before any other test can be taken. After passing Element 2, you can elect to take either Element 3A for the Technician license, or the Morse code Element 1A examination for the Novice license, or both, if you want the Technician Plus license.

In order to take the examination, "Section I" of Federal Communications Commission (FCC) Form 610, "Application For Amateur Radio Station/Operator License" must be filled out by you. This form will be given to you at the test location, and requires your name, date of birth, current mailing address, current station location, and your signature. There are also two "yes" or "no" questions, one regarding the environment and one regarding additional applications you may have with the FCC. The examiners will fill out the rest of the form. Be sure to bring identification, such as a drivers license, birth certificate, or even mail addressed to you.

Your written examination will be graded immediately, and a score of 74% is passing. This means that you must have 23 out of 30 questions correct for Element 2, and 19 out of 25 questions correct for Element 3A. The code examination, Element 1A, can be passed either by answering 7 out of 10 questions on what was sent, or copying exactly what was sent for a 1 minute period.

New computer procedures have speeded up license processing, and you will be given a telephone number that you can call to obtain your new call letters, and get on the air immediately!

Getting On The Air

You can have a lot of fun using inexpensive, low power equipment, on HF. You won't be "on top of the pile" when contacting (QSO) distant (DX) stations, but you will have great satisfaction when you do get a DX QSO. It will require extra operating ability and patience, and often these techniques will let you snare DX that the "Big Guns" miss. However, a good antenna is required, and very few city dwelling hams are able to install an effective HF antenna system. With a poor antenna, low power on HF means very few QSOs, and a minimum of 100 watts is usually needed on the Novice HF bands.

On VHF & UHF, high power is not necessary because of the high gain, easily installed antennas, that can be used to increase the effective power of your signal. A 5 to 25 watt transceiver is usually adequate.

The simplest antenna for either HF, VHF, or UHF operation, is a ground plane vertical. (Refer to pages 123 and 129). The HF "all-band" ground plane vertical will work well if mounted on the ground in a clear area. It requires a good ground system, consisting of buried wires radiating outward from its base, creating a "ground plane". The VHF and UHF ground plane verticals should be mounted high above the ground in a clear area, and connected to the station with low loss cable.

Both new and used equipment are advertised in several amateur radio publications. Write to the publishers and request or purchase a copy of their magazine, so that you can decide which ones to subscribe to. Some of the publications are:

QST - ARRL, 225 Main St., Newington, CT 06111-1494, $30/yr ($24/yr, age 65)
CQ - CQ Communications, Inc., 76 N. Broadway, Hicksville, NY 11801-2953, $25/yr
73 - 73 Amateur Radio Today, POB 50330, Boulder, CO 80321-0330, $25/yr
Amateur Radio Trader, POB 3729, Crossville, TN 38557, $15/yr
Worldradio - Worldradio Inc., 520 Calvados Ave., Sacramento, CA 95815, $15/yr

A visit to a local ham equipment store is also recommended, so that you can see first hand what is available. These stores also carry ham publications and books. The names and telephone numbers of some large suppliers are:

Amateur Electronic Supply, Inc. - 800-558-0411
Ham Radio Outlet - 800-854-6046
Henry Radio - 800-877-7979
Honolulu Electronics - 808-949-8564
Jun's Electronics - 800-882-1343
Maryland Radio Center - 800-447-7489
Michigan Radio - 800-878-4266

Radio Shack also carries a limited amount of amateur equipment. Consult the yellow pages of your telephone book for more information on electronic equipment stores near you.

RIDE THE AIRWAVES WITH ALFA & ZULU

Table of Contents

I. Novice Amateur Radio License

FCC Elements 2 & 1A

Topic	Page
1. On the Air with ALPHA & ZULU	3
2. Signal Reports & Q - Signals	7
3. Identification & Q - Signals	9
4. Amateur Radio Purpose & Rules	11
5. Definitions	13
6. Station & Operator Licenses	15
7. License Possession & Classes	17
8. Eligibility, Exam Elements, & U.S. Call Signs	19
9. Mailing Address, Lost & Renewed Licenses	21
10. Emergency Operation	23
11. Operating Your Own Station	25
12. Operating Another Station	27
13. U.S. Operation, Non-Ham QSOs, & Space Stations	29
14. Unauthorized Persons	31
15. Business Use of Amateur Radio	33
16. Third-Party & Foreign Contacts	35
17. Broadcasting, Music, Codes, & Harmful Interference	37
18. Unidentified & False Signals	39
19. Respect for Others	41
20. FM Repeaters	43
21. Simplex & Repeater Operation	45

22. Morse Code Emissions & Connections..47

23. Morse Code Operation..49

24. Voice Emissions & Connections..51

25. RTTY Emissions & Connections...53

26. Packet Emissions & Connections..55

27. Packet Operation..57

28. Direct Current, Alternating Current, & Frequency..............................59

29. Audio & Radio Frequencies...61

30. Hertz, Kilohertz, & Megahertz..63

31. Frequency & Wavelength..65

32. CW ONLY Frequencies...67

33. CW ONLY Frequency Emissions...69

34. CW, Voice, & Data Frequencies...71

35. CW, Voice, & Data Frequency Emissions..73

36. Energy, Power & Watts...75

37. High Frequency Power...77

38. Very High & Ultra High Frequency Power..79

39. Ground Wave, Sky Wave, & Sunspots..81

40. Line-of-Sight Communications..83

41. Voltage..85

42. Insulators, Conductors, Current, & Resistance................................87

43. Ohm's Law, Open & Short Circuits..89

44. Meters, Amperes, Volts, Farads, & Watts.......................................91

45. Resistor, Fuse, & Battery Symbols..93

46. Switch Symbols..95

47. Transistor & Tube Symbols	97
48. Antenna & Ground Symbols	99
49. Power Supplies	101
50. Receiver Overload	103
51. Harmonic Radiation	105
52. Harmonic Calculations	107
53. Spurious Emissions	109
54. Splatter	111
55. Standing Wave Ratio	113
56. Unusual SWR Readings, Power Meters	115
57. Antenna Feed Lines & Tuners, SWR Meters	117
58. Station Diagrams	119
59. Half-Wave Antenna Length	121
60. Quarter-Wave Vertical Length	123
61. Changing Antenna Length	125
62. The "Yagi" Beam Antenna	127
63. Vertical & Dipole Antennas	129
64. Coaxial Cable	131
65. Coaxial Cable Connections	133
66. Parallel Conductor Feed Lines	135
67. Health Risk & Antenna Location	137
68. Safety	139
69. Grounding	141
70. Lightning Protection	143
71. <u>INTERNATIONAL MORSE CODE</u>	145

II. Technician Amateur Radio License

FCC Element 3A

Topic	Page
1. Signal Reports & "Q" Signals	151
2. Identification	153
3. Emergency Operation	155
4. Radio Amateur Civil Emergency Service	159
5. Control Point & License Renewal	161
6. Broadcasting, Third-Party, & Non-Amateur Contacts	163
7. Respect for Others	165
8. Dummy Antennas	167
9. FM Repeater Operation	169
10. FM Repeater Coordination, Open & Closed Repeaters	173
11. FM Repeater Frequencies & Simplex Operation	175
12. CW & Data Modulation & Emissions	177
13. Voice Modulation & Emissions	179
14. Digital Symbol Rate	181
15. RTTY & Data Frequency Shift & Bandwidth	183
16. High & Very High Frequencies	185
17. Frequency Use & Emissions	187
18. Beacon Stations & Model Craft	189
19. Transmitter Power	191
20. RF Filters & Signal Bandwidth	193
21. Detectors, VFO's, & FM Circuits	195
22. Signal & Marker Generators, Crystal Calibrators, WWV	197

23. The Ionosphere..199

24. Ionospheric Absorption.......................................201

25. Ionospheric Changes..203

26. Troposphere VHF Communications.....................205

27. Scatter & VHF Skip...207

28. Ohm's Law...209

29. Resistors..211

30. Inductors...213

31. Inductor Cores & Symbols..................................215

32. Capacitors..217

33. Voltmeters & Ammeters......................................219

34. Wattmeters..221

35. Standing Wave Ratio & Reflectometers...............223

36. Beam Antennas..225

37. Non-Directional Antennas & Polarization.............227

38. Feed Line Losses..229

39. Baluns, Connectors, & Coax................................231

40. Health Risk & Antenna Location..........................233

41. Electrical Wiring...235

42. Safety..237

III. Binary Numbers & Question Index

1. Binary Numbers..239

2. Create Your Own Tests...240

3. Question Number-Answer-Page Number...............241

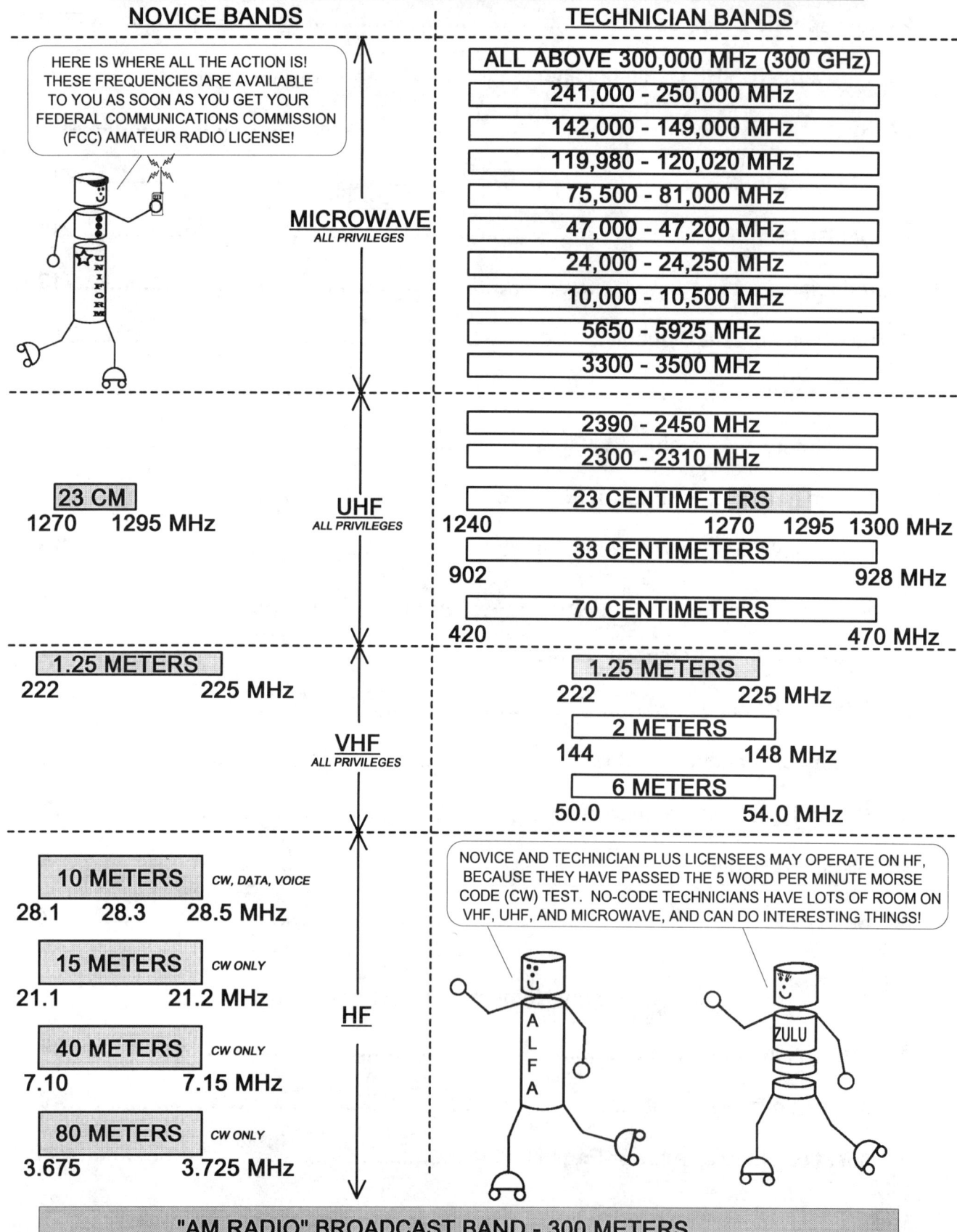

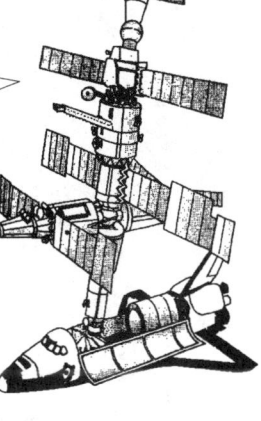

NOVICE AMATEUR RADIO LICENSE
FCC ELEMENTS 2 & 1A

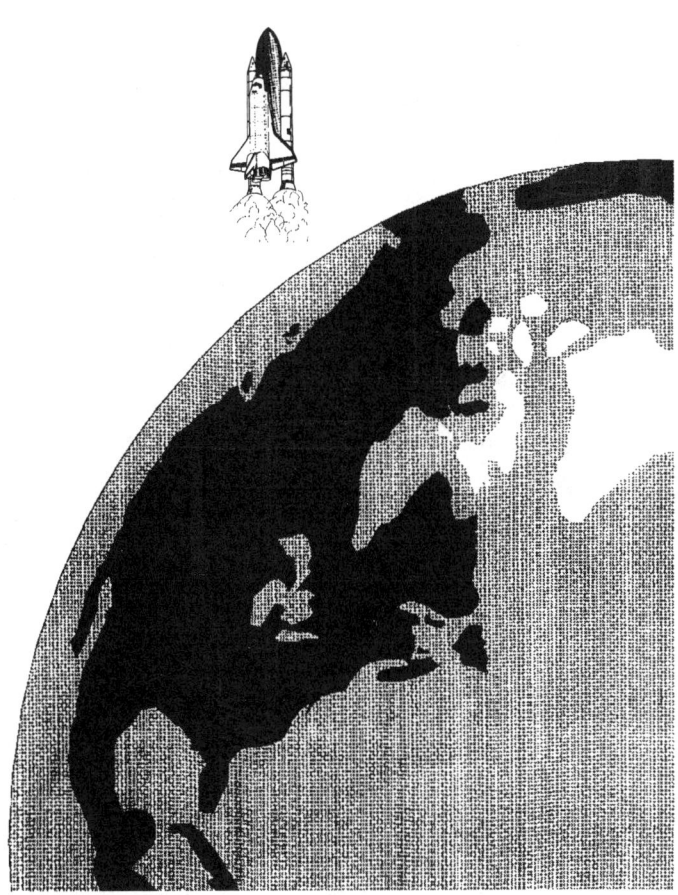

THE PHONETICOS

THE BULL — THE HORSE — THE DEER — THE ELECTRON — THE FOX

THE GOLFER — THE TRAVELER — THE INFO MAN — THE KID — THE LADY — THE MULE — NOVEMBER

THE GIRAFFE — THE PENQUIN — THE QUEEN — THE SKIER — THE DANCER — THE OFFICER — THE WINNER

THE CAT — THE TECHNICAN — DOODLE DANDY — THE ZULU

THE NUMERICOS

1 — 2 — 3 — 4 — 5 — 6 — 7 — 8 — 9 — 0

THE PUNCTUOS

COMMA — PERIOD — QUESTION — SLASH — EQUALS (PAUSE) — TRANSMISSION END — CONTACT END

THE BINARYOS

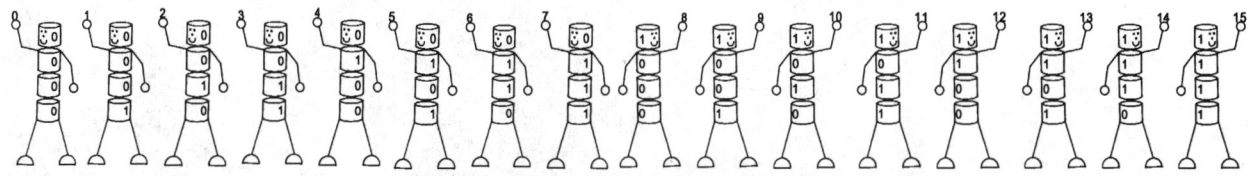

ON THE AIR WITH ALFA & ZULU
NOVICE LESSON 1

ALFA & ZULU are "Phoneticos", and ham radio operators. Their origin is the beginning and end of the phonetic alphabet, which is used on the air to make communications clearer. Their bodies are radio, or *electromagnetic* waves, in the form of Morse code letters!

STANDARD INTERNATIONAL PHONETIC ALPHABET

A - ALFA (AL FAH)	N - NOVEMBER (NO VEM BER)
B - BRAVO (BRAH VOH)	O - OSCAR (OSS CAH)
C - CHARLIE (CHAR LEE)	P - PAPA (PAH PAH)
D - DELTA (DELL TAH)	Q - QUEBEC (KEH BECK)
E - ECHO (ECK OH)	R - ROMEO (ROW ME OH)
F - FOXTROT (FOKS TROT)	S - SIERRA (SEE AIR RAH)
G - GOLF	T - TANGO (TANG GO)
H - HOTEL (HOH TELL)	U - UNIFORM (YOU NEE FORM)
I - INDIA (IN DEE AH)	V - VICTOR (VIK TAH)
J - JULIET (JEW LEE ETT)	W - WHISKEY (WISS KEY)
K - KILO (KEY LOH)	X - X-RAY (ECKS RAY)
L - LIMA (LEE MAH)	Y - YANKEE (YANG KEY)
M - MIKE	Z - ZULU (ZOO LOO)

4

ALFA: CQ CQ CQ, THIS IS ALFA ALFA SIX ALFA ALFA ALFA, AA6AAA, ALFA ALFA SIX ALFA ALFA ALFA CALLING CQ AND STANDING BY.

X-RAY: KILO, WHAT DOES THE PROCEDURAL SIGNAL "CQ" MEAN?

KILO: IT MEANS CALLING ANY STATION. IT ALSO MEANS "SEEKING YOU". ALFA IS LOOKING FOR A CONTACT WITH ANYONE ON THE AIR WHO HEARS HIM.

YANKEE: QUEBEC, WHAT IS THE CORRECT WAY TO CALL CQ WHEN USING VOICE?

QUEBEC: SAY IT THE SAME WAY ALFA DOES - SAY "CQ" THREE TIMES, FOLLOWED BY "THIS IS", FOLLOWED BY YOUR CALL SIGN SPOKEN THREE TIMES.

GOLF: HOW SHOULD YOU ANSWER A VOICE CQ CALL, SIERRA?

SIERRA: SAY THE OTHER STATION'S CALL SIGN ONCE, FOLLOWED BY "THIS IS", THEN YOUR CALL SIGN GIVEN PHONETICALLY, JUST LIKE ZULU IS SAYING.

ROMEO: JULIET, I HAVE A COUPLE OF QUESTIONS - WHAT IS THE MEANING OF THE TERM "73" AND WHAT IS MEANT BY THE TERM "DX"?

JULIET: WELL, ROMEO, 73 MEANS "BEST REGARDS" AND DX MEANS "DISTANT STATION".

ZULU: ALFA ALFA SIX ALFA ALFA ALFA THIS IS KILO ZULU SIX ZULU ZULU ZULU, OVER. (I HOPE ALFA CAN HEAR ME! IT'S FUN HERE ON 10 METERS LATELY.)

BEST REGARDS!

NOW TRY THE QUIZ ON THE NEXT PAGE!

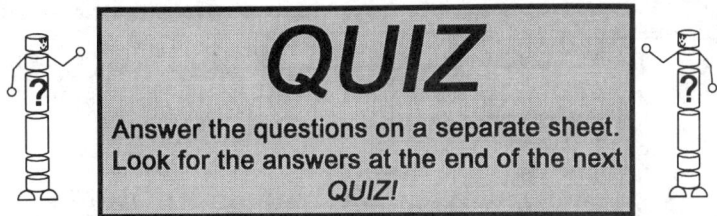

QUIZ

Answer the questions on a separate sheet. Look for the answers at the end of the next QUIZ!

N2A20
To make your call sign better understood when using voice transmissions, what should you do?
A. Use Standard International Phonetics for each letter of your call
B. Use any words which start with the same letters as your call sign for each letter of your call
C. Talk louder
D. Turn up your microphone gain

N2A08
What is the meaning of the procedural signal "CQ"?
A. "Call on the quarter hour"
B. "New antenna is being tested" (no station should answer)
C. "Only the called station should transmit"
D. "Calling any station"

N2A18
What is the correct way to call CQ when using voice?
A. Say "CQ" once, followed by "this is," followed by your call sign spoken three times
B. Say "CQ" at least five times, followed by "this is," followed by your call sign spoken once
C. Say "CQ" three times, followed by "this is," followed by your call sign spoken three times
D. Say "CQ" at least ten times, followed by "this is," followed by your call sign spoken once

N2A19
How should you answer a voice CQ call?
A. Say the other station's call sign at least ten times, followed by "this is," then your call sign at least twice
B. Say the other station's call sign at least five times phonetically, followed by "this is," then your call sign at least once
C. Say the other station's call sign at least three times, followed by "this is," then your call sign at least five times phonetically
D. Say the other station's call sign once, followed by "this is," then your call sign given phonetically

N2A12
What is the meaning of the term "73"?
A. Long distance
B. Best regards
C. Love and kisses
D. Go ahead

N2A11
What is meant by the term "DX"?
A. Best regards
B. Distant station
C. Calling any station
D. Go ahead

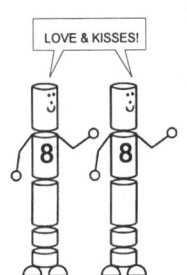

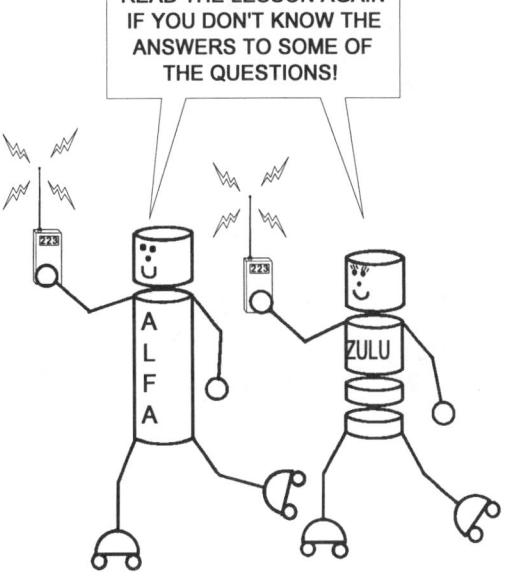

WORDSEARCH

```
R W H I S K E Y F R R I B E U U
E C H O V I C T O R J N N E Q E
G O L F T H E M X S K D E L T A
Z I B I A E E R T U C I S R L L
K U S R M O L X R A Y A N K E E
J Q L Q T A N G O A L X R Y B Q
Z I J U L I E T T U C F P R P P
E T V E N O V E M B E R A Q V G
C Z O B X I V M W Q P V P N G Q
V I K E T A F N B H O K A W M P
R I N C R J F O R B O S U U H X
N H O L H F C X R S H C P W N J
W B L Q K R Y B M M P X E K L T
```

WORD LIST

ALFA	NOVEMBER
BRAVO	OSCAR
CHARLIE	PAPA
DELTA	QUEBEC
ECHO	ROMEO
FOXTROT	SIERRA
GOLF	TANGO
HOTEL	UNIFORM
INDIA	VICTOR
JULIET	WHISKEY
KILO	XRAY
LIMA	YANKEE
MIKE	ZULU

TRY TO FIND THE NAMES OF ALL THE PHONETICOS IN THE WORDSEARCH. THEY ARE THERE!

THE NAMES GO IN ALL DIRECTIONS: UP, DOWN, BACKWARD, SIDEWAYS, AND DIAGONALLY ACROSS THE PUZZLE.

HI INDIA! DID YOU KNOW THAT ASTRONAUTS USE PHONETICS WHEN WORKING IN SPACE?

I GUESS I'M IN THE WORDSEARCH TOO - EVEN THOUGH I'VE NEVER BEEN IN SPACE!

HAVE FUN BECOMING FAMILIAR WITH THE PHONETICOS BY COMPLETING THIS WORDSEARCH!

TIME YOURSELF AND SEE HOW FAST YOU CAN WORK.

WORDSEARCH IS HARD UNTIL YOU LEARN HOW TO DO IT! THEN YOU CAN BEGIN TO SEE THE HIDDEN WORDS.

GO TO PAGE 299 FOR THE WORDSEARCH ANSWERS!

QUIZ

Answer the questions on a separate sheet. Look for the answers at the end of the next *QUIZ!*

N2A13
What are RST signal reports?
A. A short way to describe ionospheric conditions
B. A short way to describe transmitter power
C. A short way to describe signal reception
D. A short way to describe sunspot activity

N2A14
What does RST mean in a signal report?
A. Recovery, signal strength, tempo
B. Recovery, signal speed, tone
C. Readability, signal speed, tempo
D. Readability, signal strength, tone

N2A15
What is one meaning of the Q signal "QRS"?
A. Interference from static
B. Send more slowly
C. Send RST report
D. Radio station location is

N2A17
What is a QSL card?
A. A letter or postcard from an amateur pen pal
B. A Notice of Violation from the FCC
C. A written proof of communication between two amateurs
D. A postcard reminding you when your license will expire

N2A16
What is one meaning of the Q signal "QTH"?
A. Time here is
B. My name is
C. Stop sending
D. My location is

THESE QUESTIONS ARE EASY IF YOU READ THE LESSON FIRST - AND THAT'S NO BULL-ONEY!

END OF NOVICE LESSON 2!

HERE ARE SOME QSL CARDS FROM ALL OVER THE WORLD. EACH COUNTRY HAS A DIFFERENT PREFIX. HOW MANY ARE HERE?

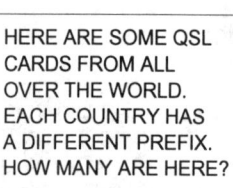

JS1ZZZ	WZ1ZZZ	UQ1ZZZ	CD1XXX
VK5ZZZ	ZL1XYZ	DL8ZZX	YU8ZXC
GM5XZY	ZS1XYZ	ZA1ZXB	N6XLK
EB6ZY	9L1ZVC	VU8ZXV	4X9XZB
KZ6ZZZ	AA6AAA	4Q7ZX	BV1ZYT
FZ8ZBC	HI8ZXE	GW8XCV	EJ9XZ
9M9ZXB	Z32XYZ	W6GOJ	W6NTR

ALL U.S. CALLS START WITH EITHER W, A, N, OR K. CAN YOU FIND THE QSL CARDS FROM THE USA? SOME FOREIGN CALLS START WITH A NUMBER.

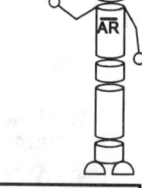

PREVIOUS QUIZ ANSWERS

N2A20 - A

N2A08 - D

N2A18 - C

N2A19 - D

N2A12 - B

N2A11 - B

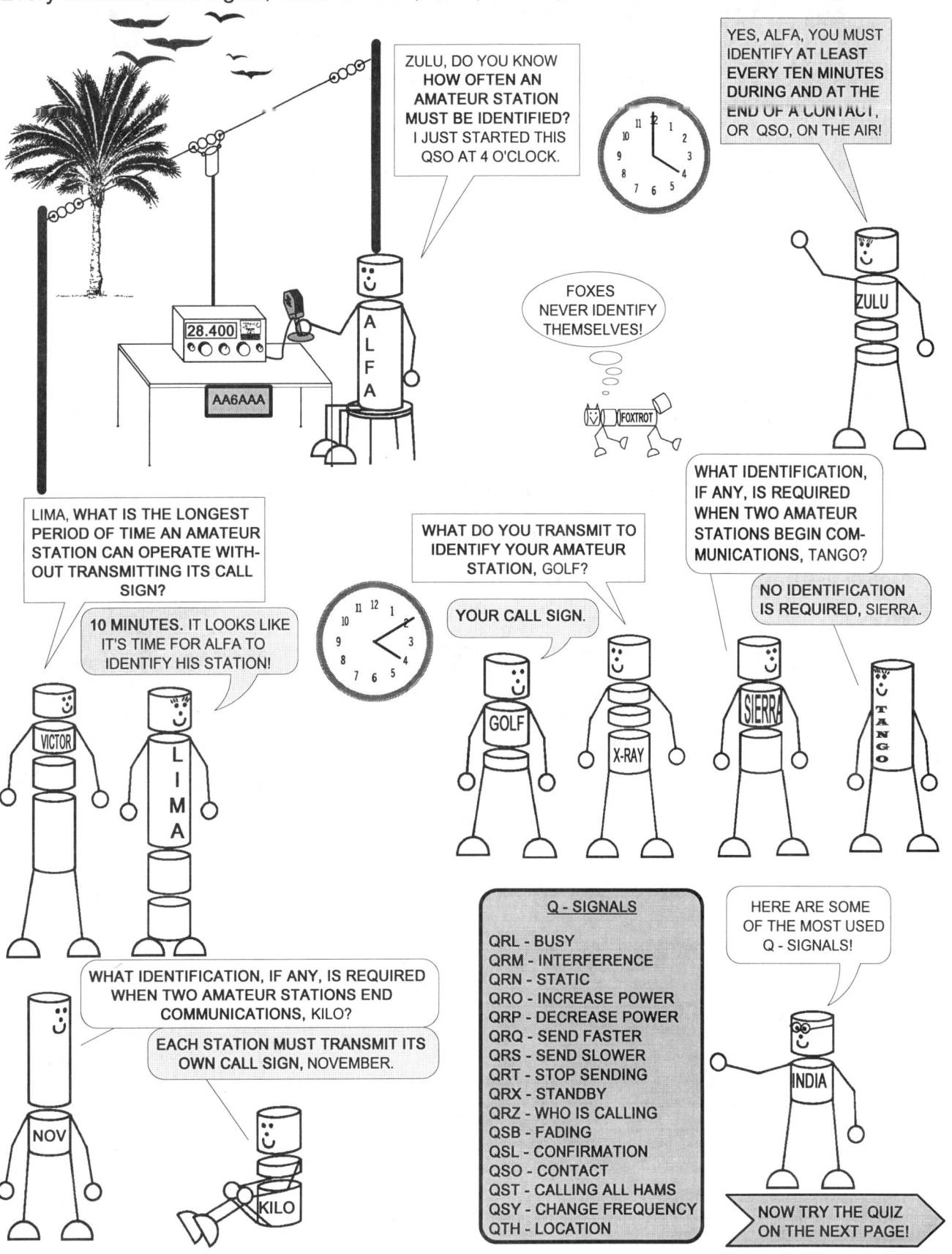

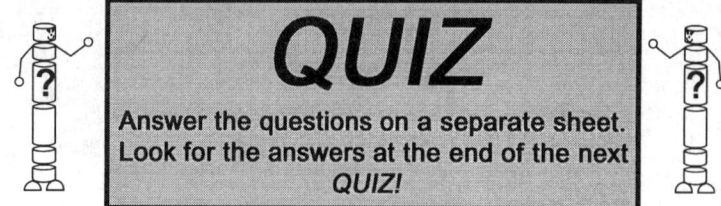

QUIZ

Answer the questions on a separate sheet. Look for the answers at the end of the next QUIZ!

N1H06
How often must an amateur station be identified?
A. At the beginning of a contact and at least every ten minutes after that
B. At least once during each transmission
C. At least every ten minutes during and at the end of a contact
D. At the beginning and end of each transmission

N1H11
What is the longest period of time an amateur station can operate without transmitting its call sign?
A. 5 minutes
B. 10 minutes
C. 15 minutes
D. 20 minutes

N1H07
What do you transmit to identify your amateur station?
A. Your "handle"
B. Your call sign
C. Your first name and your location
D. Your full name

N1H08
What identification, if any, is required when two amateur stations begin communications?
A. No identification is required
B. One of the stations must give both stations' call signs
C. Each station must transmit its own call sign
D. Both stations must transmit both call signs

N1H09
What identification, if any, is required when two amateur stations end communications?
A. No identification is required
B. One of the stations must transmit both stations' call signs
C. Each station must transmit its own call sign
D. Both stations must transmit both call signs

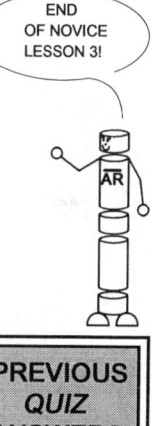

END OF NOVICE LESSON 3!

PREVIOUS QUIZ ANSWERS

N2A13 - C

N2A14 - D

N2A15 - B

N2A17 - C

N2A16 - D

AMATEUR RADIO PURPOSE & RULES
NOVICE LESSON 4

The Phoneticos were wondering one day why there are radio amateurs. Hams are different than Citizen Band, or *CB*, people. Hams have many rules and a purpose in being on the air besides chit-chatting. They also know a lot about the equipment and antennas that they operate.

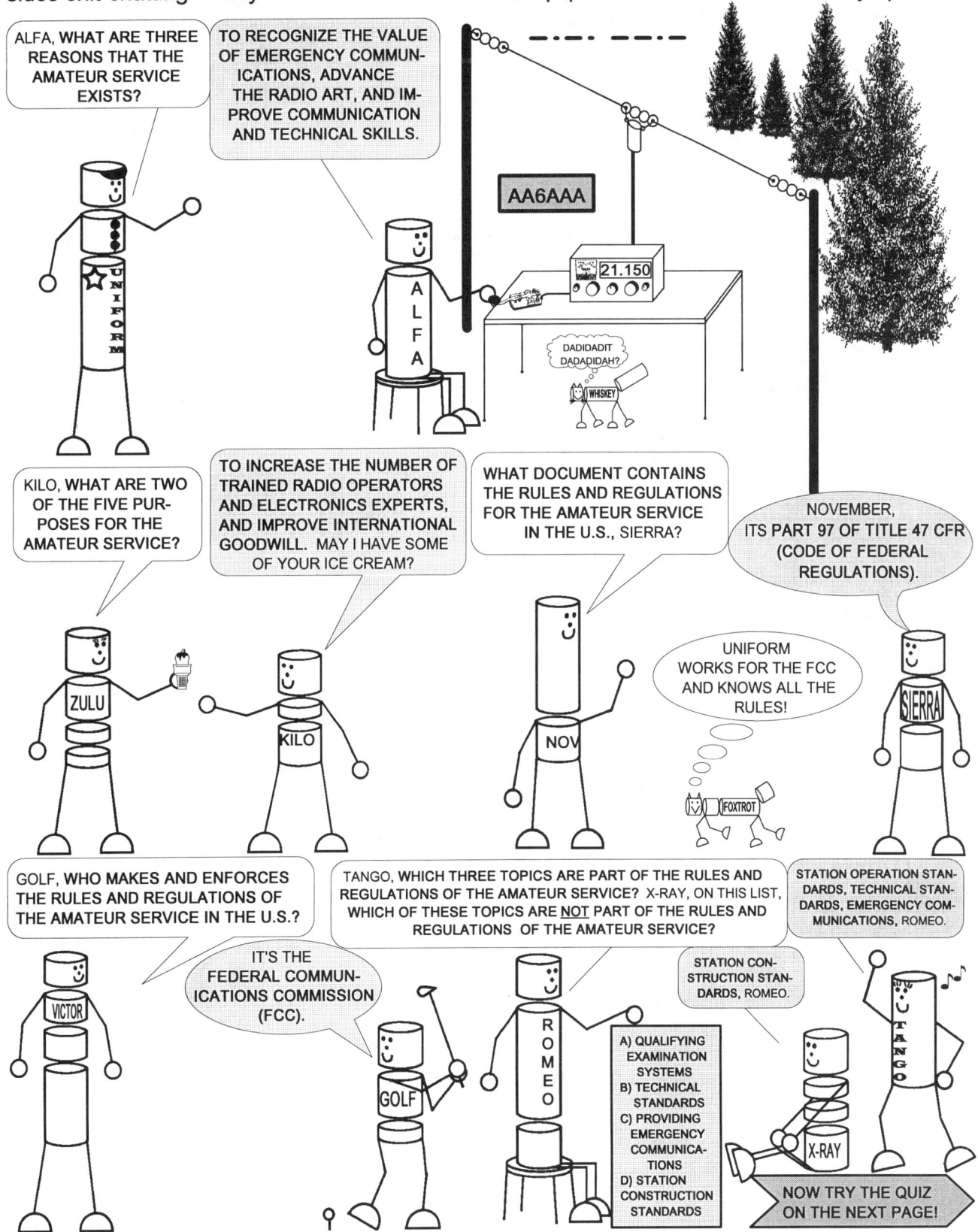

NOW TRY THE QUIZ ON THE NEXT PAGE!

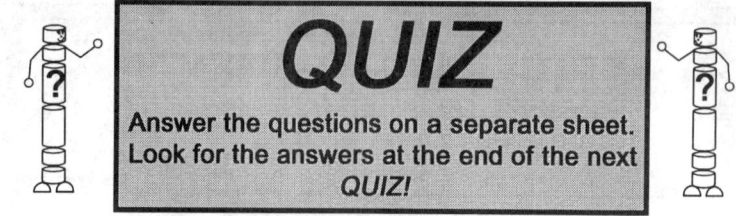

QUIZ
Answer the questions on a separate sheet. Look for the answers at the end of the next QUIZ!

N1A05
What are three reasons that the amateur service exists?
A. To recognize the value of emergency communications, advance the radio art, and improve communication and technical skills
B. To learn about business communications, increase testing by trained technicians, and improve amateur communications
C. To preserve old radio techniques, maintain a pool of people familiar with early tube-type equipment, and improve tube radios
D. To improve patriotism, preserve nationalism, and promote world peace

N1A06
What are two of the five purposes for the amateur service?
A. To protect historical radio data, and help the public understand radio history
B. To help foreign countries improve communication and technical skills, and encourage visits from foreign hams
C. To modernize radio schematic drawings, and increase the pool of electrical drafting people
D. To increase the number of trained radio operators and electronics experts, and improve international goodwill

N1A01
What document contains the rules and regulations for the amateur service in the US?
A. Part 97 of Title 47 CFR (Code of Federal Regulations)
B. The Communications Act of 1934 (as amended)
C. The Radio Amateur's Handbook
D. The minutes of the International Telecommunication Union meetings

N1A02
Who makes and enforces the rules and regulations of the amateur service in the US?
A. The Congress of the United States
B. The Federal Communications Commission (FCC)
C. The Volunteer Examiner Coordinators (VECs)
D. The Federal Bureau of Investigation (FBI)

N1A03
Which three topics are part of the rules and regulations of the amateur service?
A. Station operation standards, technical standards, emergency communications
B. Notice of Violation, common operating procedures, antenna lengths
C. Frequency band plans, repeater locations, Ohm's law
D. Station construction standards, FCC approved radios, FCC approved antennas

N1A04
Which of these topics is NOT part of the rules and regulations of the amateur service?
A. Qualifying examination systems
B. Technical standards
C. Providing emergency communications
D. Station construction standards

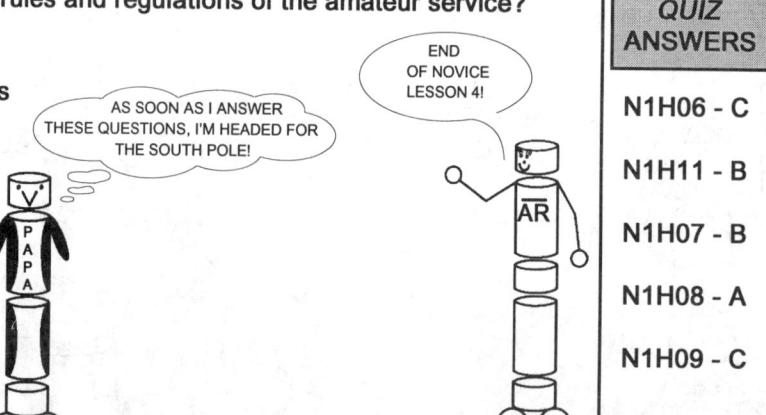

PREVIOUS QUIZ ANSWERS

N1H06 - C

N1H11 - B

N1H07 - B

N1H08 - A

N1H09 - C

DEFINITIONS
NOVICE LESSON 5

ALFA & ZULU have their licenses, and are both active radio amateurs. They studied hard to learn the theory and Morse code, and are now trying to help others to get their licenses. It would be fun if all their friends were amateurs, so that they could talk to each other wherever they went!

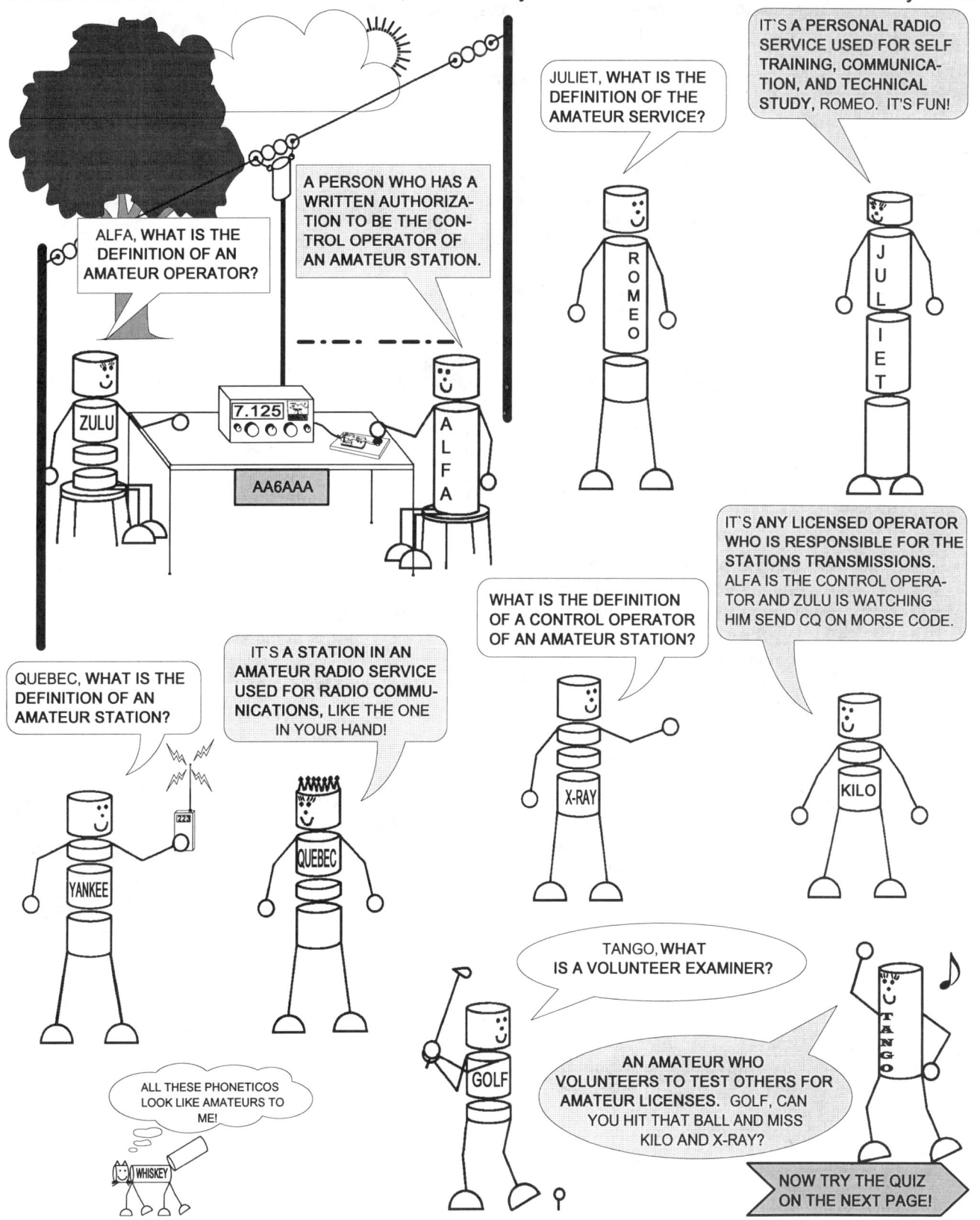

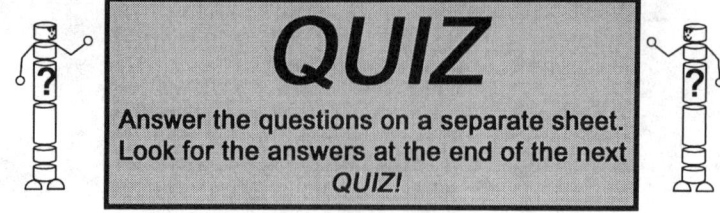

QUIZ

Answer the questions on a separate sheet. Look for the answers at the end of the next QUIZ!

N1A07
What is the definition of an amateur operator?
A. A person who has not received any training in radio operations
B. A person who has a written authorization to be the control operator of an amateur station
C. A person who has very little practice operating a radio station
D. A person who is in training to become the control operator of a radio station

N1A08
What is the definition of the amateur service?
A. A private radio service used for profit and public benefit
B. A public radio service for US citizens which requires no exam
C. A personal radio service used for self-training, communication, and technical studies
D. A private radio service used for self-training of radio announcers and technicians

N1A09
What is the definition of an amateur station?
A. A station in a public radio service used for radiocommunications
B. A station using radiocommunications for a commercial purpose
C. A station using equipment for training new radiocommunications operators
D. A station in an Amateur Radio service used for radiocommunications

N1A10
What is the definition of a control operator of an amateur station?
A. Anyone who operates the controls of the station
B. Anyone who is responsible for the station's equipment
C. Any licensed amateur operator who is responsible for the station's transmissions
D. The amateur operator with the highest class of license who is near the controls of the station

N1A11
What is a Volunteer Examiner (VE)?
A. An amateur who volunteers to check amateur teaching manuals
B. An amateur who volunteers to teach amateur classes
C. An amateur who volunteers to test others for amateur licenses
D. An amateur who volunteers to examine amateur station equipment

END OF NOVICE LESSON 5!

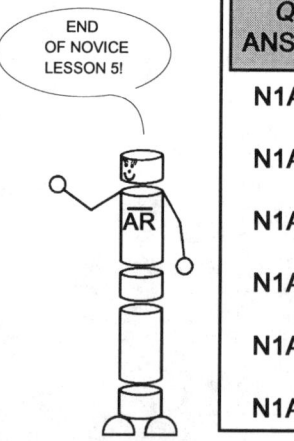

PREVIOUS QUIZ ANSWERS
N1A05 - A
N1A06 - D
N1A01 - A
N1A02 - B
N1A03 - A
N1A04 - D

THERE SURE ARE A LOT OF RULES AND DEFINITIONS IN HAM RADIO. BUT THAT'S WHY IT'S A LOT OF FUN TO BE A HAM AND PART OF A SMART GROUP OF PEOPLE!

DEER CROSSING

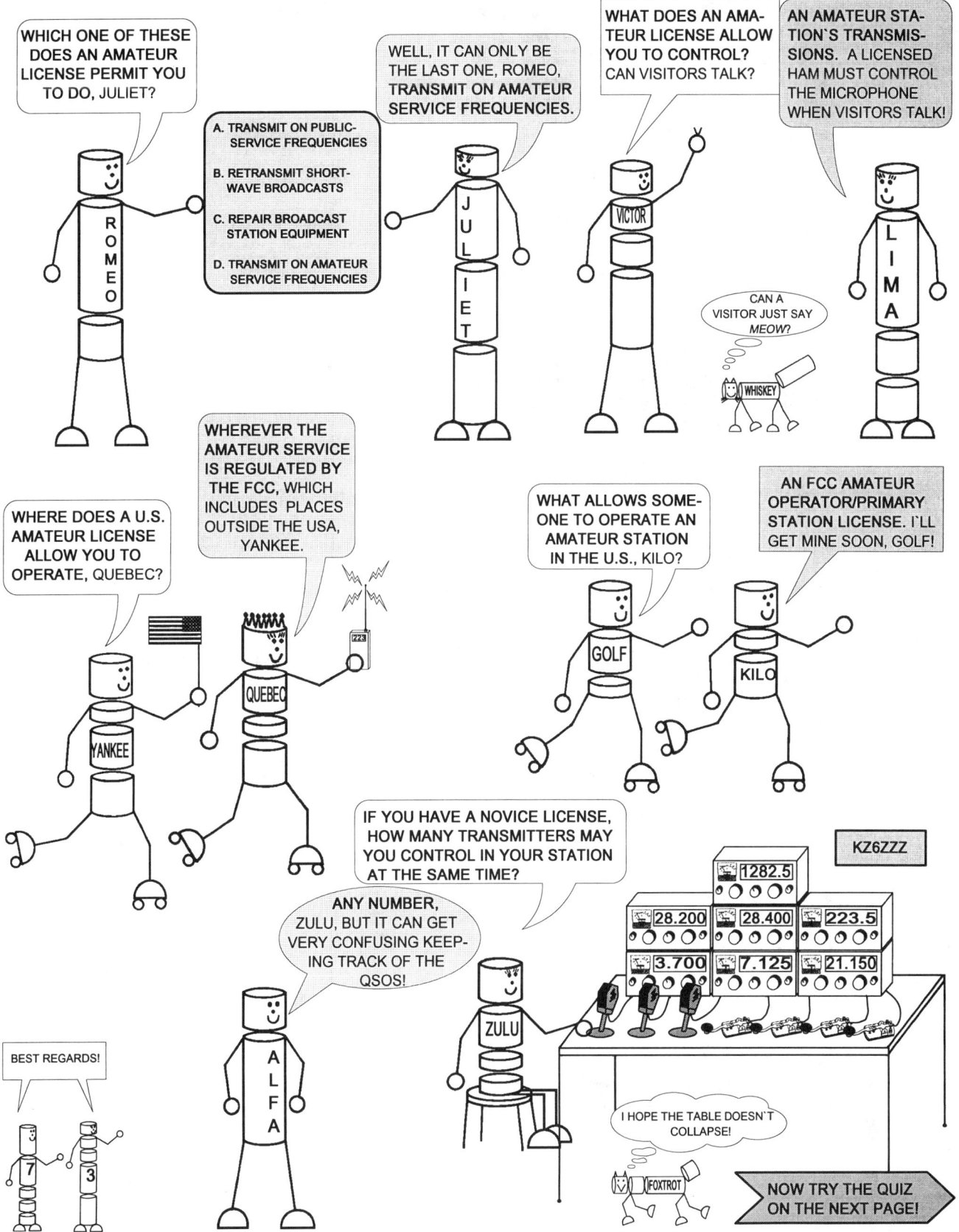

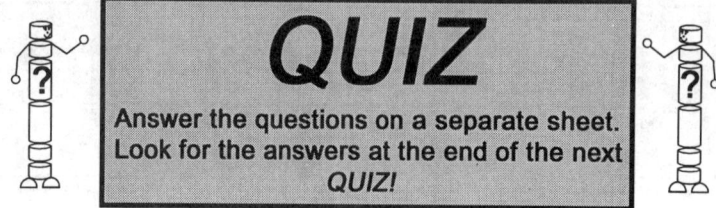

QUIZ

Answer the questions on a separate sheet. Look for the answers at the end of the next QUIZ!

N1B01
Which one of these must you have an amateur license to do?
A. Transmit on public-service frequencies
B. Retransmit shortwave broadcasts
C. Repair broadcast station equipment
D. Transmit on amateur service frequencies

N1B02
What does an amateur license allow you to control?
A. A shortwave-broadcast station's transmissions
B. An amateur station's transmissions
C. Non-commercial FM broadcast transmissions
D. Any type of transmitter, as long as it is used for non-commercial transmissions

N1B04
Where does a US amateur license allow you to operate?
A. Anywhere in the world
B. Wherever the amateur service is regulated by the FCC
C. Within 50 km of your primary station location
D. Only at your primary station location

N1B03
What allows someone to operate an amateur station in the US?
A. An FCC operator's training permit for a licensed radio station
B. An FCC Form 610 together with a license examination fee
C. An FCC amateur operator/primary station license
D. An FCC Certificate of Successful Completion of Amateur Training

N1B05
If you have a Novice license, how many transmitters may you control in your station at the same time?
A. Only one at a time
B. Only one at a time, except for emergency communications
C. Any number
D. Any number, as long as they are transmitting on different bands

PREVIOUS QUIZ ANSWERS

N1A07 - B

N1A08 - C

N1A09 - D

N1A10 - C

N1A11 - C

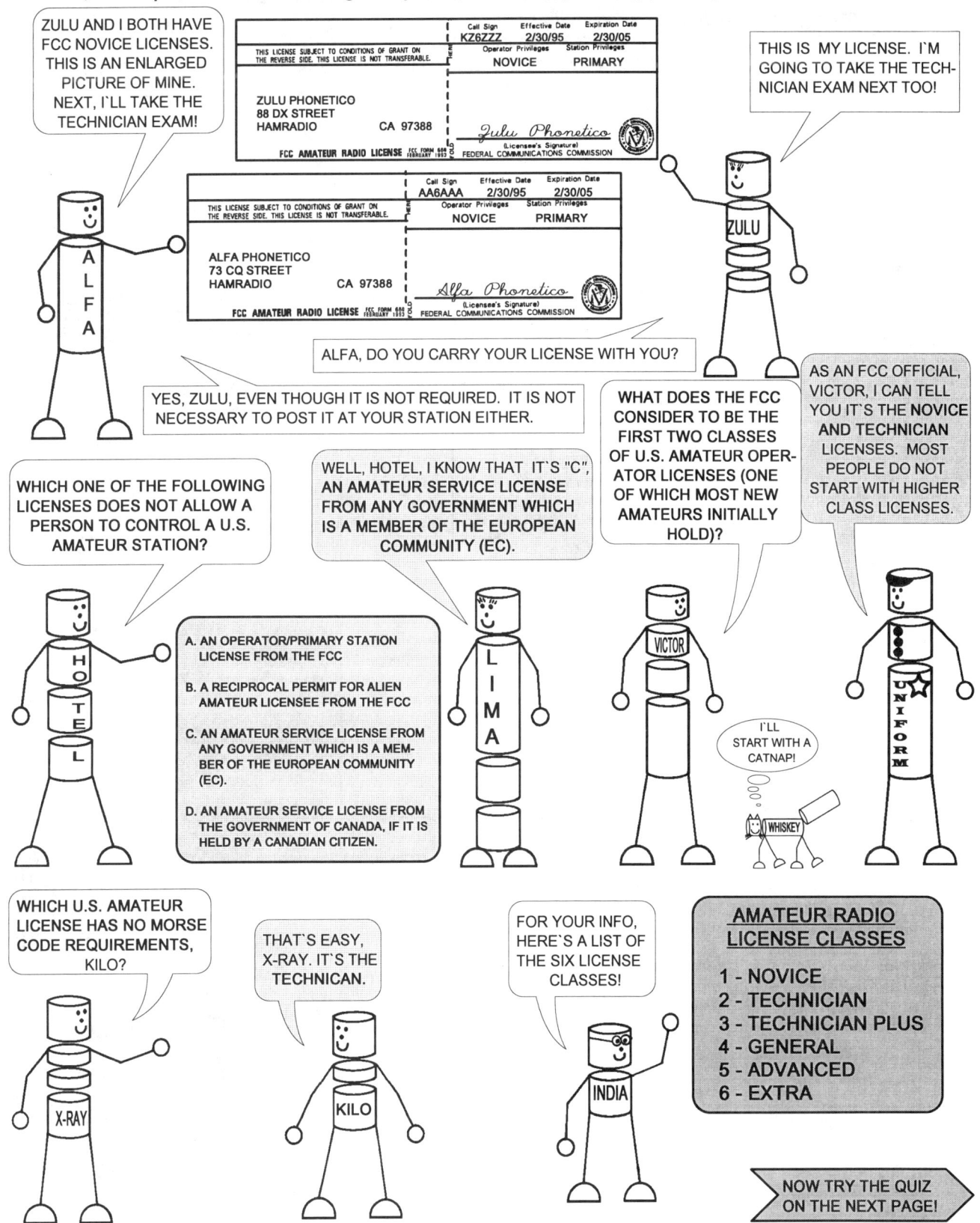

QUIZ

Answer the questions on a separate sheet. Look for the answers at the end of the next QUIZ!

N1B07
Which one of the following does not allow a person to control a US amateur station?
A. An operator/primary station license from the FCC
B. A reciprocal permit for alien amateur licensee from the FCC
C. An amateur service license from any government which is a member of the European Community (EC)
D. An amateur service license from the Government of Canada, if it is held by a Canadian citizen

N1B09
What does the FCC consider to be the first two classes of US amateur operator licenses (one of which most new amateurs initially hold)?
A. Novice and Technician
B. CB and Communicator
C. Novice and General
D. CB and Novice

N1B11
Which US amateur license has no Morse code requirements?
A. Amateur Extra
B. Advanced
C. General
D. Technician

PREVIOUS QUIZ ANSWERS
N1B01 - D
N1B02 - B
N1B04 - B
N1B03 - C
N1B05 - C

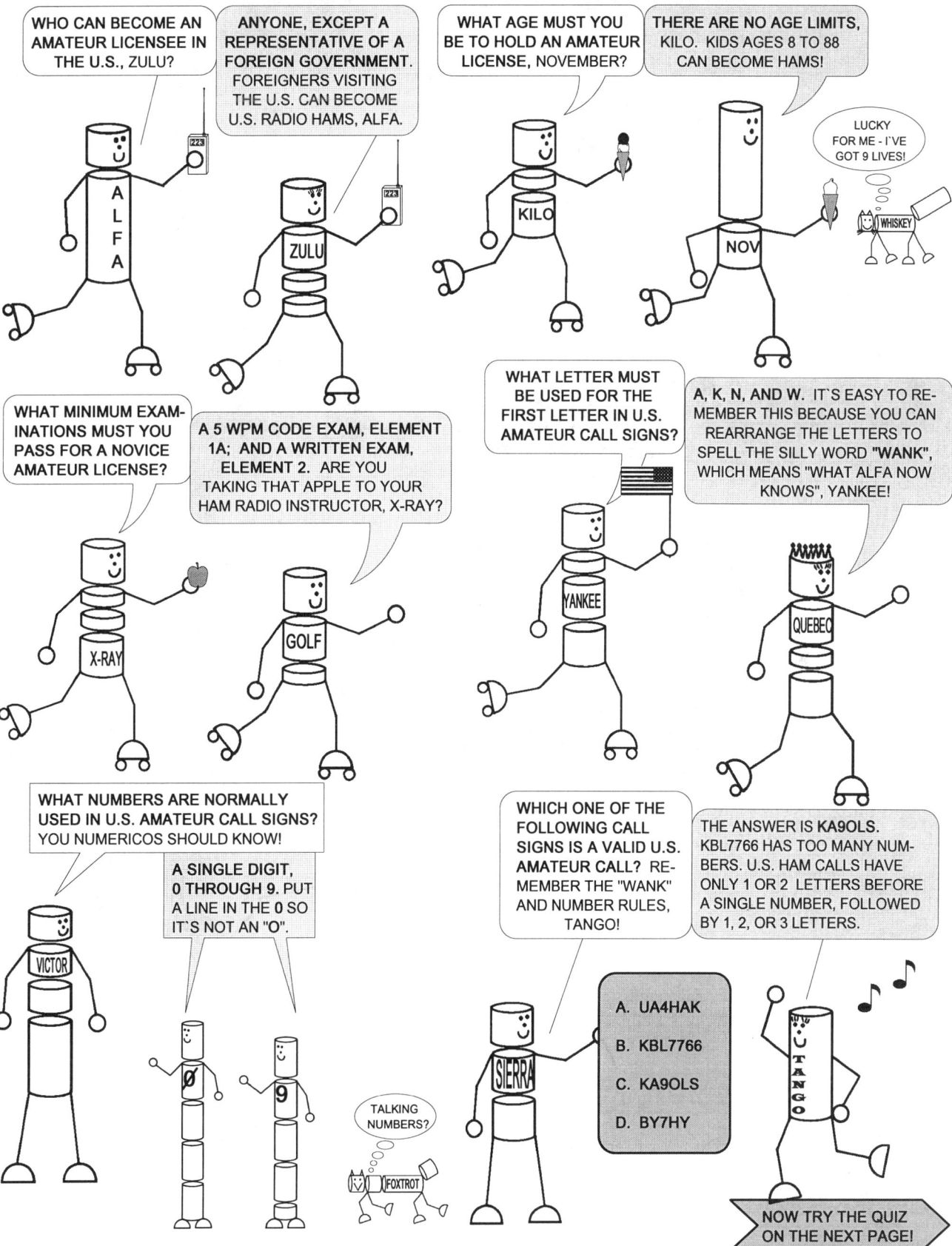

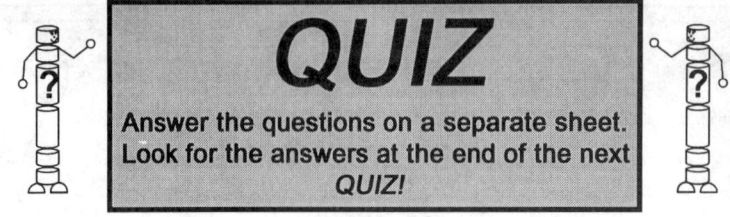

QUIZ

Answer the questions on a separate sheet. Look for the answers at the end of the next QUIZ!

N1D01
Who can become an amateur licensee in the US?
A. Anyone except a representative of a foreign government
B. Only a citizen of the United States
C. Anyone except an employee of the US government
D. Anyone

N1D02
What age must you be to hold an amateur license?
A. 14 years or older
B. 18 years or older
C. 70 years or younger
D. There are no age limits

N1D03
What minimum examinations must you pass for a Novice amateur license?
A. A written exam, Element 1(A); and a 5 WPM code exam, Element 2(A)
B. A 5 WPM code exam, Element 1(A); and a written exam, Element 3(A)
C. A 5 WPM code exam, Element 1(A); and a written exam, Element 2
D. A written exam, Element 2; and a 5 WPM code exam, Element 4

N1D08
What letters must be used for the first letter in US amateur call signs?
A. K, N, U and W
B. A, K, N and W
C. A, B, C and D
D. A, N, V and W

N1D09
What numbers are normally used in US amateur call signs?
A. Any two-digit number, 10 through 99
B. Any two-digit number, 22 through 45
C. A single digit, 1 though 9
D. A single digit, 0 through 9

N1D07
Which of the following call signs is a valid US amateur call?
A. UA4HAK
B. KBL7766
C. KA9OLS
D. BY7HY

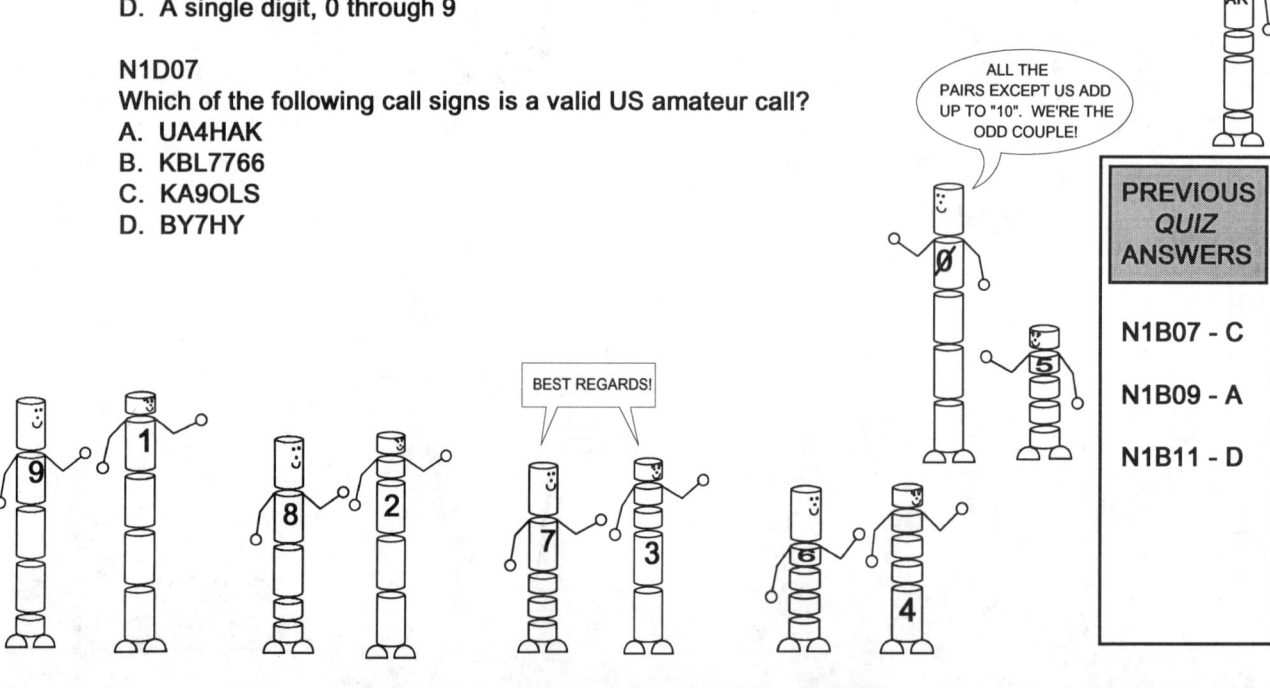

END OF NOVICE LESSON 8!

ALL THE PAIRS EXCEPT US ADD UP TO "10". WE'RE THE ODD COUPLE!

BEST REGARDS!

PREVIOUS QUIZ ANSWERS

N1B07 - C

N1B09 - A

N1B11 - D

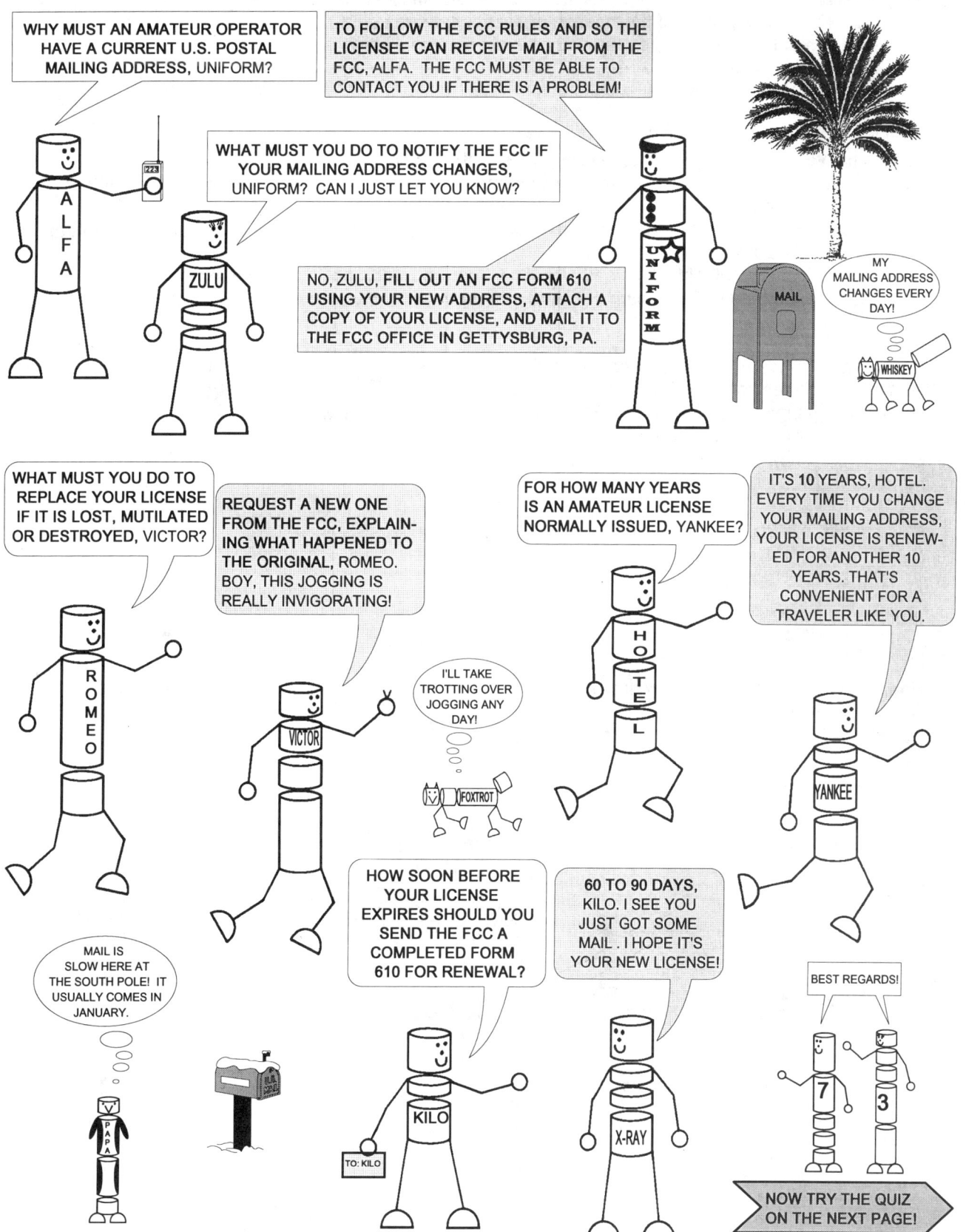

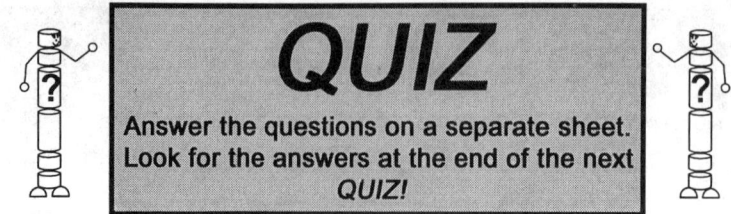

N1D04
Why must an amateur operator have a current US Postal mailing address?
A. So the FCC has a record of the location of each amateur station
B. To follow the FCC rules and so the licensee can receive mail from the FCC
C. So the FCC can send license-renewal notices
D. So the FCC can publish a call-sign directory

N1D06
What must you do to notify the FCC if your mailing address changes?
A. Fill out an FCC Form 610 using your new address, attach a copy of your license, and mail it to your local FCC Field Office
B. Fill out an FCC Form 610 using your new address, attach a copy of your license, and mail it to the FCC office in Gettysburg, PA
C. Call your local FCC Field Office and give them your new address over the phone
D. Call the FCC office in Gettysburg, PA, and give them your new address over the phone

N1D05
What must you do to replace your license if it is lost, mutilated or destroyed?
A. Nothing; no replacement is needed
B. Send a change of address to the FCC using a current FCC Form 610
C. Retake all examination elements for your license
D. Request a new one from the FCC, explaining what happened to the original

N1D10
For how many years is an amateur license normally issued?
A. 2
B. 5
C. 10
D. 15

N1D11
How soon before your license expires should you send the FCC a completed 610 for a renewal?
A. 60 to 90 days
B. within 21 days of the expiration date
C. 6 to 9 months
D. 6 months to a year

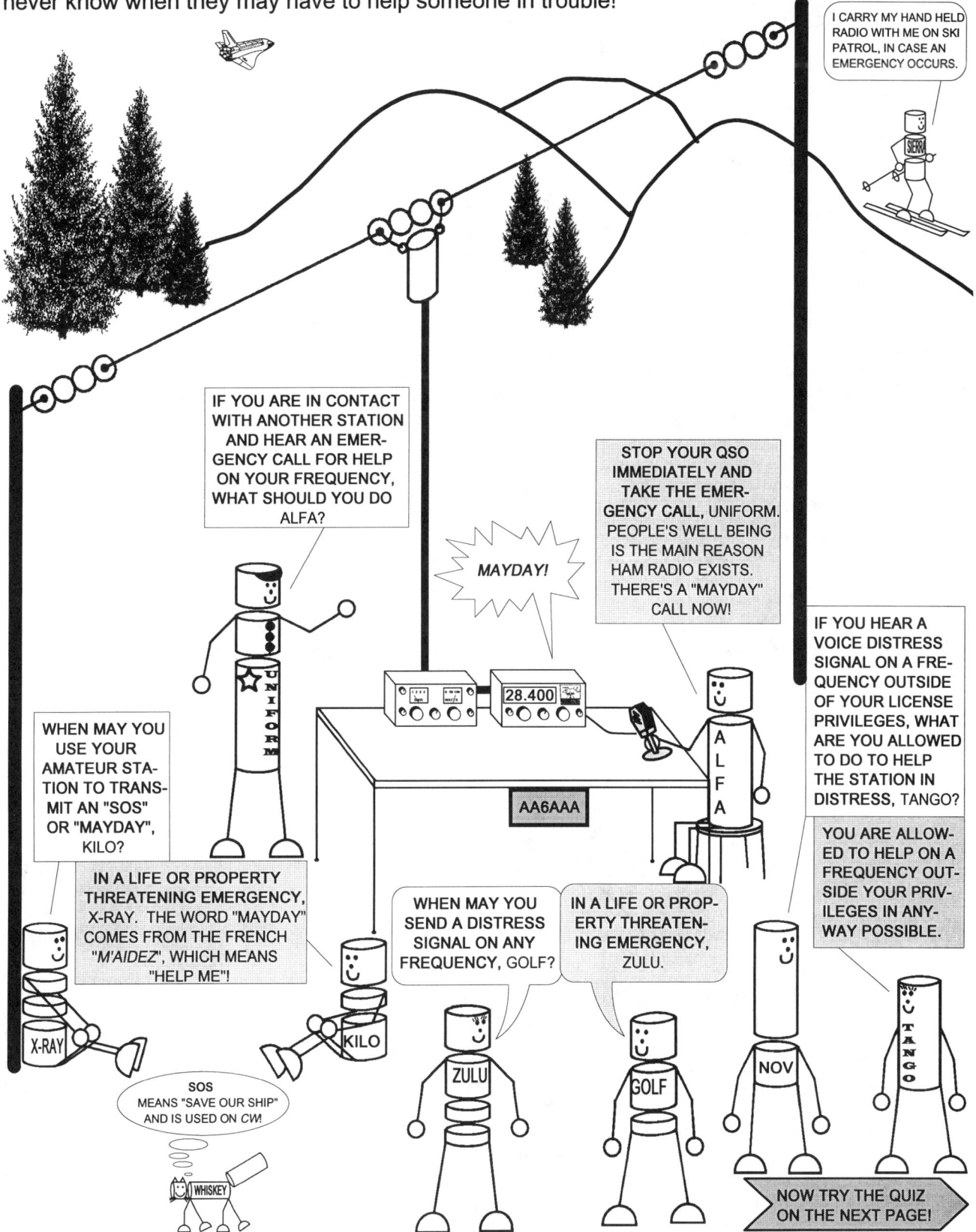

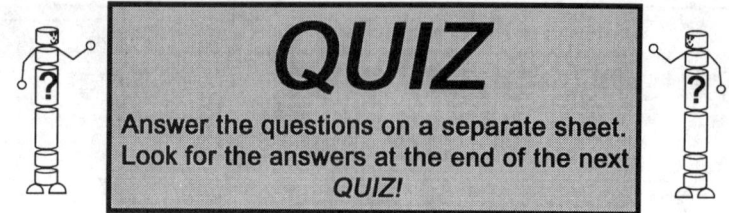

N2A04
If you are in contact with another station and you hear an emergency call for help on your frequency, what should you do?
A. Tell the calling station that the frequency is in use
B. Direct the calling station to the nearest emergency net frequency
C. Call your local Civil Preparedness Office and inform them of the emergency
D. Stop your QSO immediately and take the emergency call

N1J10
When may you use your amateur station to transmit an "SOS" or "MAYDAY"?
A. Never
B. Only at specific times (at 15 and 30 minutes after the hour)
C. In a life or property threatening emergency
D. When the National Weather Service has announced a severe weather watch

N1J11
When may you send a distress signal on any frequency?
A. Never
B. In a life or property threatening emergency
C. Only at specific times (at 15 and 30 minutes after the hour)
D. When the National Weather Service has announced a severe weather watch

N1J08
If you hear a voice distress signal on a frequency outside of your license privileges, what are you allowed to do to help the station in distress?
A. You are NOT allowed to help because the frequency of the signal is outside your privileges
B. You are allowed to help only if you keep your signals within the nearest frequency band of your privileges
C. You are allowed to help on a frequency outside your privileges only if you use international Morse code
D. You are allowed to help on a frequency outside your privileges in any way possible

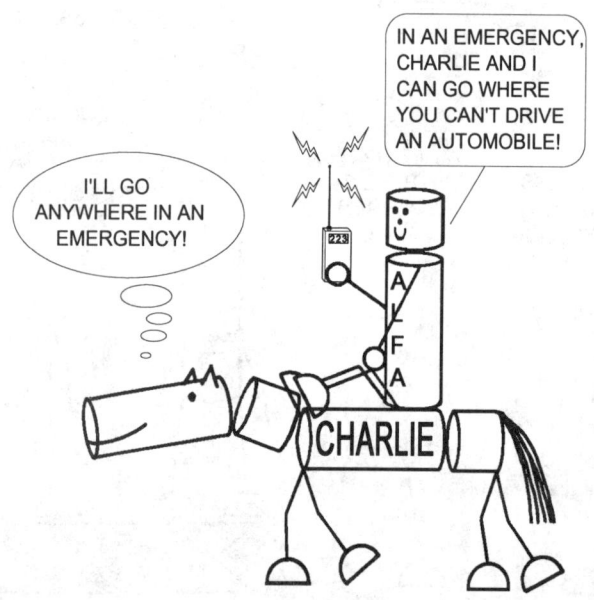

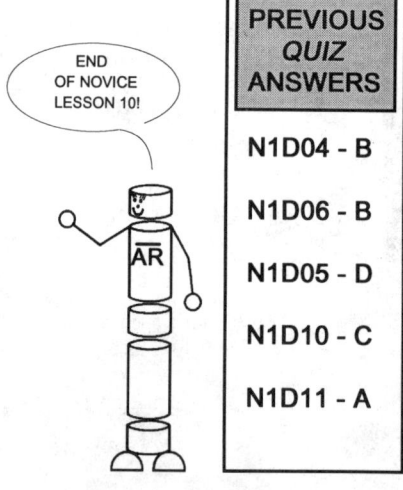

PREVIOUS QUIZ ANSWERS
N1D04 - B
N1D06 - B
N1D05 - D
N1D10 - C
N1D11 - A

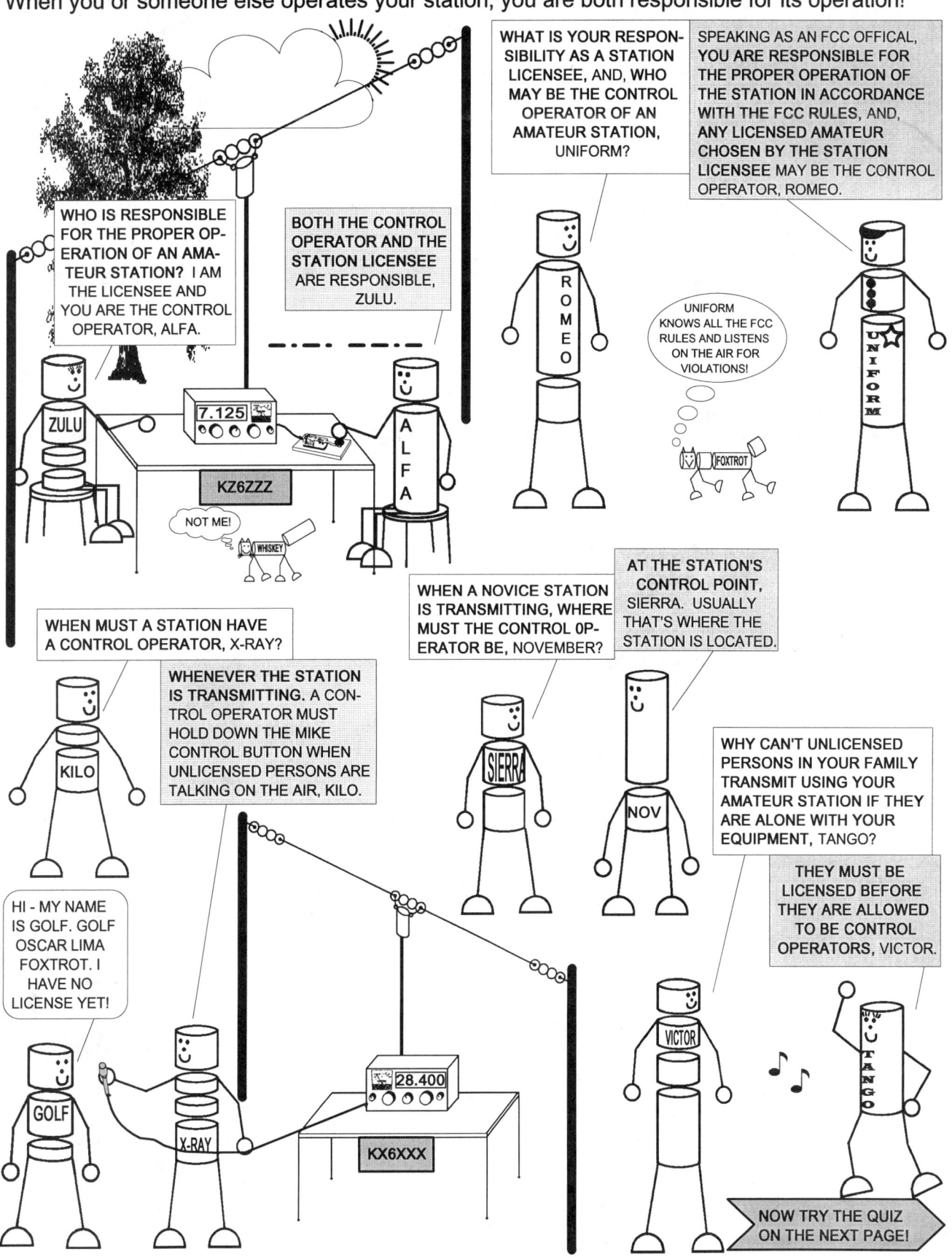

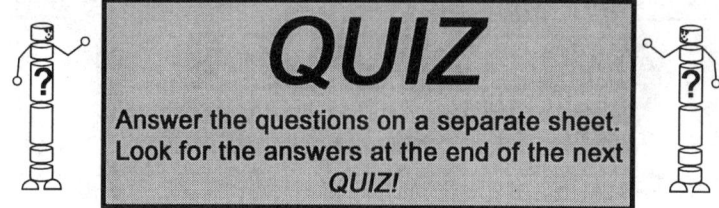

QUIZ

Answer the questions on a separate sheet. Look for the answers at the end of the next QUIZ!

N1G02
Who is responsible for the proper operation of an amateur station?
A. Only the control operator
B. Only the station licensee
C. Both the control operator and the station licensee
D. The person who owns the station equipment

N1G04
What is your responsibility as a station licensee?
A. You must allow another amateur to operate your station upon request
B. You must be present whenever the station is operated
C. You must notify the FCC if another amateur acts as the control operator
D. You are responsible for the proper operation of the station in accordance with the FCC rules

N1G05
Who may be the control operator of an amateur station?
A. Any person over 21 years of age
B. Any person over 21 years of age with a General class license or higher
C. Any licensed amateur chosen by the station licensee
D. Any licensed amateur with a Technician class license or higher

N1G09
When must an amateur station have a control operator?
A. Only when training another amateur
B. Whenever the station receiver is operated
C. Whenever the station is transmitting
D. A control operator is not needed

N1G10
When a Novice station is transmitting, where must its control operator be?
A. At the station's control point
B. Anywhere in the same building as the transmitter
C. At the station's entrance, to control entry to the room
D. Anywhere within 50 km of the station location

N1G11
Why can't unlicensed persons in your family transmit using your amateur station if they are alone with your equipment?
A. They must not use your equipment without your permission
B. They must be licensed before they are allowed to be control operators
C. They must first know how to use the right abbreviations and Q signals
D. They must first know the right frequencies and emissions for transmitting

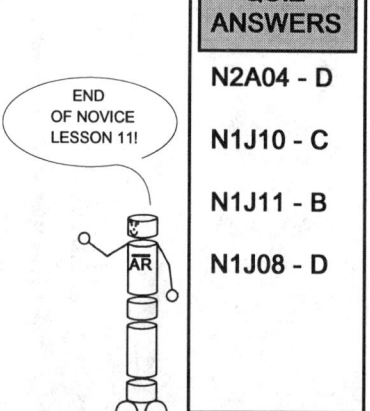

PREVIOUS QUIZ ANSWERS
N2A04 - D
N1J10 - C
N1J11 - B
N1J08 - D

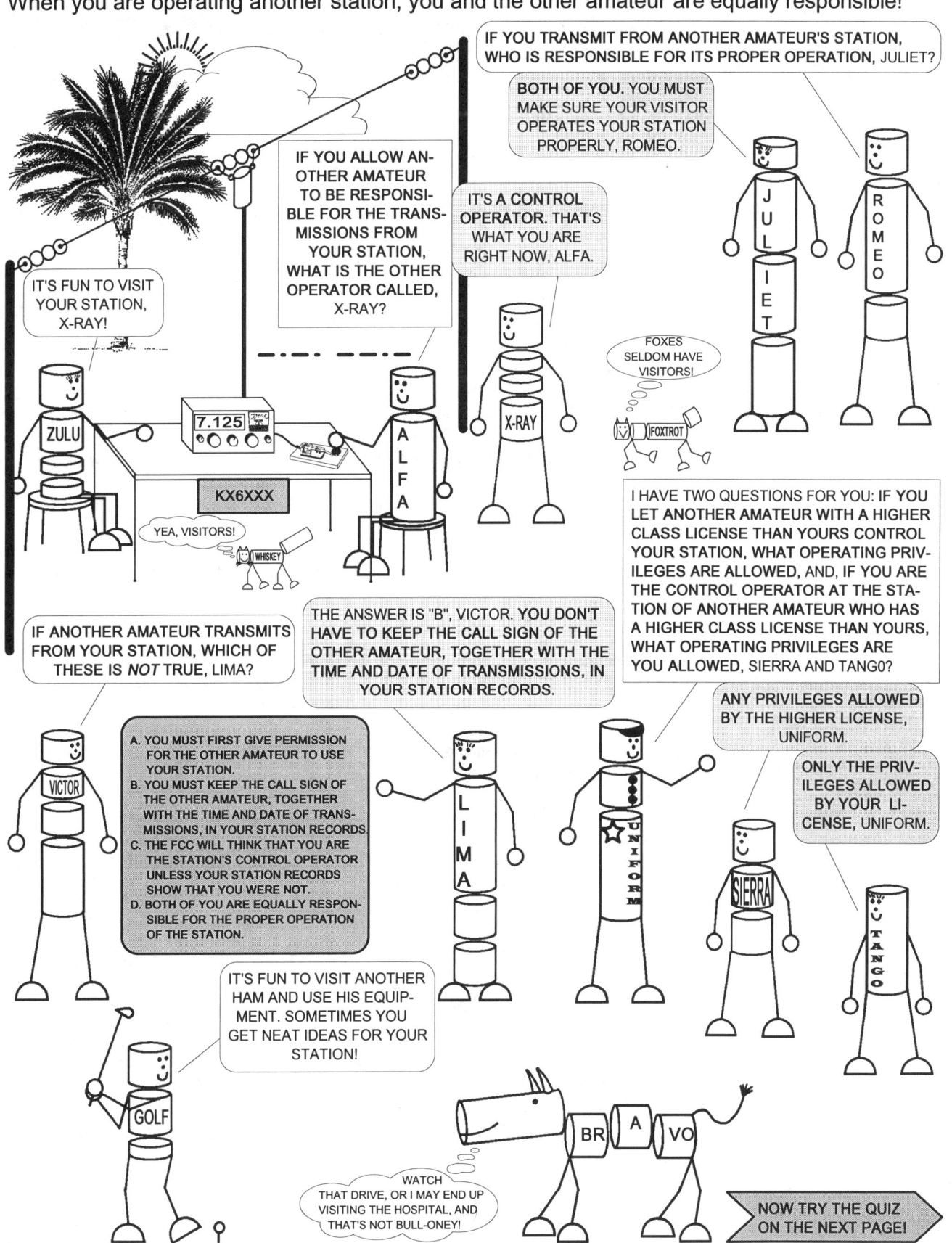

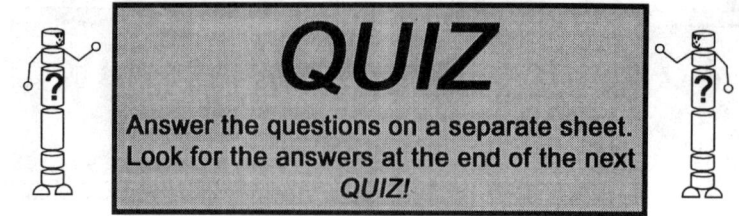

QUIZ

Answer the questions on a separate sheet. Look for the answers at the end of the next QUIZ!

N1G01
If you allow another amateur to be responsible for the transmissions from your station, what is the other operator called?
A. An auxiliary operator
B. The operations coordinator
C. A third-party operator
D. A control operator

N1G03
If you transmit from another amateur's station, who is responsible for its proper operation?
A. Both of you
B. The other amateur (the station licensee)
C. You, the control operator
D. The station licensee, unless the station records show that you were the control operator at the time

N1G06
If another amateur transmits from your station, which of these is NOT true?
A. You must first give permission for the other amateur to use your station
B. You must keep the call sign of the other amateur, together with the time and date of transmissions, in your station records
C. The FCC will think that you are the station's control operator unless your station records show that you were not
D. Both of you are equally responsible for the proper operation of the station

N1G07
If you let another amateur with a higher class license than yours control your station, what operating privileges are allowed?
A. Any privileges allowed by the higher license
B. Only the privileges allowed by your license
C. All the emission privileges of the higher license, but only the frequency privileges of your license
D. All the frequency privileges of the higher license, but only the emission privileges of your license

N1G08
If you are the control operator at the station of another amateur who has a higher class license than yours, what operating privileges are you allowed?
A. Any privileges allowed by the higher license
B. Only the privileges allowed by your license
C. All the emission privileges of the higher license, but only the frequency privileges of your license
D. All the frequency privileges of the higher license, but only the emission privileges of your license

PREVIOUS QUIZ ANSWERS

N1G02 - C
N1G04 - D
N1G05 - C
N1G09 - C
N1G10 - A
N1G11 - B

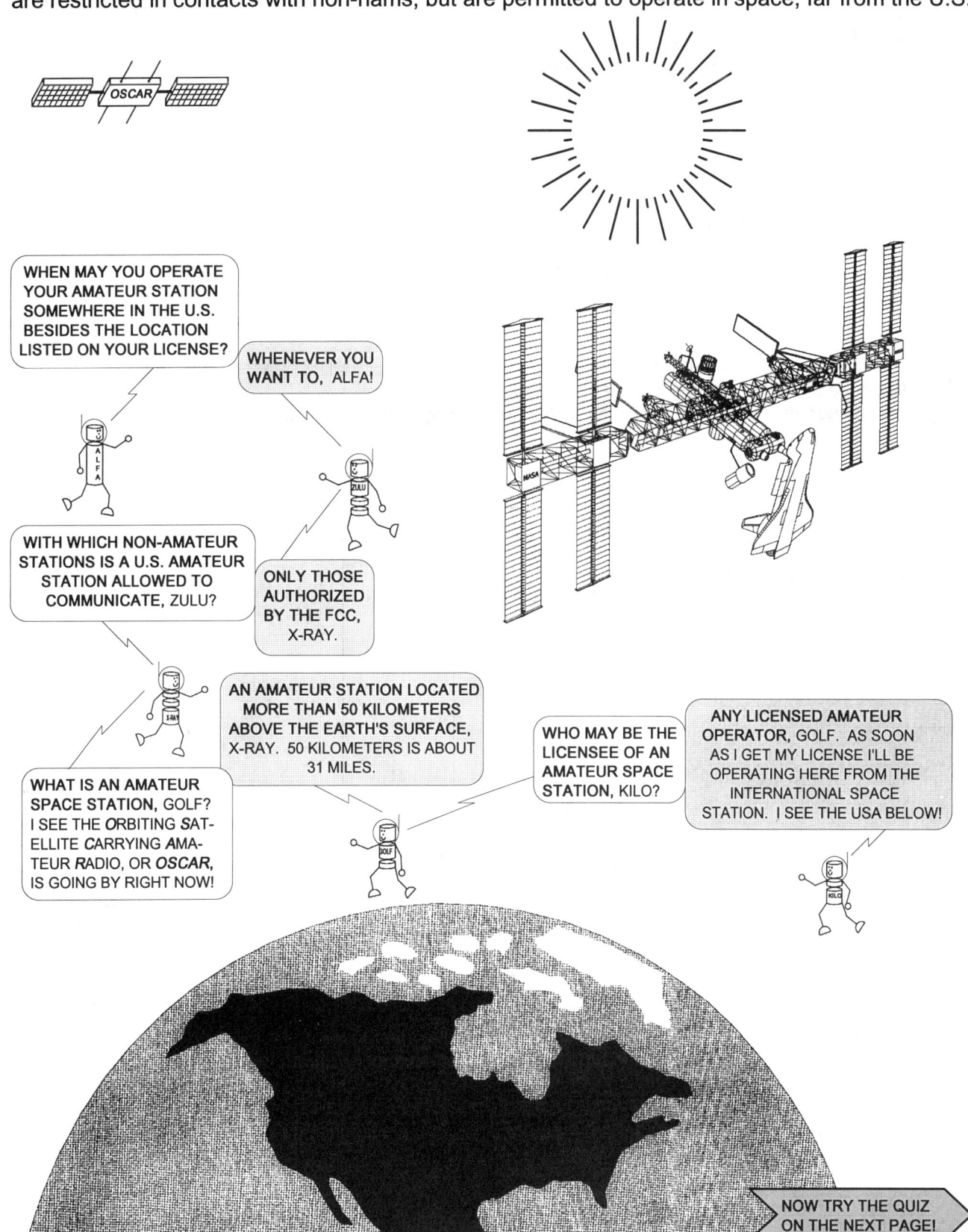

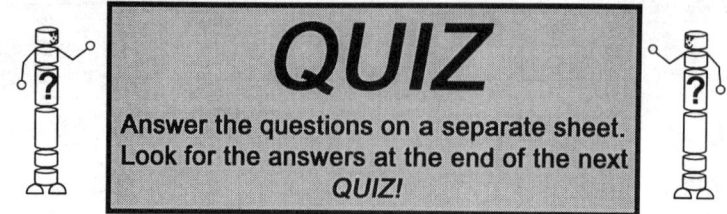

N1H01
When may you operate your amateur station somewhere in the US besides the location listed on your license?
A. Only during times of emergency
B. Only after giving proper notice to the FCC
C. During an emergency or an FCC-approved emergency practice
D. Whenever you want to

N1H02
With which non-amateur stations is a US amateur station allowed to communicate?
A. No non-amateur stations
B. All non-amateur stations
C. Only those authorized by the FCC
D. Only those who use international Morse code

N1I03
What is an amateur space station?
A. An amateur station operated on an unused frequency
B. An amateur station awaiting its new call letters from the FCC
C. An amateur station located more than 50 kilometers above the Earth's surface
D. An amateur station that communicates with Space Shuttles

N1I04
Who may be the licensee of an amateur space station?
A. An amateur holding an Amateur Extra class operator license
B. Any licensed amateur operator
C. Anyone designated by the commander of the spacecraft
D. No one unless specifically authorized by the government

UNAUTHORIZED PERSONS
NOVICE LESSON 14

Amateurs must make sure that persons without licenses do not operate their equipment when they are not present. A key operated main power switch will take care of the problem!

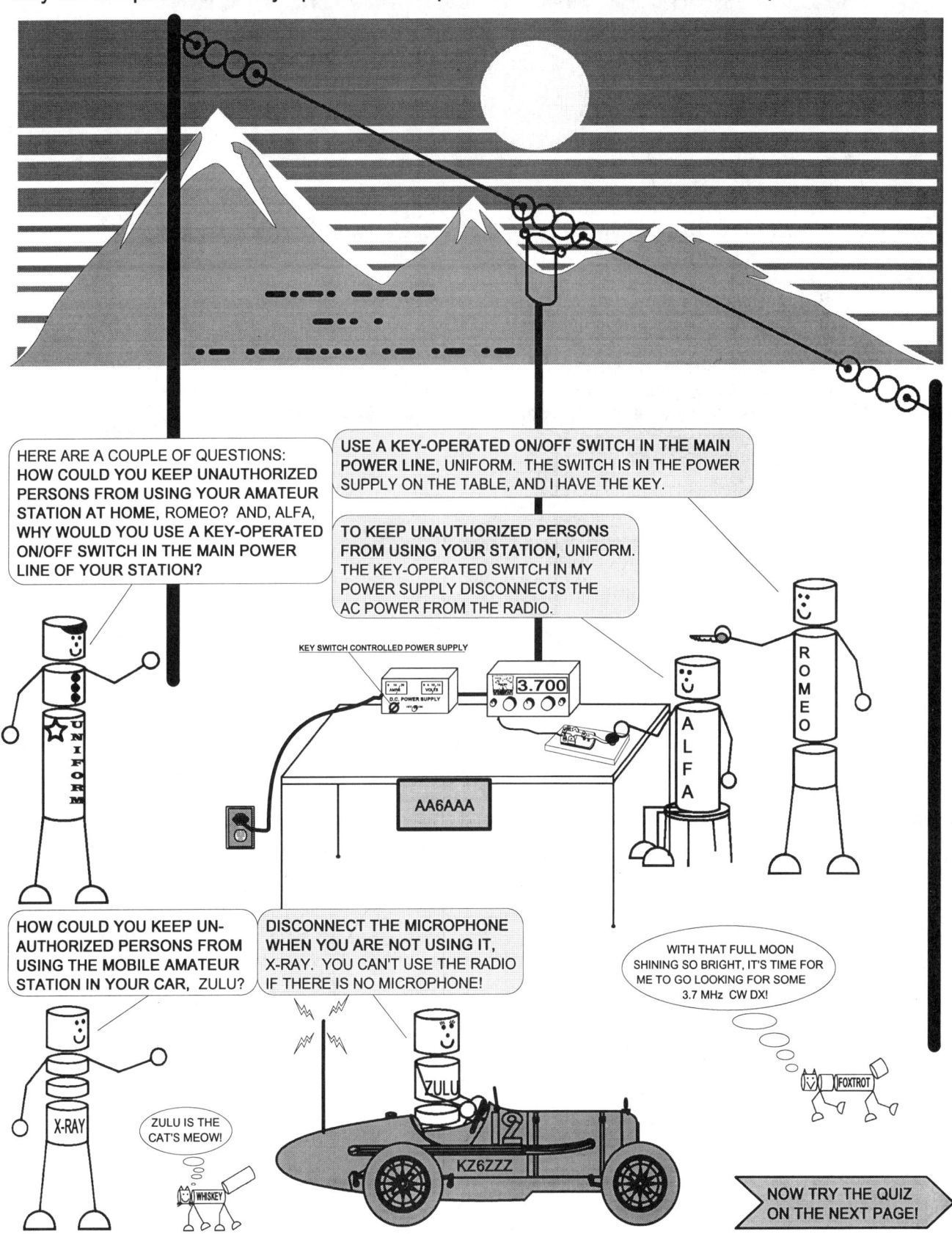

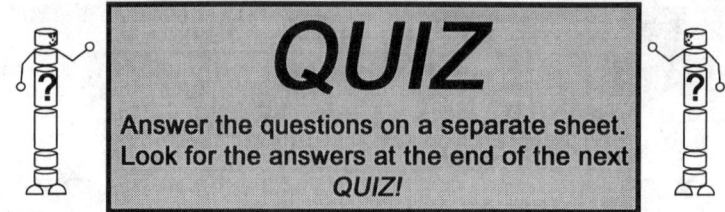

QUIZ

Answer the questions on a separate sheet.
Look for the answers at the end of the next
QUIZ!

N4A01
How could you best keep unauthorized persons from using your amateur station at home?
A. Use a carrier-operated relay in the main power line
B. Use a key-operated on/off switch in the main power line
C. Put a "Danger - High Voltage" sign in the station
D. Put fuses in the main power line

N4A03
Why would you use a key-operated on/off switch in the main power line of your station?
A. To keep unauthorized persons from using your station
B. For safety, in case the main fuses fail
C. To keep the power company from turning off your electricity during an emergency
D. For safety, to turn off the station in the event of an emergency

N4A02
How could you best keep unauthorized persons from using a mobile amateur station in your car?
A. Disconnect the microphone when you are not using it
B. Put a "do not touch" sign on the radio
C. Turn the radio off when you are not using it
D. Tune the radio to an unused frequency when you are done using it

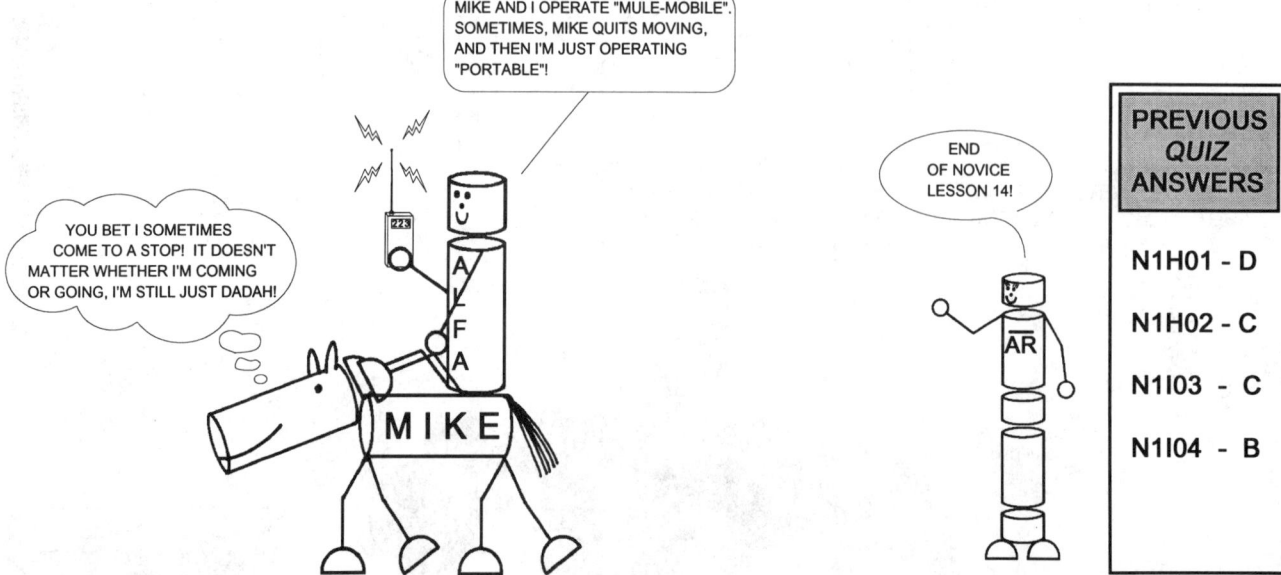

PREVIOUS *QUIZ* ANSWERS

N1H01 - D
N1H02 - C
N1I03 - C
N1I04 - B

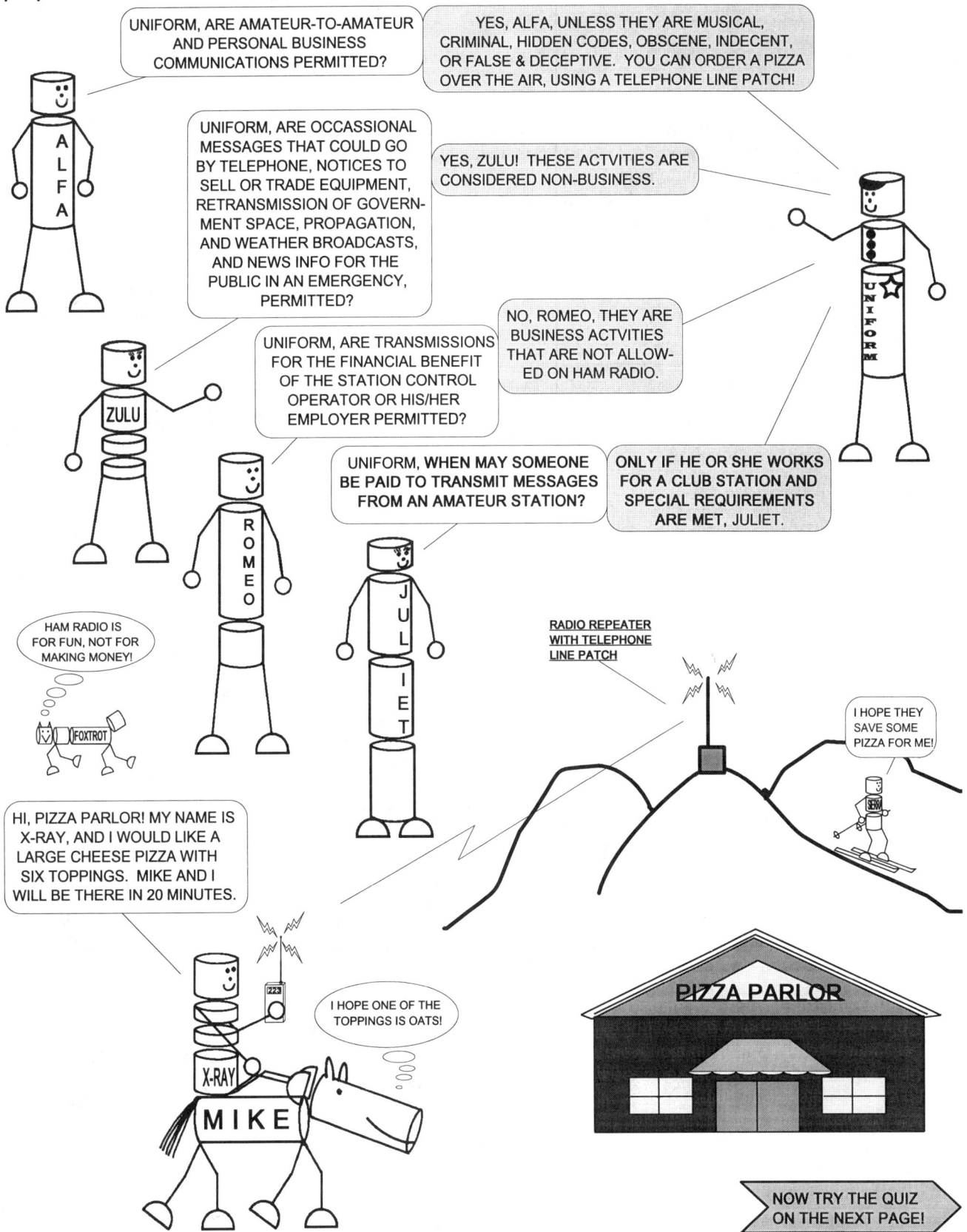

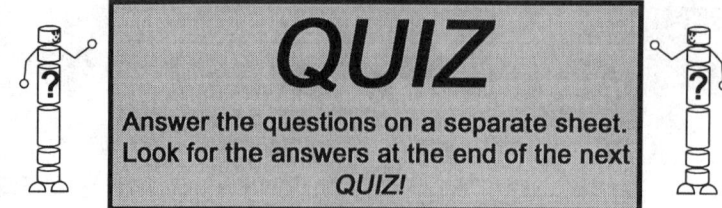

QUIZ

Answer the questions on a separate sheet. Look for the answers at the end of the next QUIZ!

N1I05
When may someone be paid to transmit messages from an amateur station?
A. Only if he or she works for a public service agency such as the Red Cross
B. Under no circumstances
C. Only if he or she reports all such payments to the IRS
D. Only if he or she works for a club station and special requirements are met

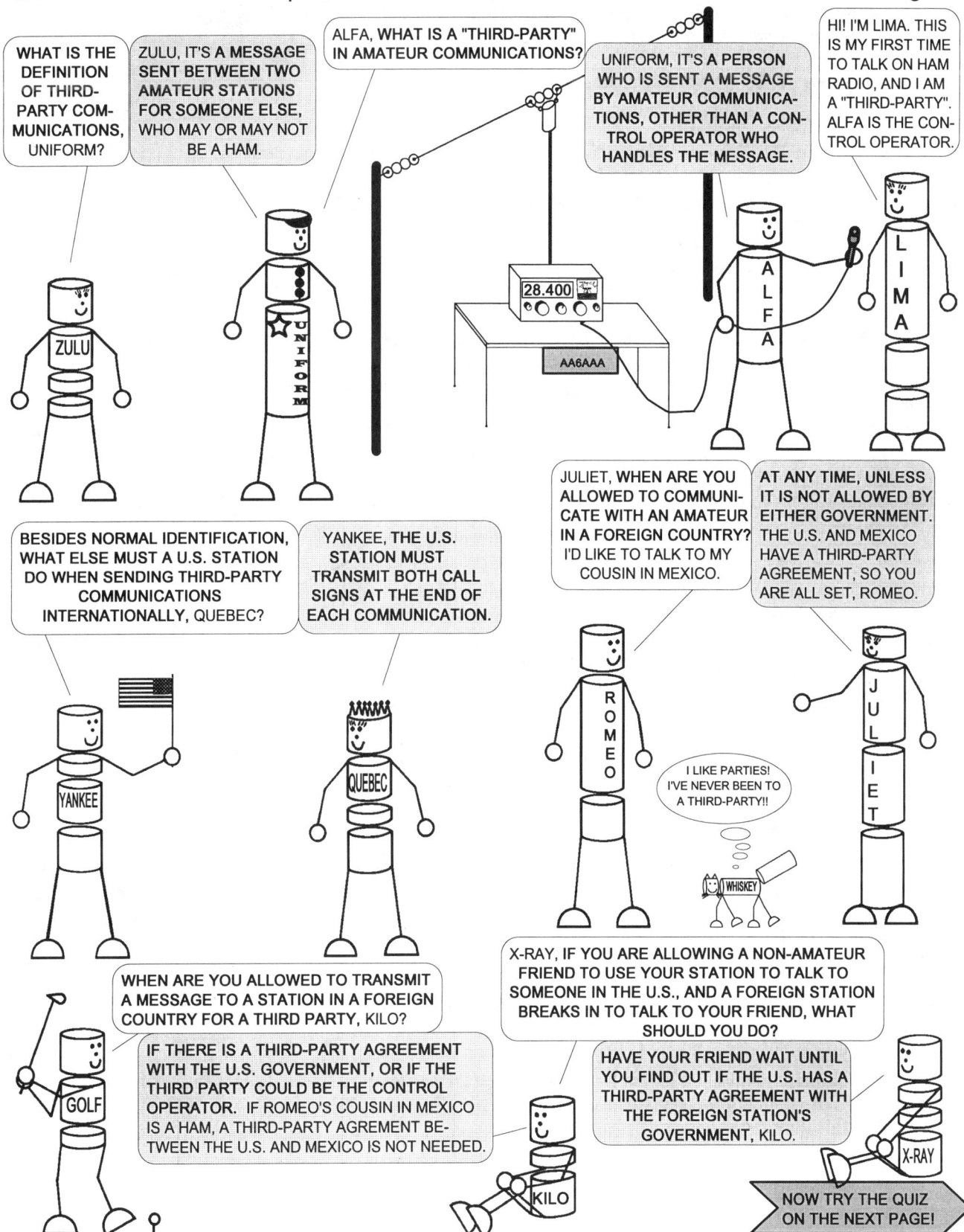

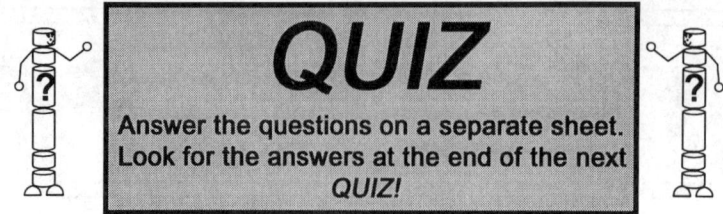

QUIZ
Answer the questions on a separate sheet. Look for the answers at the end of the next QUIZ!

N1I01
What is the definition of third-party communications?
A. A message sent between two amateur stations for someone else
B. Public service communications for a political party
C. Any messages sent by amateur stations
D. A three-minute transmission to another amateur

N1I09
What is a "third-party" in amateur communications?
A. An amateur station that breaks in to talk
B. A person who is sent a message by amateur communications other than a control operator who handles the message
C. A shortwave listener who monitors amateur communications
D. An unlicensed control operator

N1H10
Besides normal identification, what else must a US station do when sending third-party communications internationally?
A. The US station must transmit its own call sign at the beginning of each communication, and at least every ten minutes after that
B. The US station must transmit both call signs at the end of each communication
C. The US station must transmit its own call sign at the beginning of each communication, and at least every five minutes after that
D. Each station must transmit its own call sign at the end of each communication, and at least every five minutes after that

N1I02
When are you allowed to communicate with an amateur in a foreign country?
A. Only when the foreign amateur uses English
B. Only when you have permission from the FCC
C. Only when a third-party agreement exists between the US and the foreign country
D. At any time, unless it is not allowed by either government

N1I11
When are you allowed to transmit a message to a station in a foreign country for a third party?
A. Anytime
B. Never
C. Anytime, unless there is a third-party agreement between the US and the foreign government
D. If there is a third-party agreement with the US government, or if the third party could be the control operator

N1I10
If you are allowing a non-amateur friend to use your station to talk to someone in the US, and a foreign station breaks in to talk to your friend, what should you do?
A. Have your friend wait until you find out if the US has a third-party agreement with the foreign station's government
B. Stop all discussions and quickly sign off
C. Since you can talk to any foreign amateurs, your friend may keep talking as long as you are the control operator
D. Report the incident to the foreign amateur's government

PREVIOUS QUIZ ANSWERS

END OF NOVICE LESSON 16!

N1I05 - D

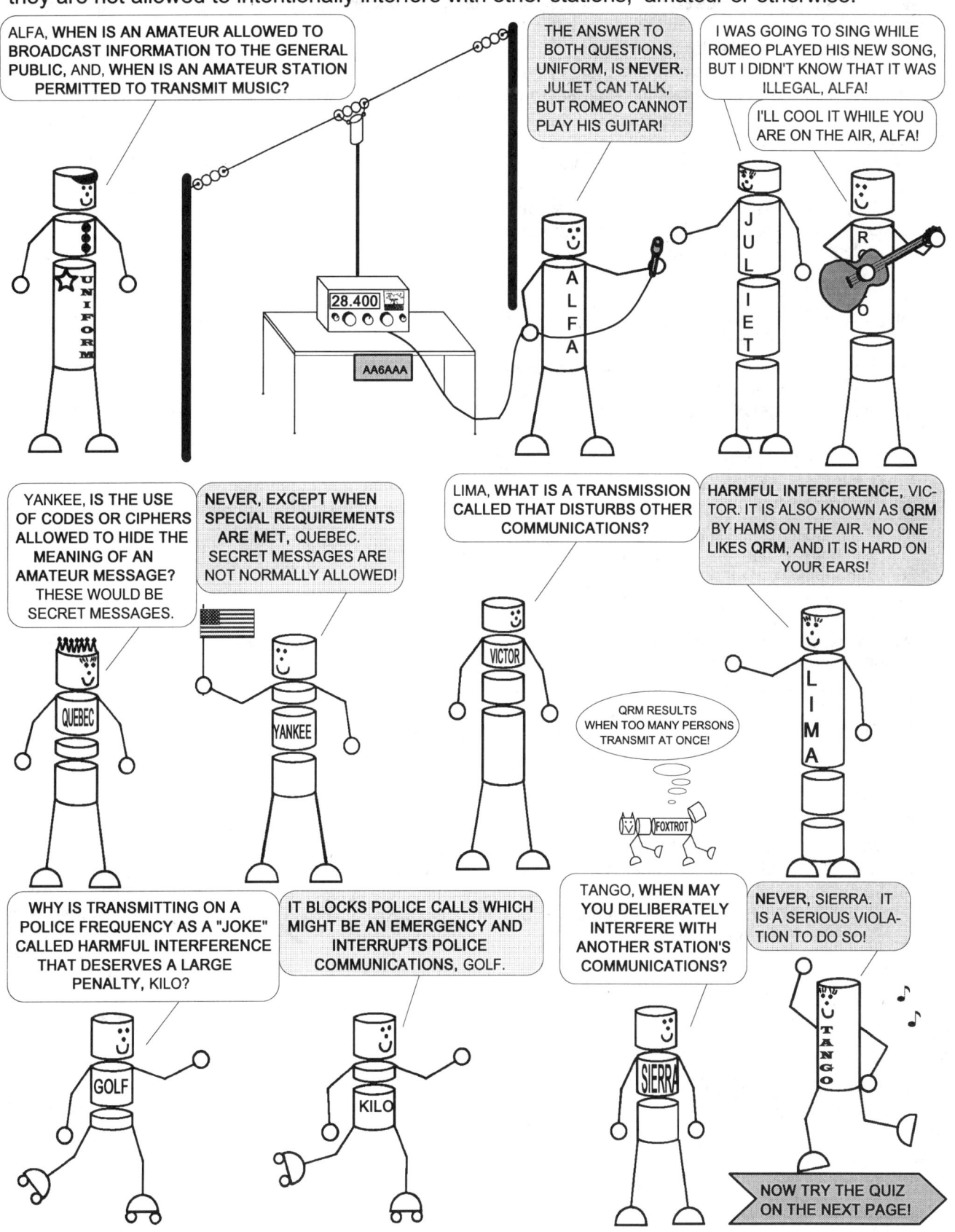

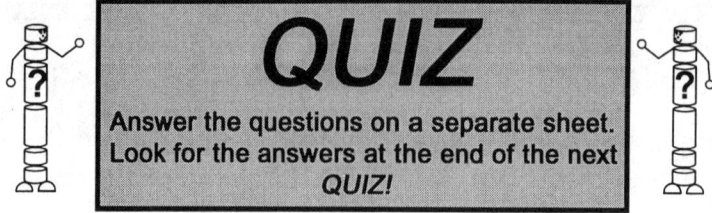

QUIZ

Answer the questions on a separate sheet. Look for the answers at the end of the next *QUIZ!*

N1I06
When is an amateur allowed to broadcast information to the general public?
A. Never
B. Only when the operator is being paid
C. Only when broadcasts last less than 1 hour
D. Only when broadcasts last longer than 15 minutes

N1I07
When is an amateur station permitted to transmit music?
A. Never
B. Only if the music played produces no spurious emissions
C. Only if it is used to jam an illegal transmission
D. Only if it is above 1280 MHz

N1I08
When is the use of codes or ciphers allowed to hide the meaning of an amateur message?
A. Only during contests
B. Only during nationally declared emergencies
C. Never, except when special requirements are met
D. Only on frequencies above 1280 MHz

N1J01
What is a transmission called that disturbs other communications?
A. Interrupted CW
B. Harmful interference
C. Transponder signals
D. Unidentified transmissions

N1J02
Why is transmitting on a police frequency as a "joke" called harmful interference that deserves a large penalty?
A. It annoys everyone who listens
B. It blocks police calls which might be an emergency and interrupts police communications
C. It is in bad taste to communicate with non-amateurs, even as a joke
D. It is poor amateur practice to transmit outside the amateur bands

N1J03
When may you deliberately interfere with another station's communications?
A. Only if the station is operating illegally
B. Only if the station begins transmitting on a frequency you are using
C. Never
D. You may expect, and cause, deliberate interference because it can't be helped during crowded band conditions

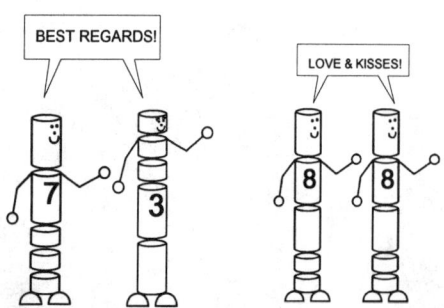

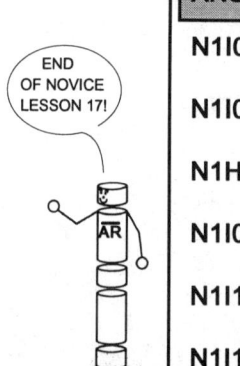

END OF NOVICE LESSON 17!

PREVIOUS QUIZ ANSWERS

N1I01 - A
N1I09 - B
N1H10 - B
N1I02 - D
N1I11 - D
N1I10 - A

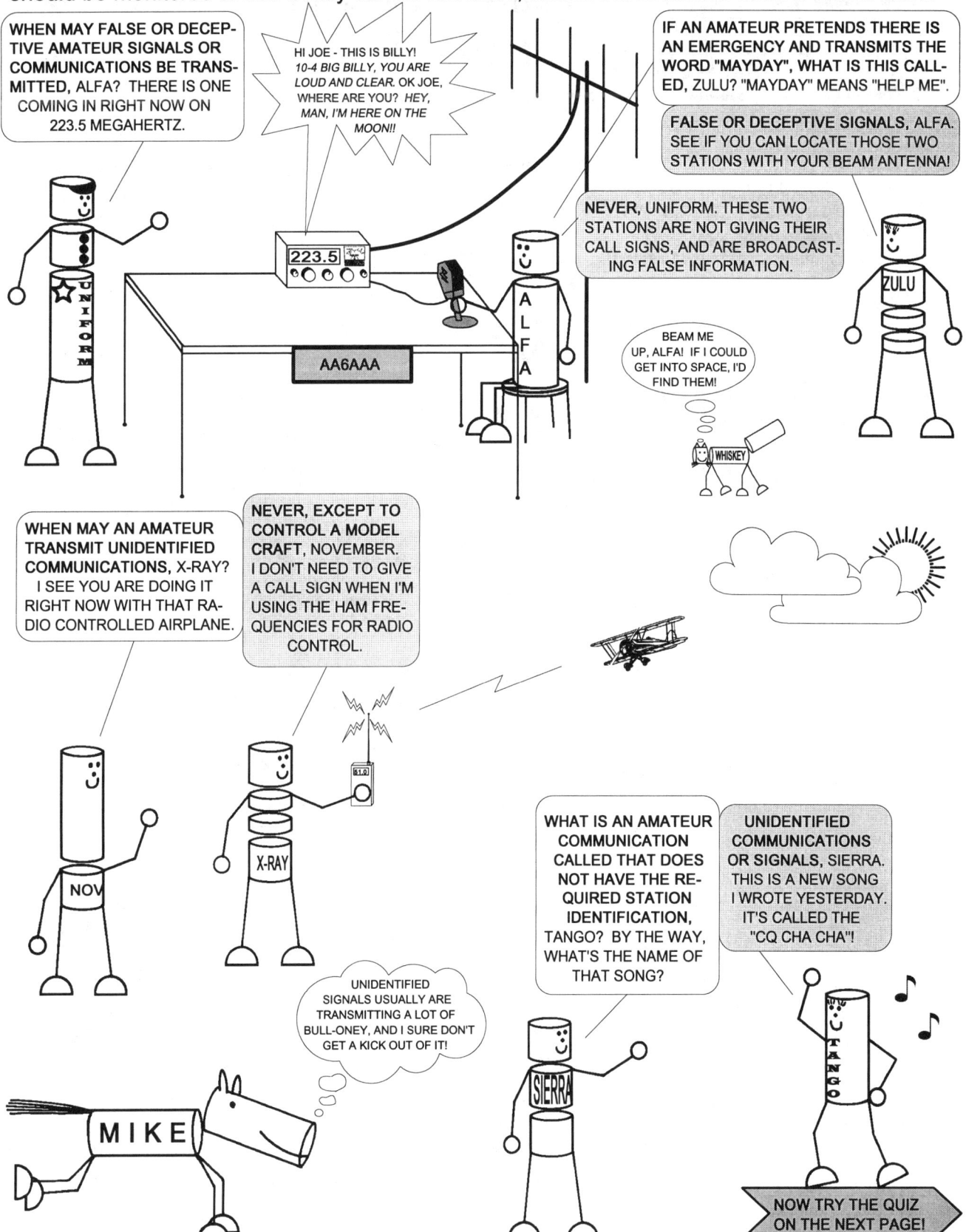

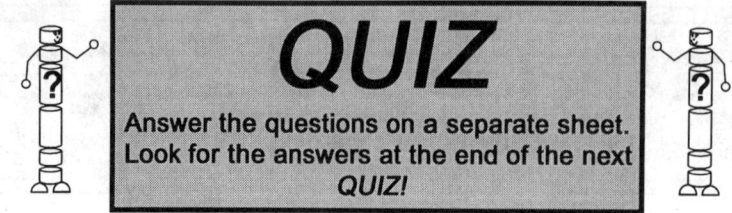

QUIZ

Answer the questions on a separate sheet. Look for the answers at the end of the next QUIZ!

N1J04
When may false or deceptive amateur signals or communications be transmitted?
A. Never
B. When operating a beacon transmitter in a "fox hunt" exercise
C. When playing a harmless "practical joke"
D. When you need to hide the meaning of a message for secrecy

N1J05
If an amateur pretends there is an emergency and transmits the word "MAYDAY," what is this called?
A. A traditional greeting in May
B. An emergency test transmission
C. False or deceptive signals
D. Nothing special; "MAYDAY" has no meaning in an emergency

N1J06
When may an amateur transmit unidentified communications?
A. Only for brief tests not meant as messages
B. Only if it does not interfere with others
C. Never, except to control a model craft
D. Only for two-way or third-party communications

N1J07
What is an amateur communication called that does not have the required station identification?
A. Unidentified communications or signals
B. Reluctance modulation
C. Test emission
D. Tactical communication

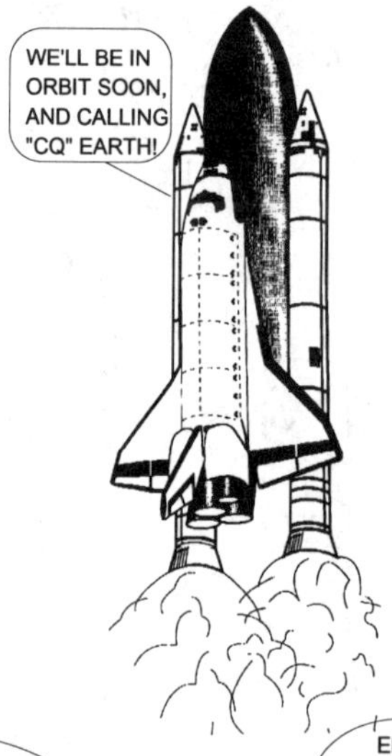

PREVIOUS QUIZ ANSWERS

N1I06 - A
N1I07 - A
N1I08 - C
N1J01 - B
N1J02 - B
N1J03 - C

RESPECT FOR OTHERS
NOVICE LESSON 19

Politeness is very important on the air, and you should use the minimum amount of power needed. It is not polite to transmit when others are on the frequency, unless you are invited to do so. If you are testing your equipment, connect it to a "dummy" antenna so no one will hear you.

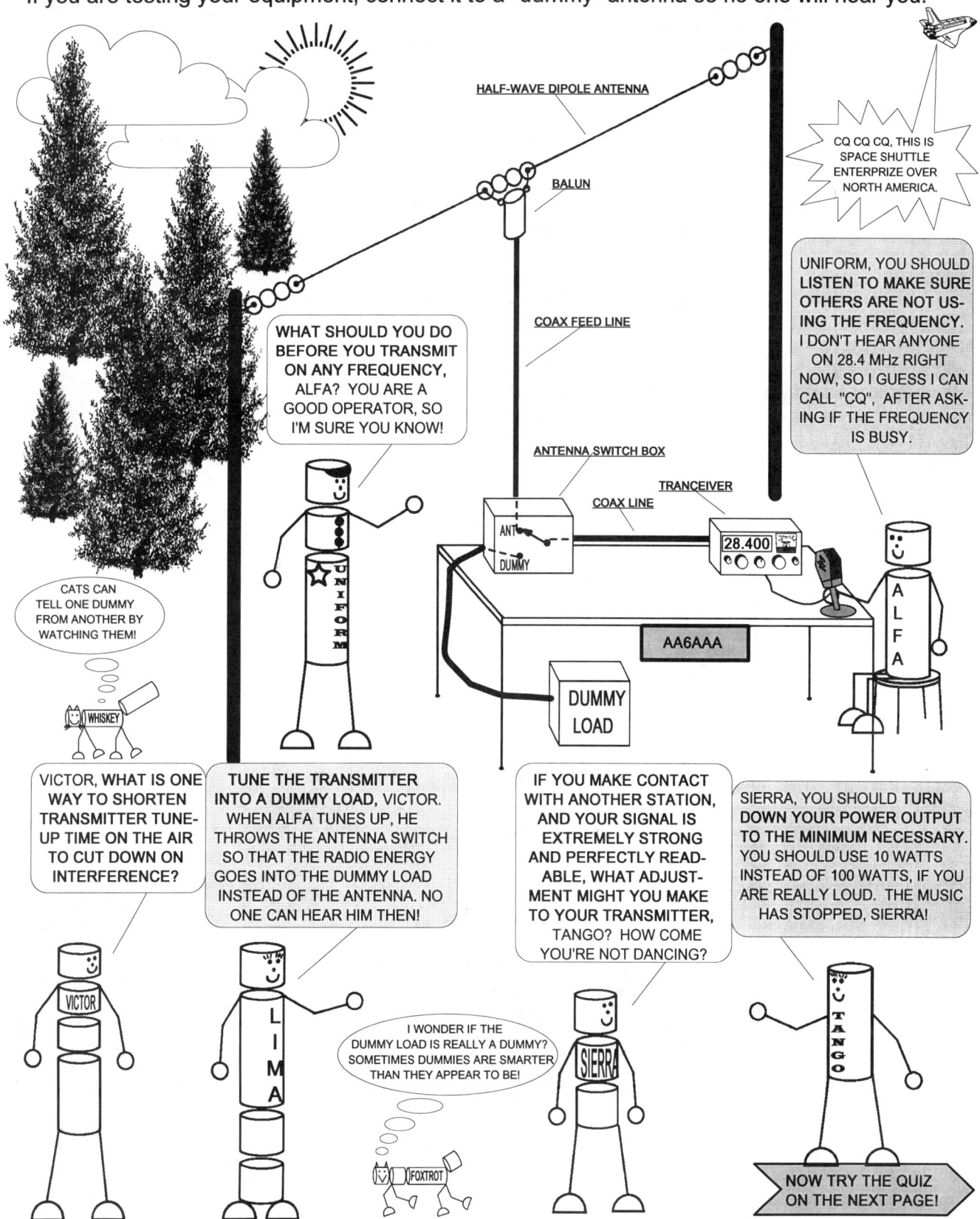

NOW TRY THE QUIZ ON THE NEXT PAGE!

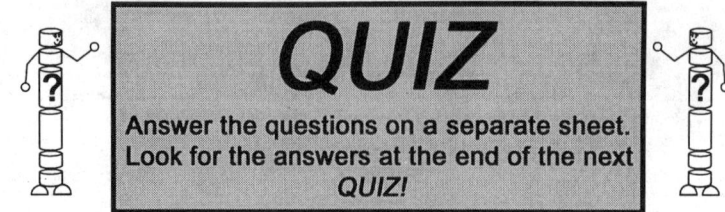

N2A01
What should you do before you transmit on any frequency?
A. Listen to make sure others are not using the frequency
B. Listen to make sure that someone will be able to hear you
C. Check your antenna for resonance at the selected frequency
D. Make sure the SWR on your antenna feed line is high enough

N2A03
What is one way to shorten transmitter tune-up time on the air to cut down on interference?
A. Use a random wire antenna
B. Tune up on 40 meters first, then switch to the desired band
C. Tune the transmitter into a dummy load
D. Use twin lead instead of coaxial-cable feed lines

N2A02
If you make contact with another station and your signal is extremely strong and perfectly readable, what adjustment might you make to your transmitter?
A. Turn on your speech processor
B. Reduce you SWR
C. Continue with your contact, making no changes
D. Turn down your power output to the minimum necessary

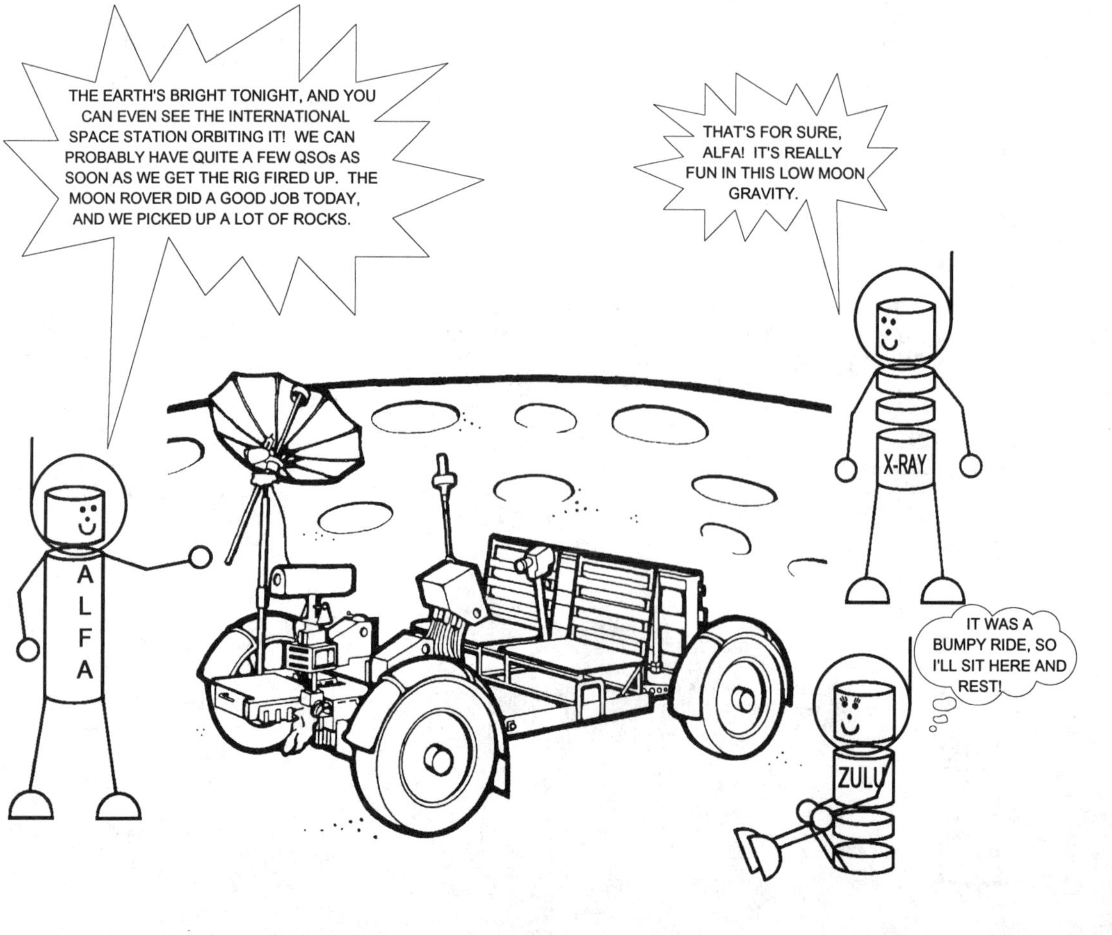

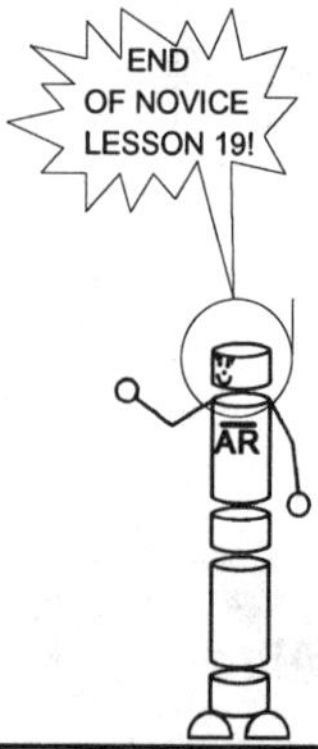

PREVIOUS QUIZ ANSWERS
N1J04 - A
N1J05 - C
N1J06 - C
N1J07 - A

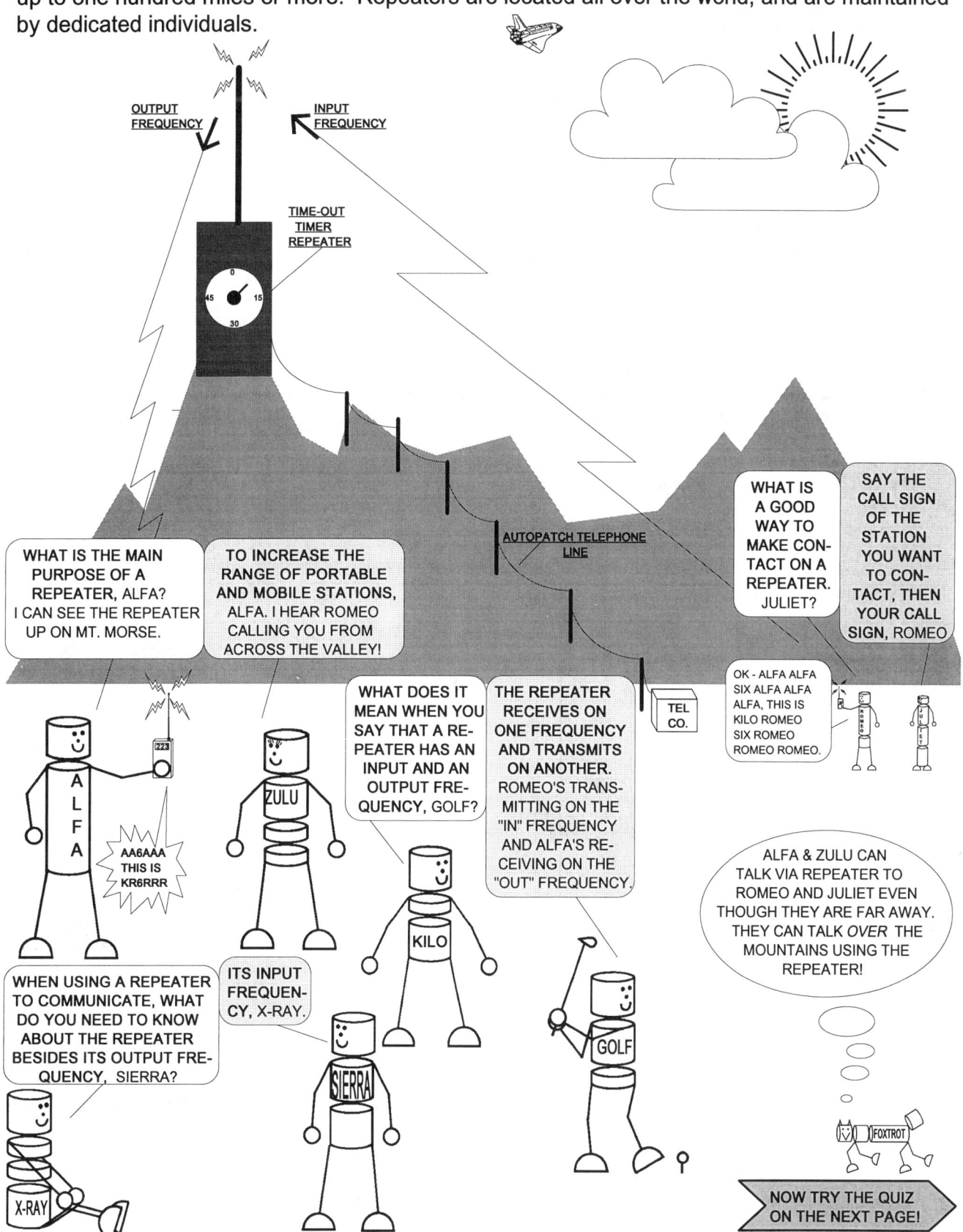

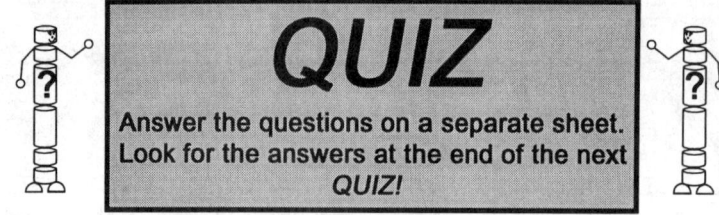

QUIZ

Answer the questions on a separate sheet. Look for the answers at the end of the next *QUIZ!*

N2B11
What is the main purpose of a repeater?
A. To make local information available 24 hours a day
B. To link amateur stations with the telephone system
C. To retransmit NOAA weather information during severe storm warnings
D. To increase the range of portable and mobile stations

N2B09
What is a good way to make contact on a repeater?
A. Say the call sign of the station you want to contact three times
B. Say the other operator's name, then your call sign three times
C. Say the call sign of the station you want to contact, then your call sign
D. Say, "Breaker, breaker," then your call sign

N2B12
What does it mean to say that a repeater has an input and an output frequency?
A. The repeater receives on one frequency and transmits on another
B. The repeater offers a choice of operating frequency, in case one is busy
C. One frequency is used to control the repeater and another is used to retransmit received signals
D. The repeater must receive an access code on one frequency before retransmitting received signals

N2B10
When using a repeater to communicate, what do you need to know about the repeater besides its output frequency?
A. Its input frequency
B. Its call sign
C. Its power level
D. Whether or not it has a phone patch

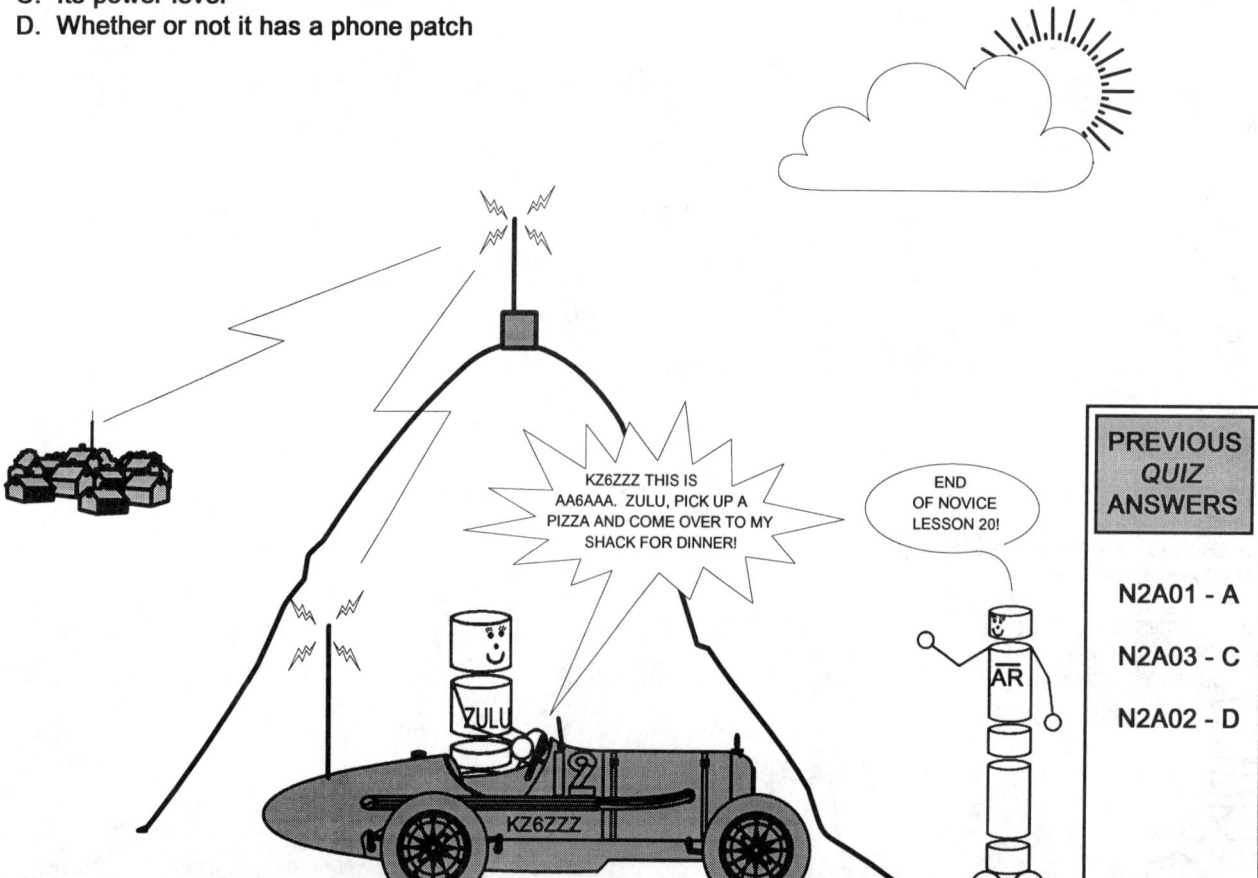

PREVIOUS *QUIZ* ANSWERS

N2A01 - A

N2A03 - C

N2A02 - D

SIMPLEX & REPEATER OPERATION
NOVICE LESSON 21

When a repeater is not needed to contact another station, *simplex*, or direct communication is used. Repeaters use *autopatch* to connect to telephone lines, time-out timers to prevent long transmissions, and subaudible tone control to prevent unwanted keying of the repeater.

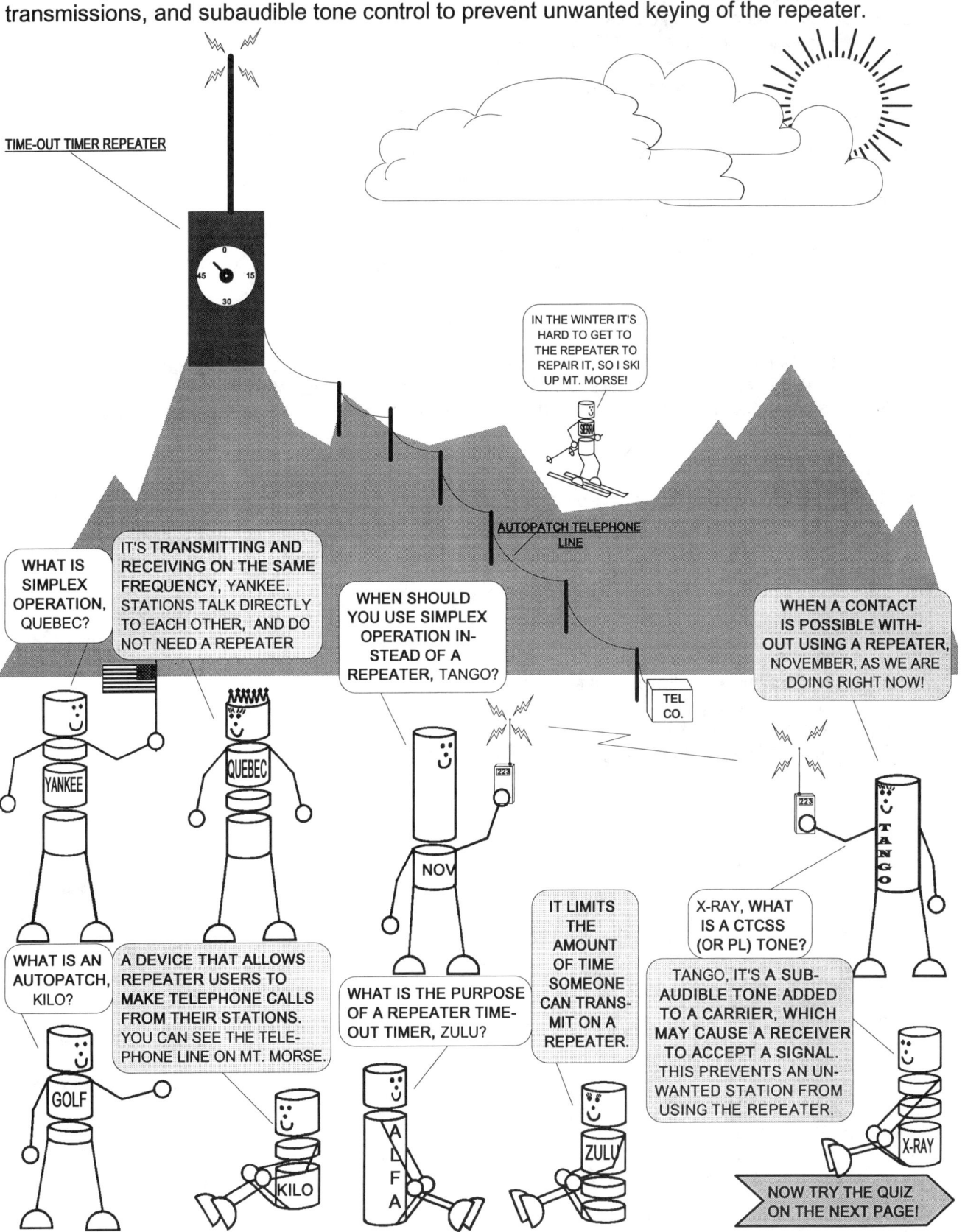

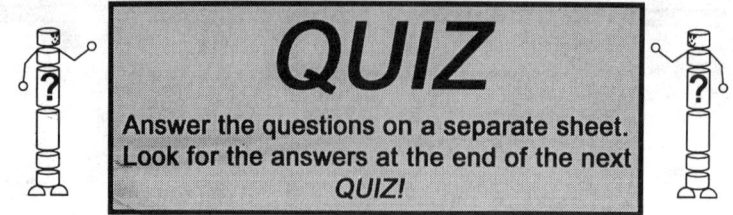

QUIZ

Answer the questions on a separate sheet. Look for the answers at the end of the next QUIZ!

N2B07
What is simplex operation?
A. Transmitting and receiving on the same frequency
B. Transmitting and receiving over a wide area
C. Transmitting on one frequency and receiving on another
D. Transmitting one-way communications

N2B08
When should you use simplex operation instead of a repeater?
A. When the most reliable communications are needed
B. When a contact is possible without using a repeater
C. When an emergency telephone call is needed
D. When you are traveling and need some local information

N2B13
What is an autopatch?
A. Something that automatically selects the strongest signal to be repeated
B. A device which connects a mobile station to the next repeater if it moves out of range of the first
C. A device that allows repeater users to make telephone calls from their stations
D. A device which locks other stations out of a repeater when there is an important conversation in progress

N2B14
What is the purpose of a repeater time-out timer?
A. It lets a repeater have a rest period after heavy use
B. It logs repeater transmit time to predict when a repeater will fail
C. It tells how long someone has been using a repeater
D. It limits the amount of time someone can transmit on a repeater

N2B15
What is a CTCSS (or PL) tone?
A. A special signal used for telecommand control of model craft
B. A sub-audible tone added to a carrier which may cause a receiver to accept a signal
C. A tone used by repeaters to mark the end of a transmission
D. A special signal used for telemetry between amateur space stations and Earth stations

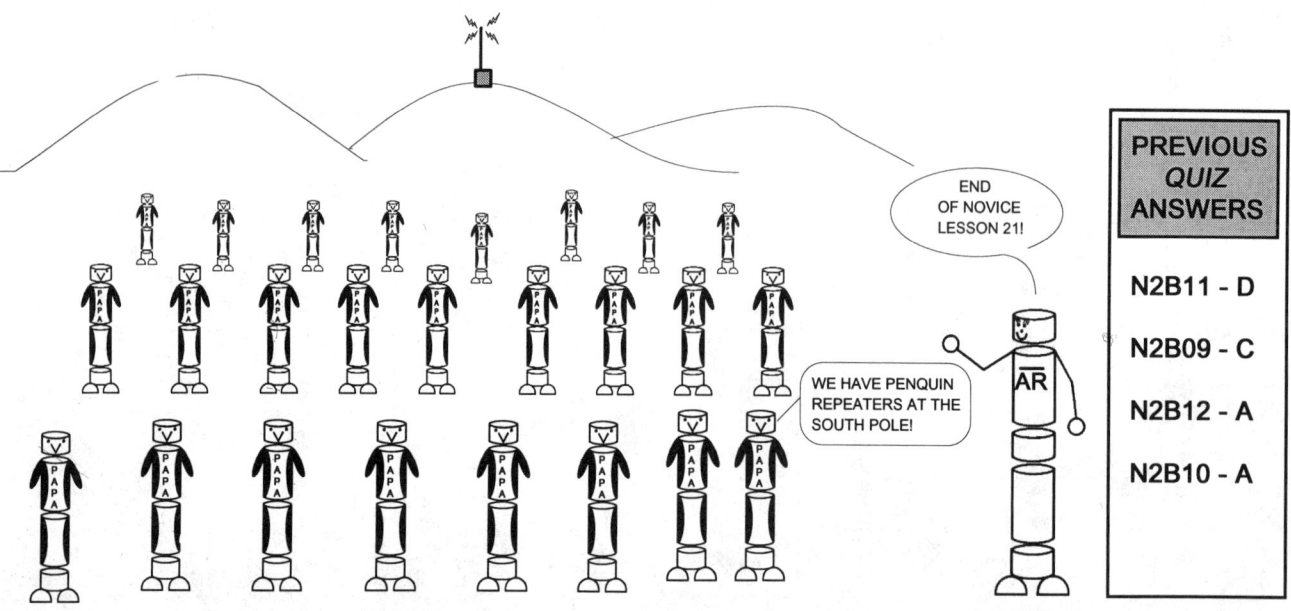

PREVIOUS QUIZ ANSWERS

N2B11 - D
N2B09 - C
N2B12 - A
N2B10 - A

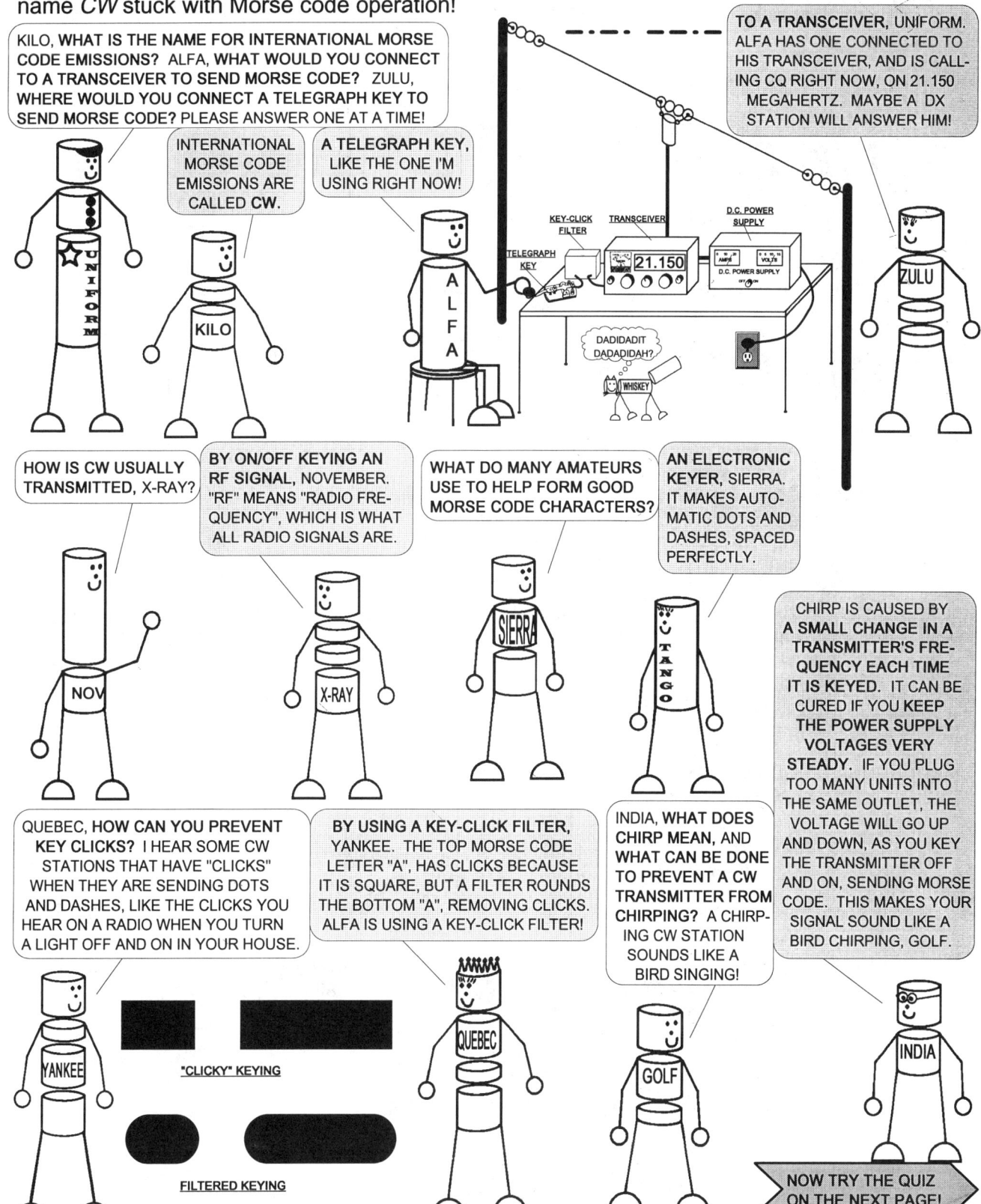

QUIZ

Answer the questions on a separate sheet. Look for the answers at the end of the next QUIZ!

N8A03
What is the name for international Morse code emissions?
A. RTTY
B. Data
C. CW
D. Phone

N7B01
What would you connect to a transceiver to send Morse code?
A. A terminal-node controller
B. A telegraph key
C. An SWR meter
D. An antenna switch

N7B02
Where would you connect a telegraph key to send Morse code?
A. To a power supply
B. To an antenna switch
C. To a transceiver
D. To an antenna

N8A01
How is CW usually transmitted?
A. By frequency-shift keying an RF signal
B. By on/off keying an RF signal
C. By audio-frequency-shift keying an oscillator tone
D. By on/off keying an audio-frequency signal

N7B03
What do many amateurs use to help form good Morse code characters?
A. A key-operated on/off switch
B. An electronic keyer
C. A key-click filter
D. A DTMF keypad

N8A07
How can you prevent key clicks?
A. By sending CW more slowly
B. By increasing power
C. By using a better power supply
D. By using a key-click filter

N8A08
What does chirp mean?
A. An overload in a receiver's audio circuit whenever CW is received
B. A high-pitched tone which is received along with a CW signal
C. A small change in a transmitter's frequency each time it is keyed
D. A slow change in transmitter frequency as the circuit warms up

N8A09
What can be done to keep a CW transmitter from chirping?
A. Add a low-pass filter
B. Use an RF amplifier
C. Keep the power supply current very steady
D. Keep the power supply voltages very steady

END OF NOVICE LESSON 22!

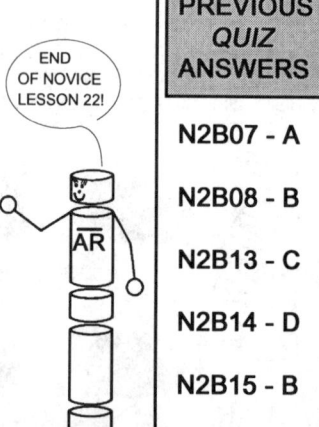

PREVIOUS QUIZ ANSWERS

N2B07 - A
N2B08 - B
N2B13 - C
N2B14 - D
N2B15 - B

MORSE CODE OPERATION
NOVICE LESSON 23

Certain procedures are followed when operating on Morse code, so that misunderstanding is reduced to a minimum. Morse code is very useful for talking to non-English speaking hams worldwide. It can work DX using low power and simple antennas. It is the most efficient form of communications, permitting the maximum number of stations to operate on ham frequencies.

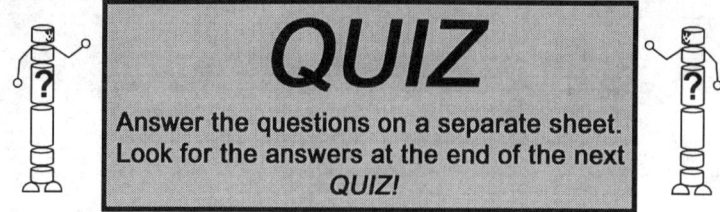

QUIZ

Answer the questions on a separate sheet. Look for the answers at the end of the next QUIZ!

N2A09
What is the meaning of the procedural signal "DE"?
A. "From" or "this is," as in "W9NGT DE N9BTT"
B. "Directional Emissions" from your antenna
C. "Received all correctly"
D. "Calling any station"

N2A05
What is the correct way to call CQ when using Morse code?
A. Send the letters "CQ" three times, followed by "DE," followed by your call sign sent once
B. Send the letters "CQ" three times, followed by "DE," followed by your call sign sent three times
C. Send the letters "CQ" ten times, followed by "DE," followed by your call sign sent once
D. Send the letters "CQ" over and over

N2A06
How should you answer a Morse code CQ call?
A. Send your call sign four times
B. Send the other station's call sign twice, followed by "DE," followed by your call sign twice
C. Send the other station's call sign once, followed by "DE," followed by your call sign four times
D. Send your call sign followed by your name, station location and a signal report

N2A07
At what speed should a Morse code CQ call be transmitted?
A. Only speeds below five WPM
B. The highest speed your keyer will operate
C. Any speed at which you can reliably receive
D. The highest speed at which you can control the keyer

N2A10
What is the meaning of the procedural signal "K"?
A. "Any station transmit"
B. "All received correctly"
C. "End of message"
D. "Called station only transmit"

THERE GOES AN OSCAR BY AGAIN! THERE WILL SOON BE EVEN MORE OSCARS, SO THAT HAMS ON THE VHF AND UHF FREQUENCIES WILL BE ABLE TO TALK WORLDWIDE ANYTIME OF THE DAY OR NIGHT. YOU CAN USE CW FOR CONTACTS ON THE OSCARS, AND IT IS USEFUL, ESPECIALLY FOR THE ONES THAT ARE ONLY OVERHEAD FOR A FEW MINUTES. YOU MUST SEND VERY FAST TO HAVE A QSO.

END OF NOVICE LESSON 23!

PREVIOUS QUIZ ANSWERS

N8A03 - C
N7B01 - B
N7B02 - C
N8A01 - B
N7B03 - B
N8A07 - D
N8A08 - C
N8A09 - D

VOICE EMISSIONS & CONNECTIONS
NOVICE LESSON 24

Voice operation is the easiest way to get acquainted with ham radio. The Phoneticos help to clarify voice operation when QRM and QRN become a problem. An "emission" is the type of signal emitted from an amateur station.

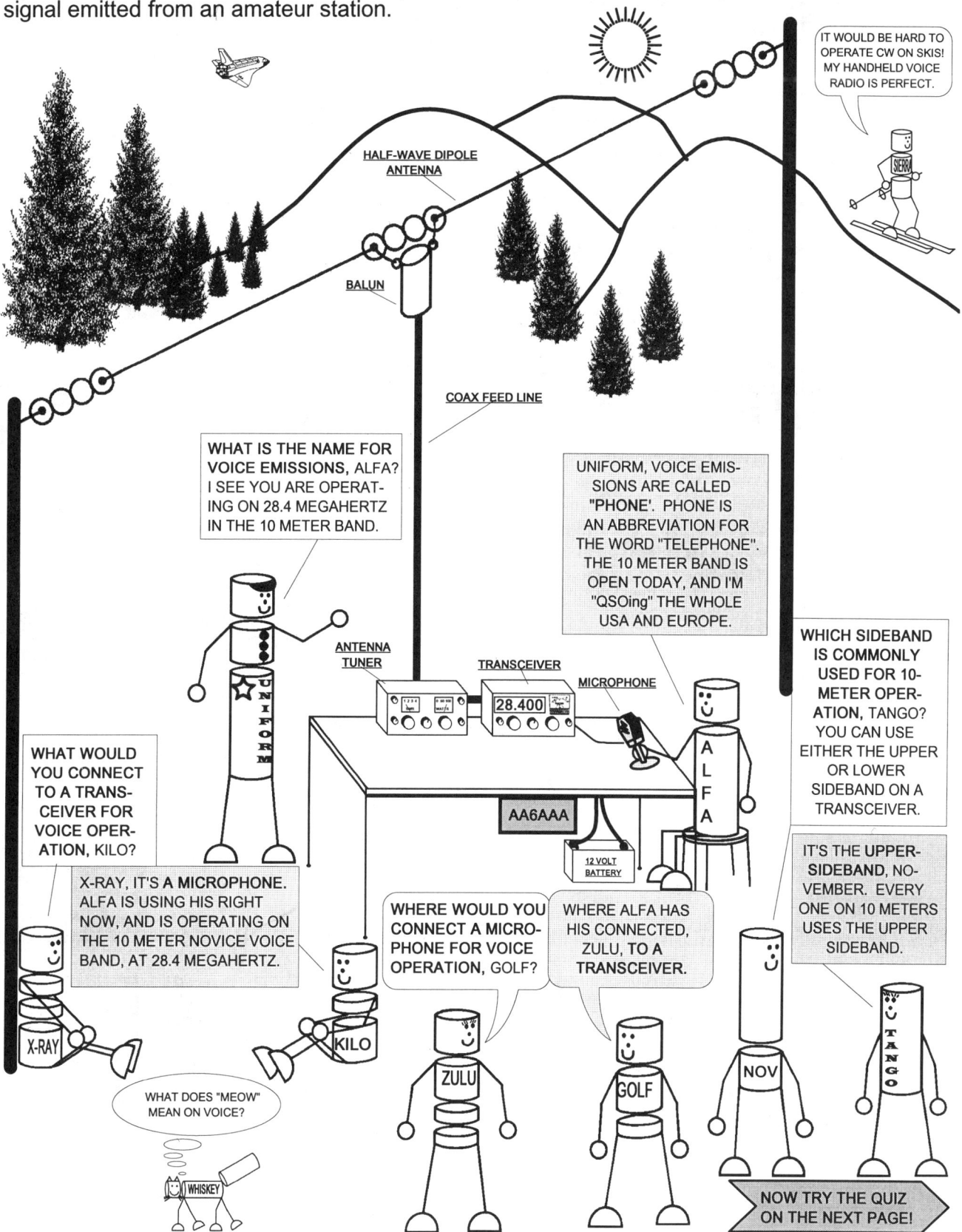

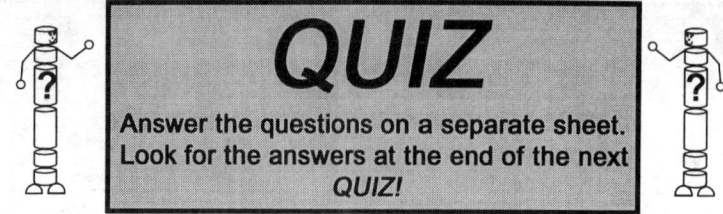

QUIZ

Answer the questions on a separate sheet. Look for the answers at the end of the next QUIZ!

N8A06
What is the name for voice emissions?
A. RTTY
B. Data
C. CW
D. Phone

N7B05
What would you connect to a transceiver for voice operation?
A. A splatter filter
B. A terminal-voice controller
C. A receiver audio filter
D. A microphone

N7B04
Where would you connect a microphone for voice operation?
A. To a power supply
B. To an antenna switch
C. To a transceiver
D. To an antenna

N8A11
Which sideband is commonly used for 10-meter phone operation?
A. Upper-sideband
B. Lower-sideband
C. Amplitude-compandored sideband
D. Double-sideband

INFO! IF A RADIO SIGNAL HAS NO INFORMATION ON IT, SUCH AS MORSE CODE KEYING OR VOICE, IT HAS NO "SIDEBANDS". WHEN CODE OR VOICE ARE USED, AN "UPPER" FREQUENCY SIDEBAND (USB), AND A "LOWER" FREQUENCY SIDEBAND (LSB) ARE CREATED. ONLY ONE OF THE SIDEBANDS IS NEEDED TO RECEIVE THE SIGNAL. ON ALL OF THE HAM BANDS, MORSE CODE IS RECEIVED ON "USB". ON HAM BANDS ABOVE 10 MHz, "USB" IS USED ON VOICE, AND ON HAM BANDS BELOW 10 MHz, "LSB" IS USED ON VOICE.

HERE COMES DELTA, AND SHE MUST BE HEADED FOR THE GREEN GRASS BACK THERE. I THINK I'LL GO SEE IF ALFA IS WORKING ANYONE ON 10 METERS. SOME DAYS THAT BAND IS REALLY HOT!

MIKE IS KICKING UP HIS HEELS, SO HE MUST BE RARING TO GO TODAY! I'LL GO LOOK AROUND IN THE MEADOW AND SEE IF ANYTHING NEW IS GROWING TO MUNCH ON, AND CHECK ON THE ANTENNA.

END OF NOVICE LESSON 24!

PREVIOUS QUIZ ANSWERS

N2A09 - A

N2A05 - B

N2A06 - B

N2A07 - C

N2A10 - A

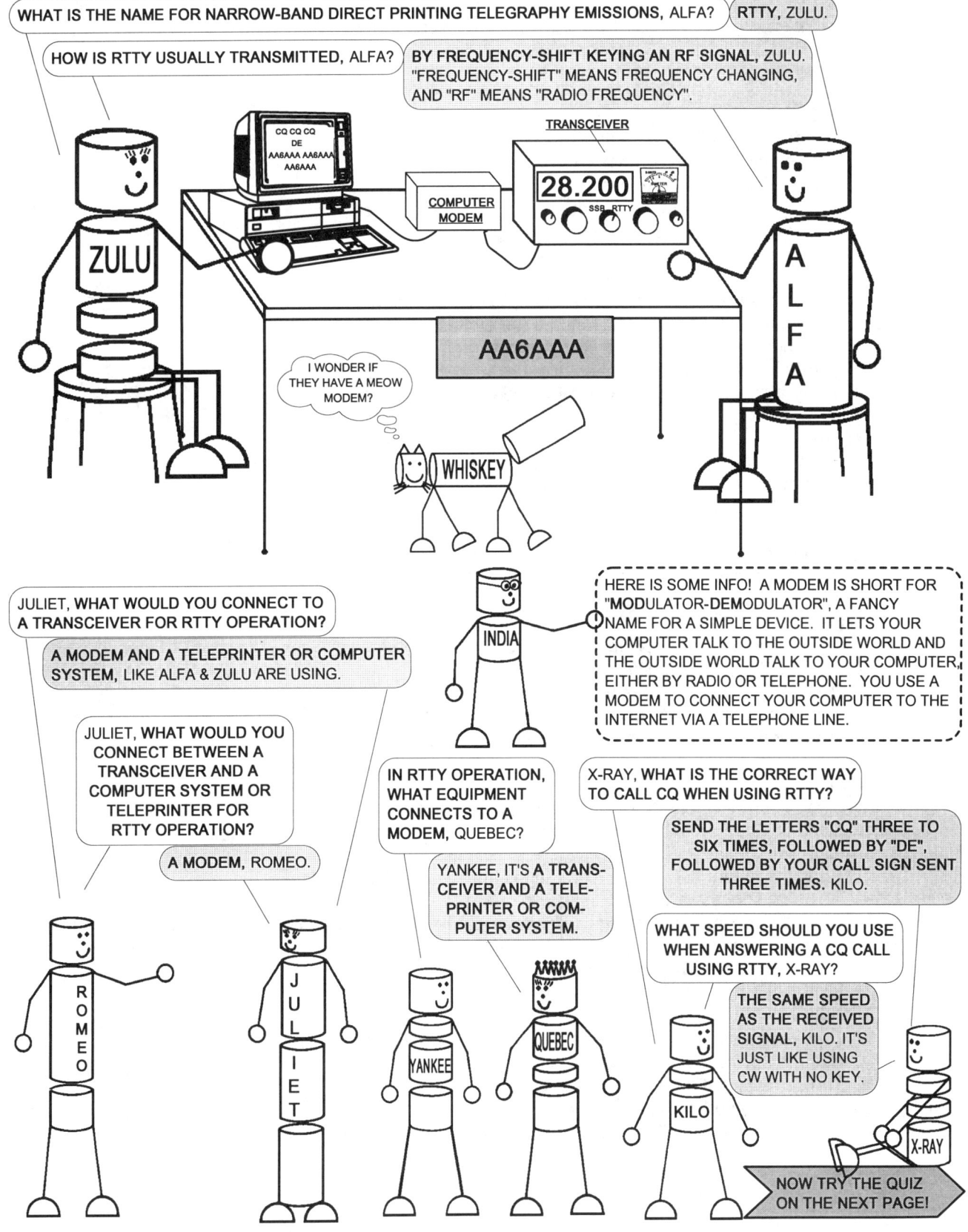

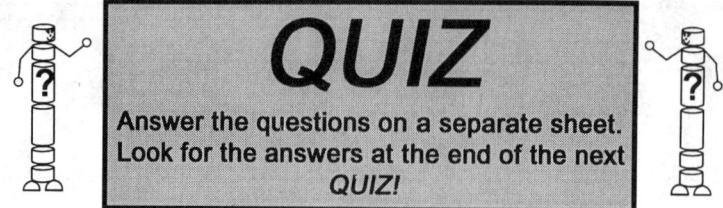

QUIZ

Answer the questions on a separate sheet. Look for the answers at the end of the next QUIZ!

N8A04
What is the name for narrow-band direct-printing telegraphy emissions?
A. RTTY
B. Data
C. CW
D. Phone

N8A02
How is RTTY usually transmitted?
A. By frequency-shift keying an RF signal
B. By on/off keying an RF signal
C. By digital pulse-code keying of an unmodulated carrier
D. By on/off keying an audio-frequency signal

N7B06
What would you connect to a transceiver for RTTY operation?
A. A modem and a teleprinter or computer system
B. A computer, a printer and a RTTY refresh unit
C. A terminal voice controller
D. A modem, a monitor and a DTMF keypad

N7B07
What would you connect between a transceiver and a computer system or teleprinter for RTTY operation?
A. An RS-232 interface
B. A DTMF keypad
C. A modem
D. A terminal-network controller

N7B10
In RTTY operation, what equipment connects to a modem?
A. A DTMF keypad, a monitor and a transceiver
B. A DTMF microphone, a monitor and a transceiver
C. A transceiver and a terminal-network controller
D. A transceiver and a teleprinter or computer system

N2B01
What is the correct way to call CQ when using RTTY?
A. Send the letters "CQ" three times, followed by "DE," followed by your call sign sent once
B. Send the letters "CQ" three to six times, followed by "DE," followed by your call sign sent three times
C. Send the letters "CQ" ten times, followed by the procedural signal "DE," followed by your call sent one time
D. Send the letters "CQ" over and over

N2B02
What speed should you use when answering a CQ call using RTTY?
A. Half the speed of the received signal
B. The same speed as the received signal
C. Twice the speed of the received signal
D. Any speed, since RTTY systems adjust to any signal speed

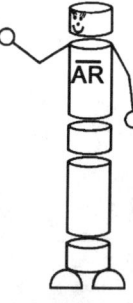

PREVIOUS *QUIZ* ANSWERS

N8A06 - D

N7B05 - D

N7B04 - C

N8A11 - A

PACKET EMISSIONS & CONNECTIONS
NOVICE LESSON 26

Packet radio is a method of sending and receiving little bundles of data and information, called packets. It is very popular, and messages can be sent worldwide via electronic bulletin boards.

KILO: WHAT IS THE NAME FOR PACKET-RADIO EMISSIONS, ALFA?

ALFA: DATA, KILO. DIGITAL RADIO IS CALLED "DATA" OPERATION.

KILO: WHAT WOULD YOU CONNECT BETWEEN A COMPUTER SYSTEM AND A TRANSCEIVER FOR PACKET-RADIO OPERATION, ALFA?

ALFA: A TERMINAL NODE CONTROLLER, KILO. IT IS CALLED A "TNC" FOR SHORT, AND IS A SMART MODEM.

Computer screen: CMD:C W6JW ***CONNECTED ENTER: B, J, K, L, R, S, HELP

PACKET TNC — DCD PTT STA CON PWR

TRANSCEIVER — 223.56 SSB FM

Callsign: AA6AAA

WHISKEY (cat thought): HOW MANY MEOWS ARE IN A PACKET?

INDIA: HERE IS SOME INFO! A TERMINAL NODE CONTROLLER, OR "TNC", IS AN ELECTRONIC BOX THAT PERMITS YOU TO TALK ON THE AIR USING YOUR COMPUTER. YOU CAN SEND MESSAGES TO HAM RADIO BULLETIN BOARDS ALL OVER THE WORLD, FOR ELECTRONIC DELIVERY TO YOUR FRIENDS. IF YOU LEAVE YOUR RADIO AND TNC ON, YOU CAN HAVE YOUR OWN PRIVATE ELECTRONIC "MAIL BOX".

ROMEO: JULIET, WHERE WOULD YOU CONNECT A TERMINAL-NODE CONTROLLER FOR PACKET-RADIO OPERATION?

JULIET: BETWEEN YOUR COMPUTER AND TRANSCEIVER, ROMEO. ALFA HAS HIS TNC CONNECTED CORRECTLY AND IS OPERATING PACKET RIGHT NOW.

YANKEE: IN PACKET-RADIO OPERATION, WHAT EQUIPMENT CONNECTS TO A TERMINAL-NODE CONTROLLER, QUEBEC?

QUEBEC: YANKEE, A TRANSCEIVER AND A TERMINAL OR COMPUTER SYSTEM. ALFA HAS HIS COMPUTER CONNECTED TO HIS TRANSCEIVER USING A TNC.

FOXTROT (thought): PACKET-RADIO IS LIKE THE INTERNET, EXCEPT YOU DON'T NEED A TELEPHONE LINE, OR PAY FEES!

NOW TRY THE QUIZ ON THE NEXT PAGE!

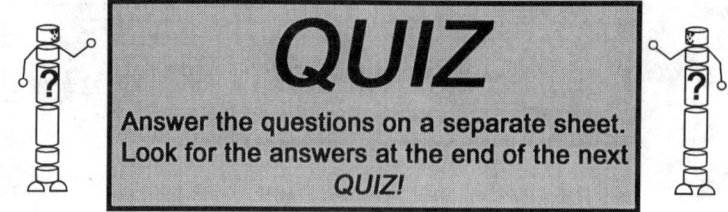

QUIZ

Answer the questions on a separate sheet. Look for the answers at the end of the next QUIZ!

N8A05
What is the name for packet-radio emissions?
A. RTTY
B. Data
C. CW
D. Phone

N7B08
What would you connect between a computer system and a transceiver for packet-radio operation?
A. A terminal-node controller
B. A DTMF keypad
C. An SWR bridge
D. An antenna tuner

N7B09
Where would you connect a terminal-node controller for packet-radio operation?
A. Between your antenna and transceiver
B. Between your computer and monitor
C. Between your computer and transceiver
D. Between your keyboard and computer

N7B11
In packet-radio operation, what equipment connects to a terminal-node controller?
A. A transceiver and a modem
B. A transceiver and a terminal or computer system
C. A DTMF keypad, a monitor and a transceiver
D. A DTMF microphone, a monitor and a transceiver

PREVIOUS QUIZ ANSWERS
N8A04 - A
N8A02 - A
N7B06 - A
N7B07 - C
N7B10 - D
N2B01 - B
N2B02 - B

PACKET OPERATION
NOVICE LESSON 27

Packet operation involves several technical terms, which describe the functions of this digital communication method.

WHAT DOES "CONNECTED" MEAN IN A PACKET-RADIO LINK, ALFA?

A TRANSMITTING STATION IS SENDING DATA TO ONLY ONE RECEIVING STATION; IT REPLIES THAT THE DATA IS BEING RECEIVED CORRECTLY, X-RAY.

WHAT DOES "MONITORING" MEAN ON A PACKET-RADIO FREQUENCY, ALFA?

A RECEIVING STATION IS DISPLAYING MESSAGES THAT MAY NOT BE SENT TO IT, AND IS NOT REPLYING TO ANY MESSAGES, X-RAY.

Computer screen: R 1296 FROM: KS6SSS TO:AA6AAA@ W6JW.#S0CA.CA USA.NA

PACKET TNC — DCD PTT STA CON PWR

TRANSCEIVER — 223.56

AA6AAA

I'VE BEEN CONNECTED AND MONITORING ALL DAY! — WHISKEY

HERE IS SOME INFO! IT IS POSSIBLE TO CONNECT TO SEVERAL DIGIPEATERS AT ONCE, AND COVER GREAT DISTANCES. IF YOU ARE NOT USING THE NETWORK THAT YOU HAVE CONNECTED, IT WILL TIME-OUT, AND DISCONNECT YOU. A VERY LOW POWER STATION WITH A NEARBY DIGIPEATER WORKS VERY WELL ON PACKET RADIO. — INDIA

ROMEO, WHAT DOES "NETWORK" MEAN IN PACKET-RADIO?

IT'S A WAY OF CONNECTING PACKET-RADIO STATIONS SO DATA CAN BE SENT OVER LONG DISTANCES, JULIET. THERE ARE PACKET STATIONS ALL OVER THE WORLD.

WHAT IS A DIGIPEATER, QUEBEC?

YANKEE, IT'S A PACKET-RADIO STATION THAT RETRANSMITS ONLY DATA THAT IS MARKED TO BE RETRANSMITTED. THERE ARE DIGIPEATERS AT MANY HIGH LOCATIONS, THAT PERMIT YOU TO CONNECT WITH DISTANT HAM BULLETIN BOARDS. THEY ARE LIKE FM REPEATERS.

DIGIPEATERS LET YOU USE A HANDHELD RADIO, A TNC, AND A PORTABLE COMPUTER TO TALK WORLD WIDE! — FOXTROT

NOW TRY THE QUIZ ON THE NEXT PAGE!

58

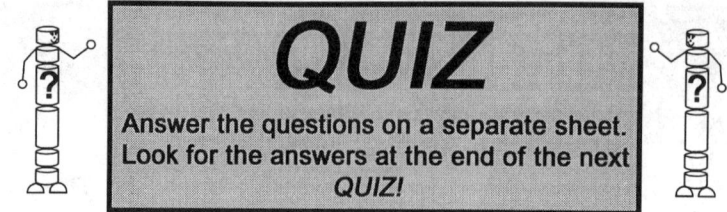

N2B03
What does "connected" mean in a packet-radio link?
A. A telephone link is working between two stations
B. A message has reached an amateur station for local delivery
C. A transmitting station is sending data to only one receiving station; it replies that the data is being received correctly
D. A transmitting and receiving station are using a digipeater, so no other contacts can take place until they are finished

N2B04
What does "monitoring" mean on a packet-radio frequency?
A. The FCC is copying all messages
B. A member of the Amateur Auxiliary to the FCC's Field Operations Bureau is copying all messages
C. A receiving station is displaying all messages sent to it, and replying that the messages are being received correctly
D. A receiving station is displaying messages that may not be sent to it, and is not replying to any message

N2B06
What does "network" mean in packet radio?
A. A way of connecting terminal-node controllers by telephone so data can be sent over long distances
B. A way of connecting packet-radio stations so data can be sent over long distances
C. The wiring connections on a terminal-node controller board
D. The programming in a terminal-node controller that rejects other callers if a station is already connected

N2B05
What is a digipeater?
A. A packet-radio station that retransmits only data that is marked to be retransmitted
B. A packet-radio station that retransmits any data that it receives
C. A repeater that changes audio signals to digital data
D. A repeater built using only digital electronics parts

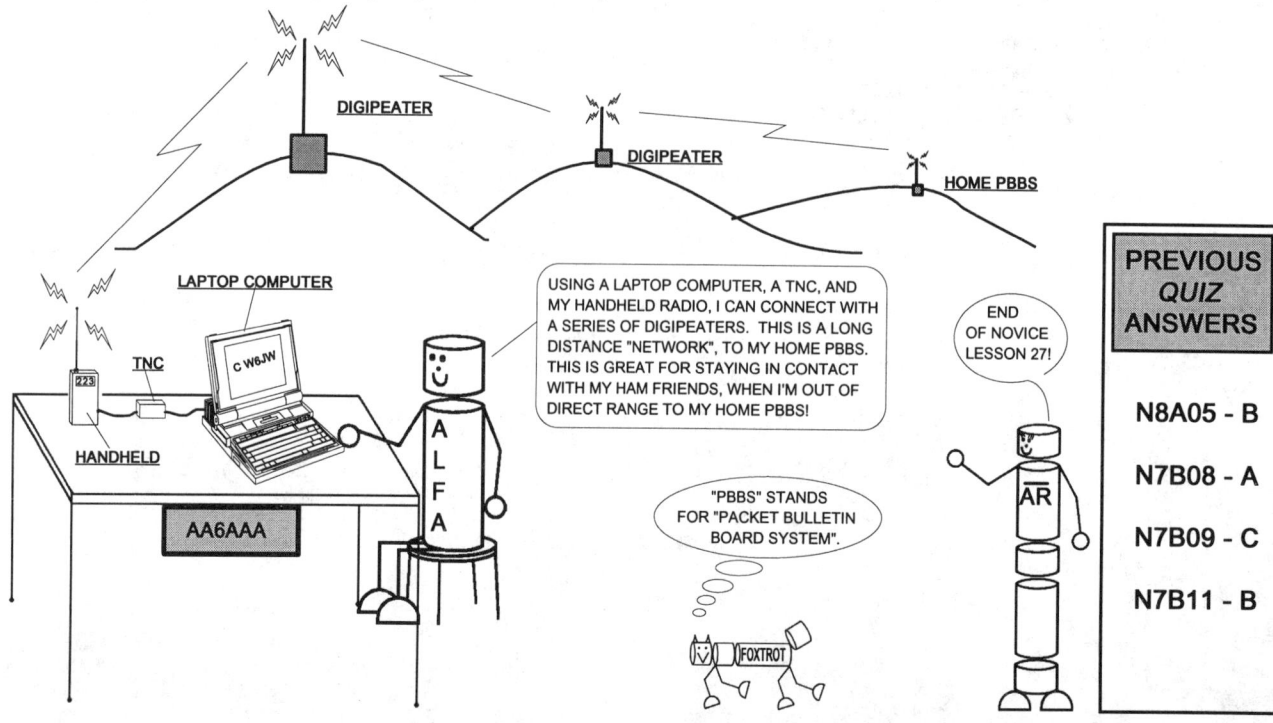

PREVIOUS QUIZ ANSWERS

N8A05 - B

N7B08 - A

N7B09 - C

N7B11 - B

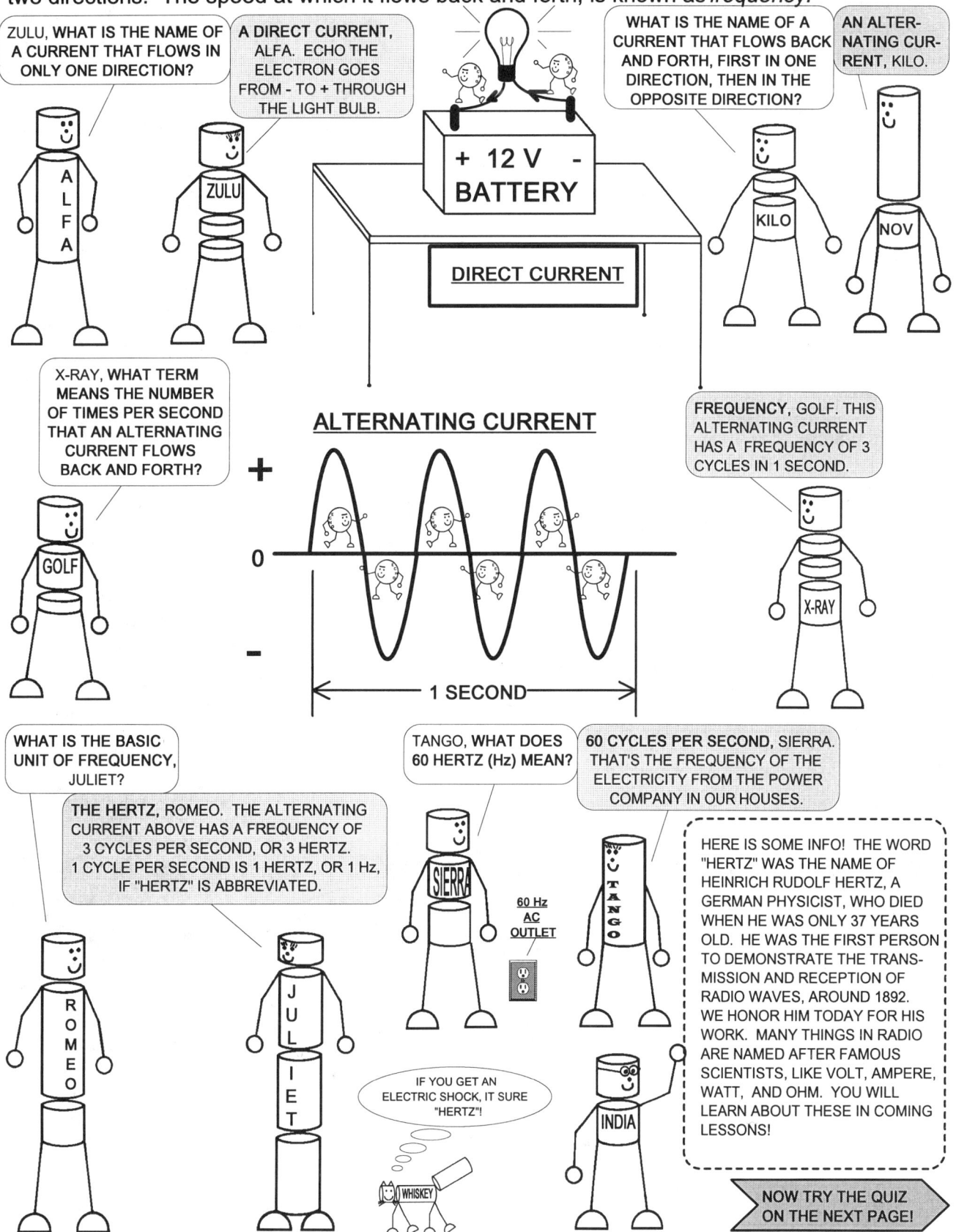

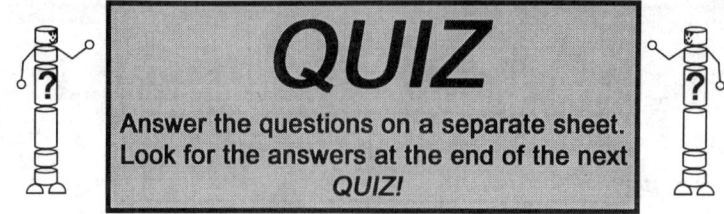

QUIZ

Answer the questions on a separate sheet. Look for the answers at the end of the next QUIZ!

N5C10
What is the name of a current that flows only in one direction?
A. An alternating current
B. A direct current
C. A normal current
D. A smooth current

N5C11
What is the name of a current that flows back and forth, first in one direction, then in the opposite direction?
A. An alternating current
B. A direct current
C. A rough current
D. A reversing current

N5D01
What term means the number of times per second that an alternating current flows back and forth?
A. Pulse rate
B. Speed
C. Wavelength
D. Frequency

N5D02
What is the basic unit of frequency?
A. The hertz
B. The watt
C. The ampere
D. The ohm

N5D11
What does 60 hertz (Hz) mean?
A. 6000 cycles per second
B. 60 cycles per second
C. 6000 meters per second
D. 60 meters per second

WE'RE ECHO THE ELECTRON & FRIENDS. THERE ARE BILLIONS AND BILLIONS OF US ALL OVER THE PLANET EARTH, AND IN THE UNIVERSE! WE ARE IN EVERY CHEMICAL ELEMENT. SOME OF US ARE FREE, AND CAN RUN FROM ONE PLACE TO ANOTHER, IF AN ELECTRIC VOLTAGE IS PLACED ON THE MATERIAL WE ARE IN. THAT'S HOW ELECTRONIC CIRCUITS OPERATE. WE ARE ALSO IN HUMAN BODIES, AND YOU MUST BE VERY CAREFUL NOT TO GET A HIGH VOLTAGE ON YOUR BODY. IF TOO MANY OF US RUN INSIDE OF YOU, WE CAN STOP YOUR HEART. SO BE VERY CAREFUL AROUND ELECTRICITY!

END OF NOVICE LESSON 28!

DANGER!! HIGH VOLTAGE!

PREVIOUS QUIZ ANSWERS

N2B03 - C
N2B04 - D
N2B06 - B
N2B05 - A

AUDIO & RADIO FREQUENCIES
NOVICE LESSON 29

Radio frequencies begin where audio frequencies end. Some humans can hear up to 20,000 cycles per second, or Hertz (Hz). Radio frequencies begin above 20,000 Hz, and extend up to 300,000,000,000 Hz. To save writing "0's", this is called 300,000,000 kilohertz, or 300,000 megahertz, or 300 gigahertz. Each new "hertz" prefix saves us from writing another three "0's"!

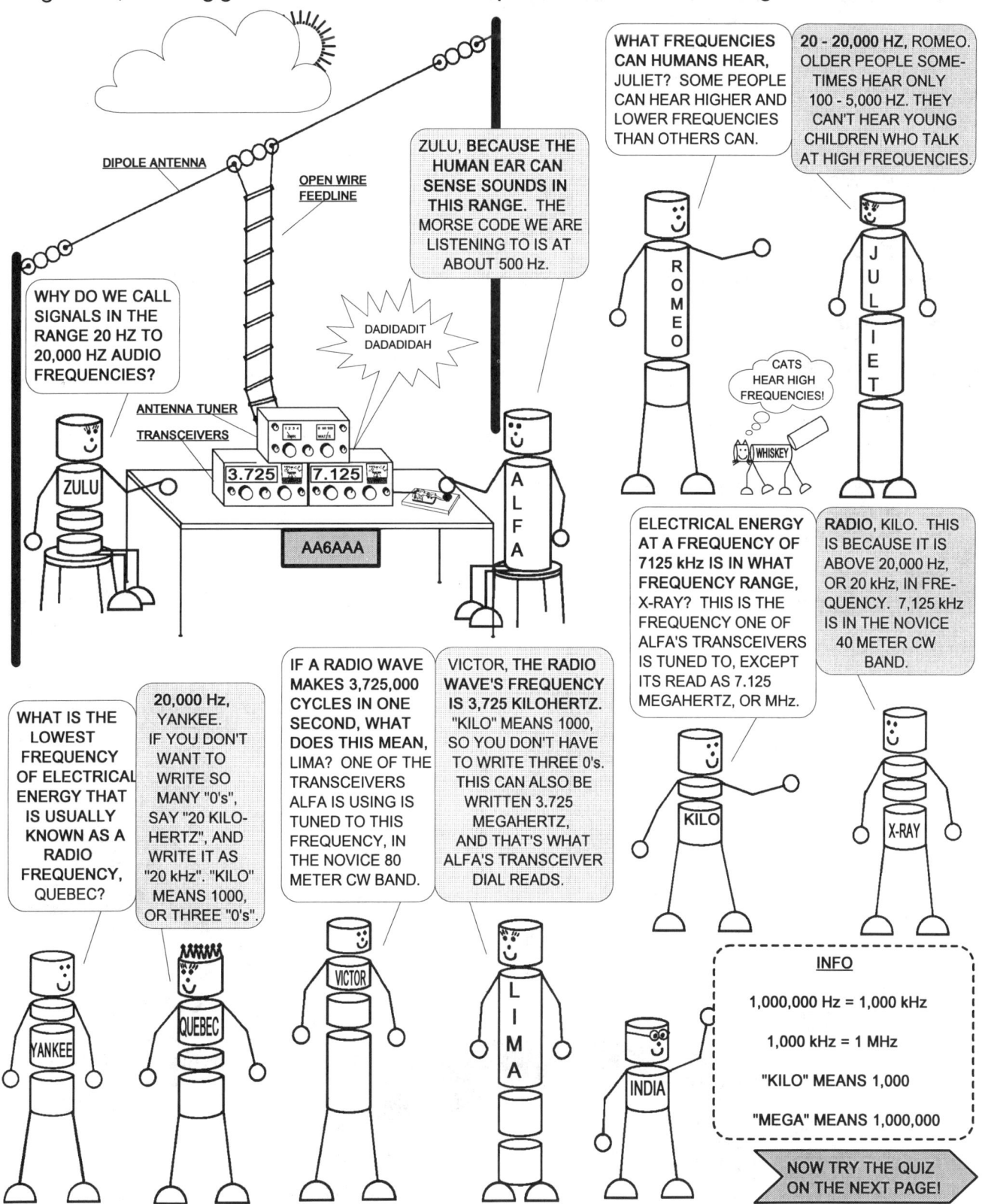

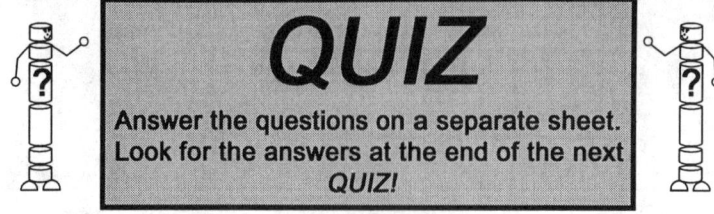

N5D04
Why do we call signals in the range 20 Hz to 20,000 Hz audio frequencies?
A. Because the human ear cannot sense anything in this range
B. Because the human ear can sense sounds in this range
C. Because this range is too low for radio energy
D. Because the human ear can sense radio waves in this range

N5D03
What frequency can humans hear?
A. 0 - 20 Hz
B. 20 - 20,000 Hz
C. 200 - 200,000 Hz
D. 10,000 - 30,000 Hz

N5D05
What is the lowest frequency of electrical energy that is usually known as a radio frequency?
A. 20 Hz
B. 2,000 Hz
C. 20,000 Hz
D. 1,000,000 Hz

N5D07
If a radio wave makes 3,725,000 cycles in one second, what does this mean?
A. The radio wave's voltage is 3,725 kilovolts
B. The radio wave's wavelength is 3,725 kilometers
C. The radio wave's frequency is 3,725 kilohertz
D. The radio wave's speed is 3,725 kilometers per second

N5D06
Electrical energy at a frequency of 7125 kHz is in what frequency range?
A. Audio
B. Radio
C. Hyper
D. Super-high

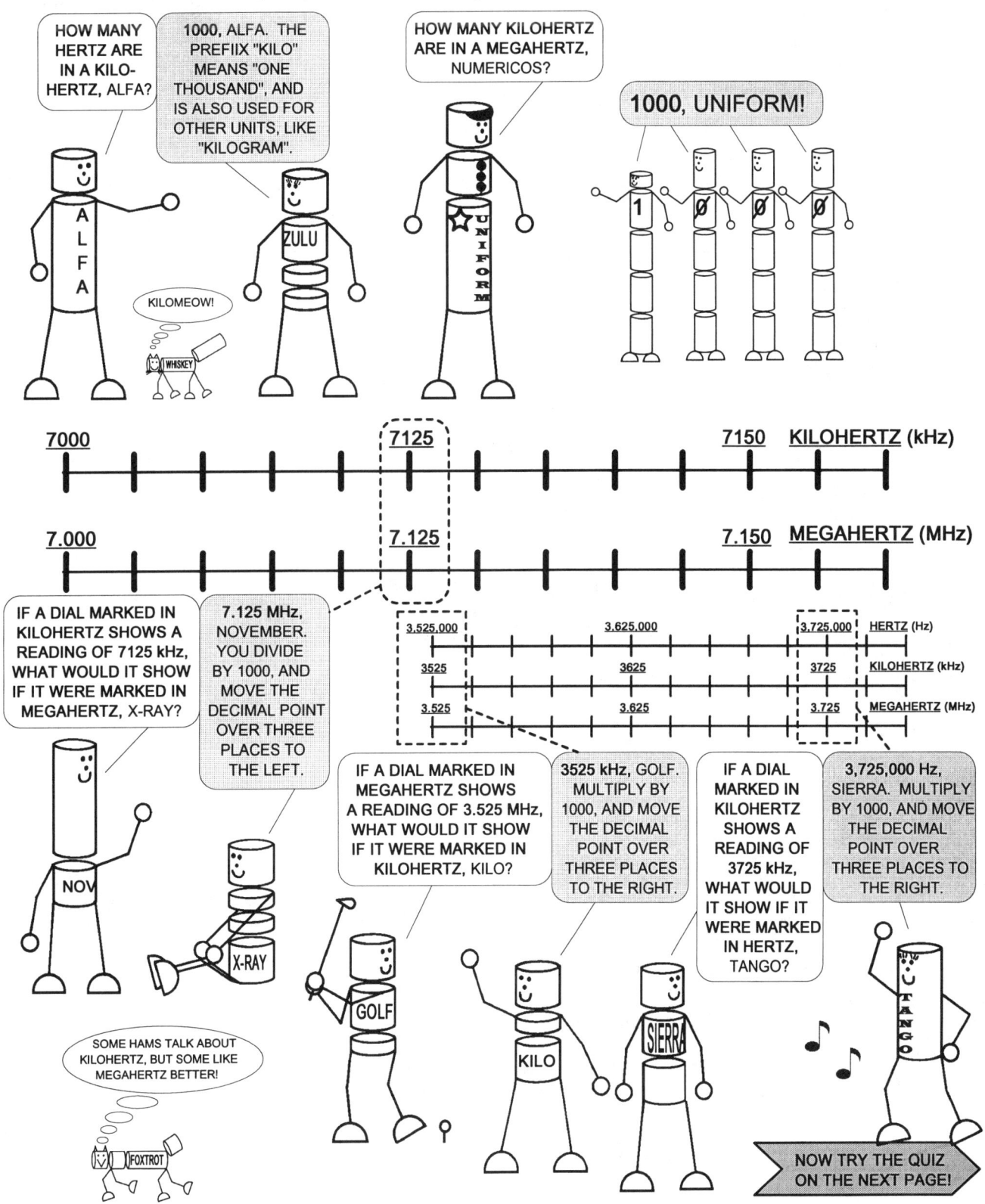

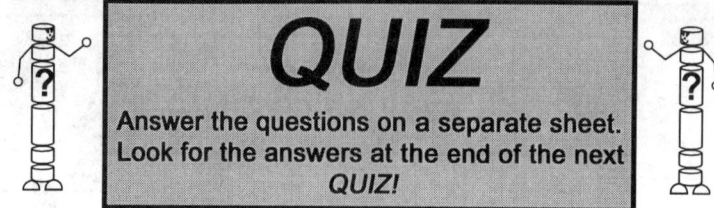

QUIZ
Answer the questions on a separate sheet. Look for the answers at the end of the next QUIZ!

N5A09
How many hertz are in a kilohertz?
A. 10
B. 100
C. 1000
D. 1000000

N5A10
How many kilohertz are in a megahertz?
A. 10
B. 100
C. 1000
D. 1000000

N5A01
If a dial marked in kilohertz shows a reading of 7125 kHz, what would it show if it were marked in megahertz?
A. 0.007125 MHz
B. 7.125 MHz
C. 71.25 MHz
D. 7,125,000 MHz

N5A02
If a dial marked in megahertz shows a reading of 3.525 MHz, what would it show if it were marked in kilohertz?
A. 0.003525 kHz
B. 35.25 kHz
C. 3525 kHz
D. 3,525,000 kHz

N5A03
If a dial marked in kilohertz shows a reading of 3725 kHz, what would it show if it were marked in hertz?
A. 3,725 Hz
B. 37.25 Hz
C. 3,725 Hz
D. 3,725,000 Hz

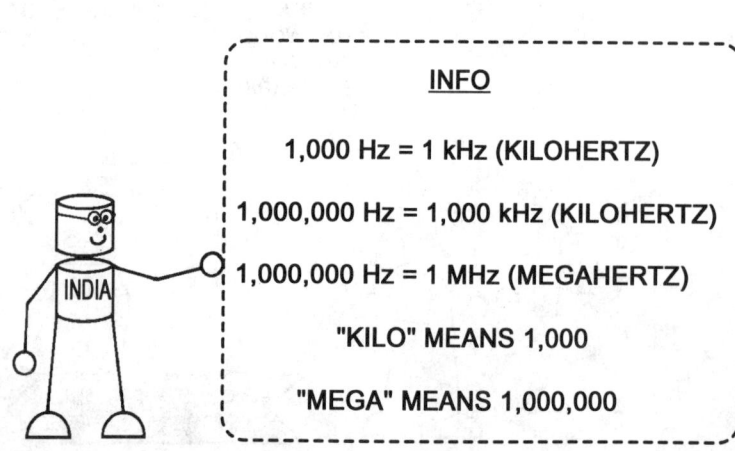

INFO

1,000 Hz = 1 kHz (KILOHERTZ)

1,000,000 Hz = 1,000 kHz (KILOHERTZ)

1,000,000 Hz = 1 MHz (MEGAHERTZ)

"KILO" MEANS 1,000

"MEGA" MEANS 1,000,000

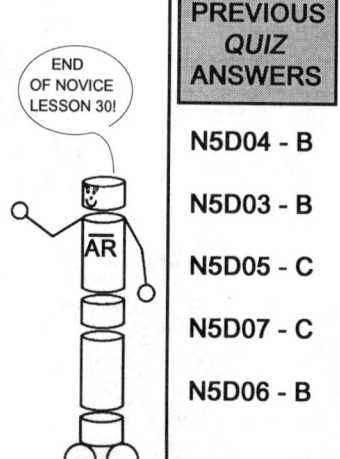

END OF NOVICE LESSON 30!

PREVIOUS QUIZ ANSWERS

N5D04 - B

N5D03 - B

N5D05 - C

N5D07 - C

N5D06 - B

FREQUENCY & WAVELENGTH
NOVICE LESSON 31

A frequency of 28.4 MHz is at a wavelength of approximately 10 meters, and hams use both terms when they talk about the popular ham band.

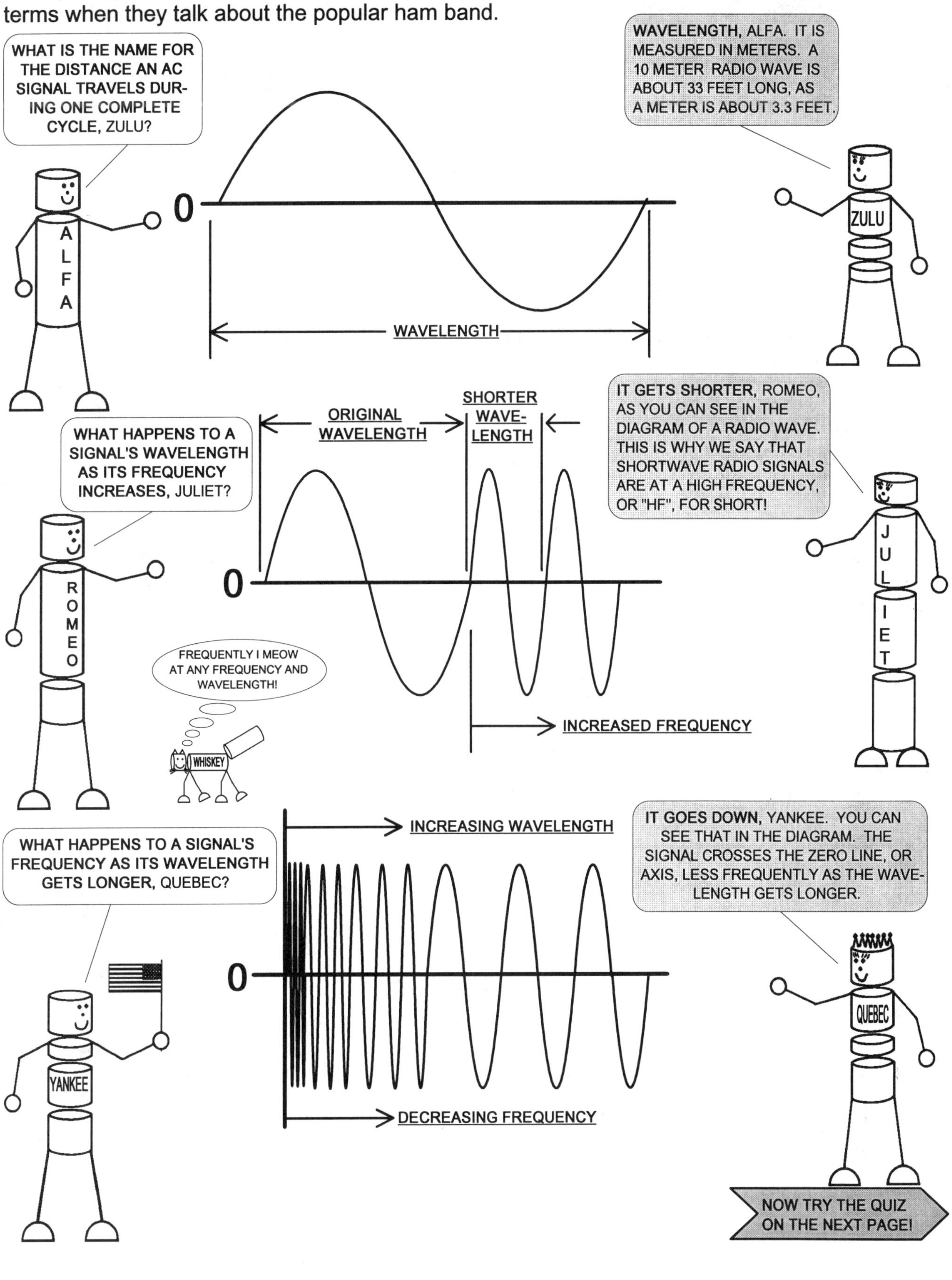

ALFA: WHAT IS THE NAME FOR THE DISTANCE AN AC SIGNAL TRAVELS DURING ONE COMPLETE CYCLE, ZULU?

ZULU: WAVELENGTH, ALFA. IT IS MEASURED IN METERS. A 10 METER RADIO WAVE IS ABOUT 33 FEET LONG, AS A METER IS ABOUT 3.3 FEET.

ROMEO: WHAT HAPPENS TO A SIGNAL'S WAVELENGTH AS ITS FREQUENCY INCREASES, JULIET?

JULIET: IT GETS SHORTER, ROMEO, AS YOU CAN SEE IN THE DIAGRAM OF A RADIO WAVE. THIS IS WHY WE SAY THAT SHORTWAVE RADIO SIGNALS ARE AT A HIGH FREQUENCY, OR "HF", FOR SHORT!

WHISKEY: FREQUENTLY I MEOW AT ANY FREQUENCY AND WAVELENGTH!

YANKEE: WHAT HAPPENS TO A SIGNAL'S FREQUENCY AS ITS WAVELENGTH GETS LONGER, QUEBEC?

QUEBEC: IT GOES DOWN, YANKEE. YOU CAN SEE THAT IN THE DIAGRAM. THE SIGNAL CROSSES THE ZERO LINE, OR AXIS, LESS FREQUENTLY AS THE WAVELENGTH GETS LONGER.

NOW TRY THE QUIZ ON THE NEXT PAGE!

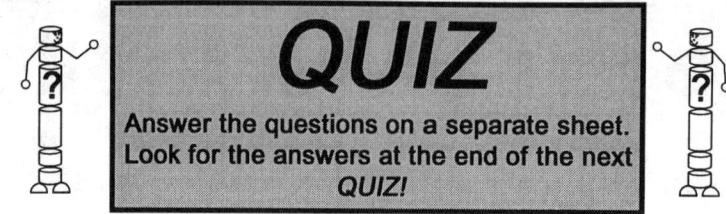

N5D08
What is the name for the distance an AC signal travels during one complete cycle?
A. Wave speed
B. Waveform
C. Wavelength
D. Wave spread

N5D09
What happens to a signal's wavelength as its frequency increases?
A. It gets shorter
B. It gets longer
C. It stays the same
D. It disappears

N5D10
What happens to a signal's frequency as its wavelength gets longer?
A. It goes down
B. It goes up
C. It stays the same
D. It disappears

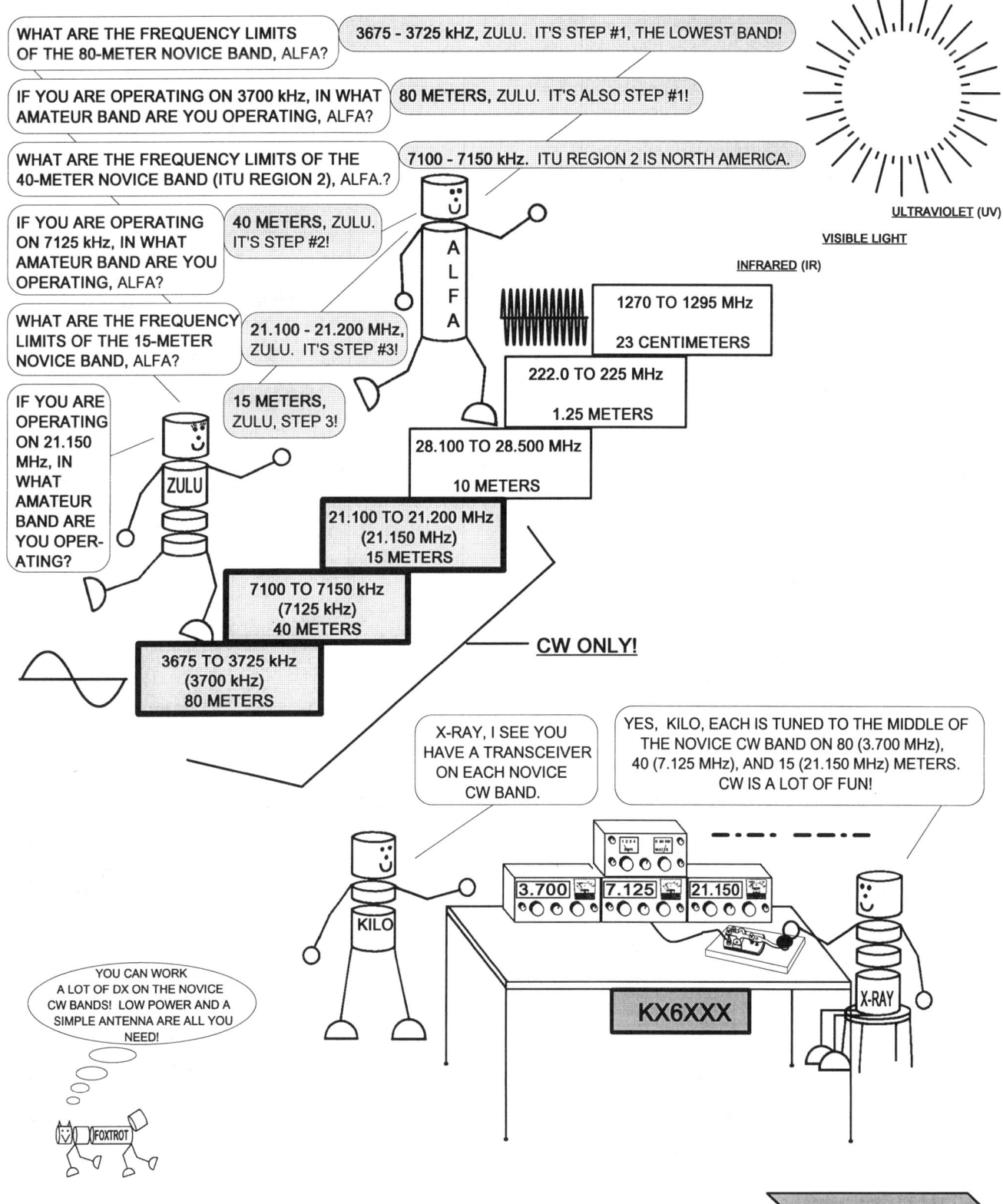

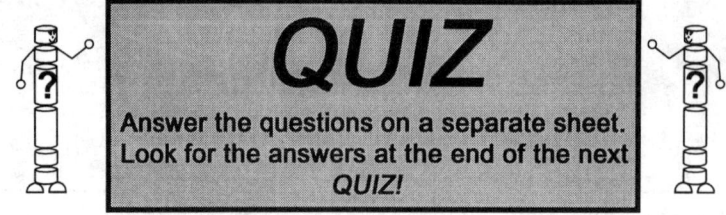

QUIZ

Answer the questions on a separate sheet. Look for the answers at the end of the next QUIZ!

N1C01
What are the frequency limits of the 80-meter Novice band?
A. 3500 - 4000 kHz
B. 3675 - 3725 kHz
C. 7100 - 7150 kHz
D. 7000 - 7300 kHz

N1C07
If you are operating on 3700 kHz, in what amateur band are you operating?
A. 80 meters
B. 40 meters
C. 15 meters
D. 10 meters

N1C02
What are the frequency limits of the 40-meter Novice band (ITU Region2)?
A. 3500 - 4000 kHz
B. 3700 - 3750 kHz
C. 7100 - 7150 kHz
D. 7000 - 7300 kHz

N1C08
If you are operating on 7125 kHz, in what amateur band are you operating?
A. 80 meters
B. 40 meters
C. 15 meters
D. 10 meters

N1C03
What are the frequency limits of the 15-meter Novice band?
A. 21.100 - 21.200 MHz
B. 21.000 - 21.450 MHz
C. 28.000 - 29.700 MHz
D. 28.100 - 28.200 MHz

N1C09
If you are operating on 21.150 MHz, in what amateur band are you operating?
A. 80 meters
B. 40 meters
C. 15 meters
D. 10 meters

NOVICES CAN OPERATE ON SEVERAL HAM BANDS, BOTH CW AND VOICE, BY LEARNING THE MORSE CODE AT 5 WPM!

END OF NOVICE LESSON 32!

PREVIOUS QUIZ ANSWERS

N5D08 - C

N5D09 - A

N5D10 - A

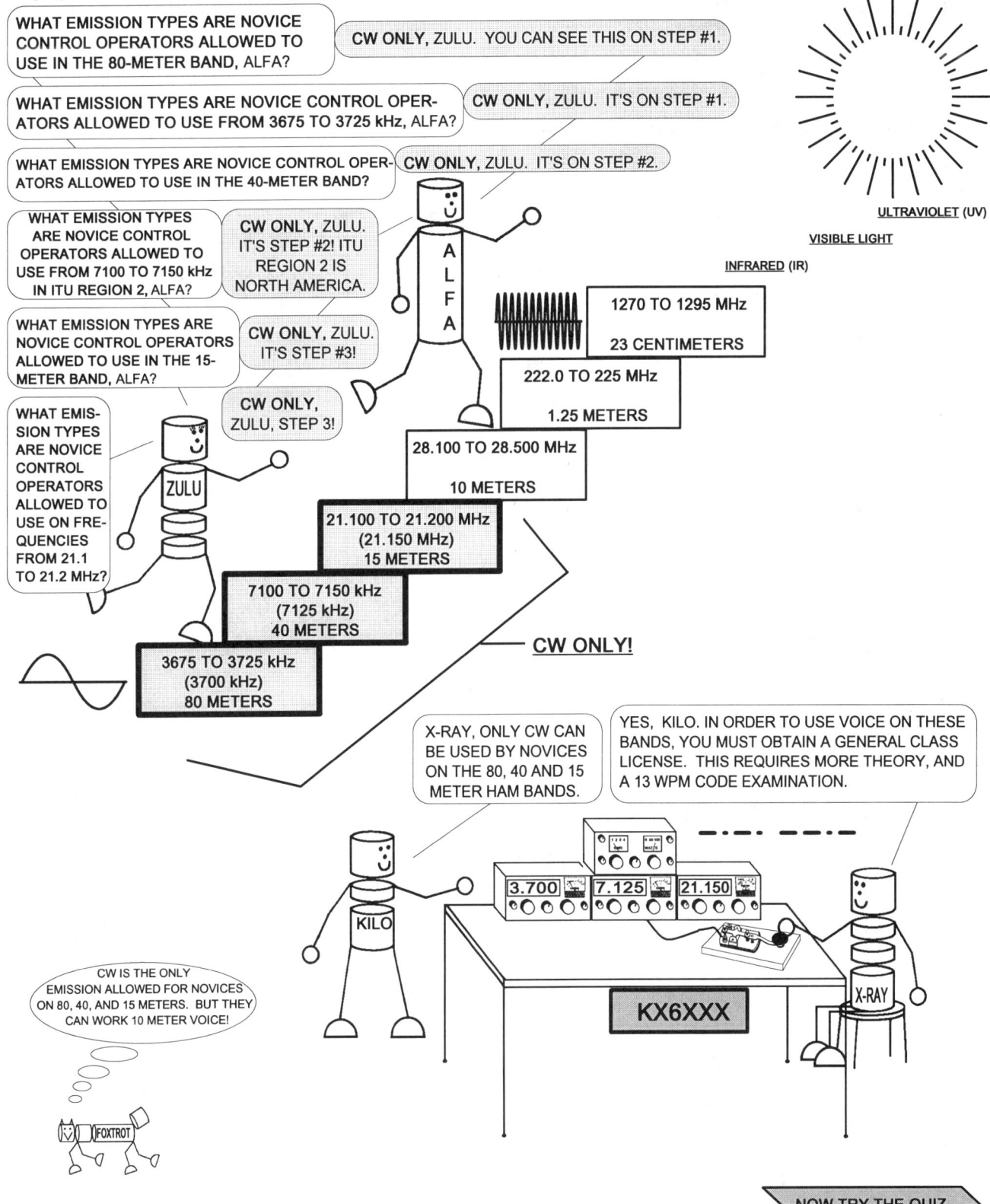

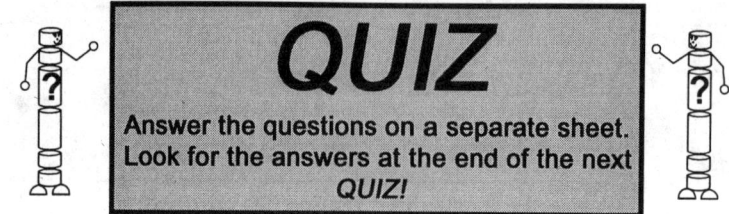

QUIZ

Answer the questions on a separate sheet. Look for the answers at the end of the next QUIZ!

N1E01
What emission types are Novice control operators allowed to use in the 80-meter band?
A. CW only
B. Data only
C. RTTY only
D. Phone only

N1E04
What emission types are Novice control operators allowed to use from 3675 to 3725 kHz?
A. Phone only
B. Image only
C. Data only
D. CW only

N1E02
What emission types are Novice control operators allowed to use in the 40-meter band?
A. CW only
B. Data only
C. RTTY only
D. Phone only

N1E05
What emission types are Novice control operators allowed to use from 7100 to 7150 kHz in ITU Region 2?
A. CW and data
B. Phone
C. Data only
D. CW only

N1E03
What emission types are Novice control operators allowed to use in the 15-meter band?
A. CW only
B. Data only
C. RTTY only
D. Phone only

N1E06
What emission types are Novice control operators allowed to use on frequencies from 21.1 to 21.2 MHz?
A. CW and data
B. CW and phone
C. Data only
D. CW only

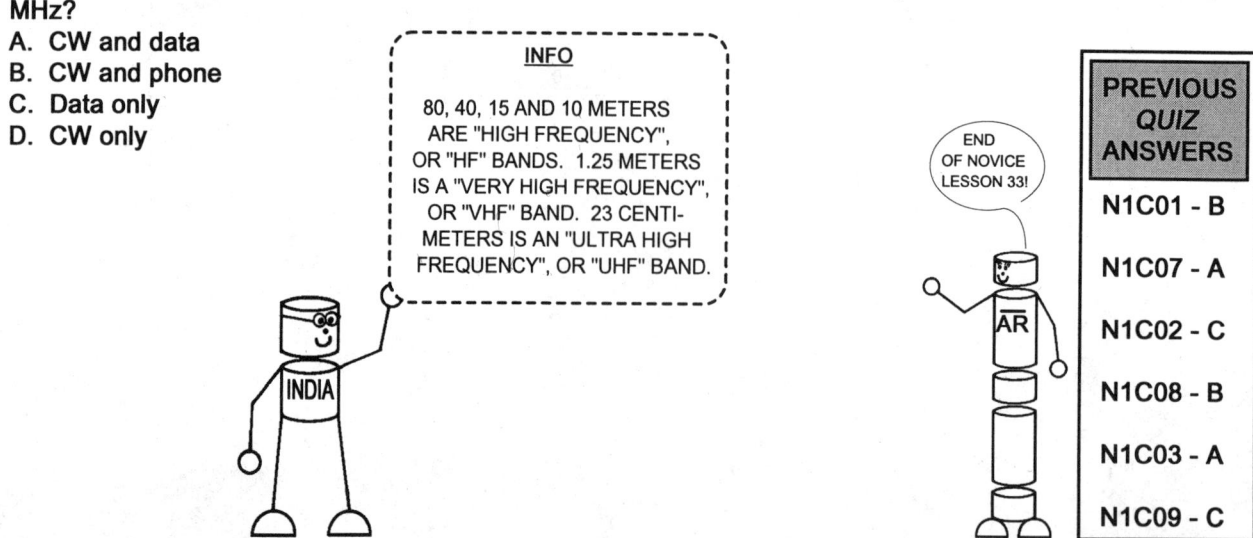

INFO

80, 40, 15 AND 10 METERS ARE "HIGH FREQUENCY", OR "HF" BANDS. 1.25 METERS IS A "VERY HIGH FREQUENCY", OR "VHF" BAND. 23 CENTIMETERS IS AN "ULTRA HIGH FREQUENCY", OR "UHF" BAND.

END OF NOVICE LESSON 33!

PREVIOUS QUIZ ANSWERS
N1C01 - B
N1C07 - A
N1C02 - C
N1C08 - B
N1C03 - A
N1C09 - C

CW, VOICE, & DATA FREQUENCIES
NOVICE LESSON 34

The Novice cw, voice, & data frequencies are those above 15 meters. The 10 meter band is open during daylight hours. The 1.25 meter and 23 centimeter (0.23 meters) are line-of-sight bands, and are good only for local QSOs, or distant QSOs using local repeaters.

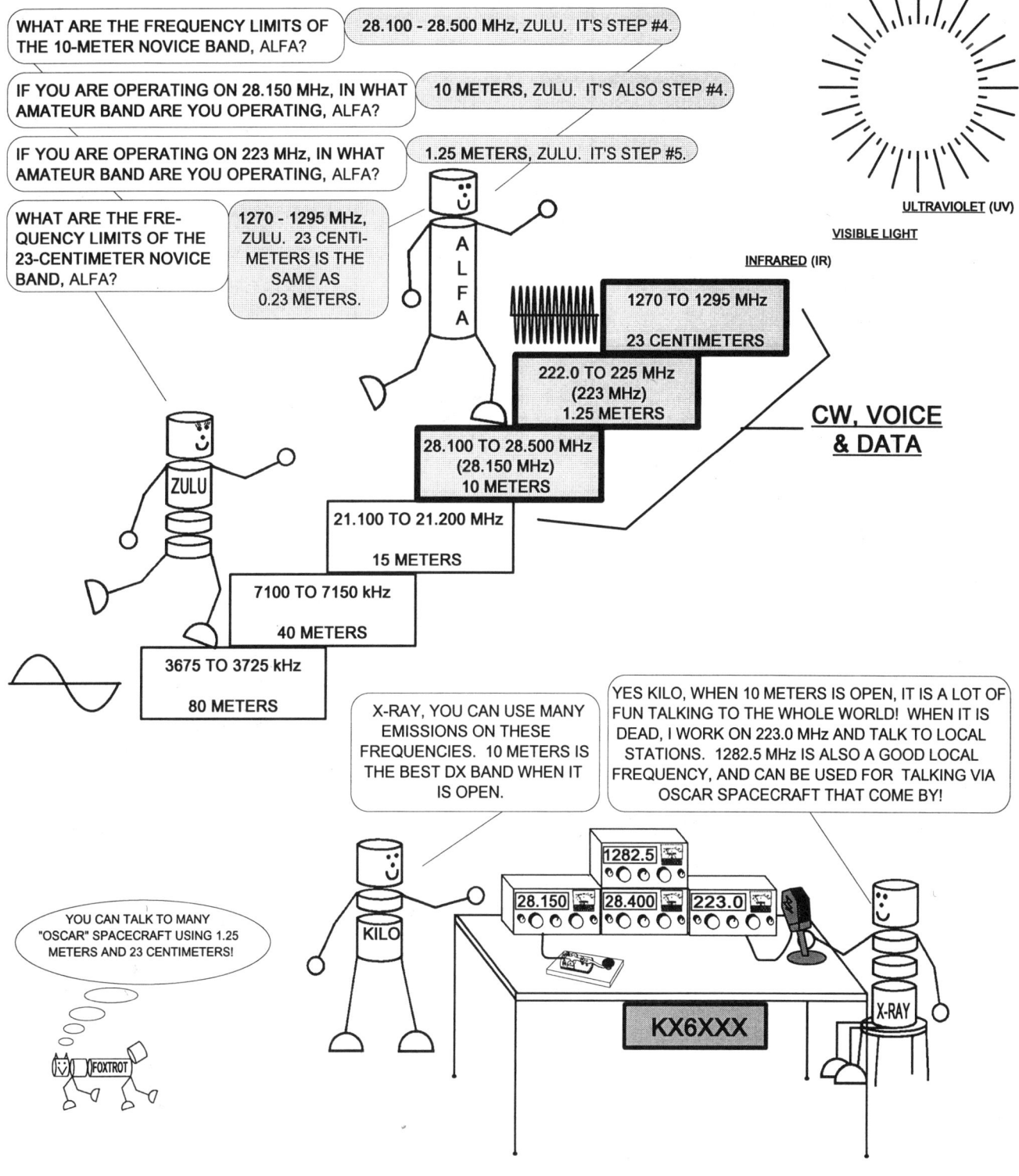

NOW TRY THE QUIZ ON THE NEXT PAGE!

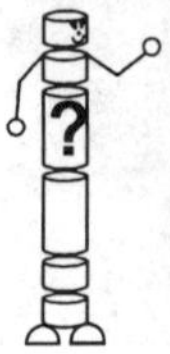

QUIZ

Answer the questions on a separate sheet. Look for the answers at the end of the next QUIZ!

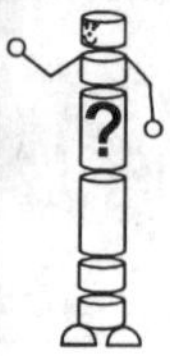

N1C04
What are the frequency limits of the 10-meter Novice band?
A. 28.000 - 28.500 MHz
B. 28.100 - 29.500 MHz
C. 28.100 - 28.500 MHz
D. 29.100 - 29.500 MHz

N1C10
If you are operating on 28.150 MHz, in what amateur band are you operating?
A. 80 meters
B. 40 meters
C. 15 meters
D. 10 meters

N1C11
If you are operating on 223 MHz, in what amateur band are you operating?
A. 15 meters
B. 10 meters
C. 2 meters
D. 1.25 meters

N1C06
What are the frequency limits of the 23-centimeter Novice band?
A. 1260 - 1270 MHz
B. 1240 - 1300 MHz
C. 1270 - 1295 MHz
D. 1240 - 1246 MHz

INFO

"SINGLE-SIDEBAND PHONE" IS THE TYPE OF VOICE OPERATION USED ON THE 10 METER BAND BY NOVICE STATIONS. ON 1.25 METERS AND 23 CENTIMETERS, FREQUENCY MODULATION, OR "FM", VOICE OPERATION IS USED.

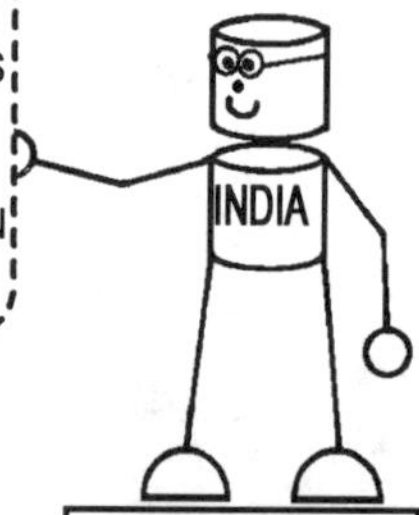

IT TAKES PRACTICE TO LEARN HOW TO TUNE IN A SINGLE-SIDEBAND (SSB) HAM SIGNAL! AT FIRST IT SOUNDS LIKE DUCKS TALKING, BUT IF YOU TUNE CAREFULLY, A VOICE BEGINS TO APPEAR. REGULAR AM RADIO STATIONS HAVE TWO SIDEBANDS, BUT HAMS ONLY NEED ONE, AND TAKE UP HALF THE SPACE ON THE AIR!

END OF NOVICE LESSON 34!

PREVIOUS QUIZ ANSWERS

N1E01 - A
N1E04 - D
N1E02 - A
N1E05 - D
N1E03 - A
N1E06 - D

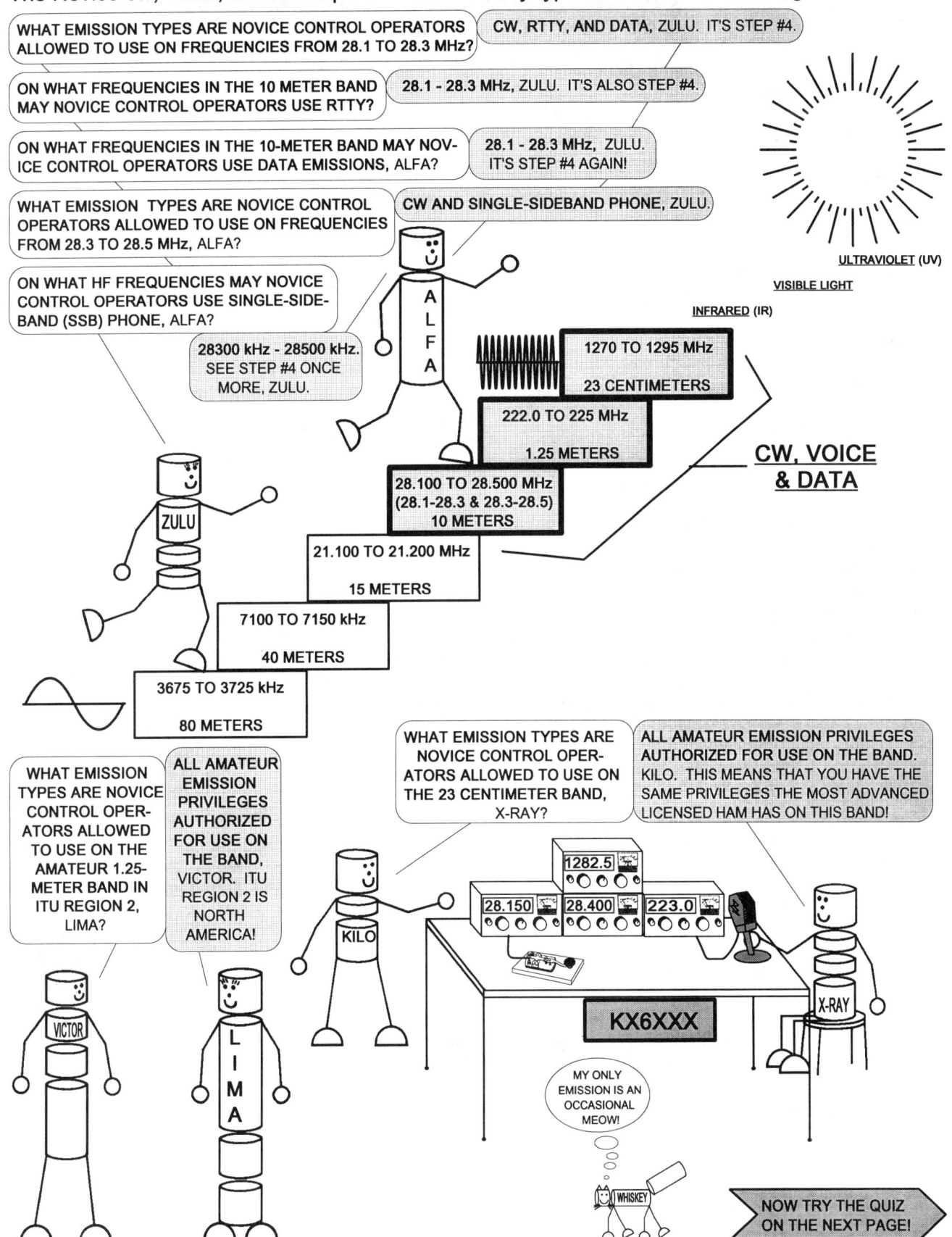

QUIZ

Answer the questions on a separate sheet. Look for the answers at the end of the next QUIZ!

N1E07
What emission types are Novice control operators allowed to use on frequencies from 28.1 to 28.3 MHz?
A. All authorized amateur emission privileges
B. Data or phone
C. CW, RTTY and data
D. CW and phone

N1E13
On what frequencies in the 10-meter band may Novice control operators use RTTY?
A. 28.0 - 28.3 MHz
B. 28.1 - 28.3 MHz
C. 28.0 - 29.3 MHz
D. 29.1 - 29.3 MHz

N1E14
On what frequencies in the 10-meter band may Novice control operators use data emissions?
A. 28.0 - 28.3 MHz
B. 28.1 - 28.3 MHz
C. 28.0 - 29.3 MHz
D. 29.1 - 29.3 MHz

N1E08
What emission types are Novice control operators allowed to use on frequencies from 28.3 to 28.5 MHz?
A. All authorized amateur emission privileges
B. CW and data
C. CW and single-sideband phone
D. Data and phone

N1E11
On what HF frequencies may Novice control operators use single-sideband (SSB) phone?
A. 3700 - 3750 kHz
B. 7100 - 7150 kHz
C. 21100 - 21200 kHz
D. 28300 - 28500 kHz

N1E09
What emission types are Novice control operators allowed to use on the amateur 1.25-meter band in ITU Region 2?
A. CW and phone
B. CW and data
C. Data and phone
D. All amateur emission privileges authorized for use on the band

N1E10
What emission types are Novice control operators allowed to use on the amateur 23-centimeter band?
A. Data and phone
B. CW and data
C. CW and phone
D. All amateur emission privileges authorized for use on the band

END OF NOVICE LESSON 35!

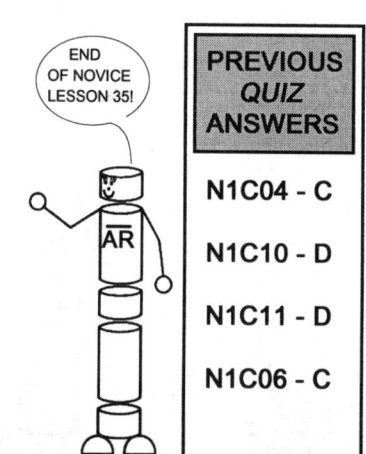

PREVIOUS QUIZ ANSWERS

N1C04 - C

N1C10 - D

N1C11 - D

N1C06 - C

ENERGY, POWER, & WATTS
NOVICE LESSON 36

Every home, or apartment, has an electric power meter that measures the amount of electricity in *watts*, or *kilowatts*, that is being used. A small "disk" inside the meter turns faster and faster as more power in kilowatts is being used. You can run an experiment to see if the disk stops, by turning off everything in your home; and turns rapidly with every light and appliance on!

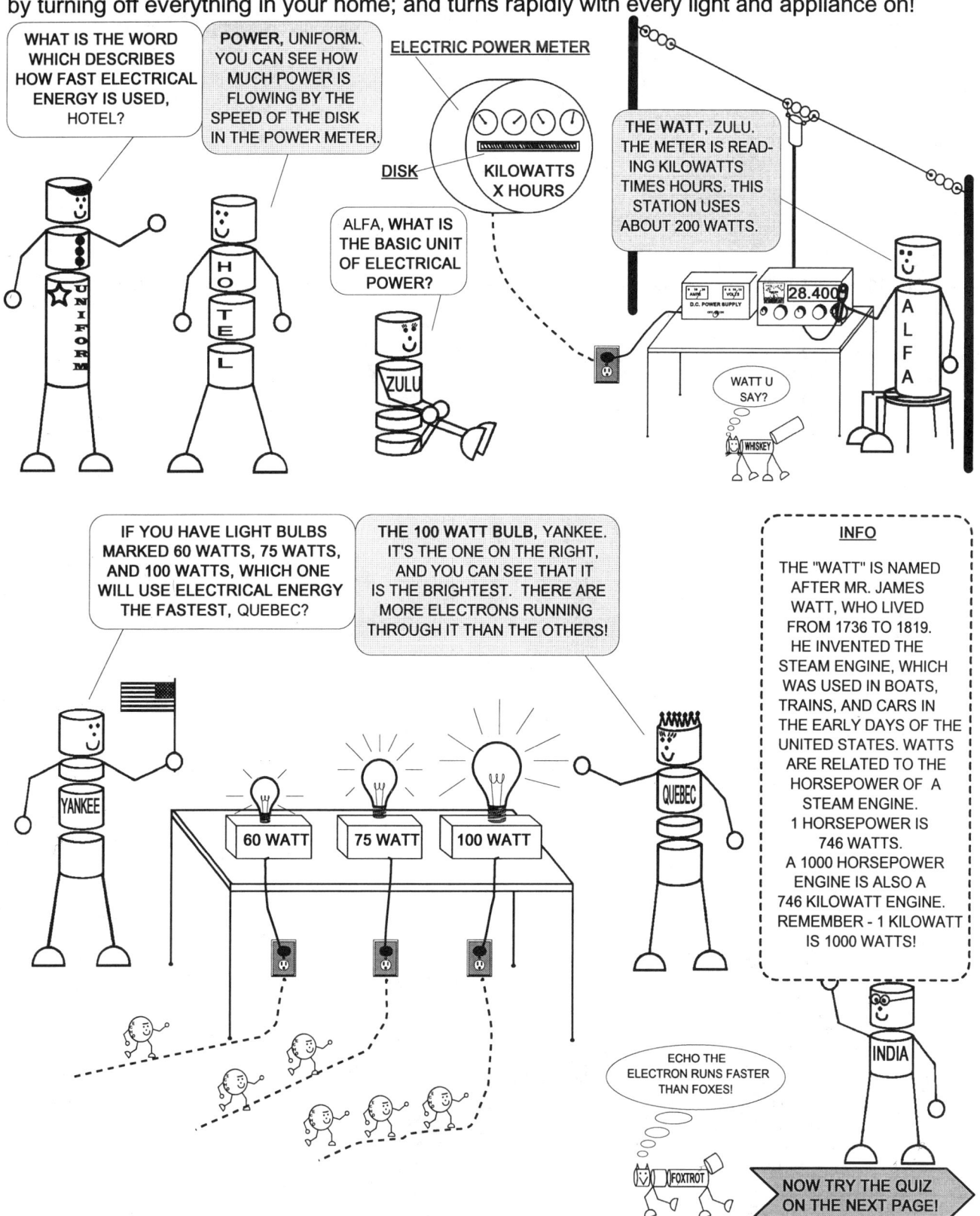

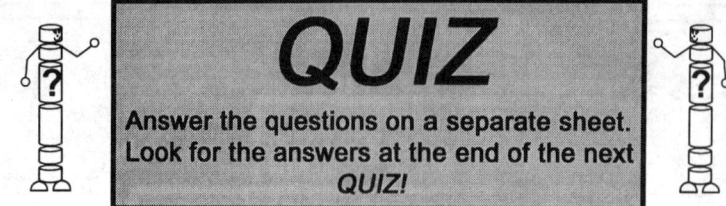

N5C05
What is the word used to describe how fast electrical energy is used?
A. Resistance
B. Current
C. Power
D. Voltage

N5C07
What is the basic unit of electrical power?
A. The ohm
B. The watt
C. The volt
D. The ampere

N5C06
If you have light bulbs marked 60 watts, 75 watts and 100 watts, which one will use electrical energy the fastest?
A. The 60 watt bulb
B. The 75 watt bulb
C. The 100 watt bulb
D. They will all be the same

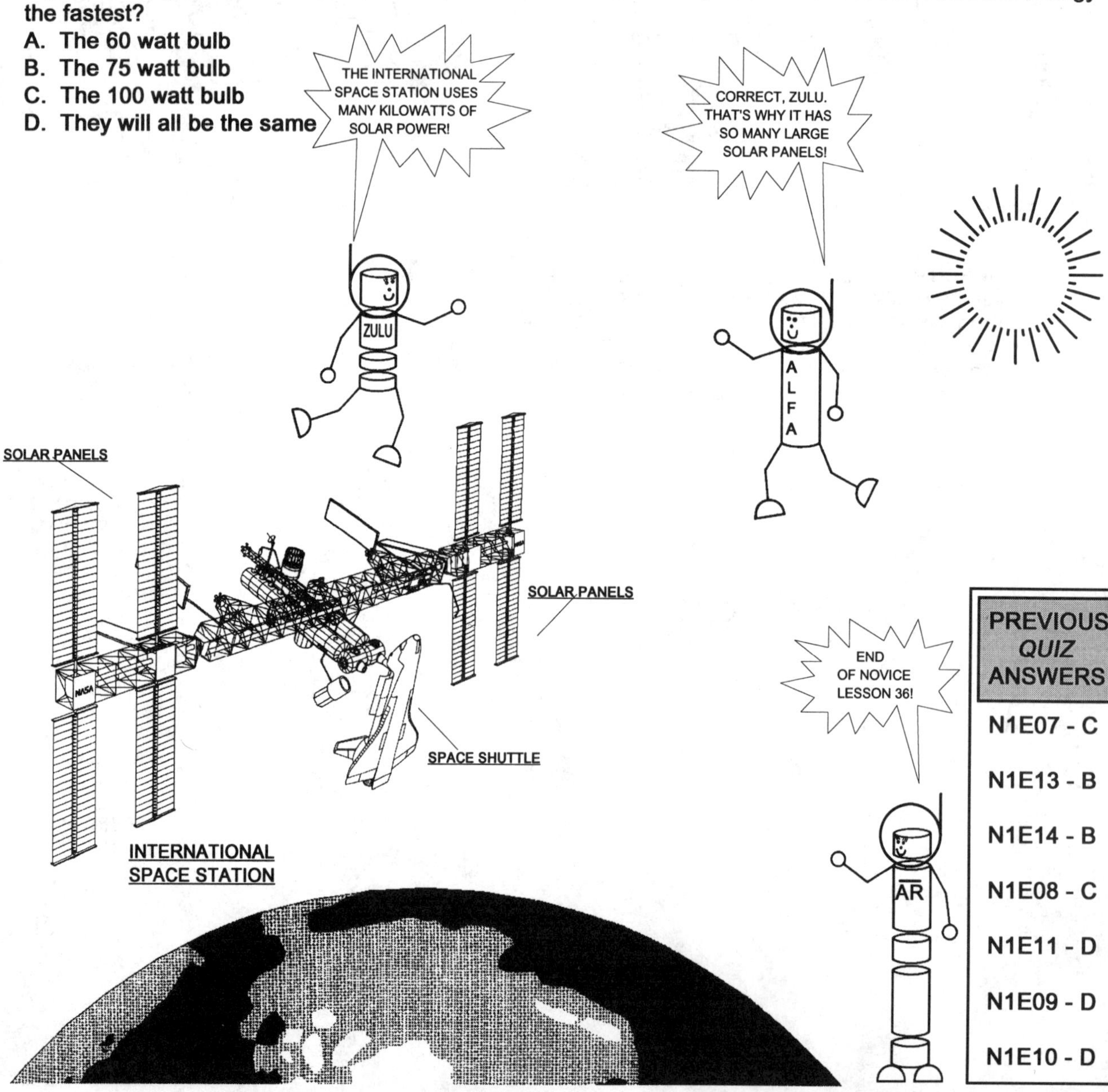

THE INTERNATIONAL SPACE STATION USES MANY KILOWATTS OF SOLAR POWER!

CORRECT, ZULU. THAT'S WHY IT HAS SO MANY LARGE SOLAR PANELS!

SOLAR PANELS
SOLAR PANELS
SPACE SHUTTLE
INTERNATIONAL SPACE STATION

END OF NOVICE LESSON 36!

PREVIOUS QUIZ ANSWERS
N1E07 - C
N1E13 - B
N1E14 - B
N1E08 - C
N1E11 - D
N1E09 - D
N1E10 - D

HIGH FREQUENCY POWER
NOVICE LESSON 37

On the Novice high frequency (HF) bands 80, 40, 15 and 10 meters, the maximum allowed power output is 200 watts PEP. "PEP" means "peak envelope power", and is a technical term used to describe the way that radio frequency (RF) power output is measured.

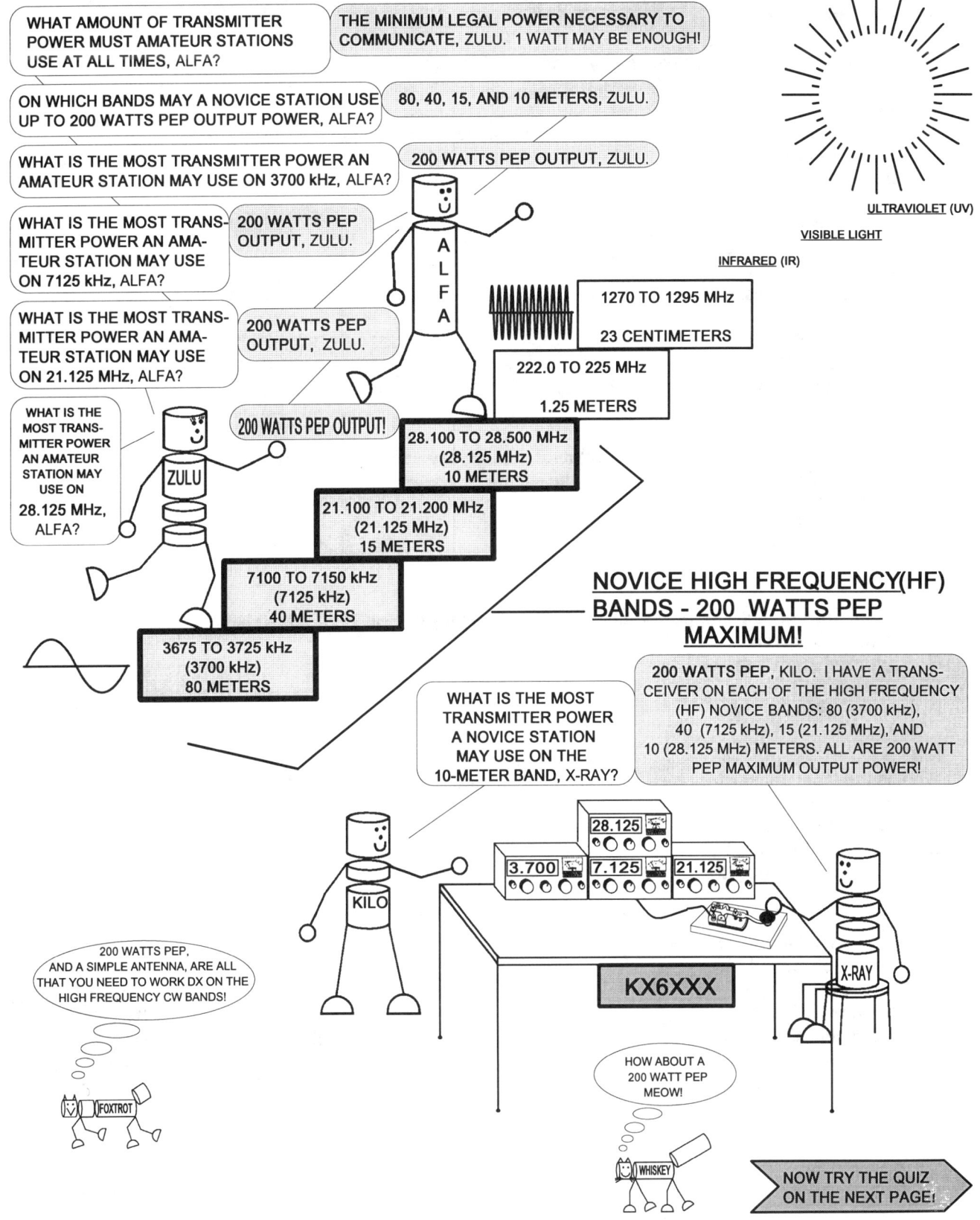

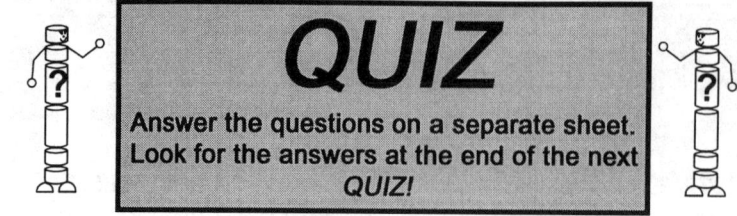

QUIZ

Answer the questions on a separate sheet. Look for the answers at the end of the next *QUIZ!*

N1F01
What amount of transmitter power must amateur stations use at all times?
A. 25 watts PEP output
B. 250 watts PEP output
C. 1500 watts PEP output
D. The minimum legal power necessary to communicate

N1F09
On which bands may a Novice station use up to 200 watts PEP output power?
A. 80, 40, 15, and 10 meters
B. 80, 40, 20, and 10 meters
C. 1.25 meters
D. 23 centimeters

N1F02
What is the most transmitter power an amateur station may use on 3700 kHz?
A. 5 watts PEP output
B. 25 watts PEP output
C. 200 watts PEP output
D. 1500 watts PEP output

N1F03
What is the most transmitter power an amateur station may use on 7125 kHz?
A. 5 watts PEP output
B. 25 watts PEP output
C. 200 watts PEP output
D. 1500 watts PEP output

N1F04
What is the most transmitter power an amateur station may use on 21.125 MHz?
A. 5 watts PEP output
B. 25 watts PEP output
C. 200 watts PEP output
D. 1500 watts PEP output

N1F05
What is the most transmitter power a Novice station may use on 28.125 MHz?
A. 5 watts PEP output
B. 25 watts PEP output
C. 200 watts PEP output
D. 1500 watts PEP output

N1F06
What is the most transmitter power a Novice station may use on the 10- meter band?
A. 5 watts PEP output
B. 25 watts PEP output
C. 200 watts PEP output
D. 1500 watts PEP output

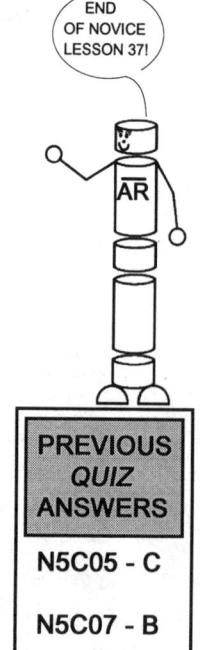

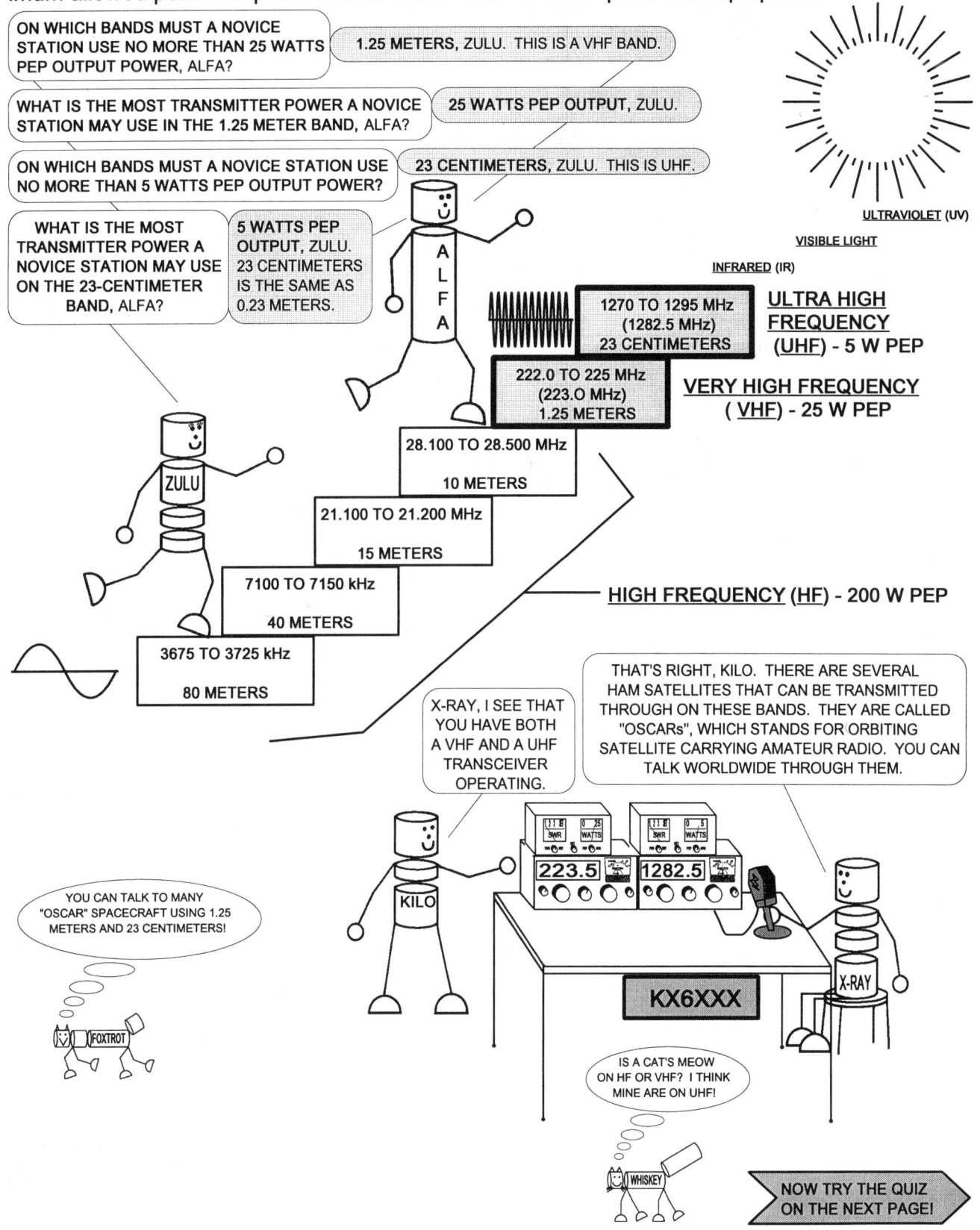

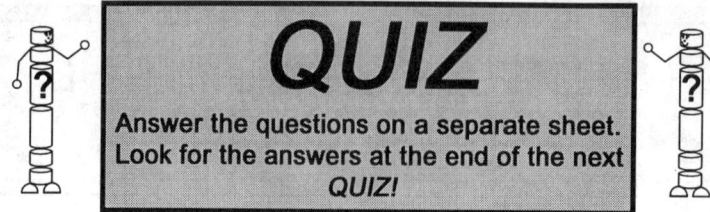

QUIZ
Answer the questions on a separate sheet. Look for the answers at the end of the next QUIZ!

N1F10
On which bands must a Novice station use no more than 25 watts PEP output power?
A. 80, 40, 15, and 10 meters
B. 80, 40, 20, and 10 meters
C. 1.25 meters
D. 23 centimeters

N1F07
What is the most transmitter power a Novice station may use on the 1.25-meter band?
A. 5 watts PEP output
B. 25 watts PEP output
C. 200 watts PEP output
D. 1500 watts PEP output

N1F11
On which bands must a Novice station use no more than 5 watts PEP output power?
A. 80, 40, 15, and 10 meters
B. 80, 40, 20, and 10 meters
C. 1.25 meters
D. 23 centimeters

N1F08
What is the most transmitter power a Novice station may use on the 23-centimeter band?
A. 5 watts PEP output
B. 25 watts PEP output
C. 200 watts PEP output
D. 1500 watts PEP output

THIS OSCAR HAS AN INPUT FREQUENCY OF 1282 MHz ON 23 CENTIMETERS AND AN OUTPUT FREQUENCY OF 223 MHz ON 1.25 METERS. I HOPE X-RAY IS TRACKING IT!

END OF NOVICE LESSON 38!

PREVIOUS QUIZ ANSWERS
N1F01 - D
N1F09 - A
N1F02 - C
N1F03 - C
N1F04 - C
N1F05 - C
N1F06 - C

GROUND-WAVE, SKY-WAVE, & SUNSPOTS
NOVICE LESSON 39

High freqeuncy (HF) radio waves can travel in several different ways, just like people. Some HF radio waves travel along the ground, and others travel in the sky. One is called a *ground-wave,* and the other is called a *sky-wave.* VHF & UHF waves travel in straight lines, from point to point. HF waves are affected by storms on the sun called *sunspots,* but VHF & UHF waves are not.

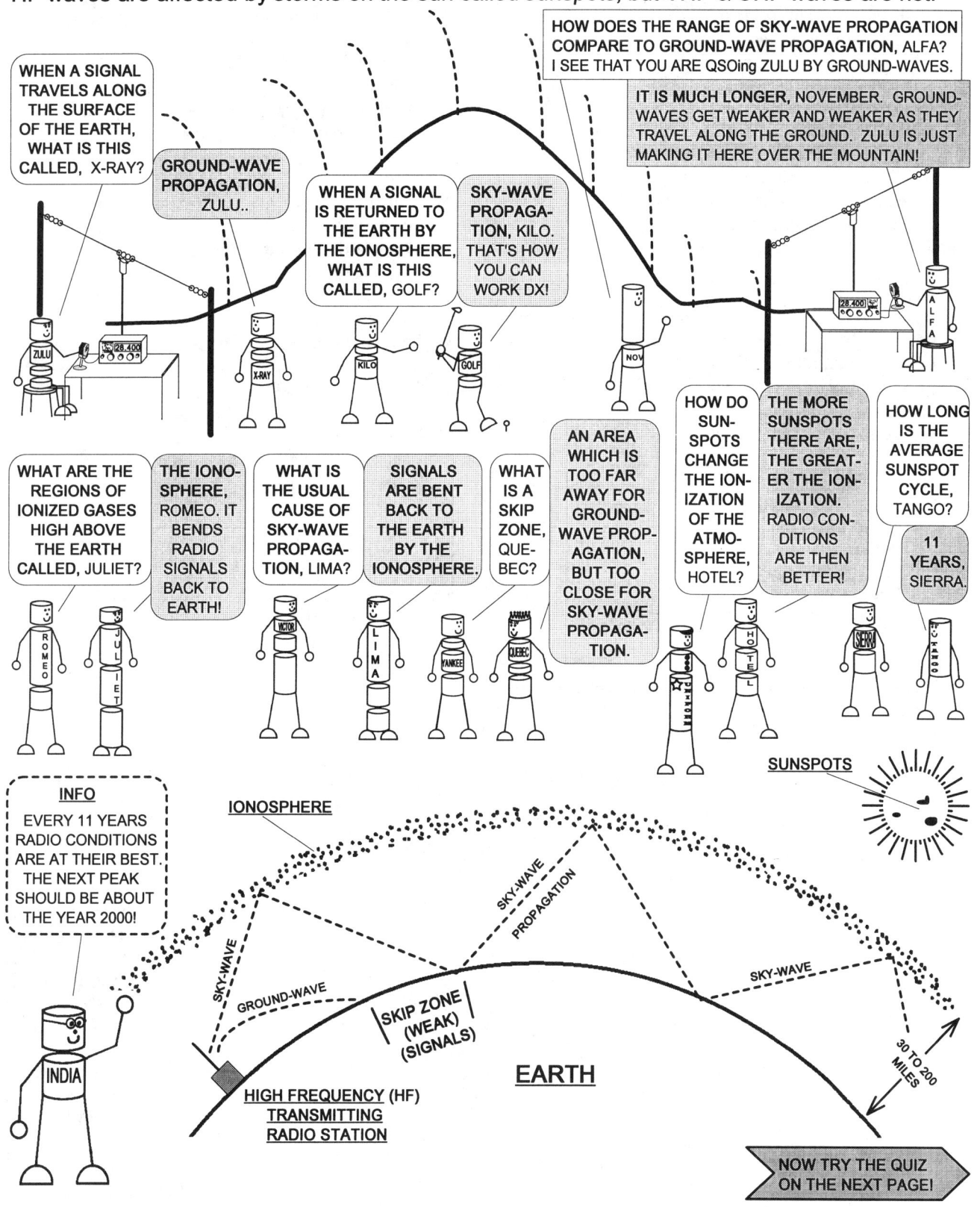

NOW TRY THE QUIZ ON THE NEXT PAGE!

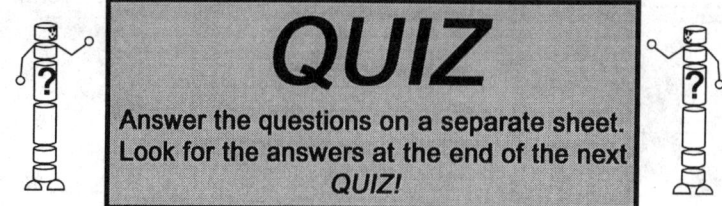

QUIZ

Answer the questions on a separate sheet. Look for the answers at the end of the next QUIZ!

N3A05
When a signal travels along the surface of the Earth, what is this called?
A. Sky-wave propagation
B. Knife-edge diffraction
C. E-region propagation
D. Ground-wave propagation

N3A07
When a signal is returned to earth by the ionosphere, what is this called?
A. Sky-wave propagation
B. Earth-moon-earth propagation
C. Ground-wave propagation
D. Tropospheric propagation

N3A06
How does the range of sky-wave propagation compare to ground-wave propagation?
A. It is much shorter
B. It is much longer
C. It is about the same
D. It depends on the weather

N3A10
What are the regions of ionized gases high above the earth called?
A. The ionosphere
B. The troposphere
C. The gas region
D. The ion zone

N3A08
What is the usual cause of sky-wave propagation?
A. Signals are reflected by a mountain
B. Signals are reflected by the moon
C. Signals are bent back to earth by the ionosphere
D. Signals are repeated by a repeater

N3A09
What is a skip zone?
A. An area covered by ground-wave propagation
B. An area covered by sky-wave propagation
C. An area which is too far away for ground-wave propagation, but to close for sky-wave propagation
D. An area which is too far away for ground-wave or sky-wave propagation

N3A11
How do sunspots change the ionization of the atmosphere?
A. The more sunspots there are, the greater the ionization
B. The more sunspots there are, the less the ionization
C. Unless there are sunspots, the ionization is zero
D. They have no effect

N3A12
How long is an average sunspot cycle?
A. 2 years
B. 5 years
C. 11 years
D. 17 years

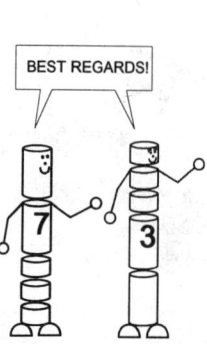

BEST REGARDS!

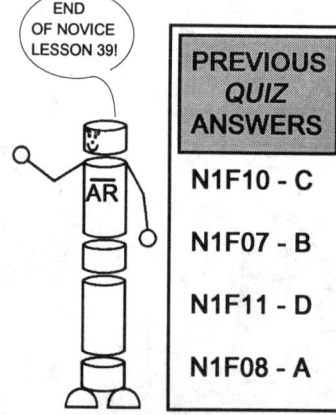

END OF NOVICE LESSON 39!

PREVIOUS QUIZ ANSWERS

N1F10 - C

N1F07 - B

N1F11 - D

N1F08 - A

LINE-OF-SIGHT COMMUNICATIONS
NOVICE LESSON 40

VHF and UHF broadcast signals, which includes FM & TV, travel in straight lines. Amateur VHF and UHF signals are exactly the same. You must be able to see the station with binoculars or a telescope. This is called "line-of-sight" communications, and is the reason that TV, FM, and amateur repeater stations are on mountain tops!

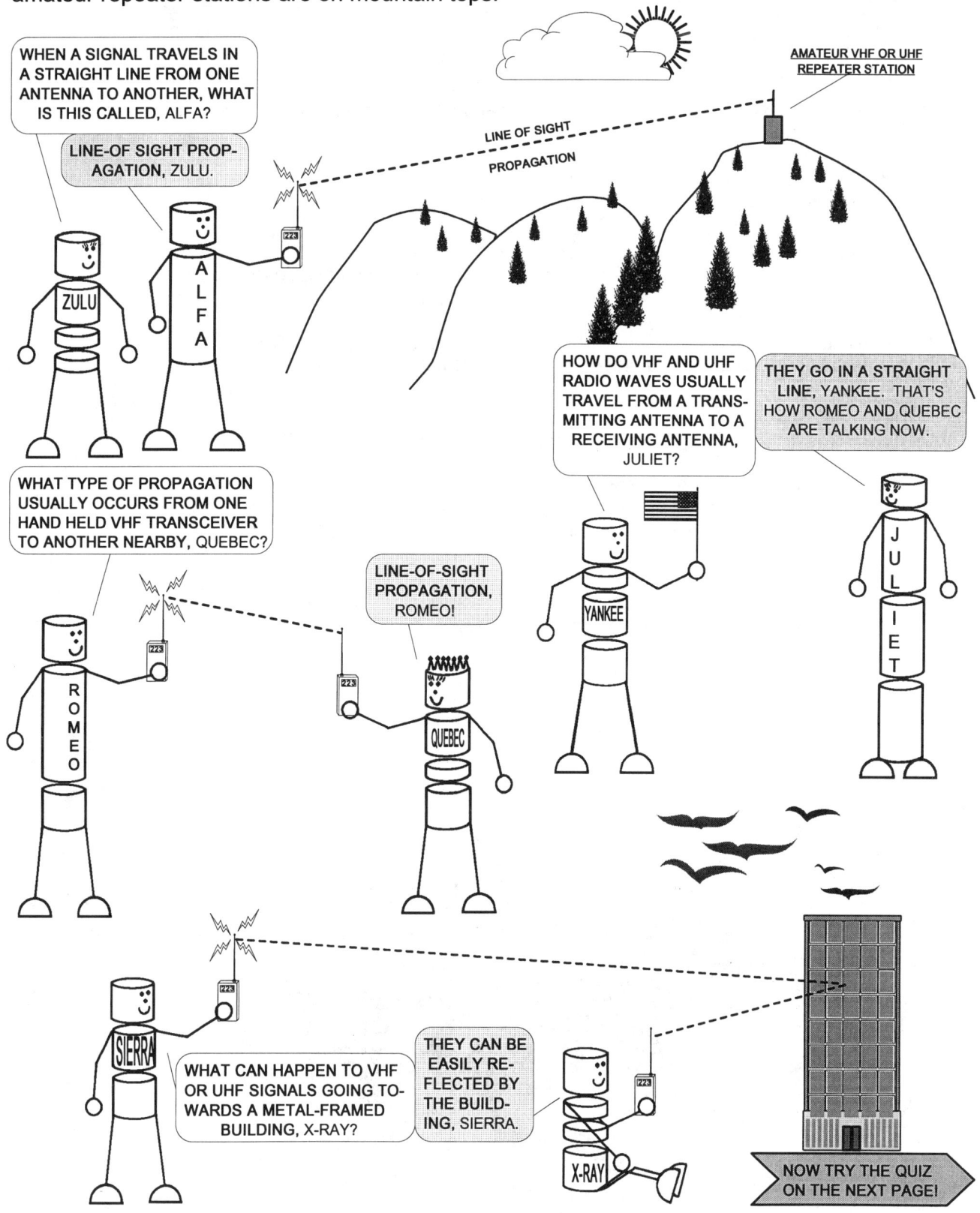

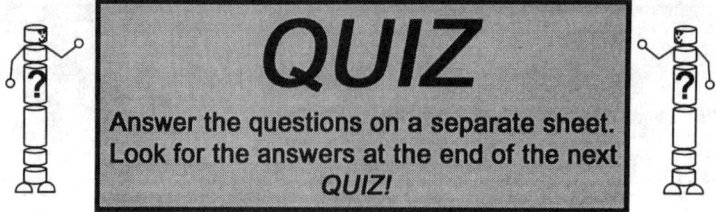

QUIZ
Answer the questions on a separate sheet. Look for the answers at the end of the next *QUIZ!*

N3A01
When a signal travels in a straight line from one antenna to another, what is this called?
A. Line-of-sight propagation
B. Straight-line propagation
C. Knife-edge diffraction
D. Tunnel propagation

N3A02
What type of propagation usually occurs from one hand held VHF transceiver to another nearby?
A. Tunnel propagation
B. Sky-wave propagation
C. Line-of-sight propagation
D. Auroral propagation

N3A03
How do VHF and UHF radio waves usually travel from a transmitting antenna to a receiving antenna?
A. They bend through the ionosphere
B. They go in a straight line
C. They wander in any direction
D. They move in a circle going either east or west from the transmitter

N3A04
What can happen to VHF or UHF signals going towards a metal-framed building?
A. They will go around the building
B. They can be bent by the ionosphere
C. They can be easily reflected by the building
D. They are sometimes scattered in the ectosphere

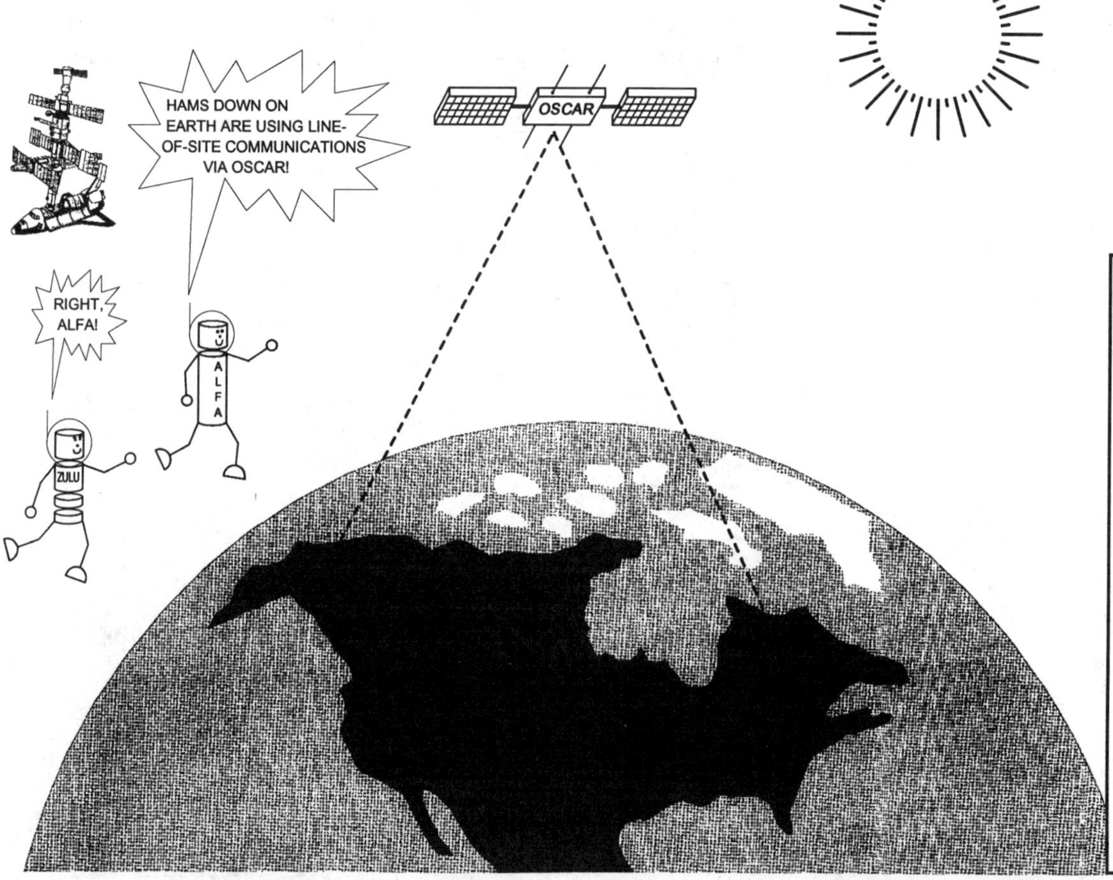

END OF NOVICE LESSON 40!

HAMS DOWN ON EARTH ARE USING LINE-OF-SITE COMMUNICATIONS VIA OSCAR!

RIGHT, ALFA!

PREVIOUS *QUIZ* ANSWERS
N3A05 - D
N3A07 - A
N3A06 - B
N3A10 - A
N3A08 - C
N3A09 - C
N3A11 - A
N3A12 - C

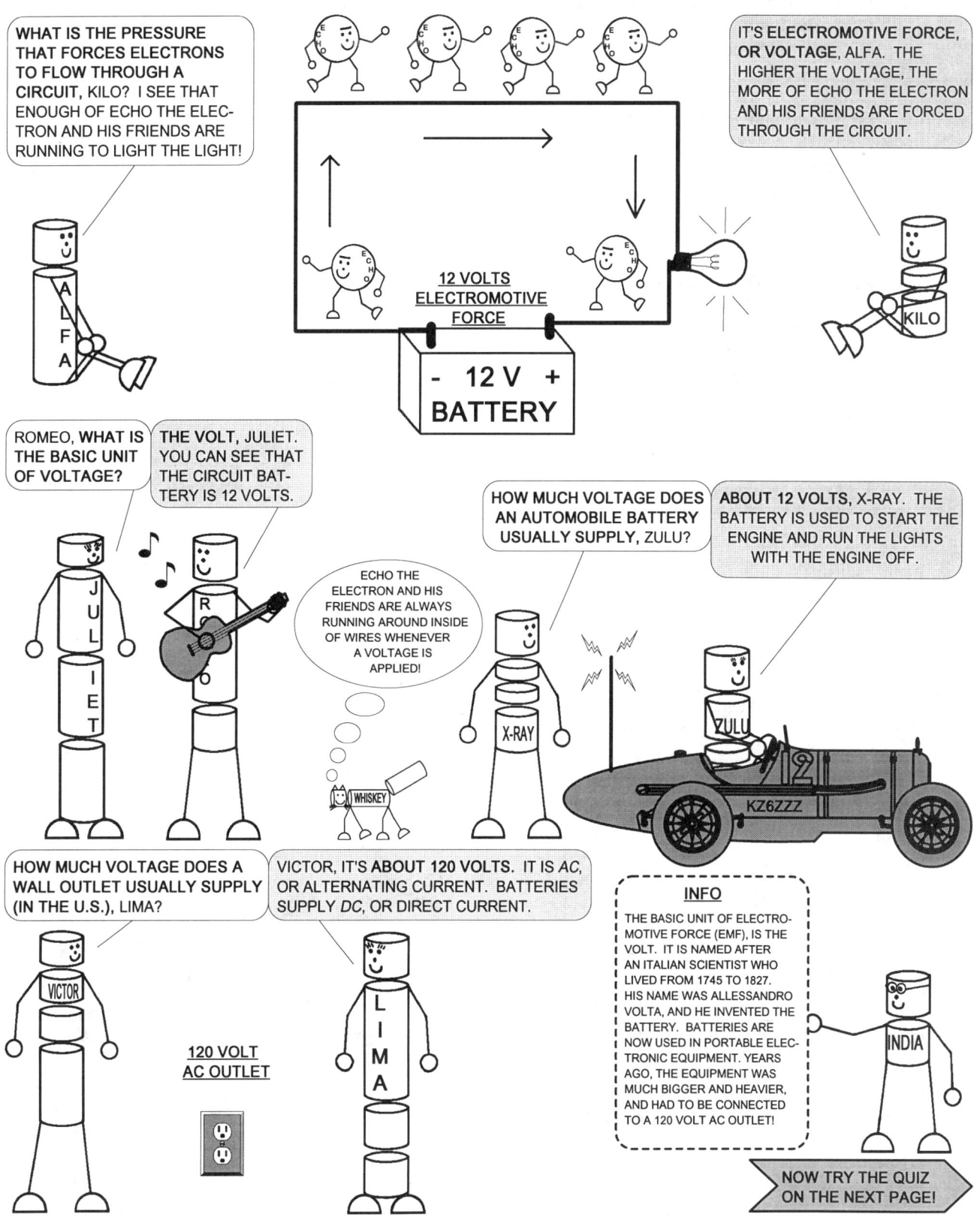

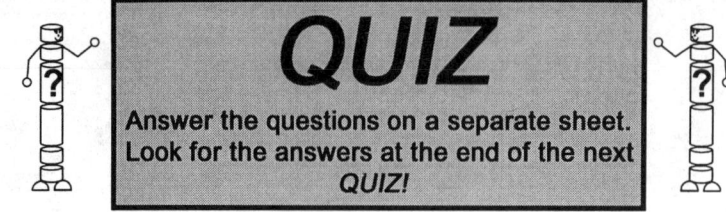

QUIZ
Answer the questions on a separate sheet. Look for the answers at the end of the next QUIZ!

N5B03
What is the pressure that forces electrons to flow through a circuit?
A. Magnetomotive force, or inductance
B. Electromotive force, or voltage
C. Farad force, or capacitance
D. Thermal force, or heat

N5B04
What is the basic unit of voltage?
A. The volt
B. The watt
C. The ampere
D. The ohm

N5B05
How much voltage does an automobile battery usually supply?
A. About 12 volts
B. About 30 volts
C. About 120 volts
D. About 240 volts

N5B06
How much voltage does a wall outlet usually supply (in the US)?
A. About 12 volts
B. About 30 volts
C. About 120 volts
D. About 480 volts

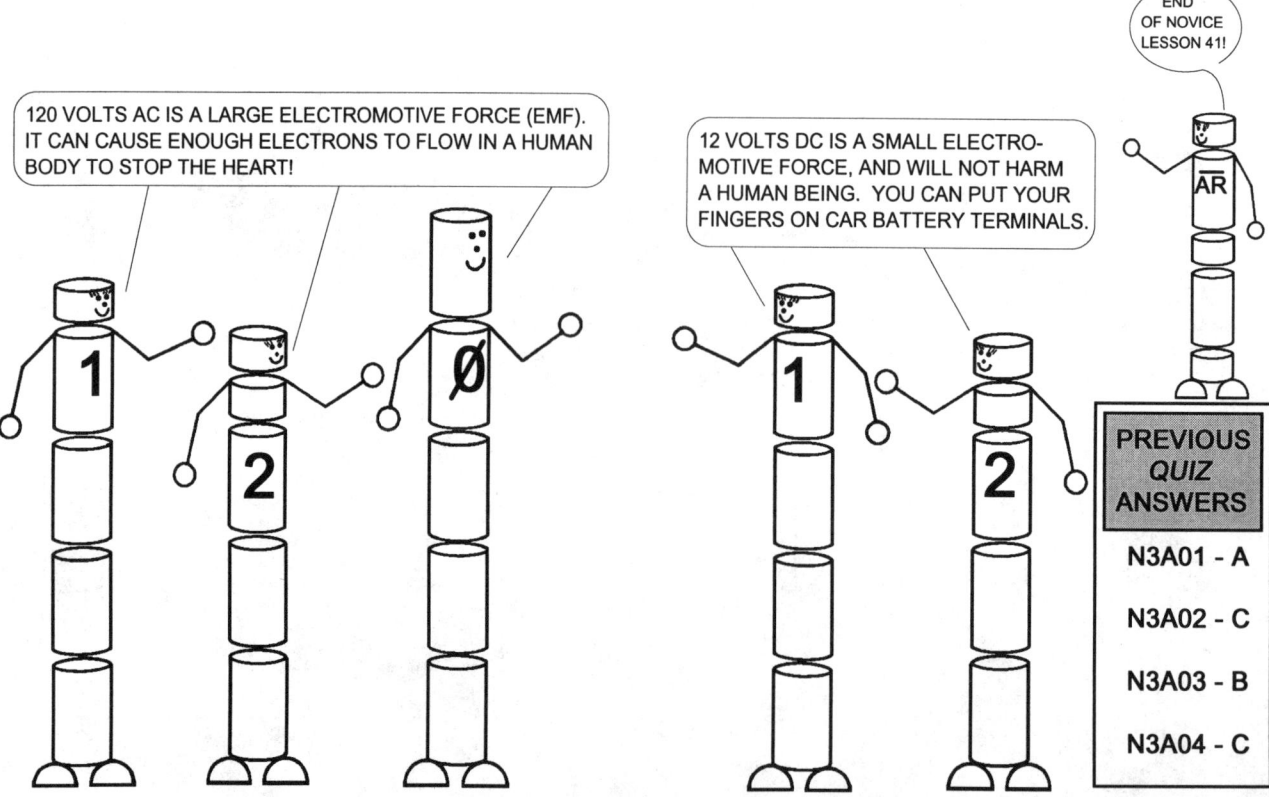

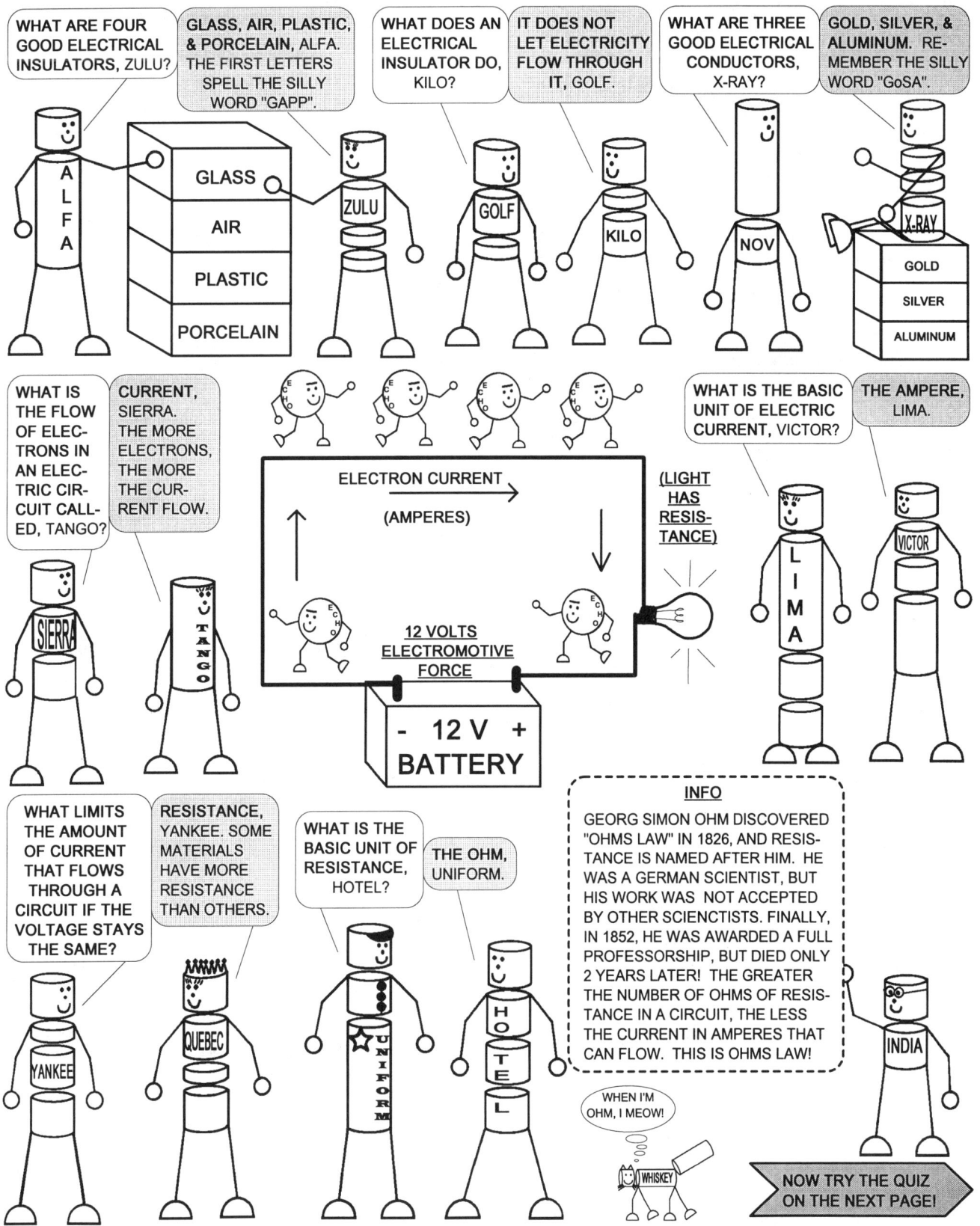

QUIZ

Answer the questions on a separate sheet. Look for the answers at the end of the next QUIZ!

N5B08
What are four good electrical insulators?
A. Glass, air, plastic, porcelain
B. Glass, wood, copper, porcelain
C. Paper, glass, air, aluminum
D. Plastic, rubber, wood, carbon

N5B09
What does an electrical insulator do?
A. It lets electricity flow through it in one direction
B. It does not let electricity flow through it
C. It lets electricity flow through it when light shines on it
D. It lets electricity flow through it

N5B07
What are three good electrical conductors?
A. Copper, gold, mica
B. Gold, silver, wood
C. Gold, silver, aluminum
D. Copper, aluminum, paper

N5B01
What is the flow of electrons in an electric circuit called?
A. Voltage
B. Resistance
C. Capacitance
D. Current

N5B02
What is the basic unit of electric current?
A. The volt
B. The watt
C. The ampere
D. The ohm

N5B10
What limits the amount of current that flows through a circuit if the voltage stays the same?
A. Reliance
B. Reactance
C. Saturation
D. Resistance

N5B11
What is the basic unit of resistance?
A. The volt
B. The watt
C. The ampere
D. The ohm

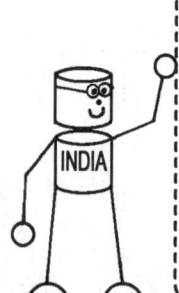

INFO
THE AMPERE IS NAMED AFTER ANDRE MARIE AMPERE, A FRENCH SCIENTIST. IN 1820, AMPERE USED ELECTRICAL MAGNETS TO INVENT THE TELEGRAPH. AN ELECTRICAL MAGNET IS A PIECE OF IRON WRAPED WITH A WIRE CONTAINING AN ELECTRICAL CURRENT. YOU CAN MAKE ONE USING AN IRON NAIL, SOME WIRE, AND A BATTERY!

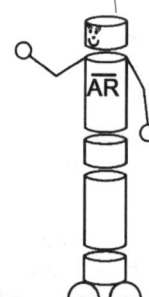

END OF NOVICE LESSON 42!

PREVIOUS QUIZ ANSWERS

N5B03 - B

N5B04 - A

N5B05 - A

N5B06 - C

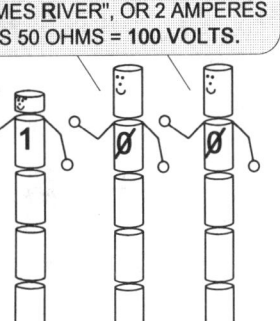

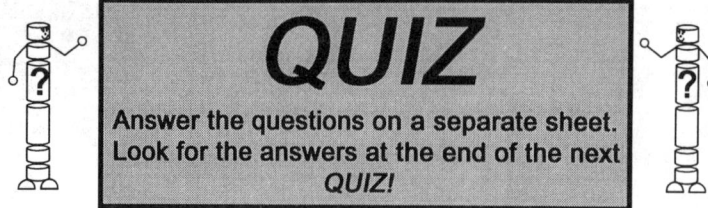

QUIZ

Answer the questions on a separate sheet. Look for the answers at the end of the next QUIZ!

N5C01
What formula shows how voltage, current and resistance relate to each other in an electric circuit?
A. Ohm's Law
B. Kirchhoff's Law
C. Ampere's Law
D. Tesla's Law

N5C03
If a 100-ohm resistor is connected to 200 volts, what is the current through the resistor?
A. 1/2 ampere
B. 2 amperes
C. 300 amperes
D. 20000 amperes

N5C04
If a current of 3 amperes flows through a resistor connected to 90 volts, what is the resistance?
A. 30 ohms
B. 93 ohms
C. 270 ohms
D. 1/30 ohm

N5C02
If a current of 2 amperes flows through a 50-ohm resistor, what is the voltage across the resistor?
A. 25 volts
B. 52 volts
C. 100 volts
D. 200 volts

N5C08
Which electrical circuit can have no current?
A. A closed circuit
B. A short circuit
C. An open circuit
D. A complete circuit

N5C09
Which electrical circuit uses too much current?
A. An open circuit
B. A dead circuit
C. A closed circuit
D. A short circuit

END OF NOVICE LESSON 43!

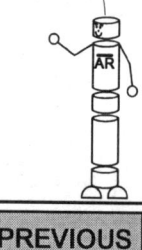

PREVIOUS QUIZ ANSWERS

N5B08 - A
N5B09 - B
N5B07 - C
N5B01 - D
N5B02 - C
N5B10 - D
N5B11 - D

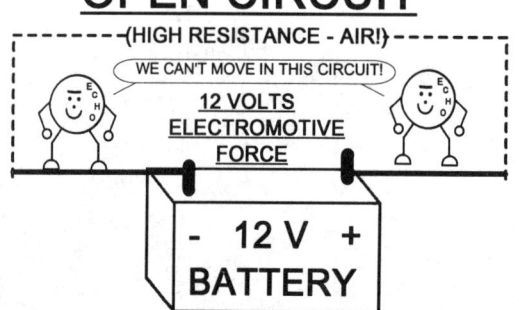

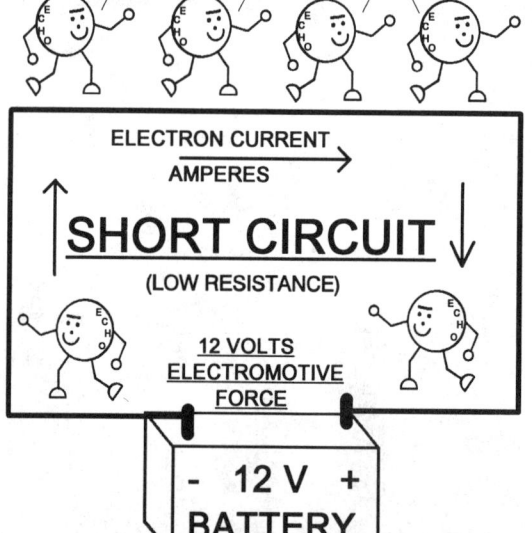

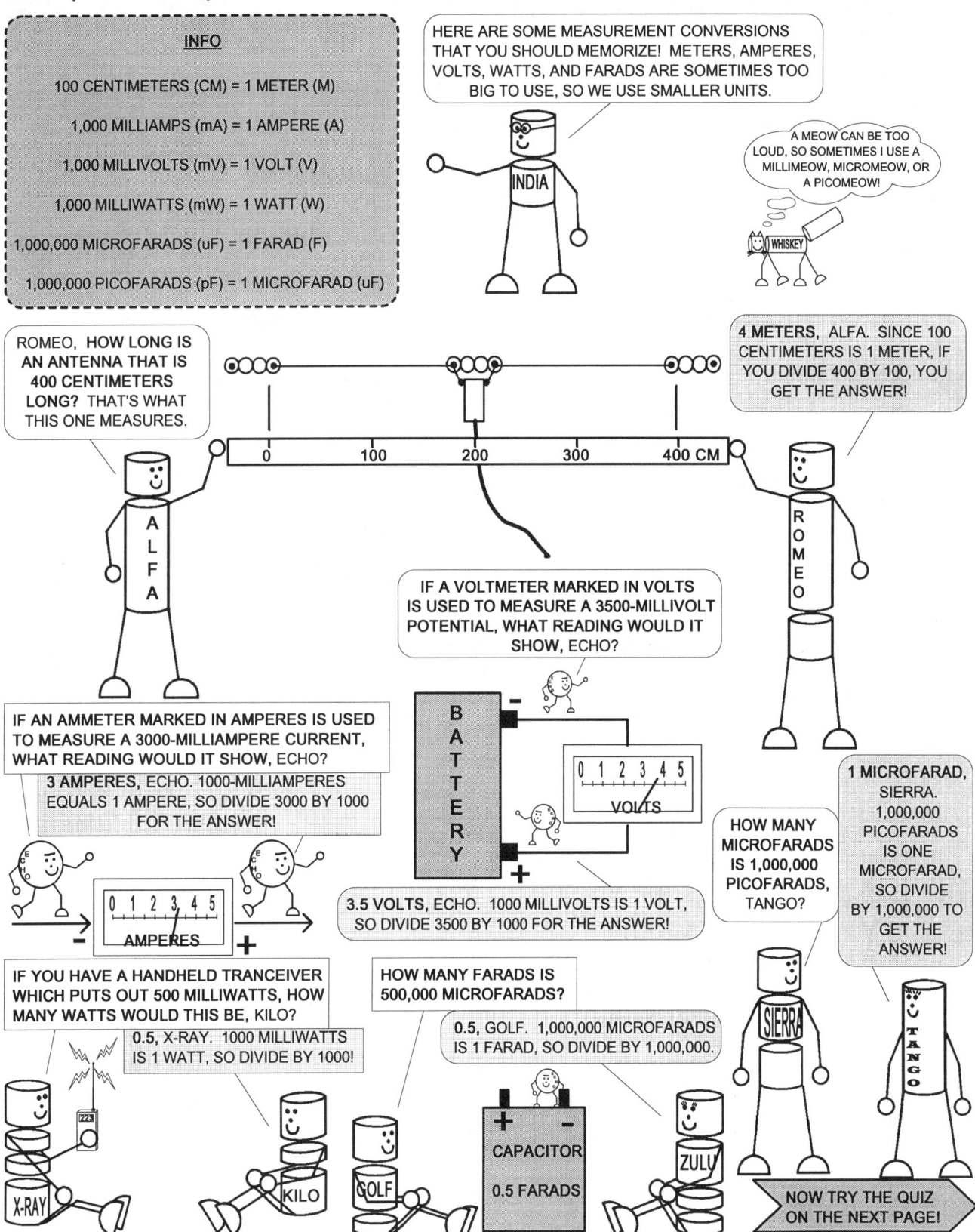

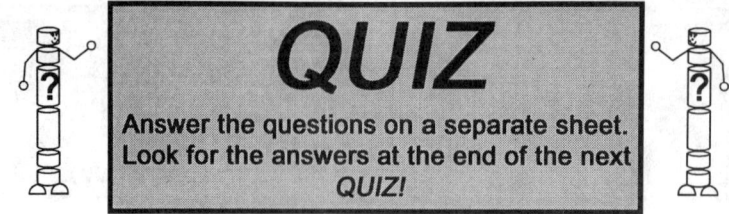

QUIZ

Answer the questions on a separate sheet. Look for the answers at the end of the next *QUIZ!*

N5A04
How long is an antenna that is 400 centimeters long?
A. 0.0004 meters
B. 4 meters
C. 40 meters
D. 40,000 meters

N5A05
If an ammeter marked in amperes is used to measure a 3000-milliampere current, what reading would it show?
A. 0.003 amperes
B. 0.3 amperes
C. 3 amperes
D. 3,000,000 amperes

N5A06
If a voltmeter marked in volts is used to measure a 3500-millivolt potential, what reading would it show?
A. 0.35 volts
B. 3.5 volts
C. 35 volts
D. 350 volts

N5A11
If you have a hand held transceiver which puts out 500 milliwatts, how many watts would this be?
A. 0.02
B. 0.5
C. 5
D. 50

N5A07
How many farads is 500,000 microfarads?
A. 0.0005 farads
B. 0.5 farads
C. 500 farads
D. 500,000,000 farads

N5A08
How many microfarads is 1,000,000 picofarads?
A. 0.001 microfarads
B. 1 microfarad
C. 1,000 microfarads
D. 1,000,000,000 microfarads

PREVIOUS QUIZ ANSWERS
N5C01 - A
N5C03 - B
N5C04 - A
N5C02 - C
N5C08 - C
N5C09 - D

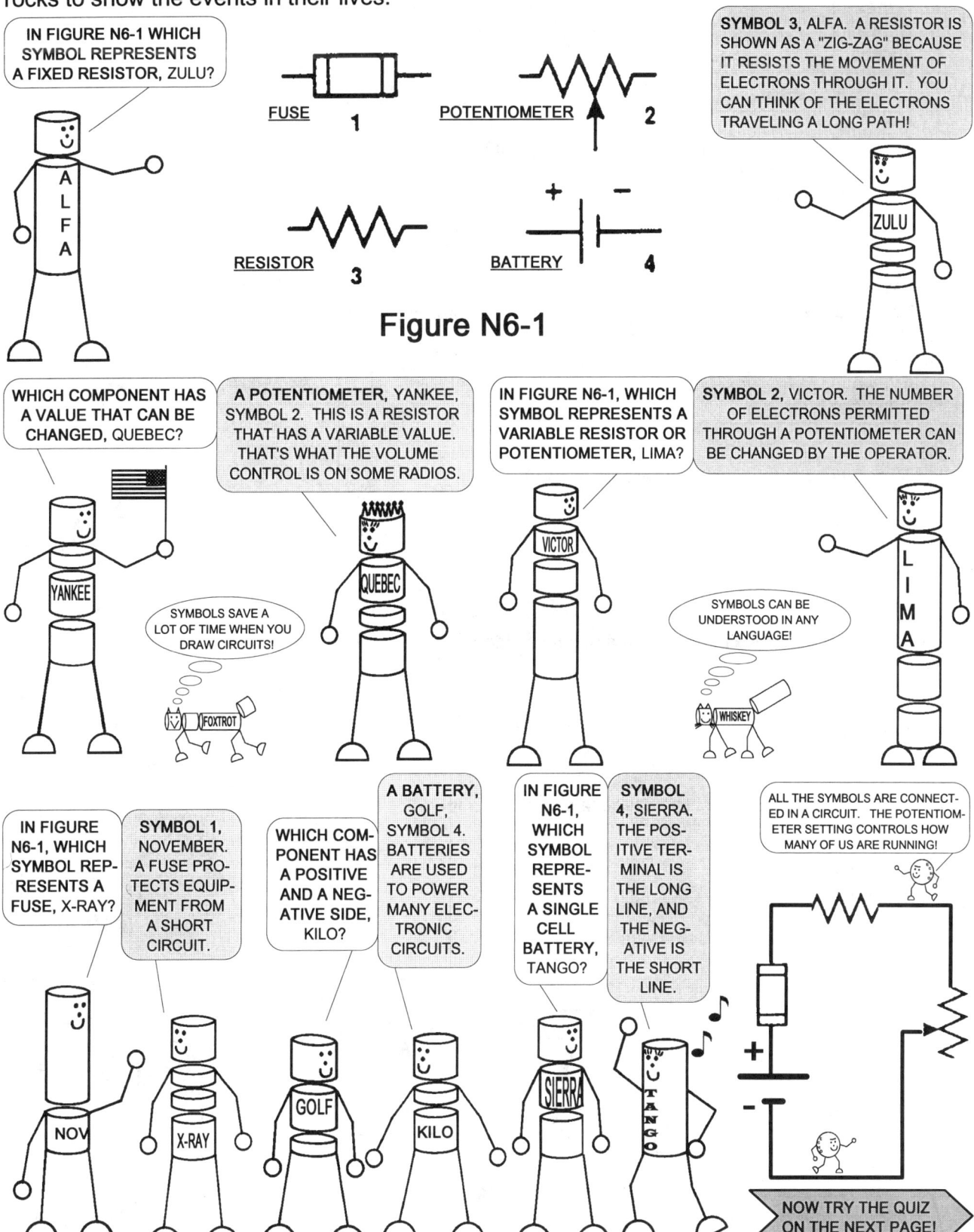

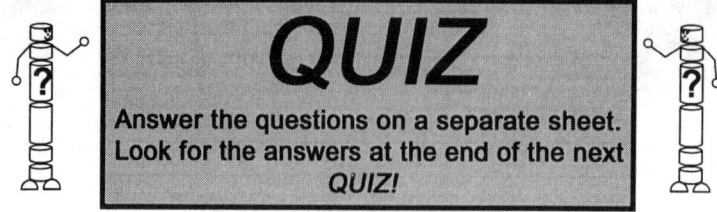

QUIZ
Answer the questions on a separate sheet. Look for the answers at the end of the next QUIZ!

N6A06
In Figure N6-1 which symbol represents a fixed resistor?
A. Symbol 1
B. Symbol 2
C. Symbol 3
D. Symbol 4

N6A04
Which component has a value that can be changed?
A. A single-cell battery
B. A potentiometer
C. A fuse
D. A resistor

N6A05
In Figure N6-1 which symbol represents a variable resistor or potentiometer?
A. Symbol 1
B. Symbol 2
C. Symbol 3
D. Symbol 4

N6A07
In Figure N6-1 which symbol represents a fuse?
A. Symbol 1
B. Symbol 2
C. Symbol 3
D. Symbol 4

N6A03
Which component has a positive and a negative side?
A. A battery
B. A potentiometer
C. A fuse
D. A resistor

N6A08
In Figure N6-1 which symbol represents a single-cell battery?
A. Symbol 1
B. Symbol 2
C. Symbol 3
D. Symbol 4

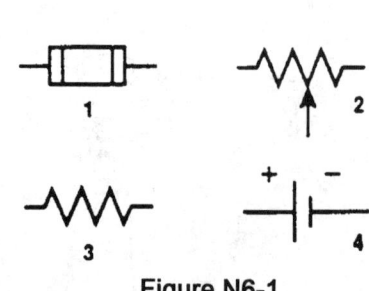

Figure N6-1

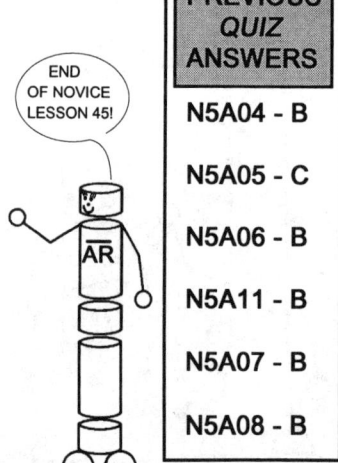

END OF NOVICE LESSON 45!

PREVIOUS QUIZ ANSWERS
N5A04 - B
N5A05 - C
N5A06 - B
N5A11 - B
N5A07 - B
N5A08 - B

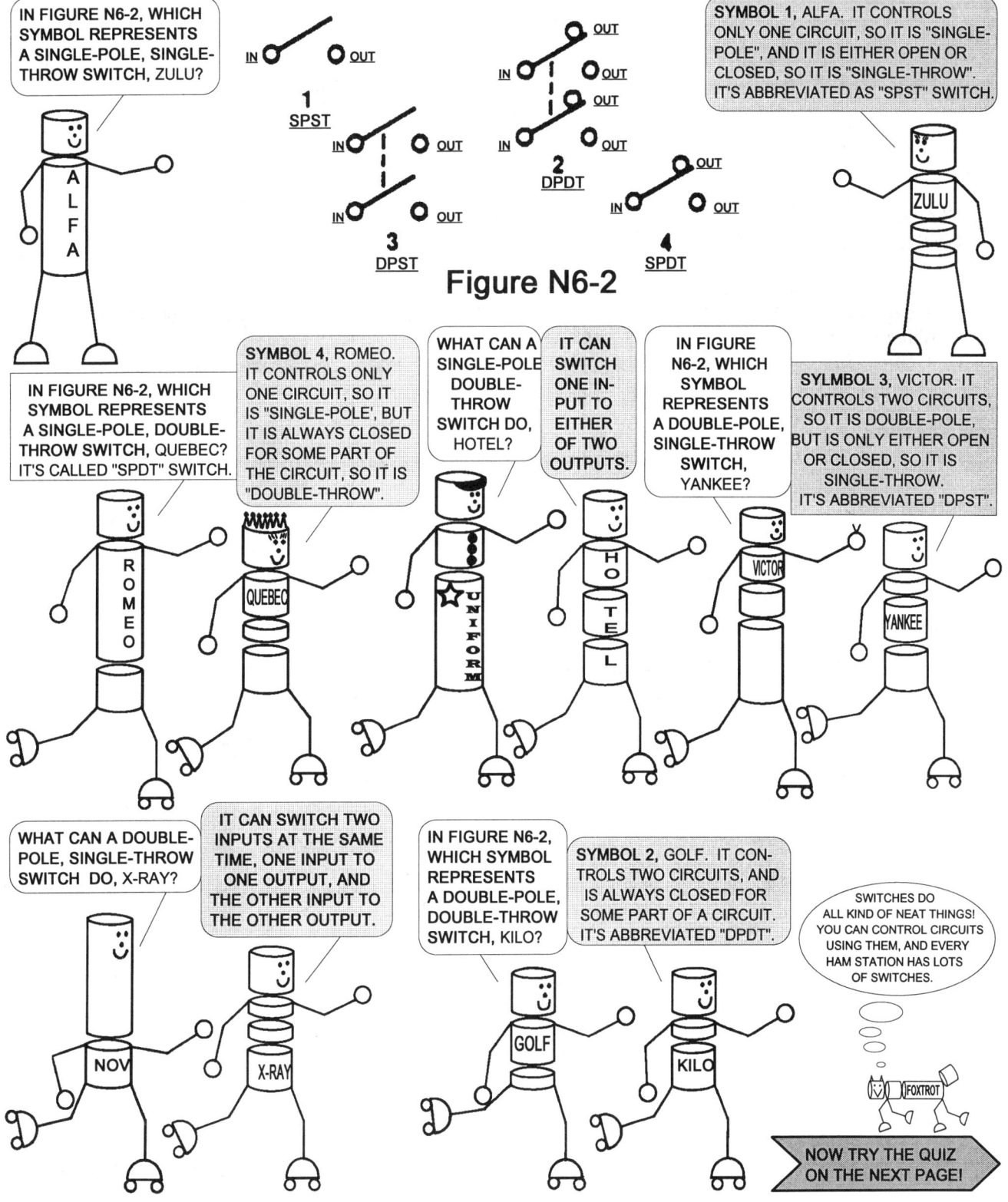

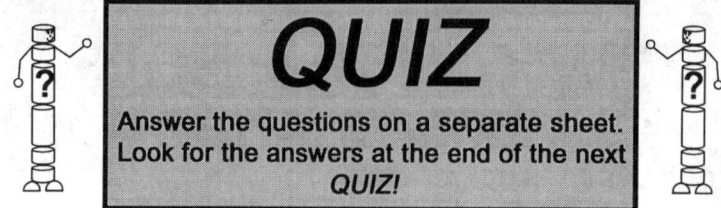

QUIZ

Answer the questions on a separate sheet. Look for the answers at the end of the next QUIZ!

N6A09
In Figure N6-2 which symbol represents a single-pole, single-throw switch?
A. Symbol 1
B. Symbol 2
C. Symbol 3
D. Symbol 4

N6A10
In Figure N6-2 which symbol represents a single-pole, double-throw switch?
A. Symbol 1
B. Symbol 2
C. Symbol 3
D. Symbol 4

N6A01
What can a single-pole, double-throw switch do?
A. It can switch one input to one output
B. It can switch one input to either of two outputs
C. It can switch two inputs at the same time, one input to either of two outputs, and the other input to either of two outputs
D. It can switch two inputs at the same time, one input to one output, and the other input to another output

N6A11
In Figure N6-2 which symbol represents a double-pole, single-throw switch?
A. Symbol 1
B. Symbol 2
C. Symbol 3
D. Symbol 4

N6A02
What can a double-pole, single-throw switch do?
A. It can switch one input to one output
B. It can switch one input to either of two outputs
C. It can switch two inputs at the same time, one input to either of two outputs, and the other input to either of two outputs
D. It can switch two inputs at the same time, one input to one output, and the other input to the other output

N6A12
In Figure N6-2 which symbol represents a double-pole, double-throw switch?
A. Symbol 1
B. Symbol 2
C. Symbol 3
D. Symbol 4

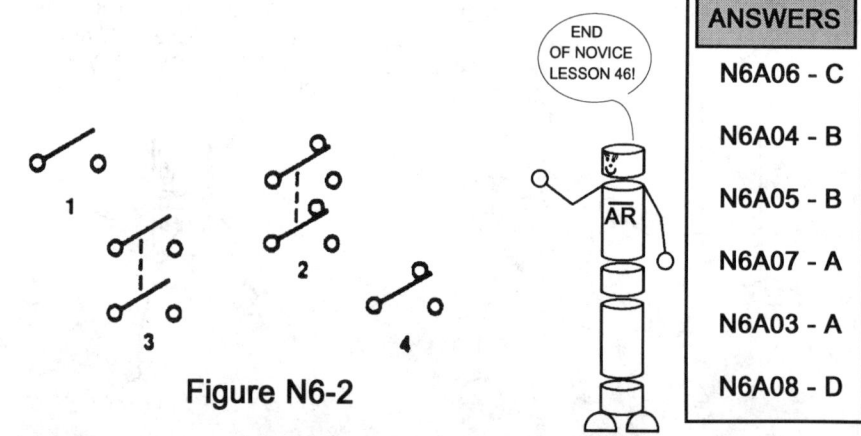

Figure N6-2

END OF NOVICE LESSON 46!

PREVIOUS QUIZ ANSWERS
N6A06 - C
N6A04 - B
N6A05 - B
N6A07 - A
N6A03 - A
N6A08 - D

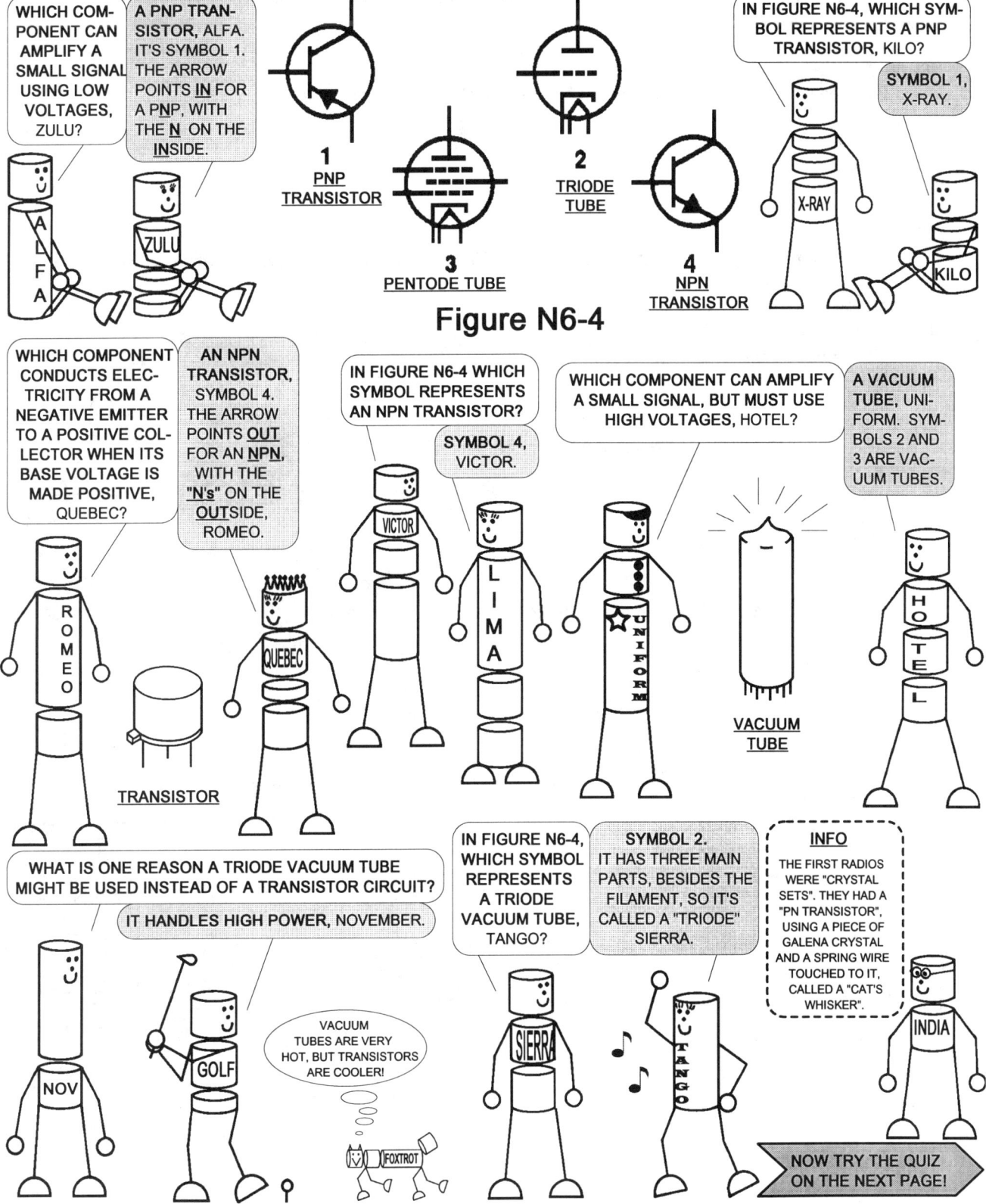

QUIZ

Answer the questions on a separate sheet.
Look for the answers at the end of the next QUIZ!

N6B01
Which component can amplify a small signal using low voltages?
A. A PNP transistor
B. A variable resistor
C. An electrolytic capacitor
D. A multiple-cell battery

N6B08
In Figure N6-4 which symbol represents a PNP transistor?
A. Symbol 1
B. Symbol 2
C. Symbol 3
D. Symbol 4

N6B02
Which component conducts electricity from a negative emitter to a positive collector when its base voltage is made positive?
A. A variable resistor
B. An NPN transistor
C. A triode vacuum tube
D. A multiple-cell battery

N6B07
In Figure N6-4 which symbol represents an NPN transistor?
A. Symbol 1
B. Symbol 2
C. Symbol 3
D. Symbol 4

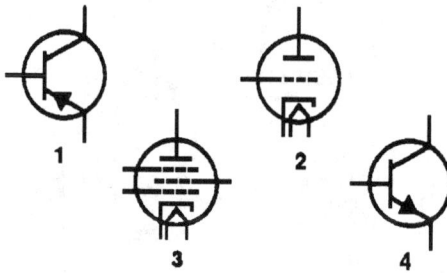

Figure N6-4

N6B11
Which component can amplify a small signal but must use high voltages?
A. A transistor
B. An electrolytic capacitor
C. A vacuum tube
D. A multiple-cell battery

N6B10
What is one reason a triode vacuum tube might be used instead of a transistor in a circuit?
A. It handles higher power
B. It uses lower voltages
C. It uses less current
D. It is much smaller

N6B09
In Figure N6-4 which symbol represents a triode vacuum tube?
A. Symbol 1
B. Symbol 2
C. Symbol 3
D. Symbol 4

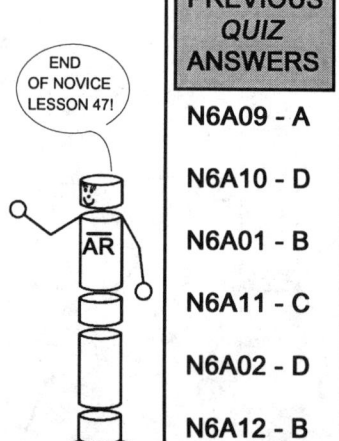

END OF NOVICE LESSON 47!

PREVIOUS QUIZ ANSWERS
N6A09 - A
N6A10 - D
N6A01 - B
N6A11 - C
N6A02 - D
N6A12 - B

ANTENNA & GROUND SYMBOLS
NOVICE LESSON 48

Antennas are used to radiate radio waves, and grounds are used with some antennas to make the radiation more efficient. Equipment and stations are grounded to prevent radio waves from traveling in unwanted places. Symbols are used to indicate an antenna or ground connection.

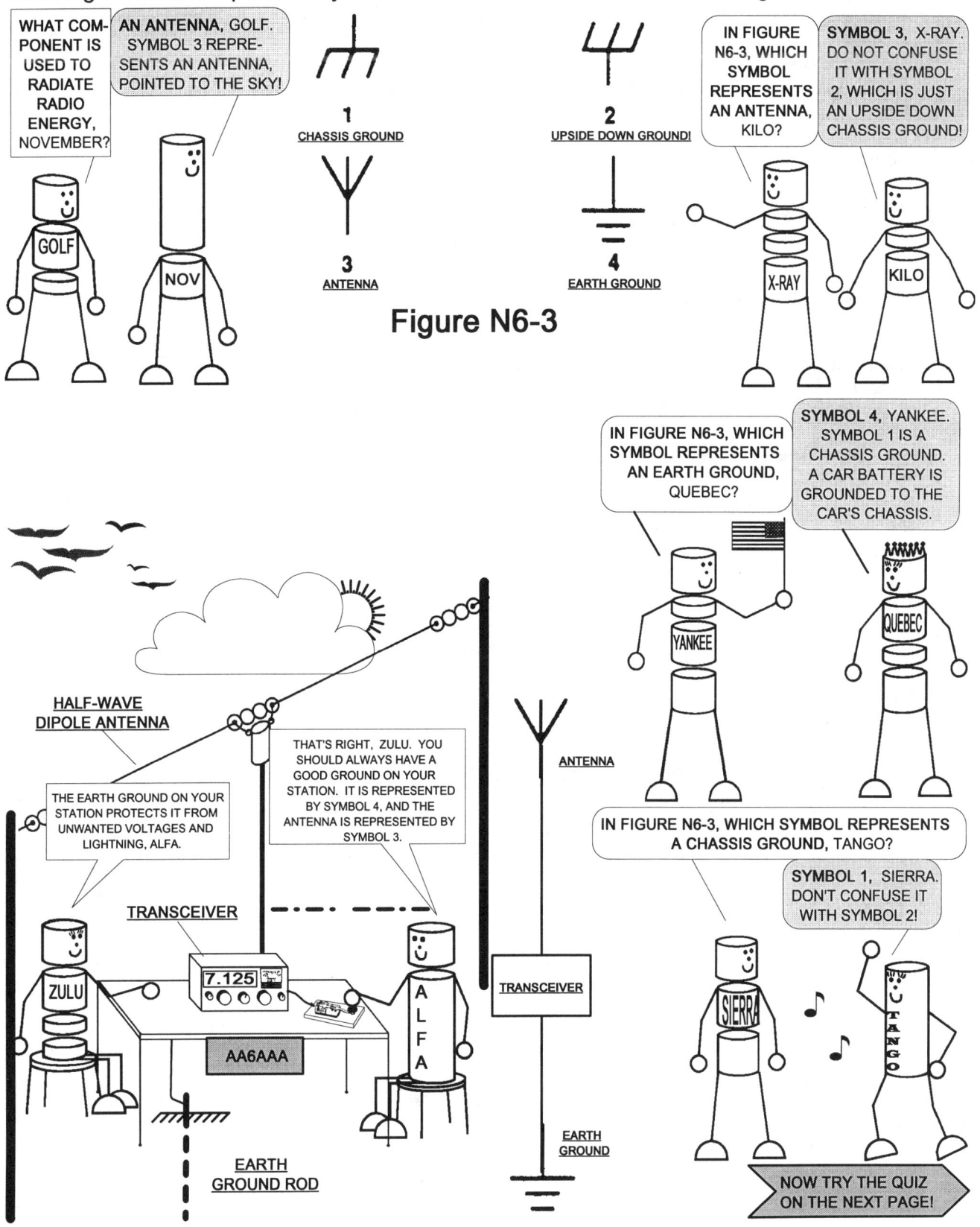

Figure N6-3

NOW TRY THE QUIZ ON THE NEXT PAGE!

QUIZ

Answer the questions on a separate sheet. Look for the answers at the end of the next QUIZ!

N6B03
Which component is used to radiate radio energy?
A. An antenna
B. An earth ground
C. A chassis ground
D. A potentiometer

N6B06
In Figure N6-3 which symbol represents an antenna?
A. Symbol 1
B. Symbol 2
C. Symbol 3
D. Symbol 4

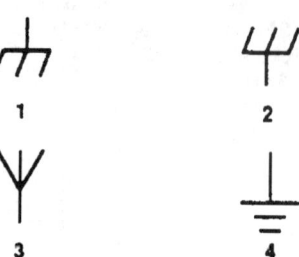

Figure N6-3

N6B04
In Figure N6-3 which symbol represents an earth ground?
A. Symbol 1
B. Symbol 2
C. Symbol 3
D. Symbol 4

N6B05
In Figure N6-3 which symbol represents a chassis ground?
A. Symbol 1
B. Symbol 2
C. Symbol 3
D. Symbol 4

THERE IS NO SYMBOL FOR A SPACECRAFT, BUT OSCAR MAKES A GREAT ANTENNA FOR YOUR SIGNAL WHEN YOU QSO THROUGH IT. AS OSCARS MOVE ACROSS THE SKY, YOU HAVE TO TRACK THEM WITH YOUR ANTENNA. SOME OSCARS ARE IN LONG "ELIPTICAL" EARTH ORBITS, SO THEY MOVE VERY SLOWLY, AND TRACKING IS VERY EASY!

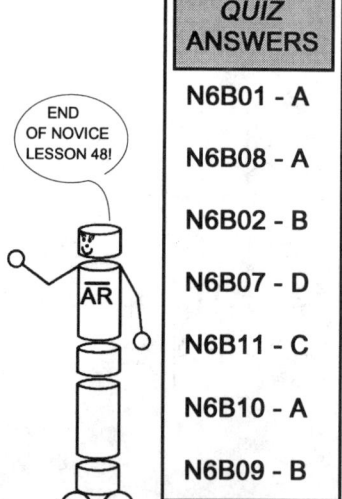

END OF NOVICE LESSON 48!

PREVIOUS QUIZ ANSWERS
N6B01 - A
N6B08 - A
N6B02 - B
N6B07 - D
N6B11 - C
N6B10 - A
N6B09 - B

POWER SUPPLIES

NOVICE LESSON 49

Transceivers operate on 12 volts DC, which is the average voltage of a car battery. A transceiver can operate either on a 12 volt DC car battery or on a 12 volt DC "power supply" in your home. This makes ham transceivers very useful in emergencies!

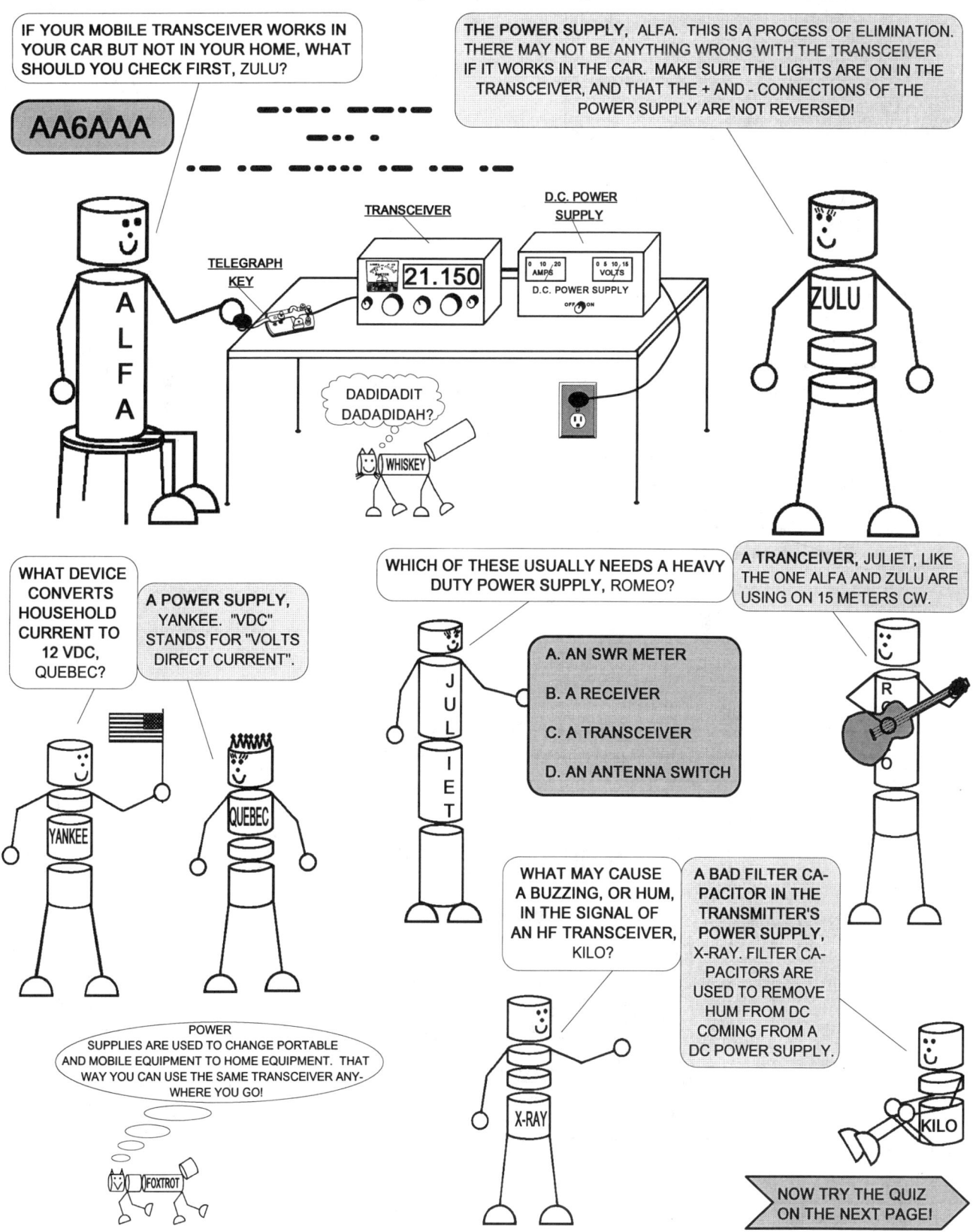

NOW TRY THE QUIZ ON THE NEXT PAGE!

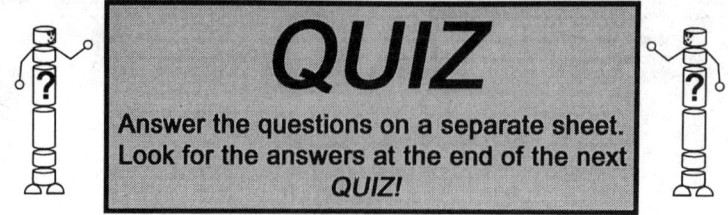

QUIZ
Answer the questions on a separate sheet. Look for the answers at the end of the next *QUIZ!*

N7A07
If your mobile transceiver works in your car but not in your home, what should you check first?
A. The power supply
B. The speaker
C. The microphone
D. The SWR meter

N7A12
What device converts household current to 12 VDC?
A. A catalytic converter
B. A low-pass filter
C. A power supply
D. An RS-232 interface

N7A13
Which of these usually needs a heavy-duty power supply?
A. An SWR meter
B. A receiver
C. A transceiver
D. An antenna switch

N8A10
What may cause a buzzing or hum in the signal of an HF transmitter?
A. Using an antenna which is the wrong length
B. Energy from another transmitter
C. Bad design of the transmitter's RF power output circuit
D. A bad filter capacitor in the transmitter's power supply

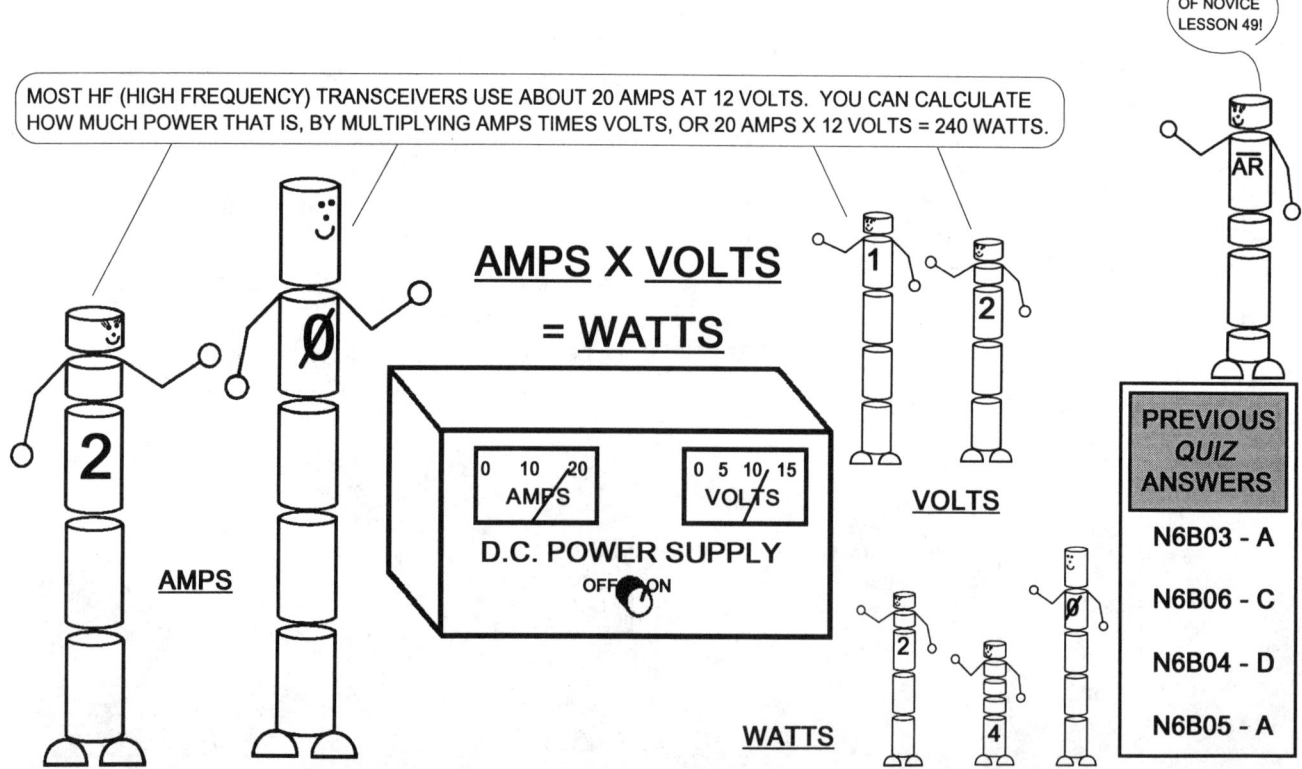

END OF NOVICE LESSON 49!

MOST HF (HIGH FREQUENCY) TRANSCEIVERS USE ABOUT 20 AMPS AT 12 VOLTS. YOU CAN CALCULATE HOW MUCH POWER THAT IS, BY MULTIPLYING AMPS TIMES VOLTS, OR 20 AMPS X 12 VOLTS = 240 WATTS.

AMPS X VOLTS = WATTS

D.C. POWER SUPPLY

PREVIOUS *QUIZ* ANSWERS

N6B03 - A
N6B06 - C
N6B04 - D
N6B05 - A

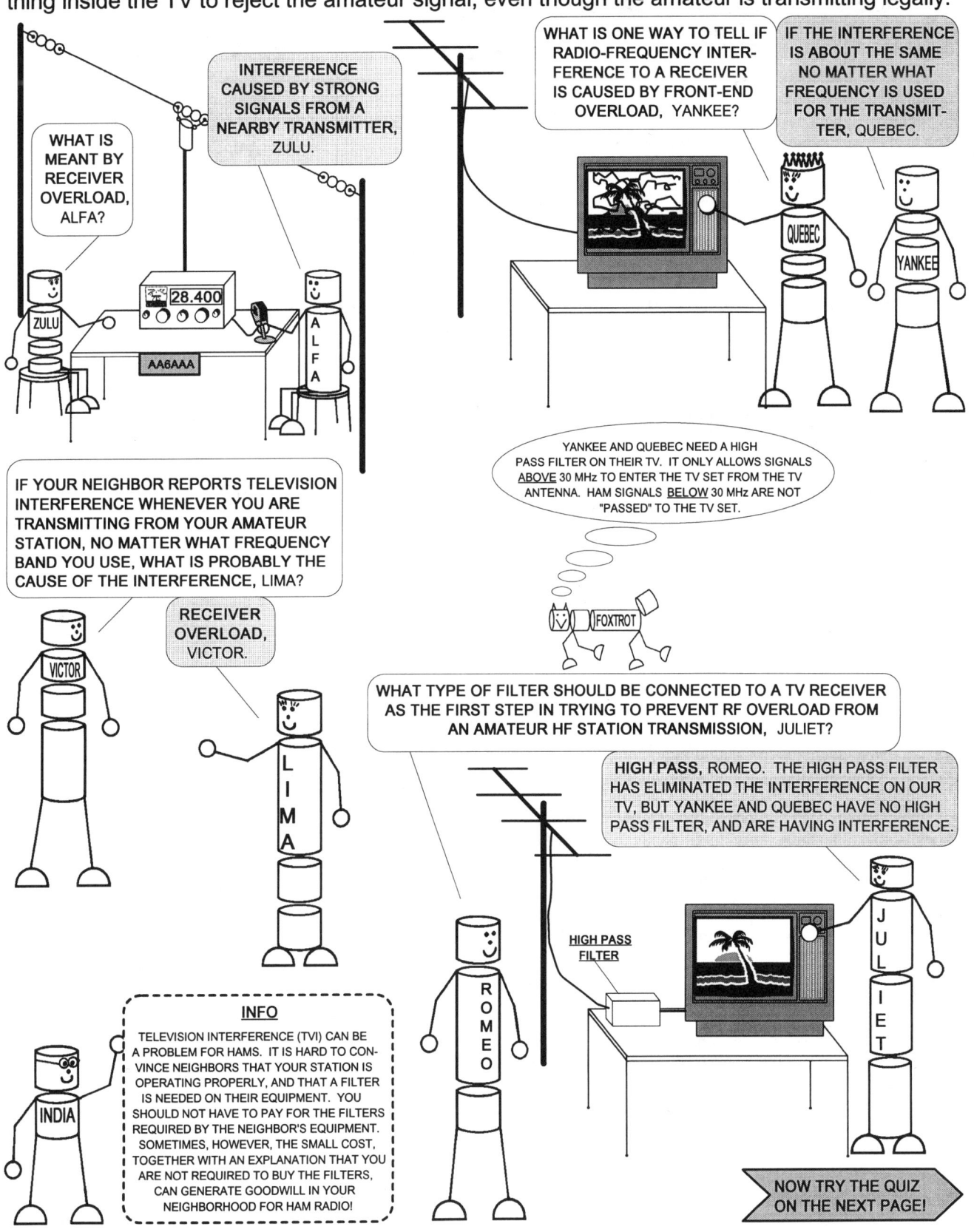

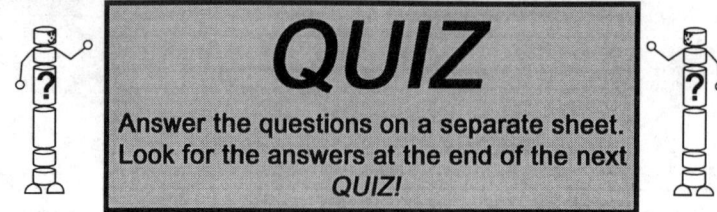

QUIZ
Answer the questions on a separate sheet. Look for the answers at the end of the next QUIZ!

N4D01
What is meant by receiver overload?
A. Too much voltage from the power supply
B. Too much current from the power supply
C. Interference caused by strong signals from a nearby transmitter
D. Interference caused by turning the volume up too high

N4D02
What is one way to tell if radio-frequency interference to a receiver is caused by front-end overload?
A. If connecting a low-pass filter to the transmitter greatly cuts down the interference
B. If the interference is about the same no matter what frequency is used for the transmitter
C. If connecting a low-pass filter to the receiver greatly cuts down the interference
D. If grounding the receiver makes the problem worse

N4D03
If your neighbor reports television interference whenever you are transmitting from your amateur station, no matter what frequency band you use, what is probably the cause of the interference?
A. Too little transmitter harmonic suppression
B. Receiver VR tube discharge
C. Receiver overload
D. Incorrect antenna length

N4D05
What type of filter should be connected to a TV receiver as the first step in trying to prevent RF overload from an amateur HF station transmission?
A. Low-pass
B. High-pass
C. Band pass
D. Notch

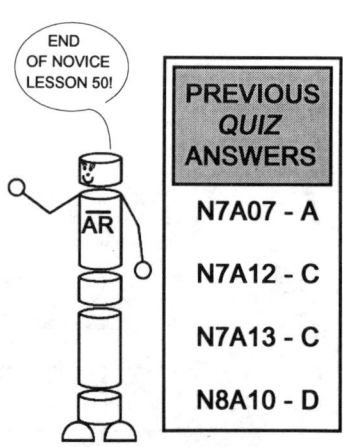

END OF NOVICE LESSON 50!

PREVIOUS QUIZ ANSWERS

N7A07 - A

N7A12 - C

N7A13 - C

N8A10 - D

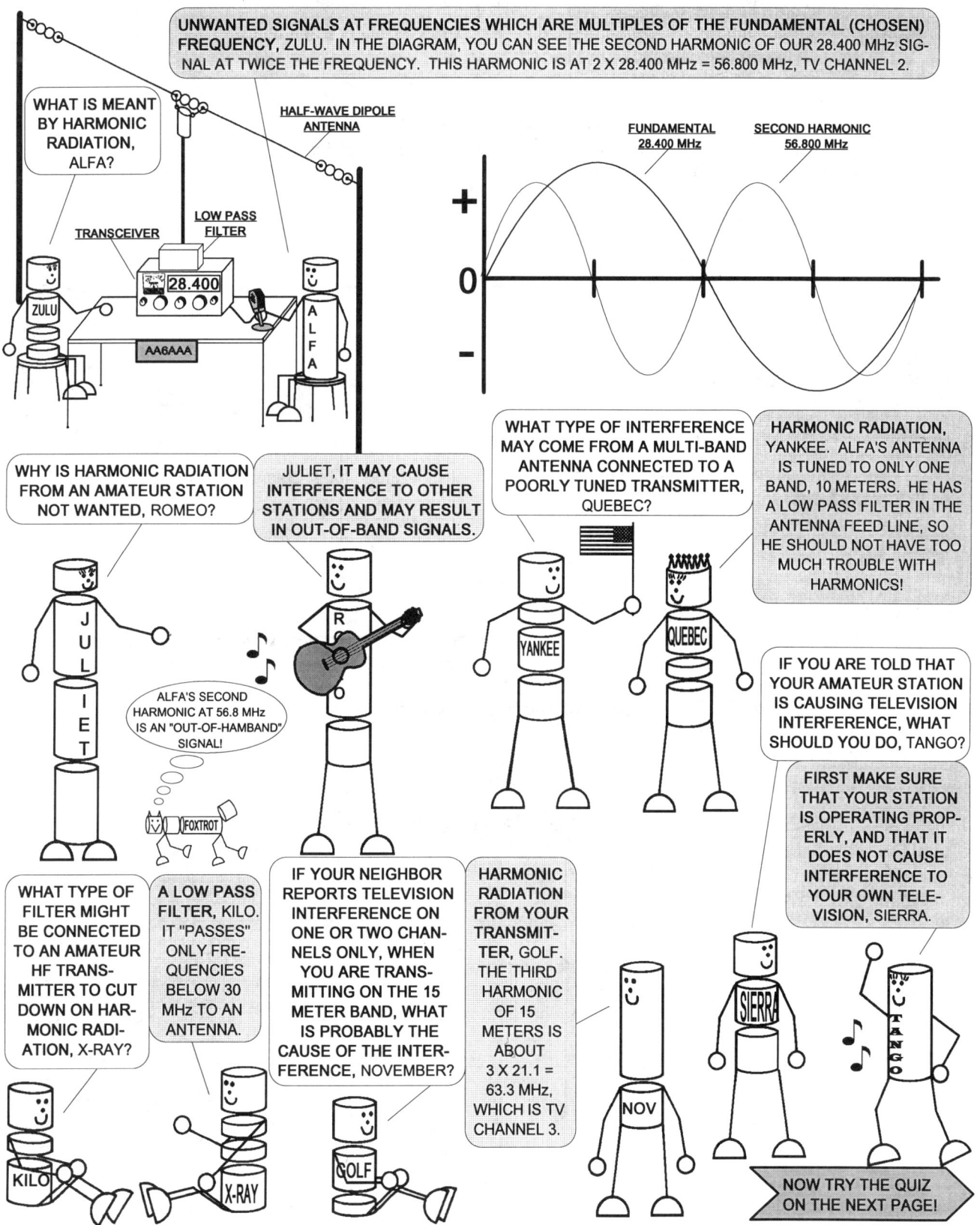

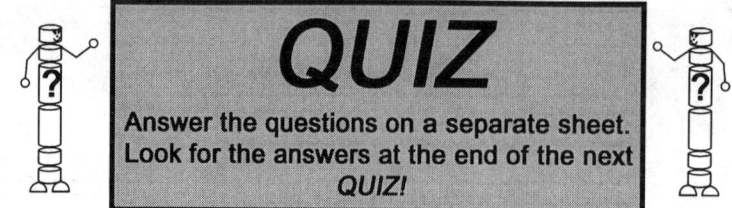

QUIZ
Answer the questions on a separate sheet. Look for the answers at the end of the next *QUIZ!*

N4D07
What is meant by harmonic radiation?
A. Unwanted signals at frequencies which are multiples of the fundamental (chosen) frequency
B. Unwanted signals that are combined with a 60-Hz hum
C. Unwanted signals caused by sympathetic vibrations from a nearby transmitter
D. Signals which cause skip propagation to occur

N4D08
Why is harmonic radiation from an amateur station not wanted?
A. It may cause interference to other stations and may result in out-of-band signals
B. It uses large amounts of electric power
C. It may cause sympathetic vibrations in nearby transmitters
D. It may cause auroras in the air

N4D09
What type of interference may come from a multi-band antenna connected to a poorly tuned transmitter?
A. Harmonic radiation
B. Auroral distortion
C. Parasitic excitation
D. Intermodulation

N4D06
What type of filter might be connected to an amateur HF transmitter to cut down on harmonic radiation?
A. A key-click filter
B. A low-pass filter
C. A high-pass filter
D. A CW filter

N4D04
If your neighbor reports television interference on one or two channels only when you are transmitting on the 15-meter band, what is probably the cause of the interference?
A. Too much low-pass filtering on the transmitter
B. De-ionization of the ionosphere near your neighbor's TV antenna
C. TV receiver front-end overload
D. Harmonic radiation from your transmitter

N4D11
If you are told that your amateur station is causing television interference, what should you do?
A. First make sure that your station is operating properly, and that it does not cause interference to your own television
B. Immediately turn off your transmitter and contact the nearest FCC office for assistance
C. Connect a high-pass filter to the transmitter output and a low-pass filter to the antenna-input terminals of the television
D. Continue operating normally, because you have no reason to worry about the interference

END OF NOVICE LESSON 51!

PREVIOUS *QUIZ* ANSWERS

N4D01 - C

N4D02 - B

N4D03 - C

N4D05 - B

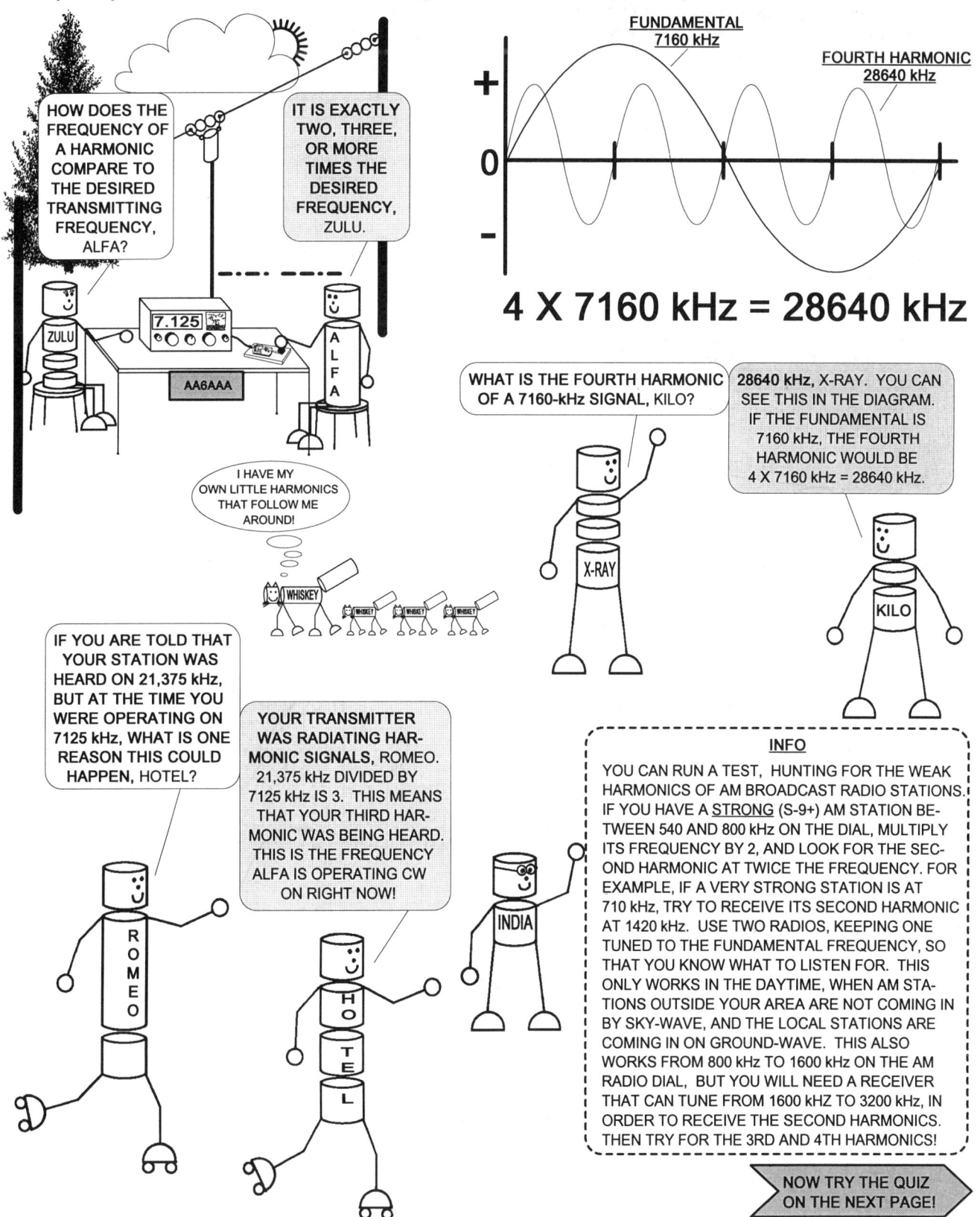

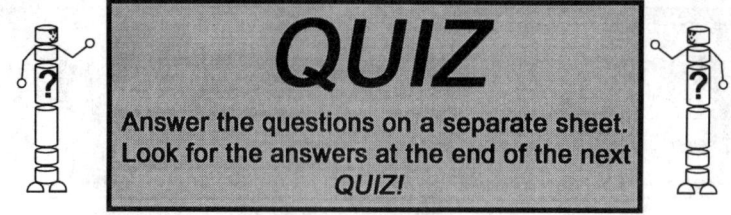

N8B01
How does the frequency of a harmonic compare to the desired transmitting frequency?
A. It is slightly more than the desired frequency
B. It is slightly less than the desired frequency
C. It is exactly two, or three, or more times the desired frequency
D. It is much less than the desired frequency

N8B02
What is the fourth harmonic of a 7160-kHz signal?
A. 28,640 kHz
B. 35,800 kHz
C. 28,160 kHz
D. 1790 kHz

N8B03
If you are told your station was heard on 21,375 kHz, but at the time you were operating on 7125 kHz, what is one reason this could happen?
A. Your transmitter's power-supply filter capacitor was bad
B. You were sending CW too fast
C. Your transmitter was radiating harmonic signals
D. Your transmitter's power-supply filter choke was bad

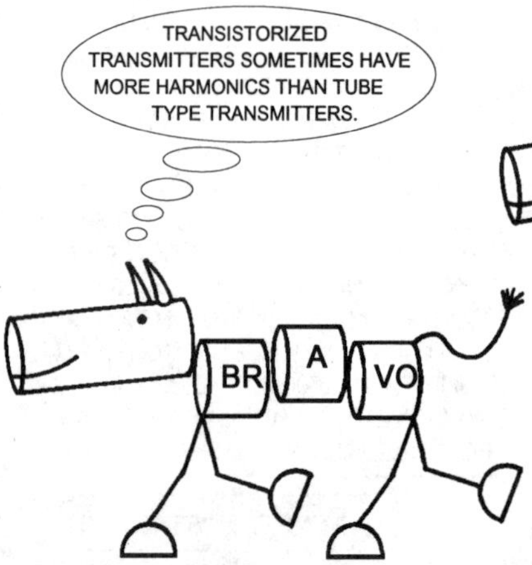

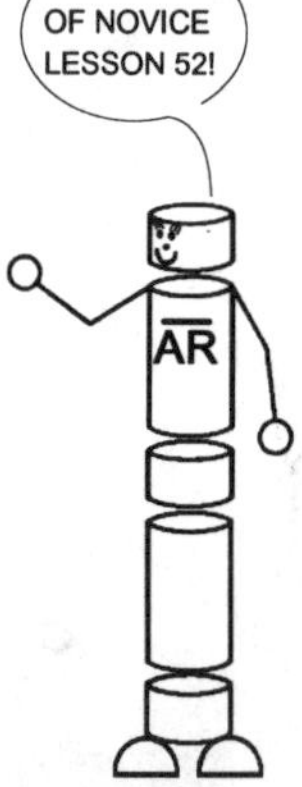

PREVIOUS QUIZ ANSWERS

N4D07 - A
N4D08 - A
N4D09 - A
N4D06 - B
N4D04 - D
N4D11 - A

SPURIOUS EMISSIONS
NOVICE LESSON 53

Radio frequency (RF) energy, that is radiated on the air at undesired frequencies, is called *spurious emissions*. It does nothing to provide the desired communications, and only interferes with others.

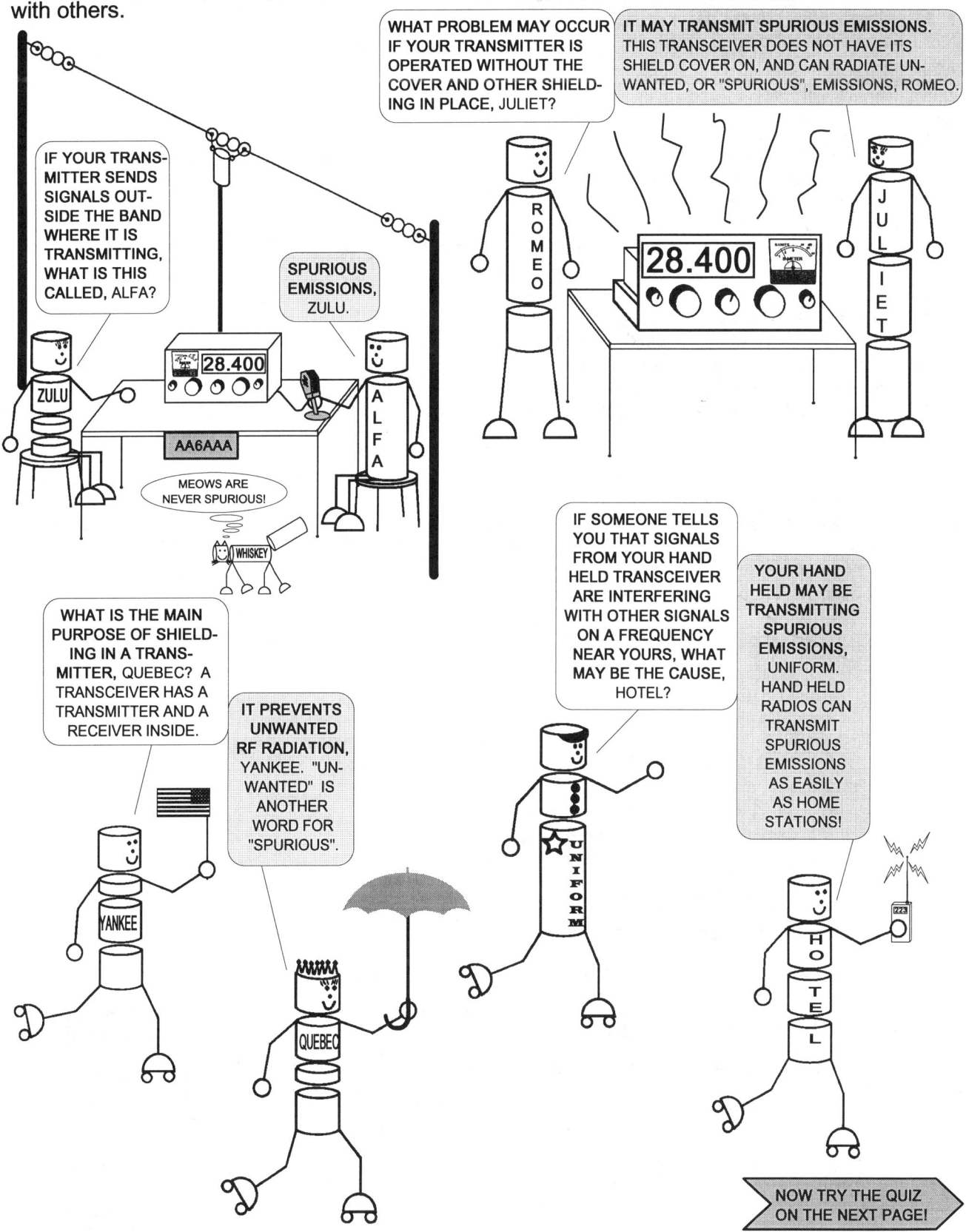

NOW TRY THE QUIZ ON THE NEXT PAGE!

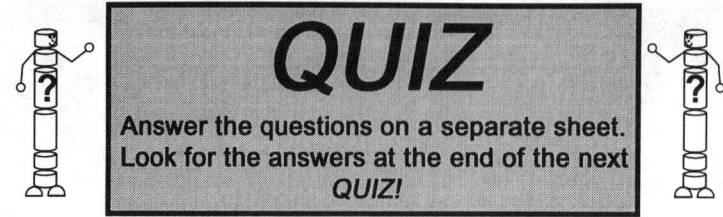

QUIZ
Answer the questions on a separate sheet. Look for the answers at the end of the next QUIZ!

N8B05
If your transmitter sends signals outside the band where it is transmitting, what is this called?
A. Off-frequency emissions
B. Transmitter chirping
C. Side tones
D. Spurious emissions

N8B06
What problem may occur if your transmitter is operated without the cover and other shielding in place?
A. It may transmit spurious emissions
B. It may transmit a chirpy signal
C. It may transmit a weak signal
D. It may interfere with other stations operating near its frequency

N4D10
What is the main purpose of shielding in a transmitter?
A. It gives the low-pass filter a solid support
B. It helps the sound quality of transmitters
C. It prevents unwanted RF radiation
D. It helps keep electronic parts warmer and more stable

N8B04
If someone tells you that signals from your hand held transceiver are interfering with other signals on a frequency near yours, what may be the cause?
A. You may need a power amplifier for your hand held
B. Your hand held may have chirp from weak batteries
C. You may need to turn the volume up on your hand held
D. Your hand held may be transmitting spurious emissions

INFO

HARMONICS ARE SPURIOUS EMISSIONS, BUT SPURIOUS EMISSIONS ARE NOT NECESSARILY HARMONICS! SPURIOUS EMISSIONS CAN BE AT ANY FREQUENCY. HARMONICS ARE ALWAYS AT EXACT MULTIPLES OF THE FUNDAMENTAL FREQUENCY. THEY ARE ALWAYS 2, 3, 4, 5, 6, OR MORE, TIMES THE FUNDAMENTAL FREQUENCY.

WHEN YOU ARE ON THE AIR, YOU WILL OCCASIONALLY HEAR SPURIOUS EMISSIONS. BY TUNING YOUR RECEIVER AROUND THE HAM BAND, OR EVEN OUTSIDE OF IT, YOU CAN SOMETIMES DETERMINE WHERE THEY ARE COMING FROM. IF IT IS ANOTHER HAM, YOU SHOULD LET HIM OR HER KNOW, THAT HIS OR HER EQUIPMENT IS NOT OPERATING PROPERLY!

RADIO HAMS ARE SELF-POLICING. THE FEDERAL COMMUNICATIONS COMMISSION (FCC) DOES NOT ALWAYS MONITOR AMATEUR BANDS, BUT DEPENDS ON HAMS TO DO THE MONITORING FOR THEM. THIS IS WHY THE AMATEUR SERVICE IS HELD IN HIGH REGARD BY THE FCC!

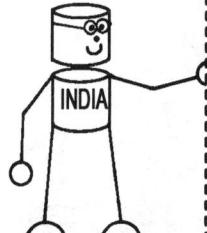

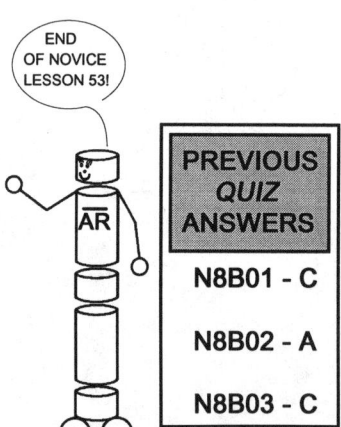

END OF NOVICE LESSON 53!

PREVIOUS QUIZ ANSWERS

N8B01 - C

N8B02 - A

N8B03 - C

SPLATTER
NOVICE LESSON 54

If you talk too loudly into a microphone, or turn up the microphone "gain", or volume, too high when operating voice on either single-sideband (SSB), or frequency modulation (FM), *splatter* can occur. Splatter interferes with other stations, and sounds like a shotgun being fired nearby.

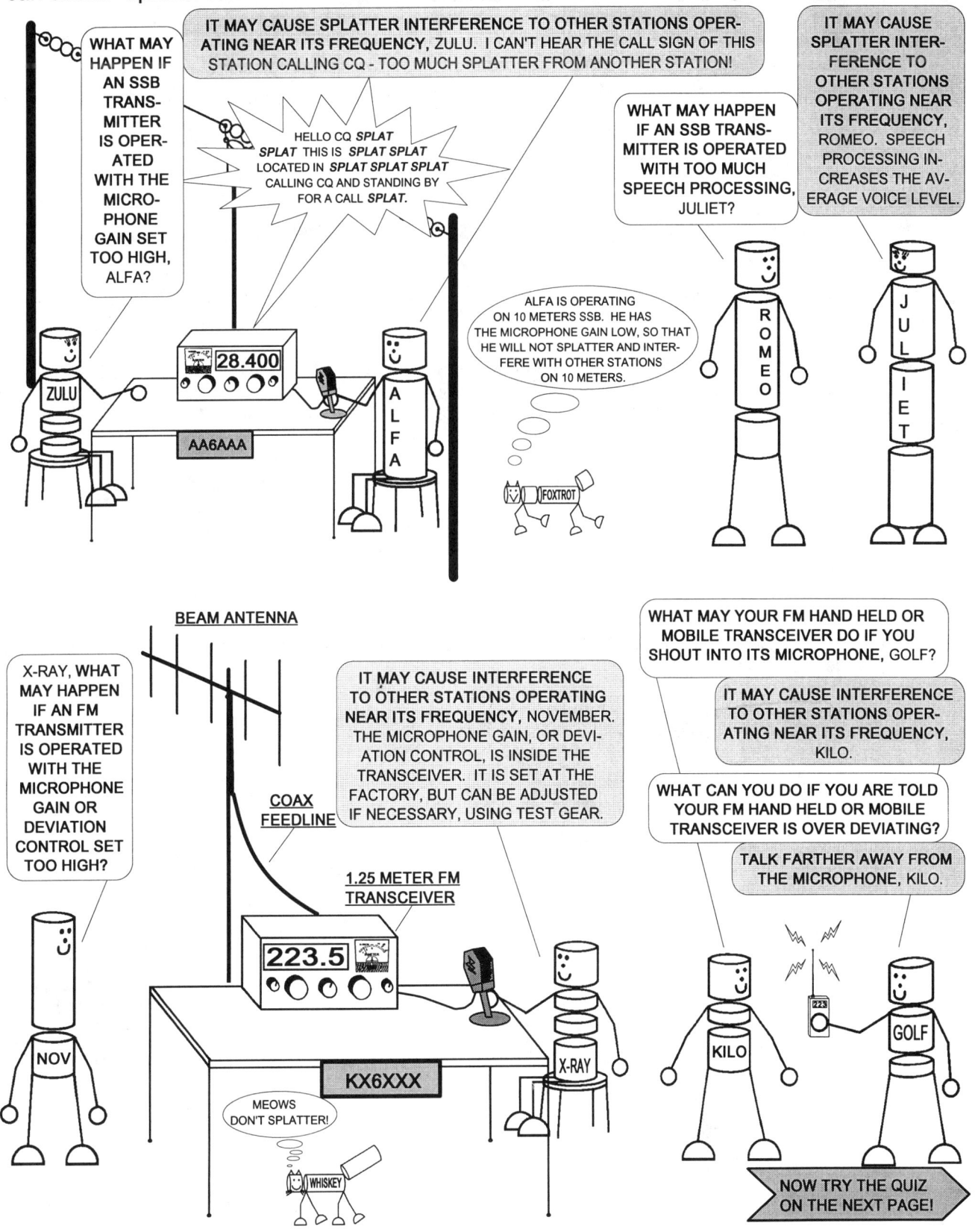

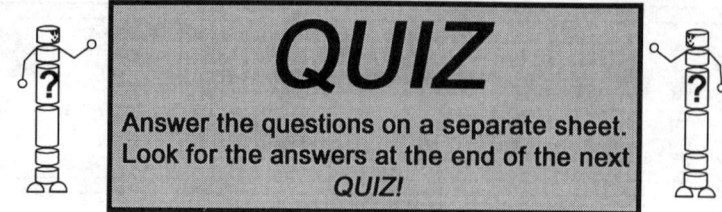

N8B07
What may happen if an SSB transmitter is operated with the microphone gain set too high?
A. It may cause digital interference to computer equipment
B. It may cause splatter interference to other stations operating near its frequency
C. It may cause atmospheric interference in the air around the antenna
D. It may cause interference to other stations operating on a higher frequency band

N8B08
What may happen if an SSB transmitter is operated with too much speech processing?
A. It may cause digital interference to computer equipment
B. It may cause splatter interference to other stations operating near its frequency
C. It may cause atmospheric interference in the air around the antenna
D. It may cause interference to other stations operating on a higher frequency band

N8B09
What may happen if an FM transmitter is operated with the microphone gain or deviation control set too high?
A. It may cause digital interference to computer equipment
B. It may cause interference to other stations operating near its frequency
C. It may cause atmospheric interference in the air around the antenna
D. It may cause interference to other stations operating on a higher frequency band

N8B10
What may your FM hand held or mobile transceiver do if you shout into its microphone?
A. It may cause digital interference to computer equipment
B. It may cause interference to other stations operating near its frequency
C. It may cause atmospheric interference in the air around the antenna
D. It may cause interference to other stations operating on a higher frequency band

N8B11
What can you do if you are told your FM hand held or mobile transceiver is over deviating?
A. Talk louder into the microphone
B. Let the transceiver cool off
C. Change to a higher power level
D. Talk farther away from the microphone

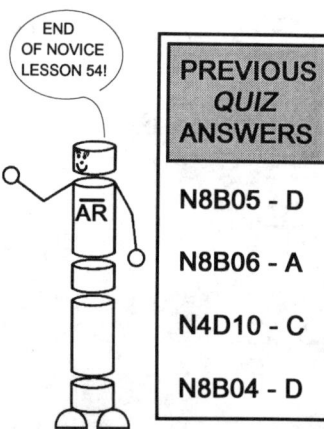

PREVIOUS QUIZ ANSWERS

N8B05 - D

N8B06 - A

N4D10 - C

N8B04 - D

STANDING WAVE RATIO (SWR)
NOVICE LESSON 55

Standing wave ratio, or *SWR*, is a measure of how well an antenna system is tuned. The best possible SWR is 1:1. A 1.5:1 SWR, or less, is acceptable. A 2:1 SWR is poor, and a 4:1 SWR is very poor! A good SWR helps prevent harmonic radiation.

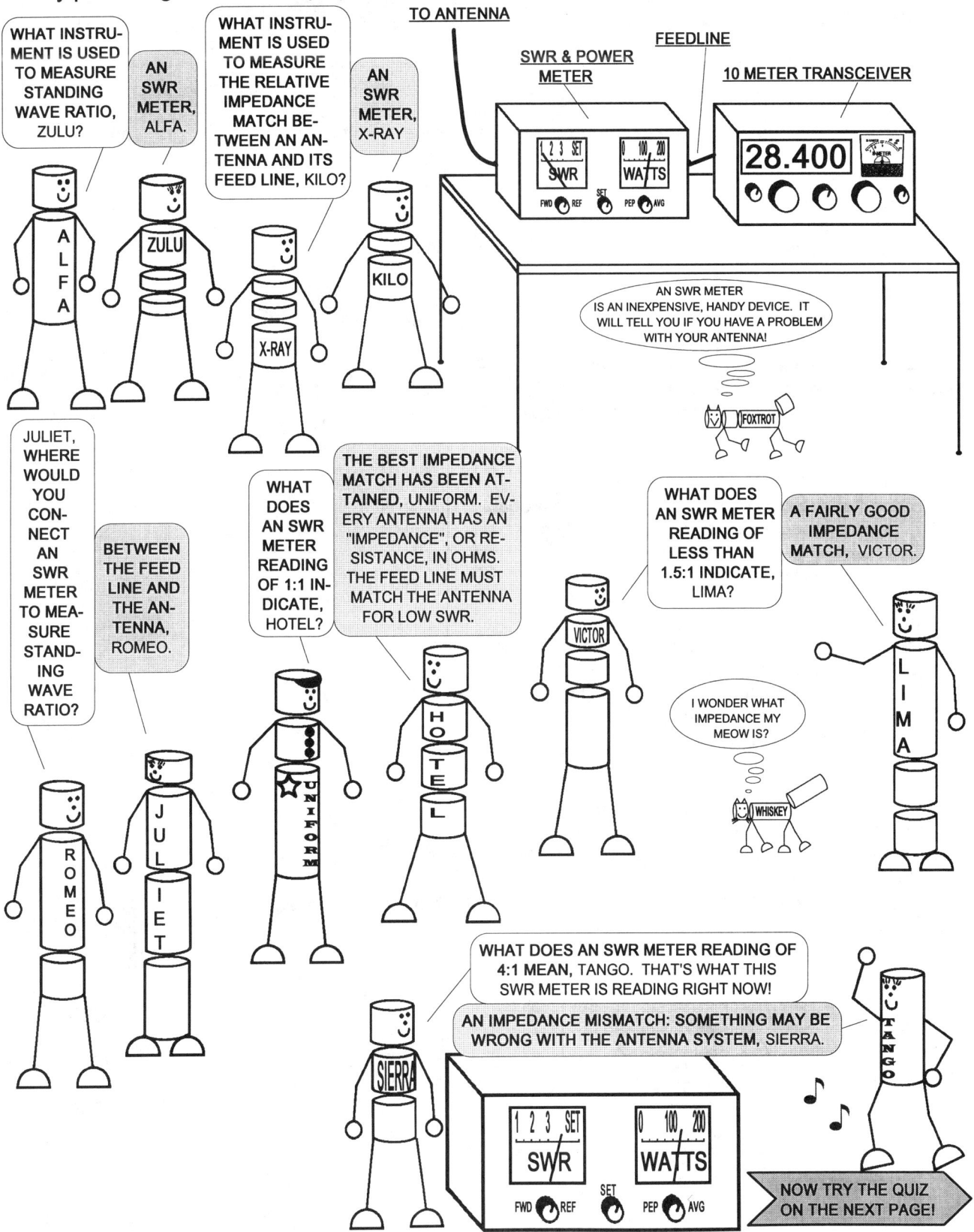

NOW TRY THE QUIZ ON THE NEXT PAGE!

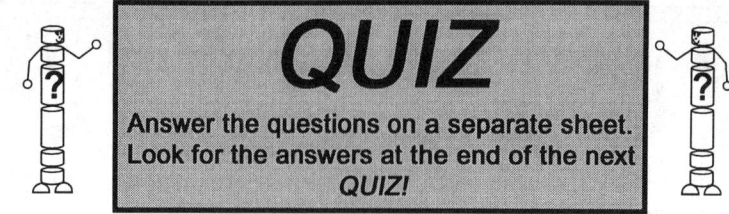

QUIZ
Answer the questions on a separate sheet. Look for the answers at the end of the next QUIZ!

N4C01
What instrument is used to measure standing wave ratio?
A. An ohmmeter
B. An ammeter
C. An SWR meter
D. A current bridge

N4C02
What instrument is used to measure the relative impedance match between an antenna and its feed line?
A. An ammeter
B. An ohmmeter
C. A voltmeter
D. An SWR meter

N4C03
Where would you connect an SWR meter to measure standing wave ratio?
A. Between the feed line and the antenna
B. Between the transmitter and the power supply
C. Between the transmitter and the receiver
D. Between the transmitter and the ground

N4C04
What does an SWR reading of 1:1 mean?
A. An antenna for another frequency band is probably connected
B. The best impedance match has been attained
C. No power is going to the antenna
D. The SWR meter is broken

N4C05
What does an SWR reading of less than 1.5:1 mean?
A. An impedance match which is too low
B. An impedance mismatch; something may be wrong with the antenna system
C. A fairly good impedance match
D. An antenna gain of 1.5

N4C06
What does an SWR reading of 4:1 mean?
A. An impedance match which is too low
B. An impedance match which is good, but not the best
C. An antenna gain of 4
D. An impedance mismatch; something may be wrong with the antenna system

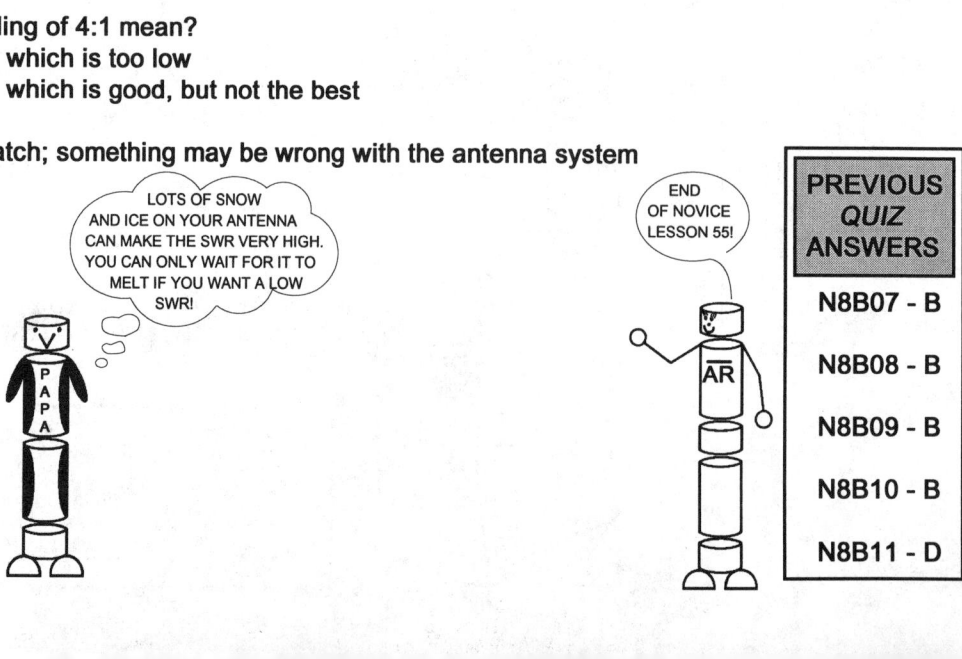

PREVIOUS QUIZ ANSWERS

N8B07 - B

N8B08 - B

N8B09 - B

N8B10 - B

N8B11 - D

UNUSUAL SWR READINGS, POWER METERS
NOVICE LESSON 56

An SWR meter can tell you how your antenna is performing. If the SWR reading is "jumpy", you know that there is a short, or loose connection somewhere in your antenna system. If the reading is very high, the antenna system is detuned, open, or shorted. A difference in SWR reading from one end of the band to the other, indicates that an antenna is too long or too short.

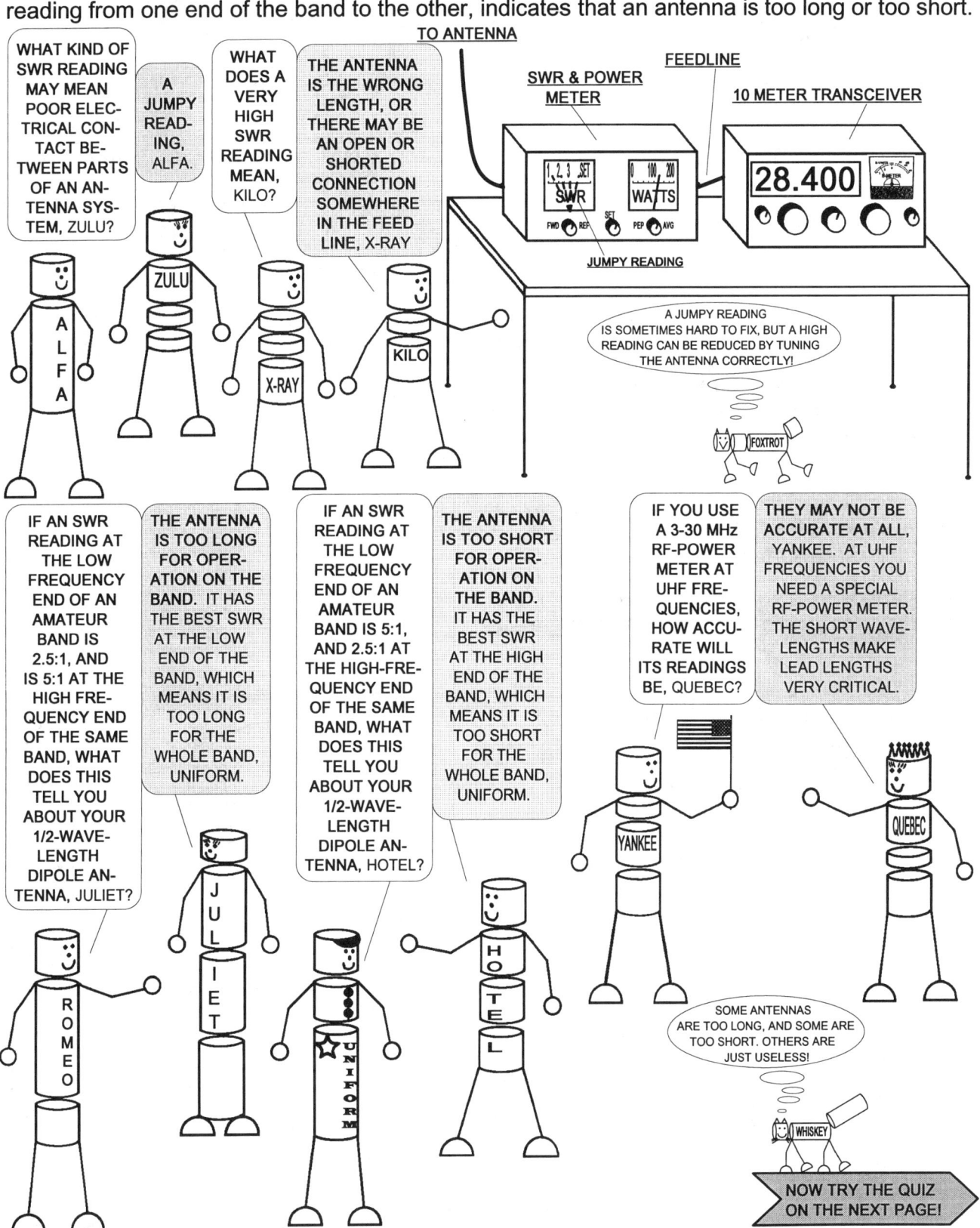

NOW TRY THE QUIZ ON THE NEXT PAGE!

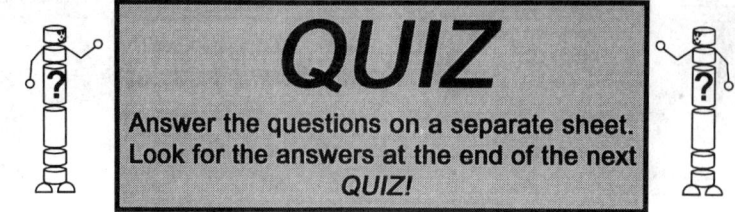

N4C07
What kind of SWR reading may mean poor electrical contact between parts of an antenna system?
A. A jumpy reading
B. A very low reading
C. No reading at all
D. A negative reading

N4C08
What does a very high SWR reading mean?
A. The antenna is the wrong length, or there may be an open or shorted connection somewhere in the feed line
B. The signals coming from the antenna are unusually strong, which means very good radio conditions
C. The transmitter is putting out more power than normal, showing that it is about to go bad
D. There is a large amount of solar radiation, which means very poor radio conditions

N4C09
If an SWR reading at the low frequency end of an amateur band is 2.5:1, and is 5:1 at the high frequency end of the same band, what does this tell you about your 1/2-wavelength dipole antenna?
A. The antenna is broadbanded
B. The antenna is too long for operation on the band
C. The antenna is too short for operation on the band
D. The antenna is just right for operation on the band

N4C10
If an SWR reading at the low frequency end of an amateur band is 5:1, and 2.5:1 at the high frequency end of the same band, what does this tell you about your 1/2-wavelength dipole antenna?
A. The antenna is broadbanded
B. The antenna is too long for operation on the band
C. The antenna is too short for operation on the band
D. The antenna is just right for operation on the band

N4C11
If you use a 3-30 MHz RF-power meter at UHF frequencies, how accurate will its readings be?
A. They may not be accurate at all
B. They will be accurate enough to get by
C. They will be accurate but the readings must be divided by two
D. They will be accurate but the readings must be multiplied by two

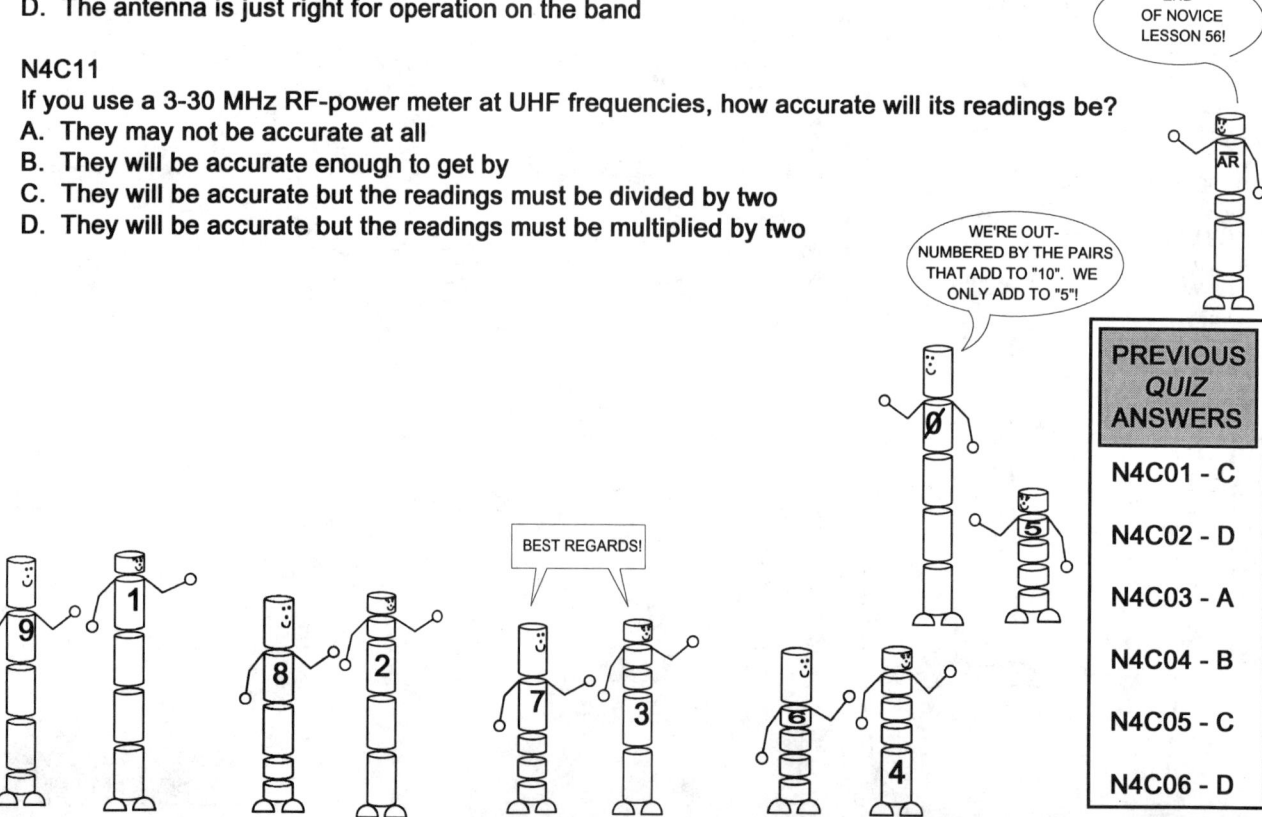

PREVIOUS QUIZ ANSWERS

N4C01 - C
N4C02 - D
N4C03 - A
N4C04 - B
N4C05 - C
N4C06 - D

ANTENNA FEED LINES & TUNERS, SWR METERS
NOVICE LESSON 57

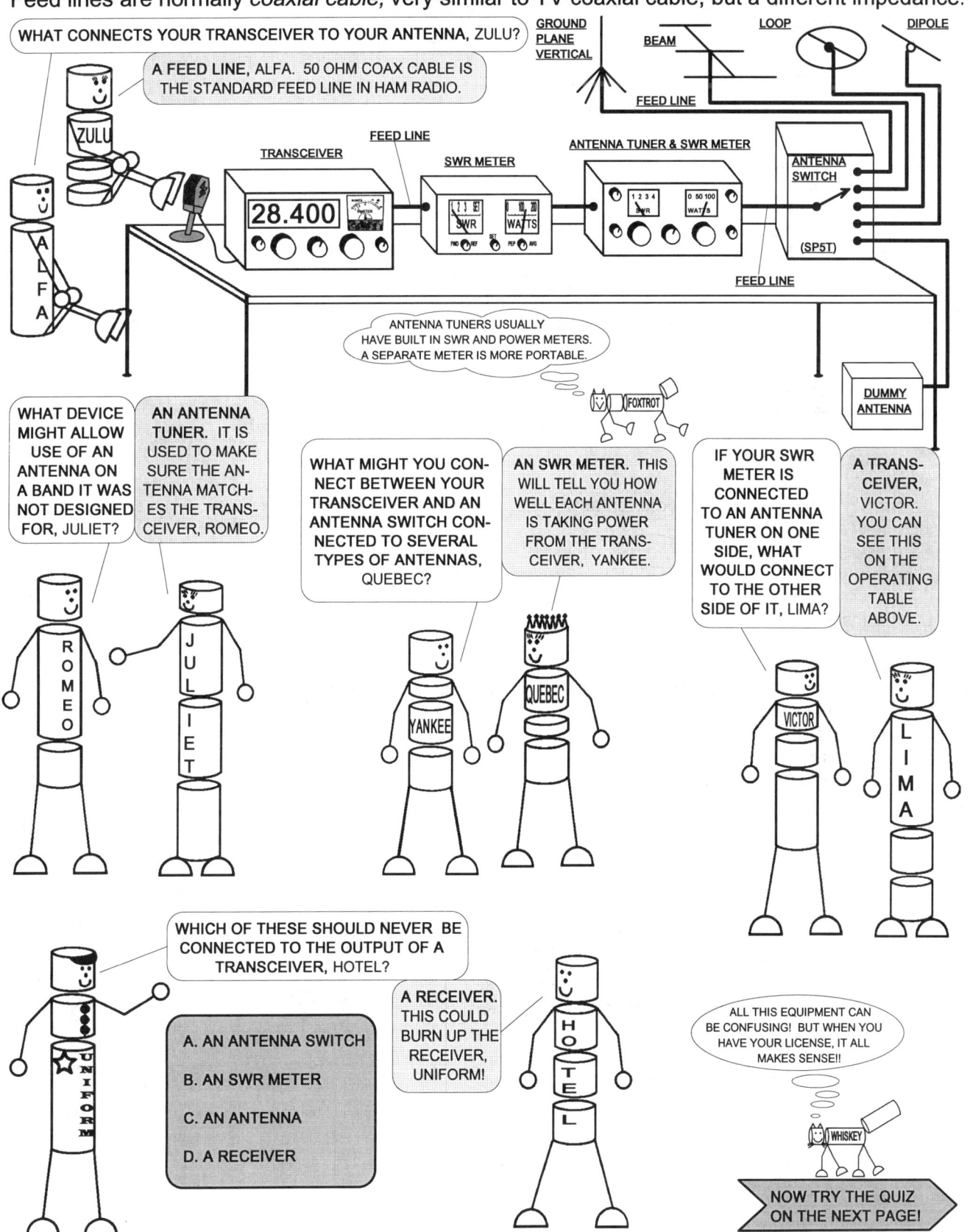

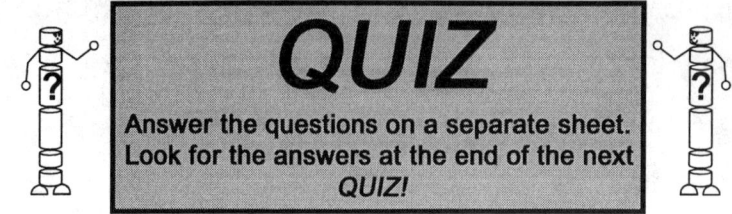

N7A03
What connects your transceiver to your antenna?
A. A dummy load
B. A ground wire
C. The power cord
D. A feed line

N7A02
What device might allow use of an antenna on a band it was not designed for?
A. An SWR meter
B. A low-pass filter
C. An antenna tuner
D. A high-pass filter

N7A04
What might you connect between your transceiver and an antenna switch connected to several types of antennas?
A. A high-pass filter
B. An SWR meter
C. A key click filter
D. A mixer

N7A05
If your SWR meter is connected to an antenna tuner on one side, what would you connect to the other side of it?
A. A power supply
B. An antenna
C. An antenna switch
D. A transceiver

N7A06
Which of these should never be connected to the output of a transceiver?
A. An antenna switch
B. An SWR meter
C. An antenna
D. A receiver

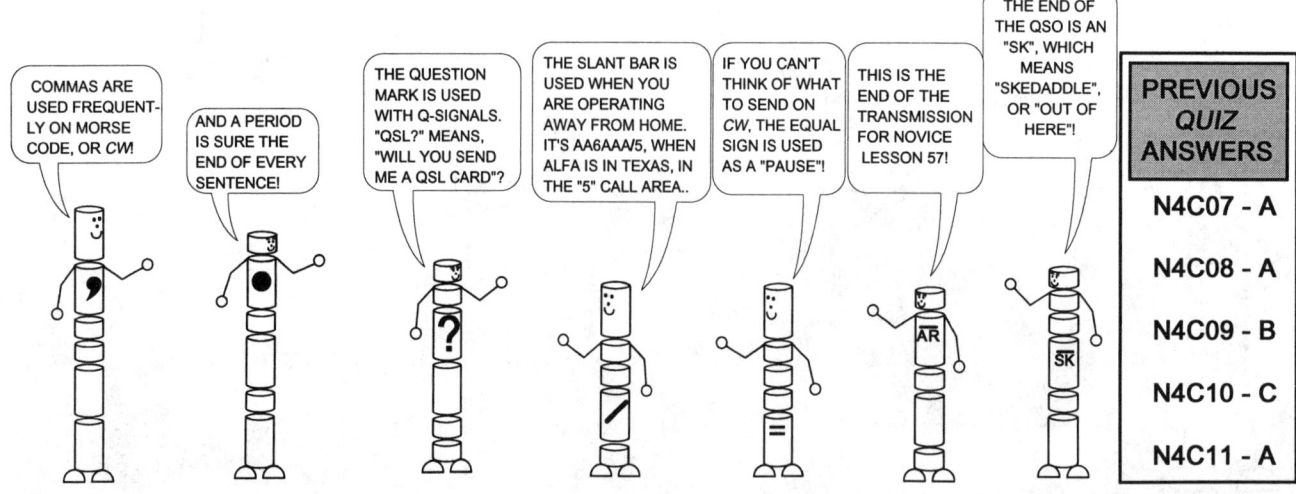

STATION DIAGRAMS
NOVICE LESSON 58

Diagrams can be made which show the interconnection between parts of a station. This is easier than drawing pictures of the actual equipment.

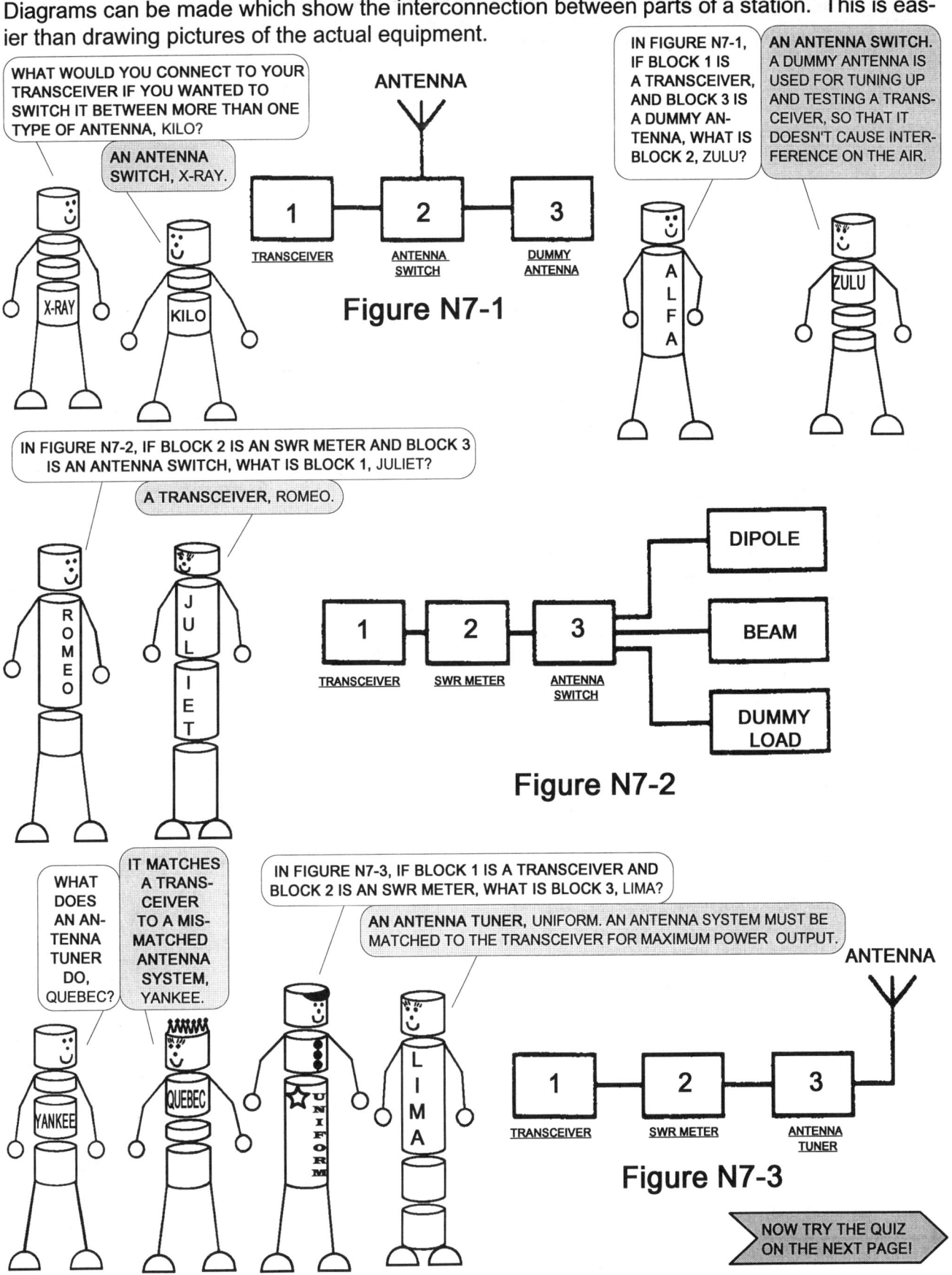

Figure N7-1

Figure N7-2

Figure N7-3

NOW TRY THE QUIZ ON THE NEXT PAGE!

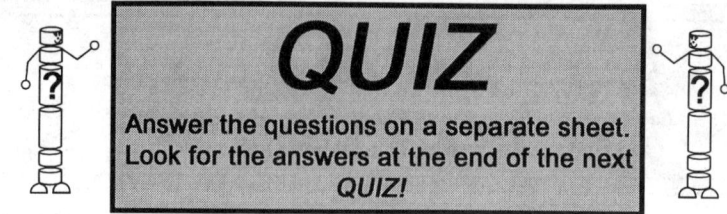

QUIZ

Answer the questions on a separate sheet. Look for the answers at the end of the next QUIZ!

N7A01
What would you connect to your transceiver if you wanted to switch it between more than one type of antenna?
A. A terminal-node switch
B. An antenna switch
C. A telegraph key switch
D. A high-pass filter

N7A09
In Figure N7-1, if block 1 is a transceiver and block 3 is a dummy antenna what is block 2?
A. A terminal-node switch
B. An antenna switch
C. A telegraph key switch
D. A high-pass filter

Figure N7-1

N7A10
In Figure N7-2, if block 2 is an SWR meter and block 3 is an antenna switch, what is block 1?
A. A transceiver
B. A high-pass filter
C. An antenna tuner
D. A modem

N7A08
What does an antenna tuner do?
A. It matches a transceiver to a mismatched antenna system
B. It helps a receiver automatically tune in stations that are far away
C. It switches an antenna system to a transceiver when sending, and to a receiver when listening
D. It switches a transceiver between different kinds of antennas connected to one feed line

Figure N7-2

N7A11
In Figure N7-3, if block 1 is a transceiver and block 2 is an SWR meter, what is block 3?
A. An antenna switch
B. An antenna tuner
C. A key-click filter
D. A terminal-node controller

Figure N7-3

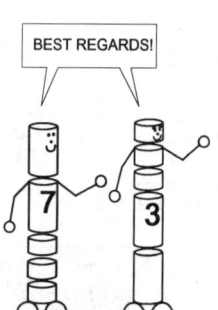

END OF NOVICE LESSON 58!

PREVIOUS QUIZ ANSWERS

N7A03 - D
N7A02 - C
N7A04 - B
N7A05 - D
N7A06 - D

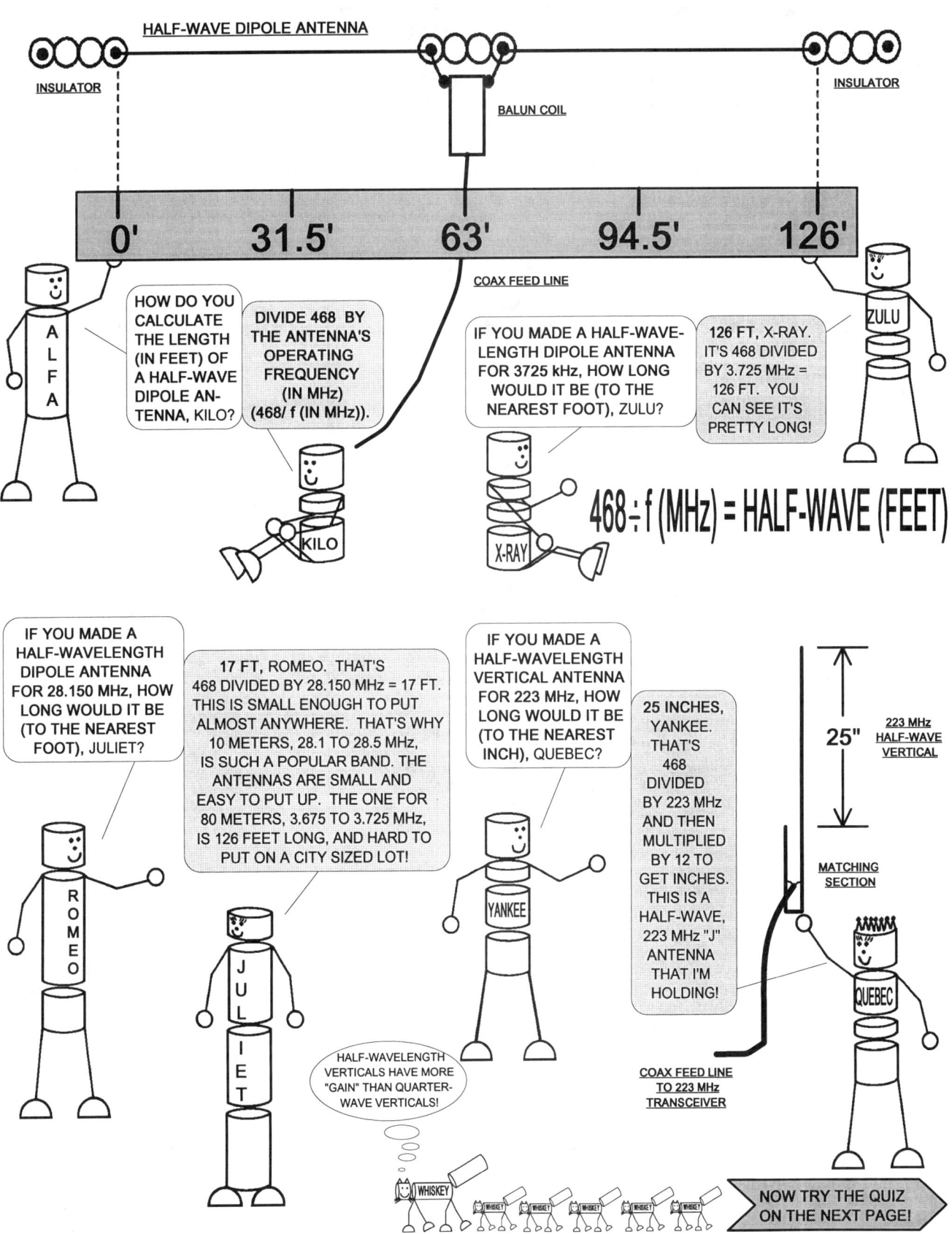

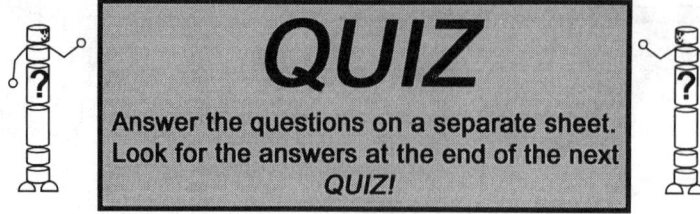

QUIZ
Answer the questions on a separate sheet. Look for the answers at the end of the next QUIZ!

N9A01
How do you calculate the length (in feet) of a half-wavelength dipole antenna?
A. Divide 150 by the antenna's operating frequency (in MHz) [150/f(in MHz)]
B. Divide 234 by the antenna's operating frequency (in MHz) [234/f (in MHz)]
C. Divide 300 by the antenna's operating frequency (in MHz) [300/f (in MHz)]
D. Divide 468 by the antenna's operating frequency (in MHz) [468/f (in MHz)]

N9A03
If you made a half-wavelength dipole antenna for 3725 kHz, how long would it be (to the nearest foot)?
A. 126 ft
B. 81 ft
C. 63 ft
D. 40 ft

N9A04
If you made a half-wavelength dipole antenna for 28.150 MHz, how long would it be (to the nearest foot)?
A. 22 ft
B. 11 ft
C. 17 ft
D. 34 ft

N9A07
If you made a half-wavelength vertical antenna for 223 MHz, how long would it be (to the nearest inch)?
A. 112 inches
B. 50 inches
C. 25 inches
D. 12 inches

THE ORBITING SATELLITES CARRYING AMATEUR RADIO, OR OSCARs, HAVE INTERESTING ANTENNA SYSTEMS. THEY MUST RECEIVE EARTH SIGNALS NO MATTER WHERE THEY ARE IN SPACE, AND ALSO TRANSMIT TO THE EARTH. AT THE SAME TIME, THE SOLAR PANELS MUST ALWAYS FACE THE SUN!

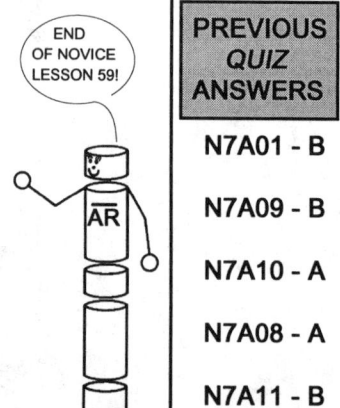

END OF NOVICE LESSON 59!

PREVIOUS QUIZ ANSWERS

N7A01 - B

N7A09 - B

N7A10 - A

N7A08 - A

N7A11 - B

QUARTER-WAVELENGTH VERTICAL LENGTH
NOVICE LESSON 60

Vertical antennas are easy to build and install. They take up very little space on the ground, and can be very efficient if a good ground wire, or "radial", system is installed underneath them.

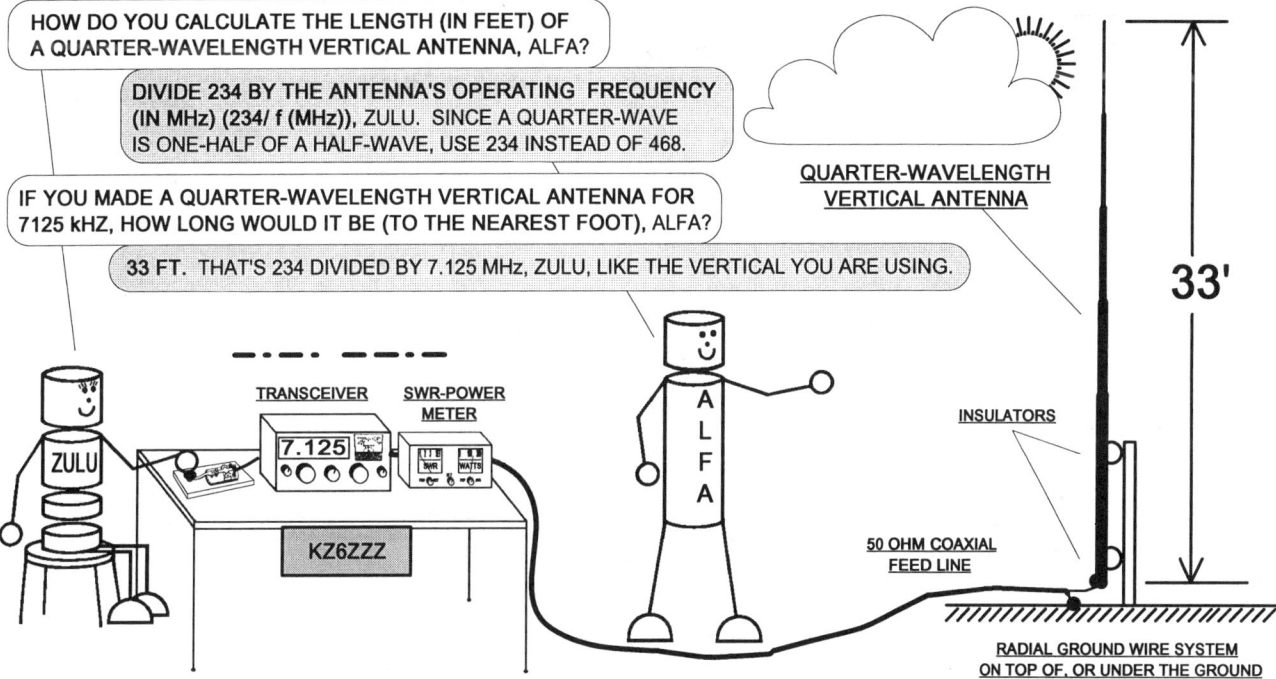

234 ÷ f (MHz) = QUARTER-WAVE (FEET)

INFO

VERTICAL ANTENNAS ARE THEORETICALLY BETTER THAN HORIZONTAL ANTENNAS, BUT THEY REQUIRE A GOOD GROUND RADIAL SYSTEM. RADIALS ARE LENGTHS OF WIRE, EITHER BURIED IN THE GROUND OR ON TOP OF IT. THEY ARE CONNECTED TO THE GROUND SIDE OF THE COAXIAL FEED LINE AT THE ANTENNA. THEY ARE USUALLY A QUARTER-WAVELENGTH LONG, AND CAN BE CALCULATED BY THE SAME FORMULA USED TO DETERMINE THE LENGTH OF THE QUARTER-WAVELENGTH VERTICAL ANTENNA.

VERTICALS MUST BE INSTALLED IN A CLEAR LOCATION. NEARBY BUILDINGS CAN ABSORB THE ENERGY FROM THE ANTENNA, AND PREVENT IT FROM WORKING WELL. VERTICALS FOR 15 METERS (11 FT), AND 10 METERS (8 FT), CAN BE MOUNTED HIGH ABOVE GROUND. 80 METER (66 FT), AND 40 METER (33 FT) VERTICALS ARE TOO TALL, AND ARE USUALLY MOUNTED ON THE GROUND. ZULU'S 40 METER, 7.125 MHz, QUARTER-WAVELENGTH, 33 FOOT VERTICAL, IS MOUNTED ON THE GROUND.

NOW TRY THE QUIZ ON THE NEXT PAGE!

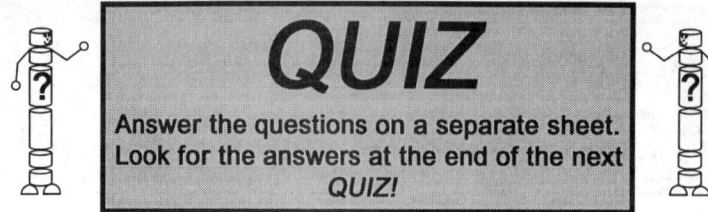

N9A02
How do you calculate the length (in feet) of a quarter-wavelength vertical antenna?
A. Divide 150 by the antenna's operating frequency (in MHz) [150/f (in MHz)]
B. Divide 234 by the antenna's operating frequency (in MHz) [234/f (in MHz)]
C. Divide 300 by the antenna's operating frequency (in MHz) [300/f (in MHz)]
D. Divide 468 by the antenna's operating frequency (in MHz) [468/f (in MHz)]

N9A05
If you made a quarter-wavelength vertical antenna for 7125 kHz, how long would it be (to the nearest foot)?
A. 11 ft
B. 16 ft
C. 21 ft
D. 33 ft

N9A06
If you made a quarter-wavelength vertical antenna for 21.125 MHz, how long would it be (to the nearest foot)?
A. 7 ft
B. 11 ft
C. 14 ft
D. 22 ft

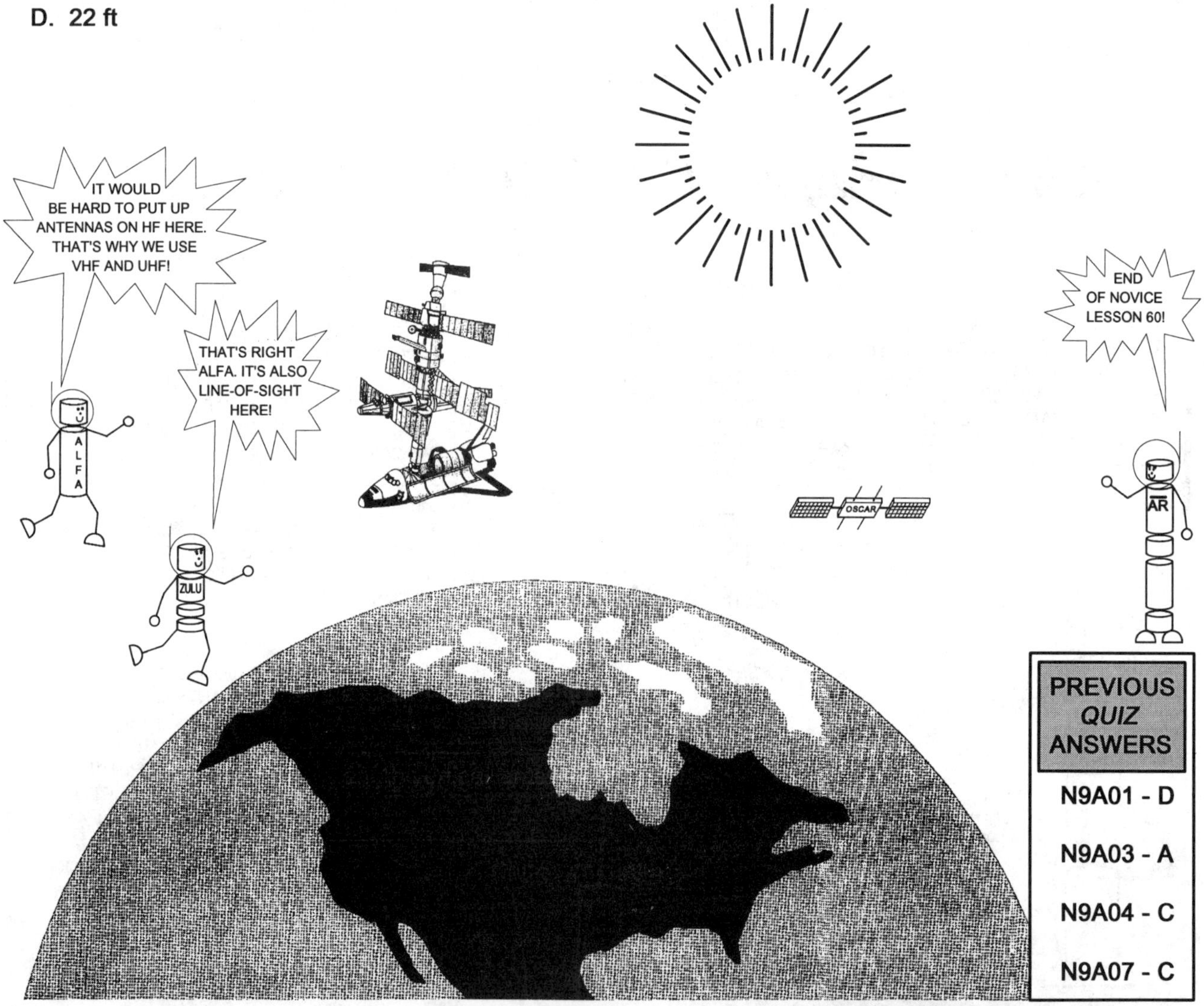

IT WOULD BE HARD TO PUT UP ANTENNAS ON HF HERE. THAT'S WHY WE USE VHF AND UHF!

THAT'S RIGHT ALFA. IT'S ALSO LINE-OF-SIGHT HERE!

END OF NOVICE LESSON 60!

PREVIOUS *QUIZ* ANSWERS
N9A01 - D
N9A03 - A
N9A04 - C
N9A07 - C

CHANGING ANTENNA LENGTH
NOVICE LESSON 61

Changing the length of an antenna is like changing the length of a string on a musical instrument. The longer the string, the lower the frequency of the musical note.

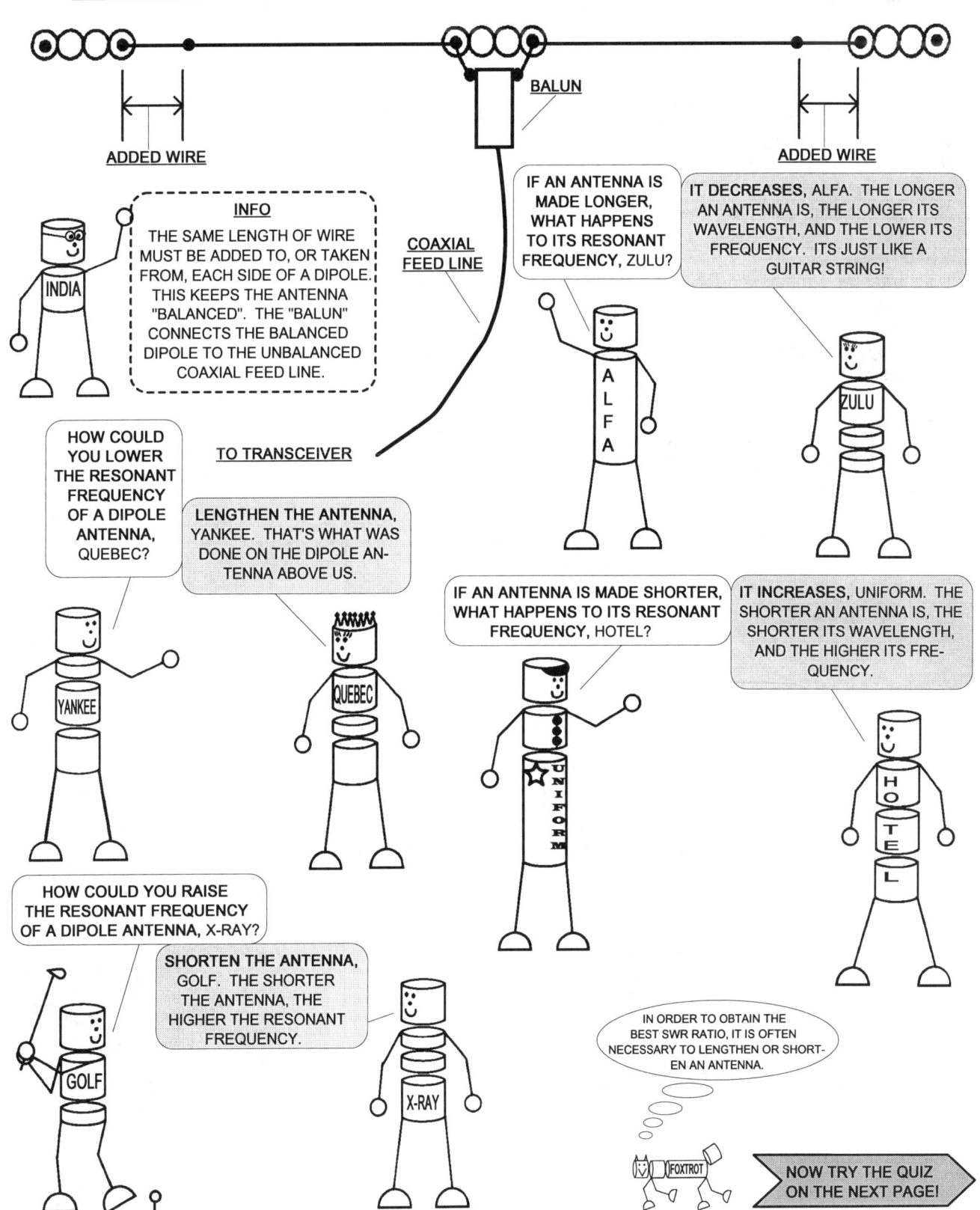

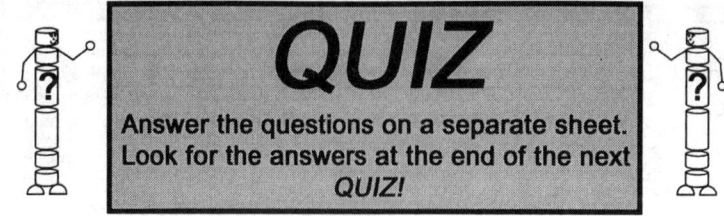

QUIZ
Answer the questions on a separate sheet. Look for the answers at the end of the next QUIZ!

N9A08
If an antenna is made longer, what happens to its resonant frequency?
A. It decreases
B. It increases
C. It stays the same
D. It disappears

N9A10
How could you lower the resonant frequency of a dipole antenna?
A. Lengthen the antenna
B. Shorten the antenna
C. Use less feed line
D. Use a smaller size feed line

N9A09
If an antenna is made shorter, what happens to its resonant frequency?
A. It decreases
B. It increases
C. It stays the same
D. It disappears

N9A11
How could you raise the resonant frequency of a dipole antenna?
A. Lengthen the antenna
B. Shorten the antenna
C. Use more feed line
D. Use a larger size feed line

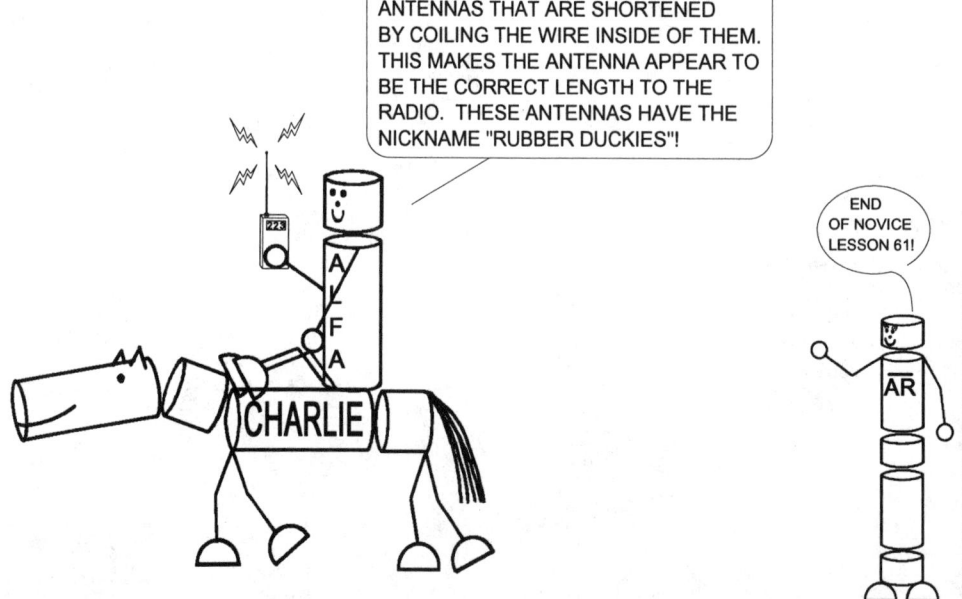

PREVIOUS QUIZ ANSWERS

N9A02 - B

N9A05 - D

N9A06 - B

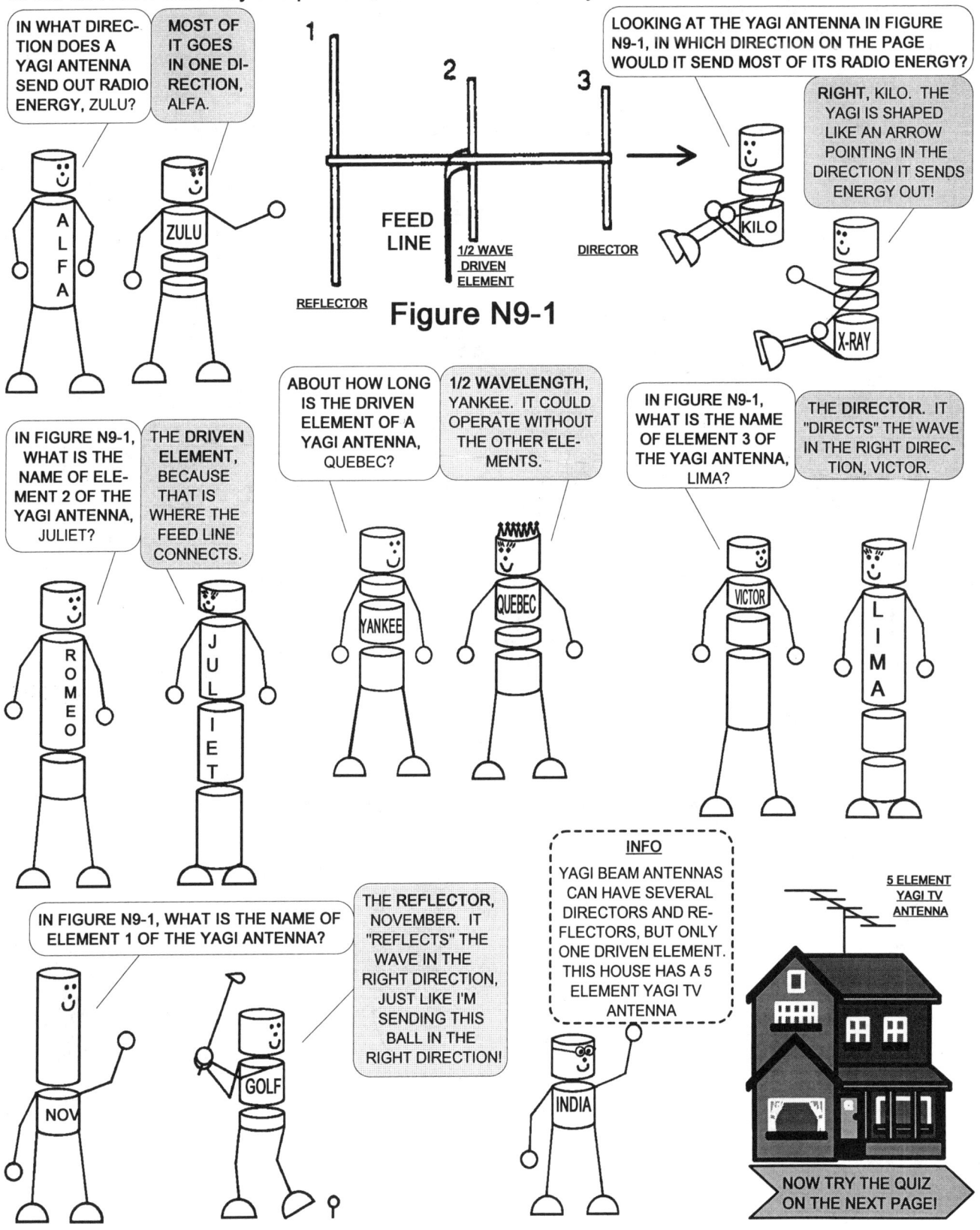

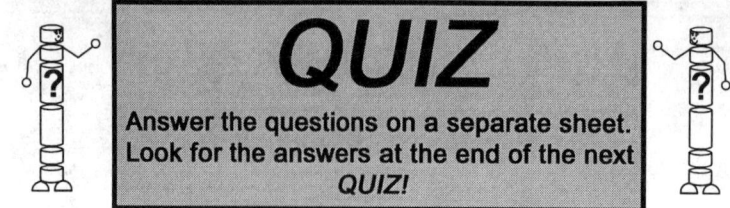

N9B01
In what direction does a Yagi antenna send out radio energy?
A. It goes out equally in all directions
B. Most of it goes in one direction
C. Most of it goes equally in two opposite directions
D. Most of it is aimed high into the air

N9B06
Looking at the Yagi antenna in Figure N9-1, in which direction on the page would it send most of its radio energy?
A. Left
B. Right
C. Top
D. Bottom

N9B03
In Figure N9-1, what is the name of element 2 of the Yagi antenna?
A. Director
B. Reflector
C. Boom
D. Driven element

N9B02
About how long is the driven element of a Yagi antenna?
A. 1/4 wavelength
B. 1/3 wavelength
C. 1/2 wavelength
D. 1 wavelength

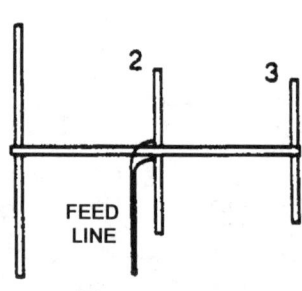

Figure N9-1

N9B04
In Figure N9-1, what is the name of element 3 of the Yagi antenna?
A. Director
B. Reflector
C. Boom
D. Driven element

N9B05
In Figure N9-1, what is the name of element 1 of the Yagi antenna?
A. Director
B. Reflector
C. Boom
D. Driven element

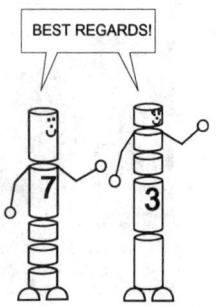
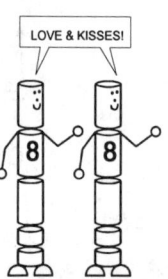
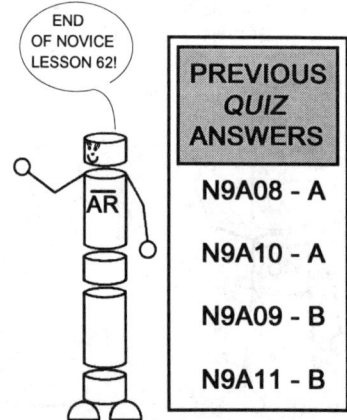

PREVIOUS QUIZ ANSWERS
N9A08 - A
N9A10 - A
N9A09 - B
N9A11 - B

VERTICAL & DIPOLE ANTENNAS
NOVICE LESSON 63

Vertical and dipole antennas have unique characteristics. These characteristics should be kept in mind when an antenna is chosen for a particular purpose, or ham band.

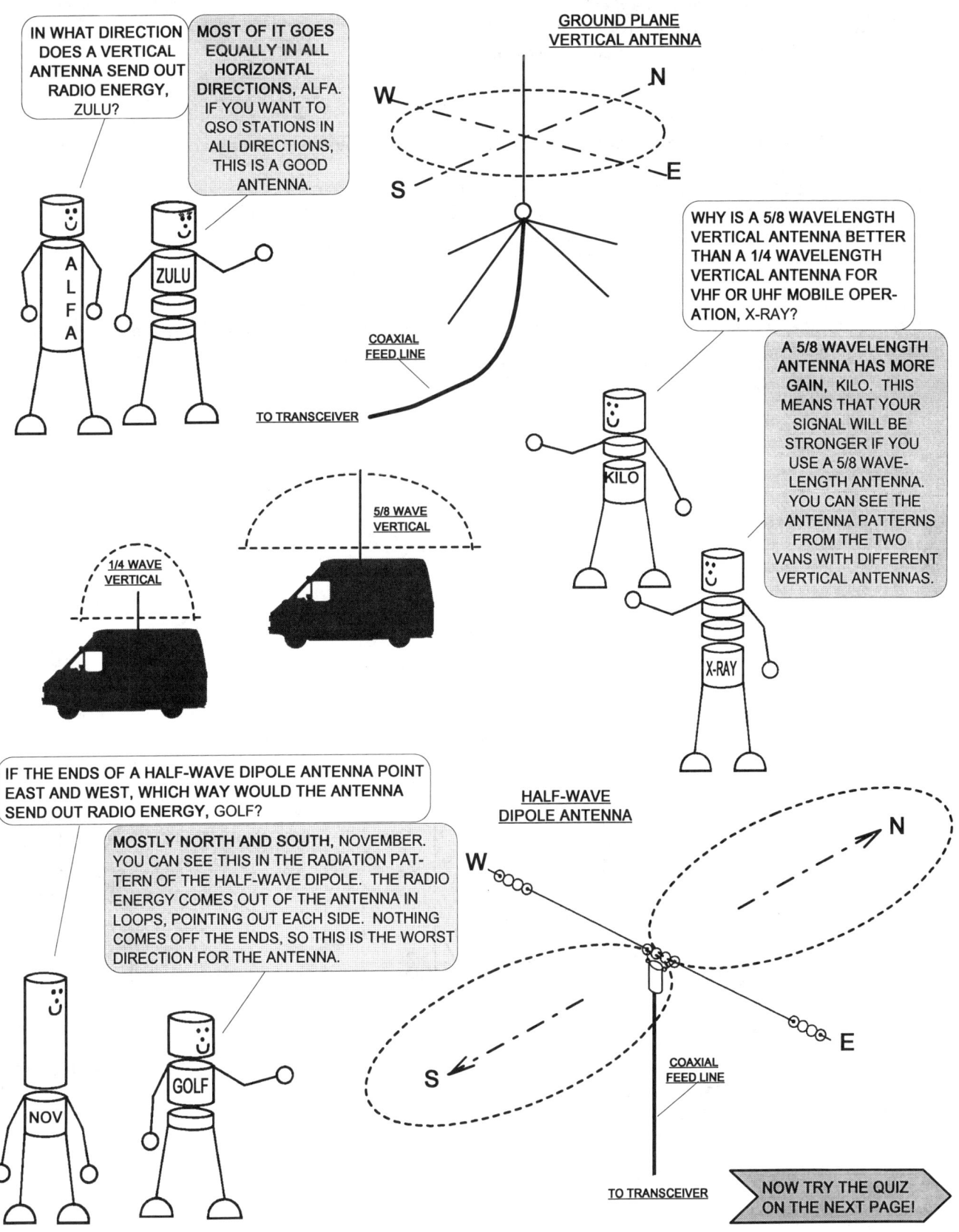

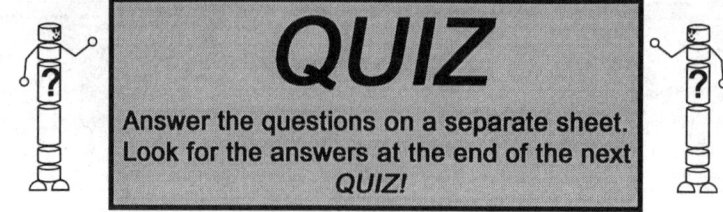

N9B08
In what direction does a vertical antenna send out radio energy?
A. Most of it goes in two opposite directions
B. Most of it goes high into the air
C. Most of it goes equally in all horizontal directions
D. Most of it goes in one direction

N9B07
Why is a 5/8-wavelength vertical antenna better than a 1/4-wavelength vertical antenna for VHF or UHF mobile operations?
A. A 5/8-wavelength antenna can handle more power
B. A 5/8-wavelength antenna has more gain
C. A 5/8-wavelength antenna has less corona loss
D. A 5/8-wavelength antenna is easier to install on a car

N9B09
If the ends of a half-wave dipole antenna point east and west, which way would the antenna send out radio energy?
A. Equally in all directions
B. Mostly up and down
C. Mostly north and south
D. Mostly east and west

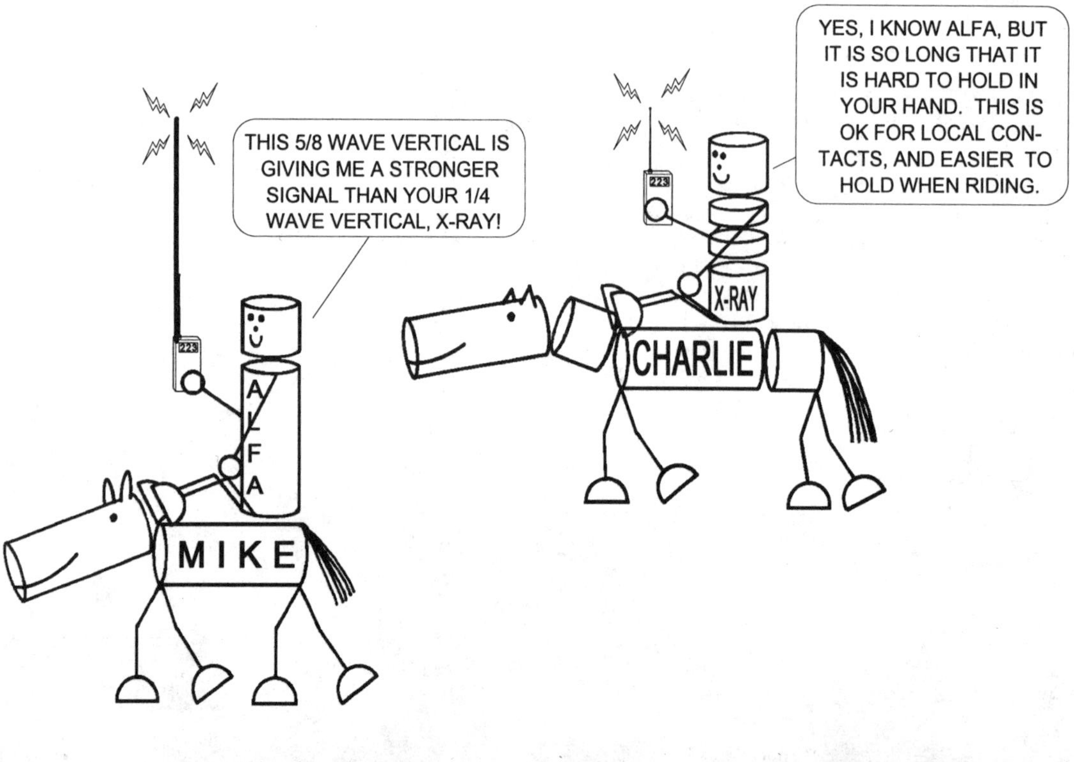

PREVIOUS QUIZ ANSWERS

N9B01 - B
N9B06 - B
N9B03 - D
N9B02 - C
N9B04 - A
N9B05 - B

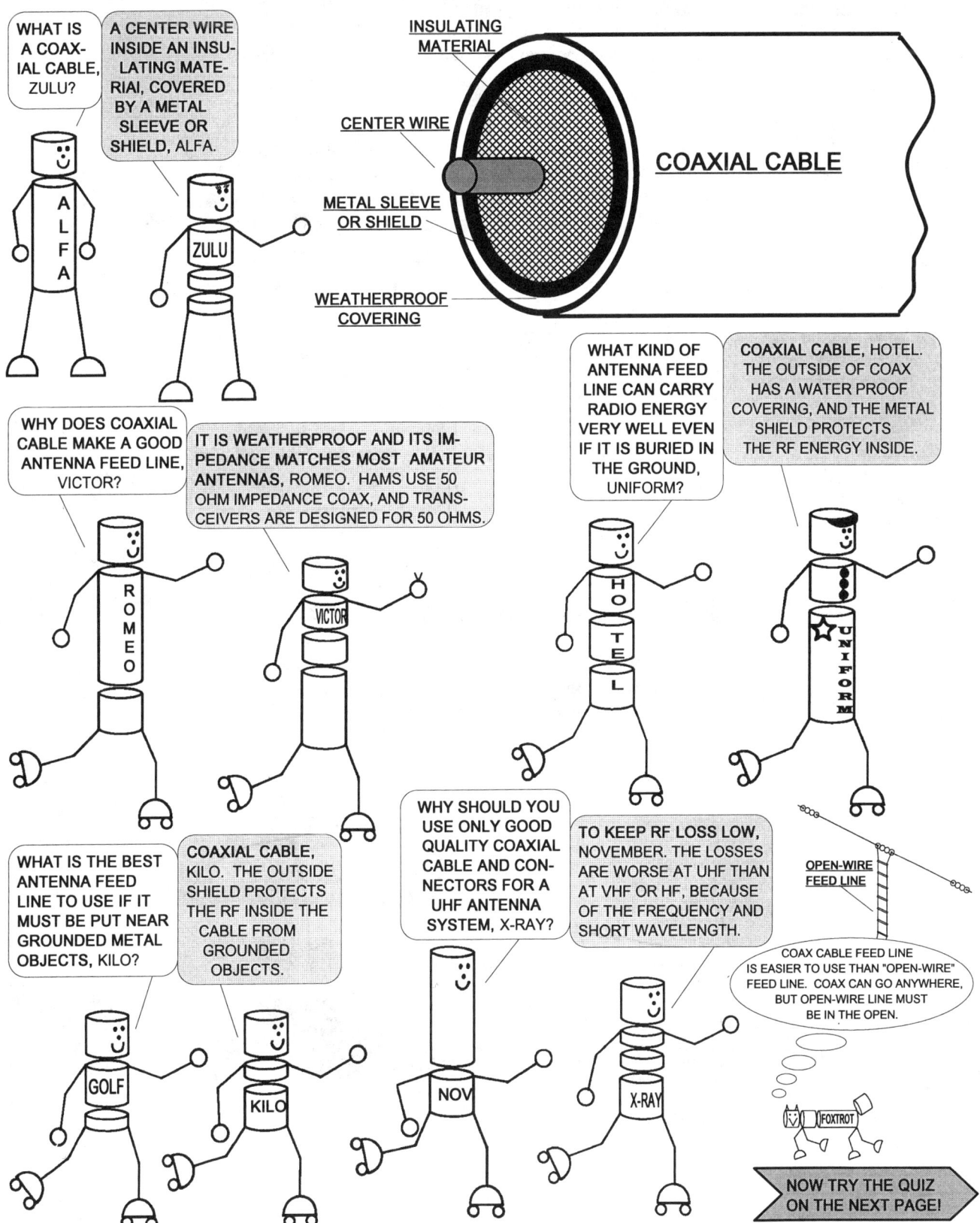

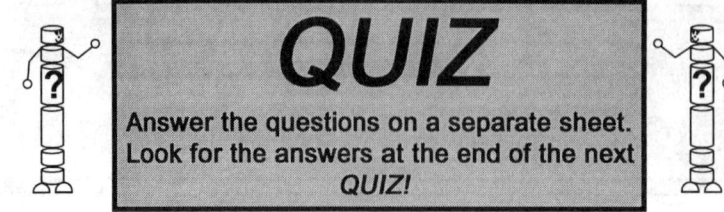

QUIZ
Answer the questions on a separate sheet. Look for the answers at the end of the next QUIZ!

N9C01
What is a coaxial cable?
A. Two wires side-by-side in a plastic ribbon
B. Two wires side-by-side held apart by insulating rods
C. Two wires twisted around each other in a spiral
D. A center wire inside an insulating material covered by a metal sleeve or shield

N9C02
Why does coaxial cable make a good antenna feed line?
A. You can make it at home, and its impedance matches most amateur antennas
B. It is weatherproof, and its impedance matches most amateur antennas
C. It is weatherproof, and its impedance is higher than that of most amateur antennas
D. It can be used near metal objects, and its impedance is higher than that of most amateur antennas

N9C03
Which kind of antenna feed line can carry radio energy very well even if it is buried in the ground?
A. Twin lead
B. Coaxial cable
C. Parallel conductor
D. Twisted pair

N9C04
What is the best antenna feed line to use if it must be put near grounded metal objects?
A. Coaxial cable
B. Twin lead
C. Twisted pair
D. Ladder-line

N4B04
Why should you use only good quality coaxial cable and connectors for a UHF antenna system?
A. To keep RF loss low
B. To keep television interference high
C. To keep the power going to your antenna system from getting too high
D. To keep the standing wave ratio of your antenna system high

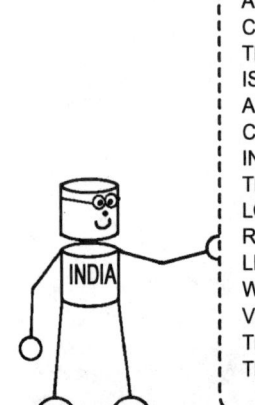

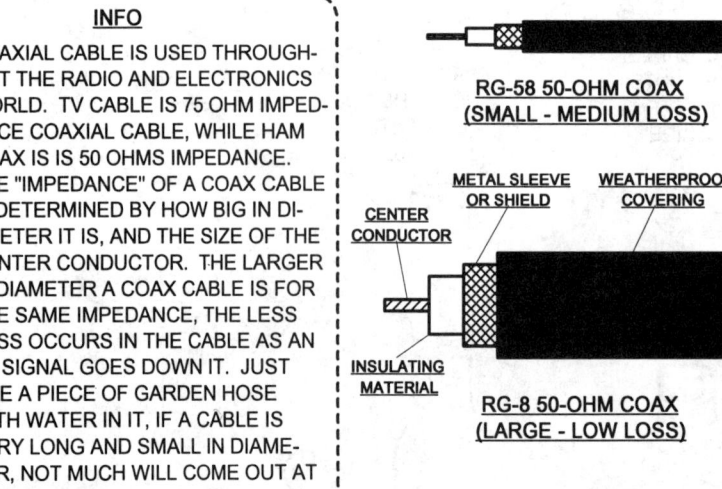

INFO
COAXIAL CABLE IS USED THROUGHOUT THE RADIO AND ELECTRONICS WORLD. TV CABLE IS 75 OHM IMPEDANCE COAXIAL CABLE, WHILE HAM COAX IS IS 50 OHMS IMPEDANCE. THE "IMPEDANCE" OF A COAX CABLE IS DETERMINED BY HOW BIG IN DIAMETER IT IS, AND THE SIZE OF THE CENTER CONDUCTOR. THE LARGER IN DIAMETER A COAX CABLE IS FOR THE SAME IMPEDANCE, THE LESS LOSS OCCURS IN THE CABLE AS AN RF SIGNAL GOES DOWN IT. JUST LIKE A PIECE OF GARDEN HOSE WITH WATER IN IT, IF A CABLE IS VERY LONG AND SMALL IN DIAMETER, NOT MUCH WILL COME OUT AT THE FAR END!

END OF NOVICE LESSON 64!

PREVIOUS QUIZ ANSWERS

N9B08 - C

N9B07 - B

N9B09 - C

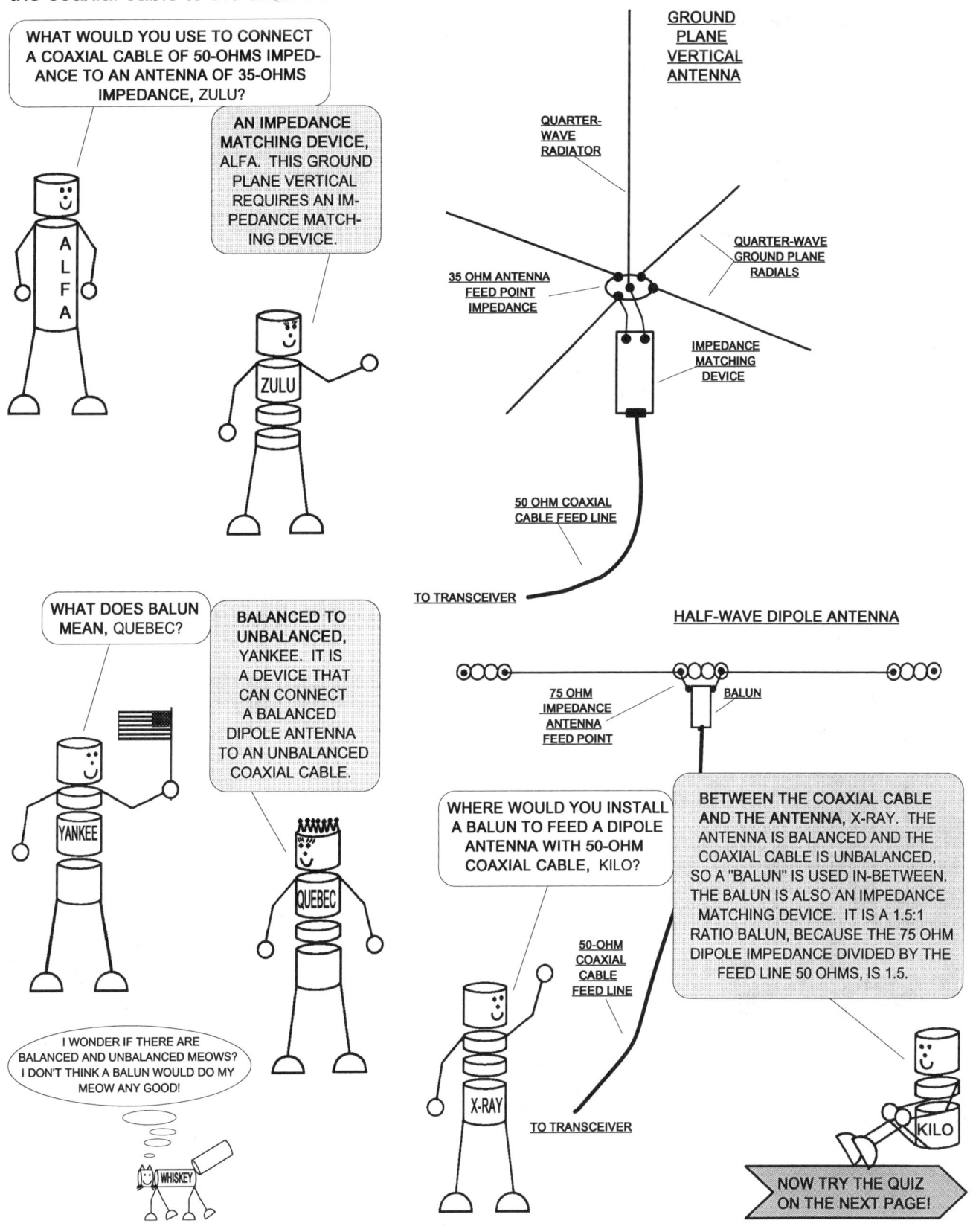

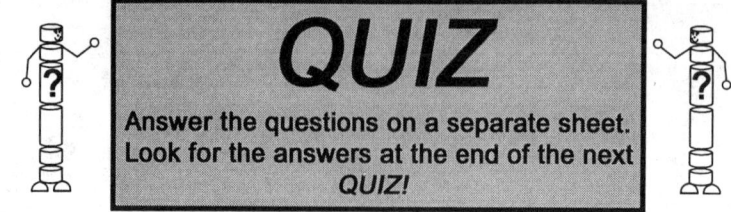

N9C09
What would you use to connect a coaxial cable of 50-ohms impedance to an antenna of 35-ohms impedance?
A. A terminating resistor
B. An SWR meter
C. An impedance matching device
D. A low-pass filter

N9C10
What does balun mean?
A. Balanced antenna network
B. Balanced unloader
C. Balanced unmodulator
D. Balanced to unbalanced

N9C11
Where would you install a balun to feed a dipole antenna with 50-ohm coaxial cable?
A. Between the coaxial cable and the antenna
B. Between the transmitter and the coaxial cable
C. Between the antenna and the ground
D. Between the coaxial cable and the ground

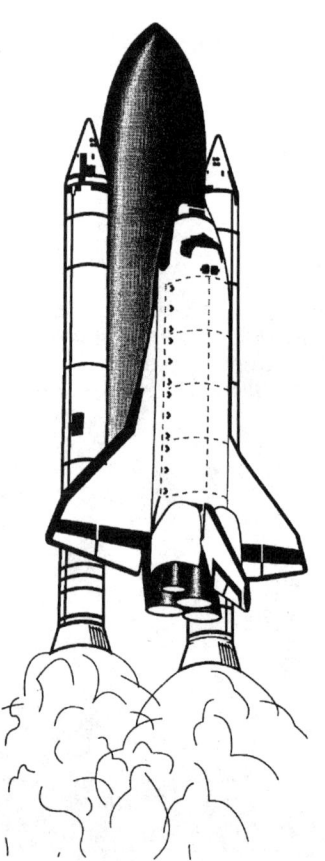
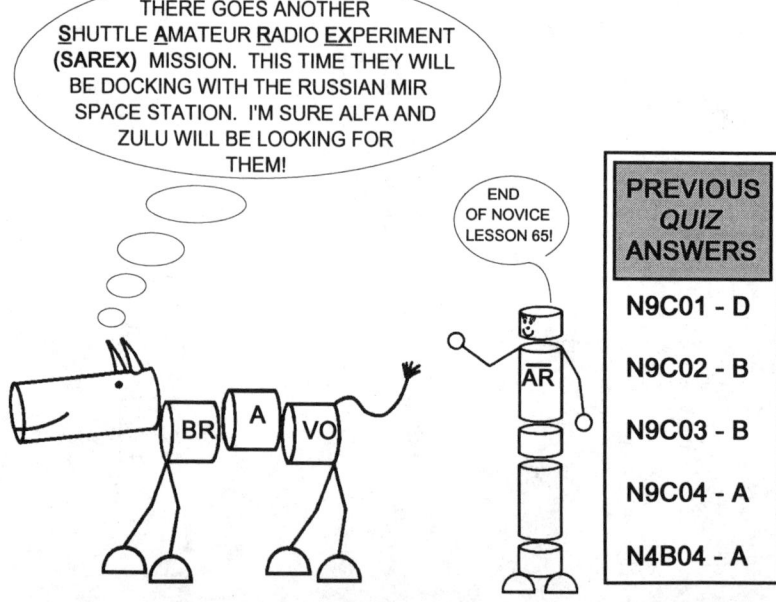

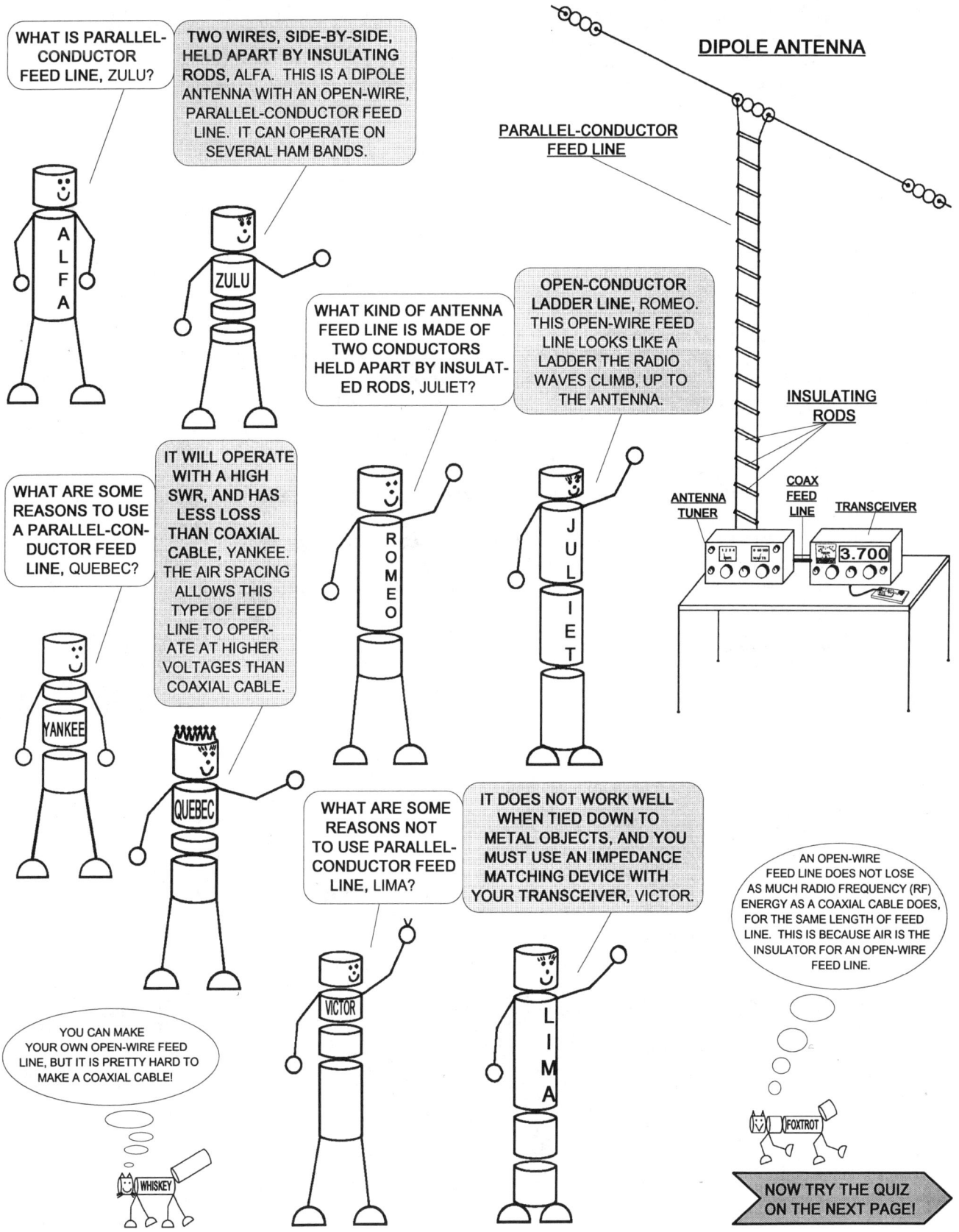

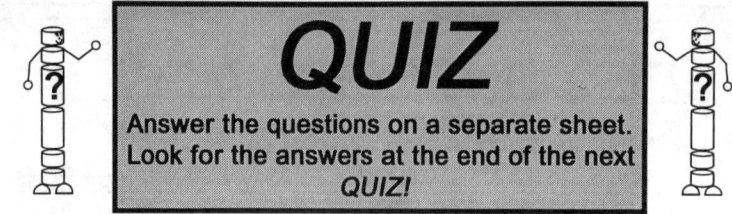

N9C05
What is parallel-conductor feed line?
A. Two wires twisted around each other in a spiral
B. Two wires side-by-side held apart by insulating rods
C. A center wire inside an insulating material which is covered by a metal sleeve or shield
D. A metal pipe which is as wide or slightly wider than a wavelength of the signal it carries

N9C08
What kind of antenna feed line is made of two conductors held apart by insulated rods?
A. Coaxial cable
B. Open-conductor ladder line
C. Twin lead in a plastic ribbon
D. Twisted pair

N9C06
What are some reasons to use parallel-conductor feed line?
A. It has low impedance, and will operate with a high SWR
B. It will operate with a high SWR, and it works well when tied down to metal objects
C. It has a low impedance, and has less loss than coaxial cable
D. It will operate with a high SWR, and has less loss than coaxial cable

N9C07
What are some reasons not to use parallel-conductor feed line?
A. It does not work well when tied down to metal objects, and you must use an impedance matching device with your transceiver
B. It is difficult to make at home, and it does not work very well with a high SWR
C. It does not work well when tied down to metal objects, and it cannot operate under high power
D. You must use an impedance matching device with your transceiver, and it does not work very well with a high SWR

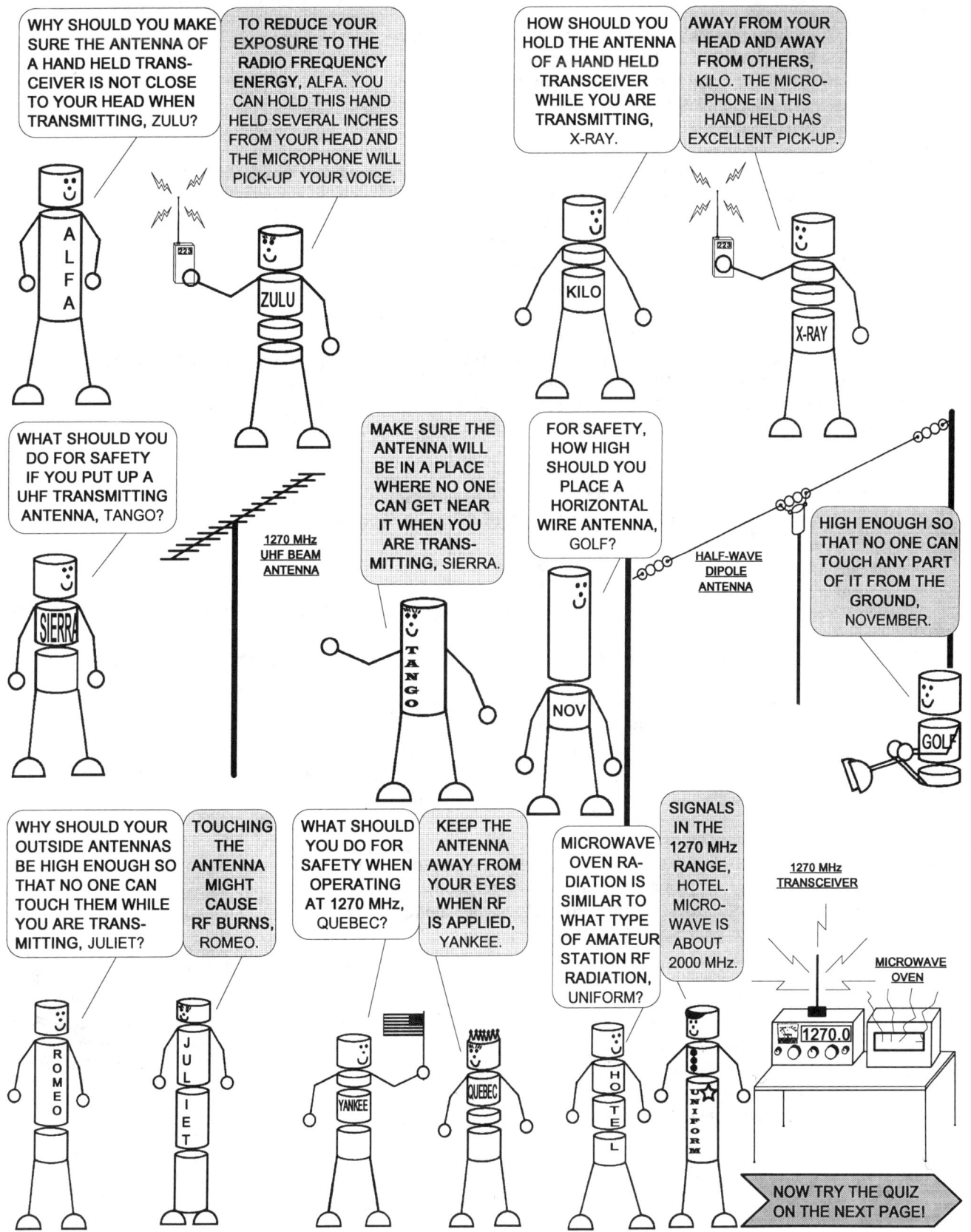

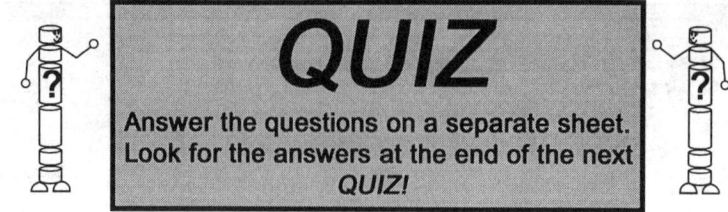

QUIZ
Answer the questions on a separate sheet.
Look for the answers at the end of the next *QUIZ!*

N4B05
Why should you make sure the antenna of a hand held transceiver is not close to your head when transmitting?
A. To help the antenna radiate energy equally in all directions
B. To reduce your exposure to the radio-frequency energy
C. To use your body to reflect the signal in one direction
D. To keep static charges from building up

N9B10
How should you hold the antenna of a hand held transceiver while you are transmitting?
A. Away from your head and away from others
B. Pointed towards the station you are contacting
C. Pointed away from the station you are contacting
D. Pointed down to bounce the signal off the ground

N4B02
What should you do for safety if you put up a UHF transmitting antenna?
A. Make sure the antenna will be in a place where no one can get near it when you are transmitting
B. Make sure that RF field screens are in place
C. Make sure the antenna is near the ground to keep its RF energy pointing in the correct direction
D. Make sure you connect an RF leakage filter at the antenna feed point

N4B10
For safety, how high should you place a horizontal wire antenna?
A. High enough so that no one can touch any part of it from the ground
B. As close to the ground as possible
C. Just high enough so you can easily reach it for adjustments or repairs
D. Above high-voltage electrical lines

N9B11
Why should your outside antennas be high enough so that no one can touch them while you are transmitting?
A. Touching the antenna might cause television interference
B. Touching the antenna might cause RF burns
C. Touching the antenna might radiate harmonics
D. Touching the antenna might reflect the signal back to the transmitter and cause damage

N4B01
What should you do for safety when operating at 1270 MHz?
A. Make sure that an RF leakage filter is installed at the antenna feed point
B. Keep antenna away from your eyes when RF is applied
C. Make sure the standing wave ratio is low before you conduct a test
D. Never use a shielded horizontally polarized antenna

N4B06
Microwave oven radiation is similar to what type of amateur station RF radiation?
A. Signals in the 3.5 MHz range
B. Signals in the 21 MHz range
C. Signals in the 50 MHz range
D. Signals in the 1270 MHz range

END OF NOVICE LESSON 67!

PREVIOUS *QUIZ* ANSWERS

N9C05 - B

N9C08 - B

N9C06 - D

N9C07 - A

SAFETY
NOVICE LESSON 68

Safety is always important. Amateurs sometimes have antennas that are mounted on towers high above the ground. Certain precautions must be taken when working on these antennas. In addition, radiation and high voltage hazards are involved with some types of equipment.

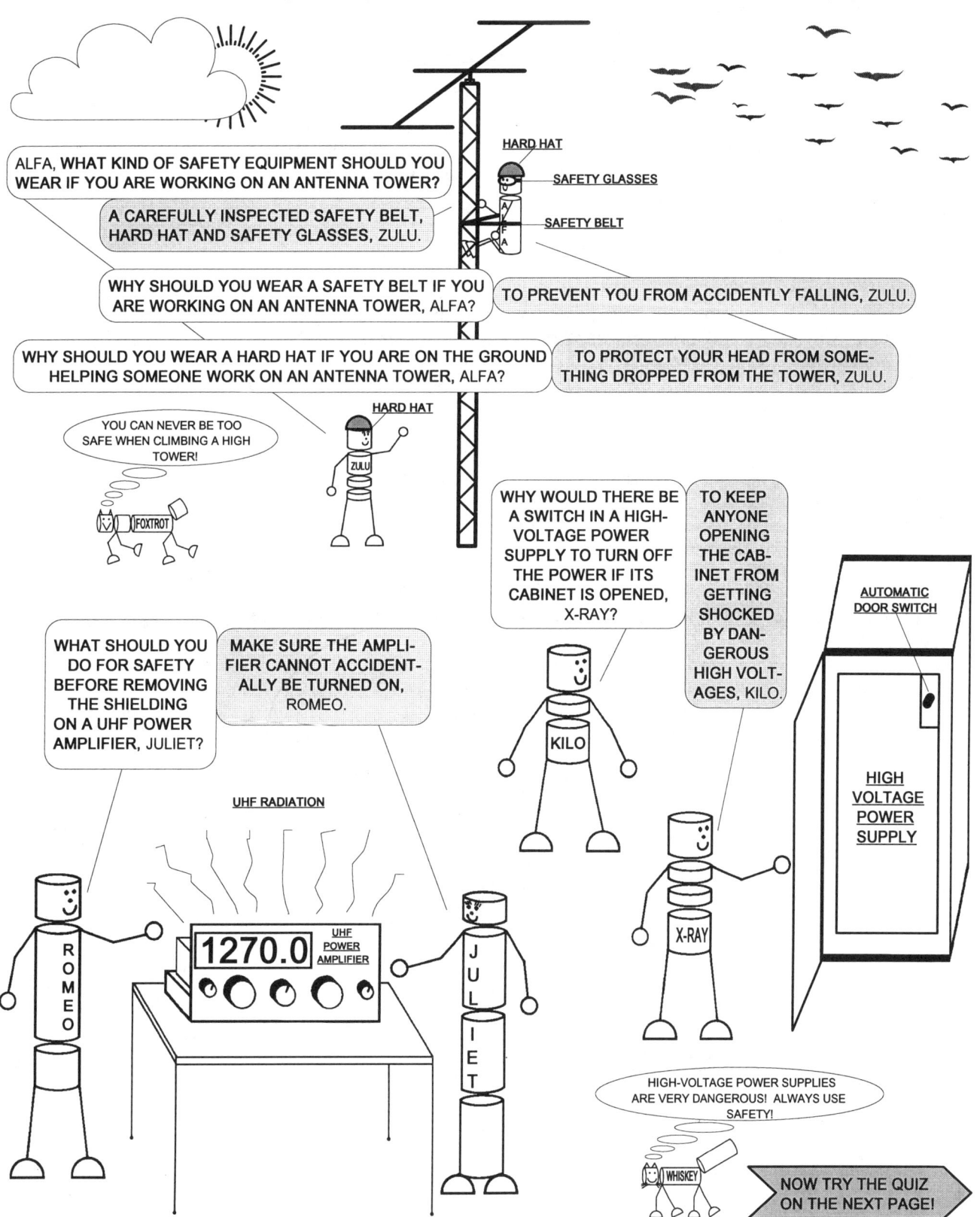

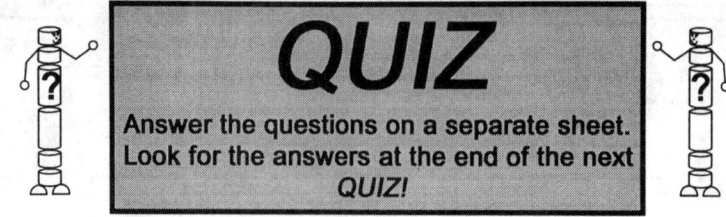

QUIZ

Answer the questions on a separate sheet. Look for the answers at the end of the next *QUIZ!*

N4B08
What kind of safety equipment should you wear if you are working on an antenna tower?
A. A grounding chain
B. A reflective vest of approved color
C. A flashing red, yellow or white light
D. A carefully inspected safety belt, hard hat and safety glasses

N4B09
Why should you wear a safety belt if you are working on an antenna tower?
A. To safely hold your tools so they don't fall and injure someone on the ground
B. To keep the tower from becoming unbalanced while you are working
C. To safely bring any tools you might use up and down the tower
D. To prevent you from accidentally falling

N4B11
Why should you wear a hard hat if you are on the ground helping someone work on an antenna tower?
A. So you won't be hurt if the tower should accidentally fall
B. To keep RF energy away from your head during antenna testing
C. To protect your head from something dropped from the tower
D. So someone passing by will know that work is being done on the tower and will stay away

N4B03
What should you do for safety before removing the shielding on a UHF power amplifier?
A. Make sure all RF screens are in place at the antenna feed line
B. Make sure the antenna feed line is properly grounded
C. Make sure the amplifier cannot accidentally be turned on
D. Make sure that RF leakage filters are connected

N4B07
Why would there be a switch in a high-voltage power supply to turn off the power if its cabinet is opened?
A. To keep dangerous RF radiation from leaking out through an open cabinet
B. To keep dangerous RF radiation from coming in through an open cabinet
C. To turn the power supply off when it is not being used
D. To keep anyone opening the cabinet from getting shocked by dangerous high voltages

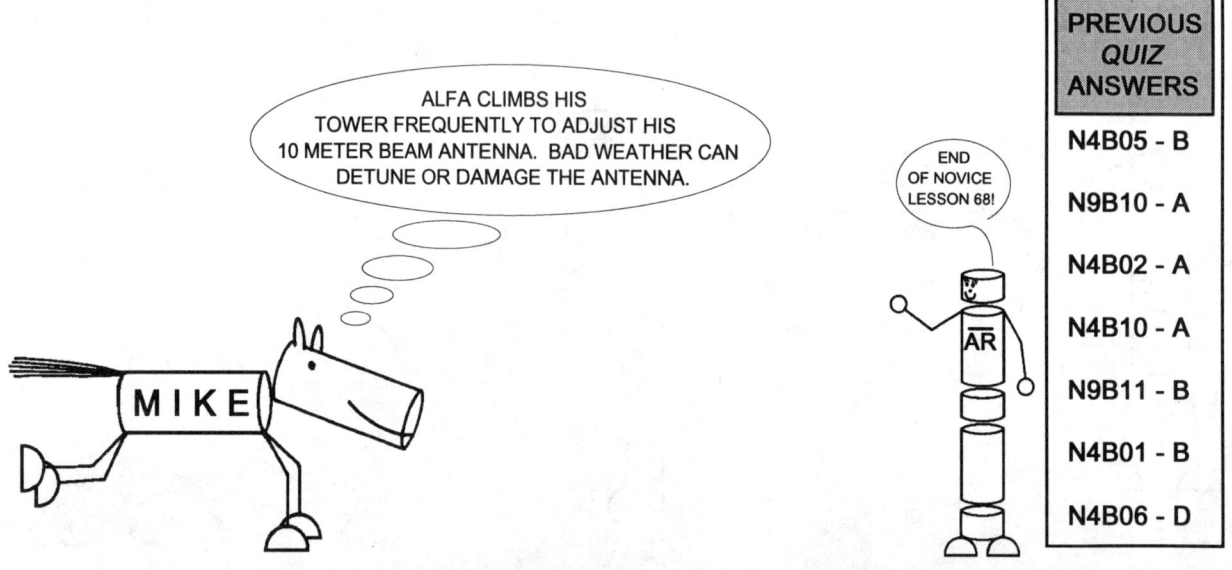

PREVIOUS *QUIZ* ANSWERS

N4B05 - B
N9B10 - A
N4B02 - A
N4B10 - A
N9B11 - B
N4B01 - B
N4B06 - D

GROUNDING
NOVICE LESSON 69

"Grounding" means electrically connecting to the earth. It is a method for preventing electrical shock, and radio frequency energy (RF) "hot spots".

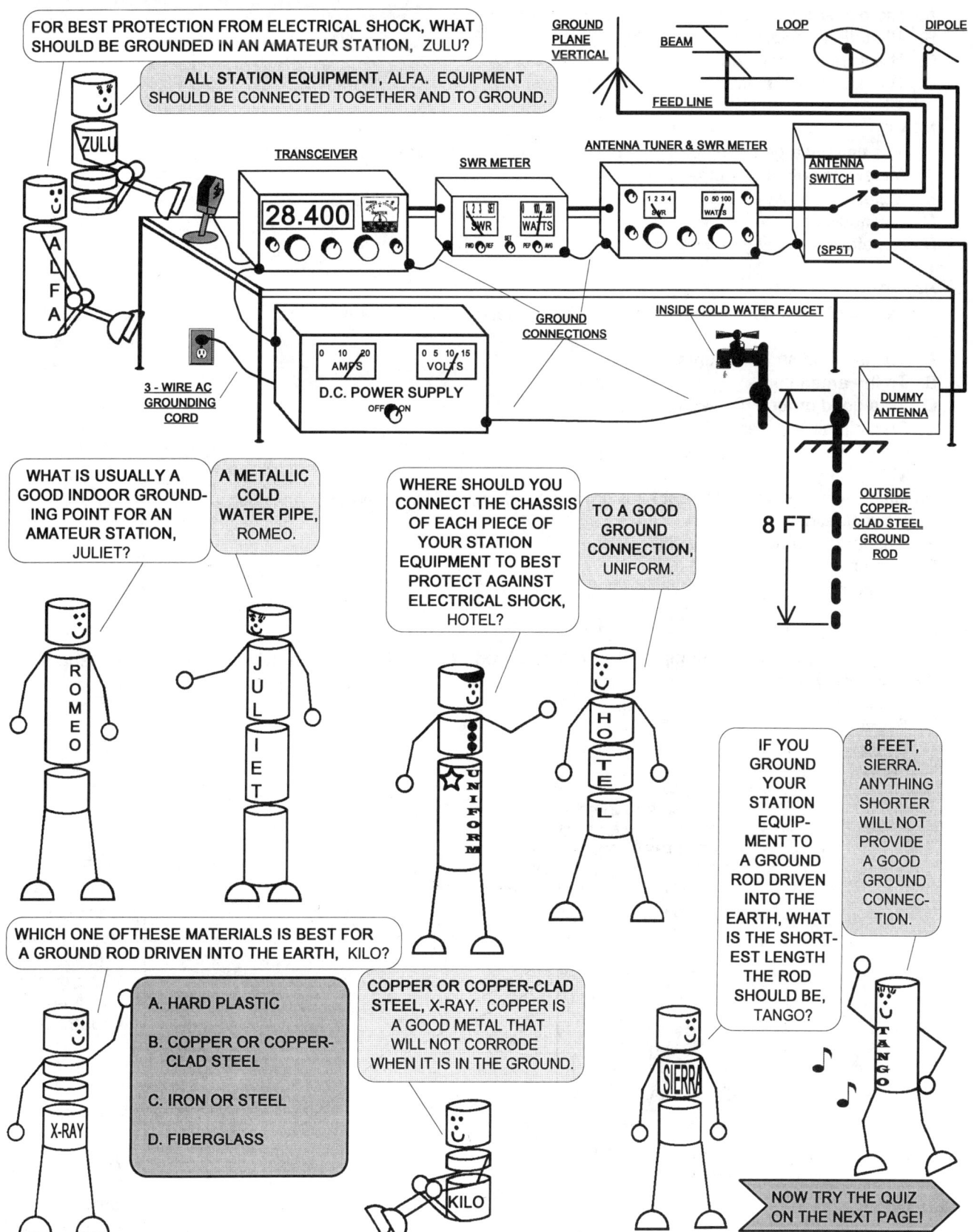

Now try the quiz on the next page!

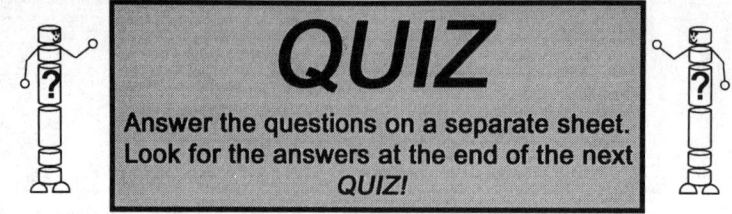

QUIZ
Answer the questions on a separate sheet.
Look for the answers at the end of the next QUIZ!

N4A07
For best protection from electrical shock, what should be grounded in an amateur station?
A. The power supply primary
B. All station equipment
C. The antenna feed line
D. The AC power mains

N4A08
What is usually a good indoor grounding point for an amateur station?
A. A metallic cold water pipe
B. A plastic cold water pipe
C. A window screen
D. A metallic natural gas pipe

N4A09
Where should you connect the chassis of each piece of your station equipment to best protect against electrical shock?
A. To insulated shock mounts
B. To the antenna
C. To a good ground connection
D. To a circuit breaker

N4A10
Which of these materials is best for a ground rod driven into the earth?
A. Hard plastic
B. Copper or copper-clad steel
C. Iron or steel
D. Fiberglass

N4A11
If you ground your station equipment to a ground rod driven into the earth, what is the shortest length the rod should be?
A. 4 feet
B. 6 feet
C. 8 feet
D. 10 feet

GROUNDING IS VERY IMPORTANT IN AN AMATEUR STATION. IT KEEPS THE RF ENERGY UNDER CONTROL, AND CAN HELP TO REDUCE INTERFERENCE WITH RADIO AND TELEVISION.

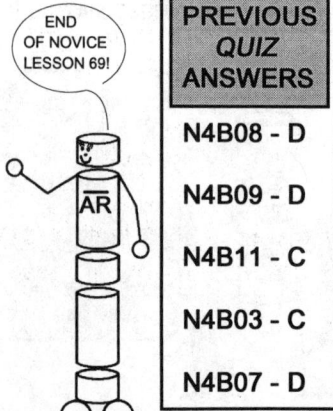

END OF NOVICE LESSON 69!

PREVIOUS QUIZ ANSWERS

N4B08 - D
N4B09 - D
N4B11 - C
N4B03 - C
N4B07 - D

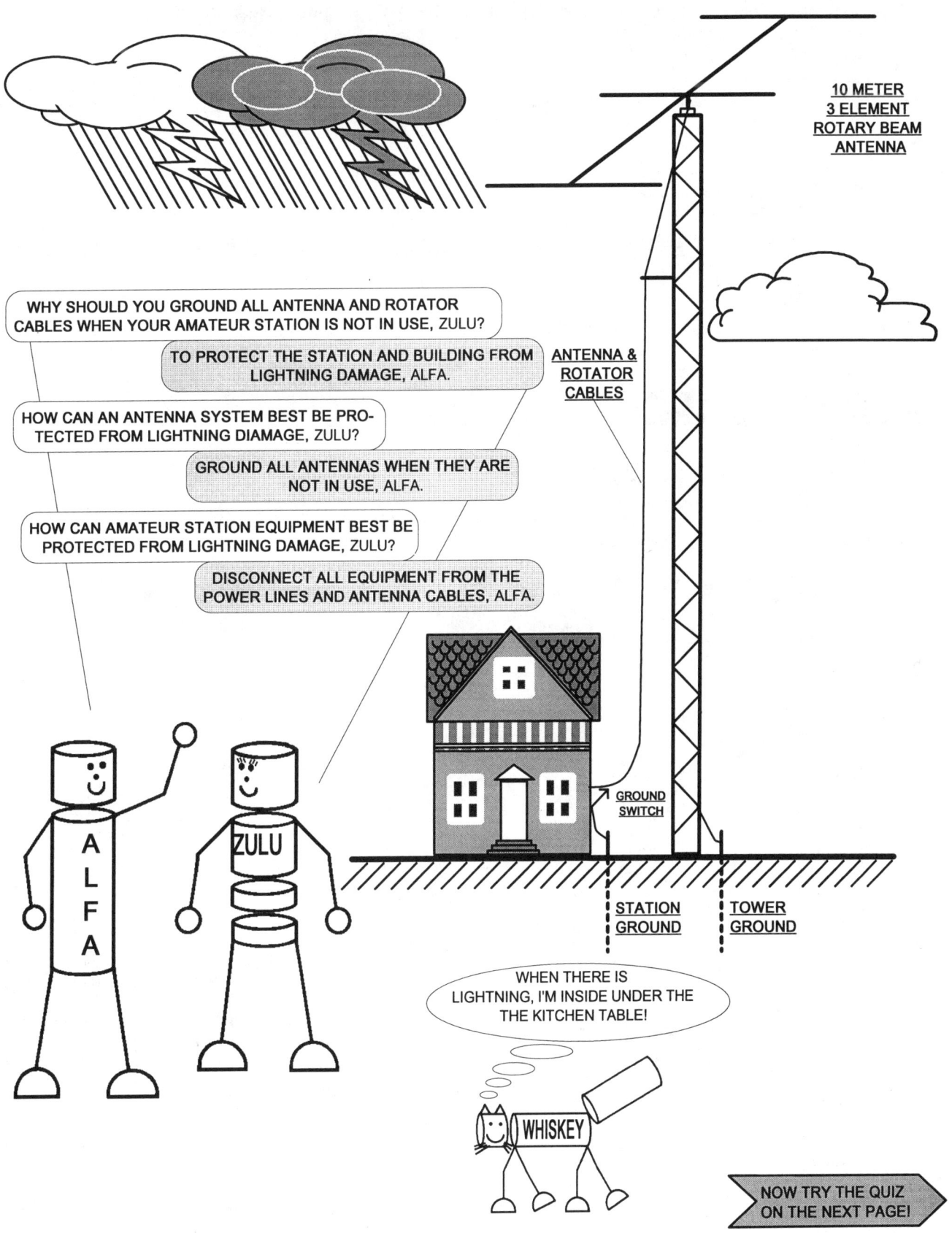

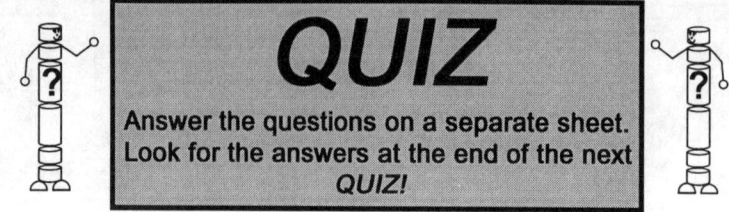

QUIZ

Answer the questions on a separate sheet. Look for the answers at the end of the next QUIZ!

N4A04
Why should you ground all antenna and rotator cables when your amateur station is not in use?
A. To lock the antenna system in one position
B. To avoid radio frequency interference
C. To save electricity
D. To protect the station and building from lightning damage

N4A05
How can an antenna system best be protected from lightning damage?
A. Install a balun at the antenna feed point
B. Install an RF choke in the antenna feed line
C. Ground all antennas when they are not in use
D. Install a fuse in the antenna feed line

N4A06
How can amateur station equipment best be protected from lightning damage?
A. Use heavy insulation on the wiring
B. Never turn off the equipment
C. Disconnect the ground system from all radios
D. Disconnect all equipment from the power lines and antenna cables

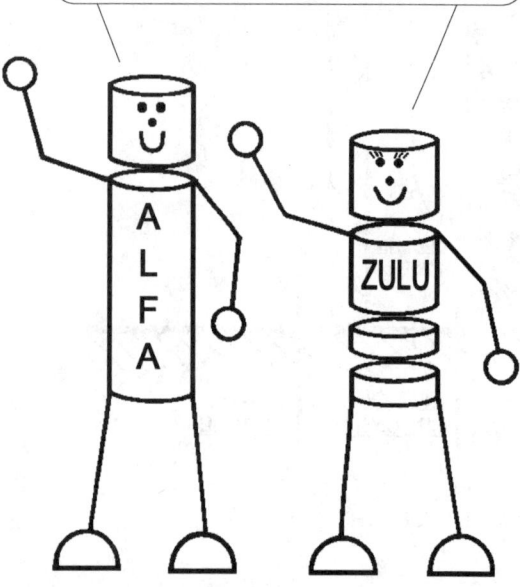

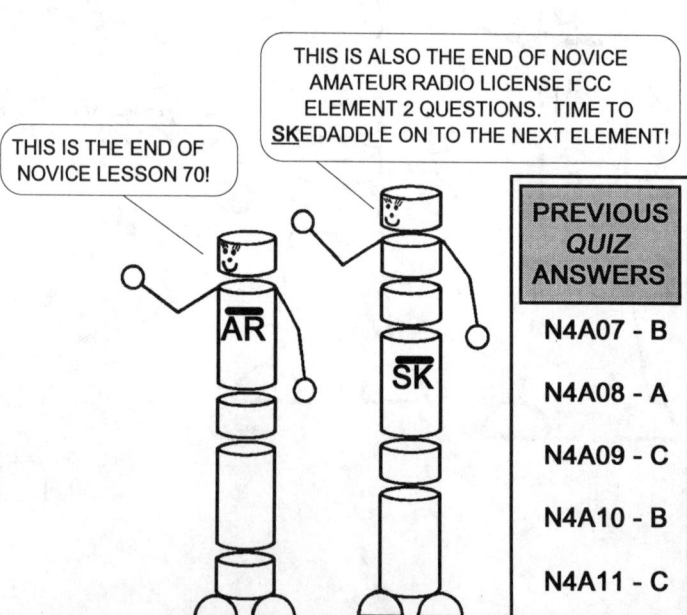

PREVIOUS QUIZ ANSWERS
N4A07 - B
N4A08 - A
N4A09 - C
N4A10 - B
N4A11 - C

INTERNATIONAL MORSE CODE
NOVICE LESSON 71

The International Morse Code was the first method of radio communication. The following Morse code letters, numbers, and punctuation, must be received at 5 words per minute (WPM) in order to pass Federal Communications Commission (FCC) Element 1A. A dash (dah) is three dots (dits) long. The spacing between dits and dahs in one letter is 1 dit; the spacing between letters in a word is 3 dits; and the spacing between words is 7 dits, as follows:

I LIKE CODE

A DIDAH
B DADIDIDIT
C DADIDADIT
D DADIDIT
E DIT
F DIDIDADIT
G DADADIT
H DIDIDIDIT
I DIDIT
J DIDADADAH
K DADIDAH
L DIDADIDIT
M DADAH
N DADIT
O DADADAH
P DIDADADIT
Q DADADIDAH
R DIDADIT
S DIDIDIT
T DAH
U DIDIDAH
V DIDIDIDAH
W DIDADAH
X DADIDIDAH
Y DADIDADAH
Z DADADIDIT

1 DIDADADADAH
2 DIDIDADADAH
3 DIDIDIDADAH
4 DIDIDIDIDAH
5 DIDIDIDIDIT
6 DADIDIDIDIT
7 DADADIDIDIT
8 DADADADIDIT
9 DADADADADIT
0 DADADADADAH

Period . (AAA) DIDADIDADIDAH
Comma , (MIM) DADADIDIDADAH
Question mark ? (IMI) DIDIDADIDIT
Slant bar / (DN) DADIDIDADIT
End Transmission (AR) DIDADIDADIT
End of QSO (SK) DIDIDIDADIDAH
Pause or Equal = (BT) DADIDIDIDAH

FILL IN THE BLANKS:

DIDIDIDIT DIDIT   DADADIT DIDIDAH DIDADIT DIDIDAH
___ ___   ___ ___ ___ ___

DADADIDIDADAH DAH DIDIDIT DIT   DADAH DADADAH DIDADIT DIDIDIT DIT
___ ___ ___ ___   ___ ___ ___ ___ ___

DADIDIDIT DADADAH DADIDIT DIT   DIDIT DIDIDIT   DIDIDADIT DIDIDAH DADIT
___ ___ ___ ___   ___ ___   ___ ___ ___

DIDADIDADIDAH ___

DIDIT DAH   DIDIDIT DIDIDAH DIDADIT DIT
___ ___   ___ ___ ___ ___

DIDIT DIDIDIT   DIDAH DIDADIT DIDIDADIT DIDAH
___ ___   ___ ___ ___ ___

DIDADIDADIDAH ___

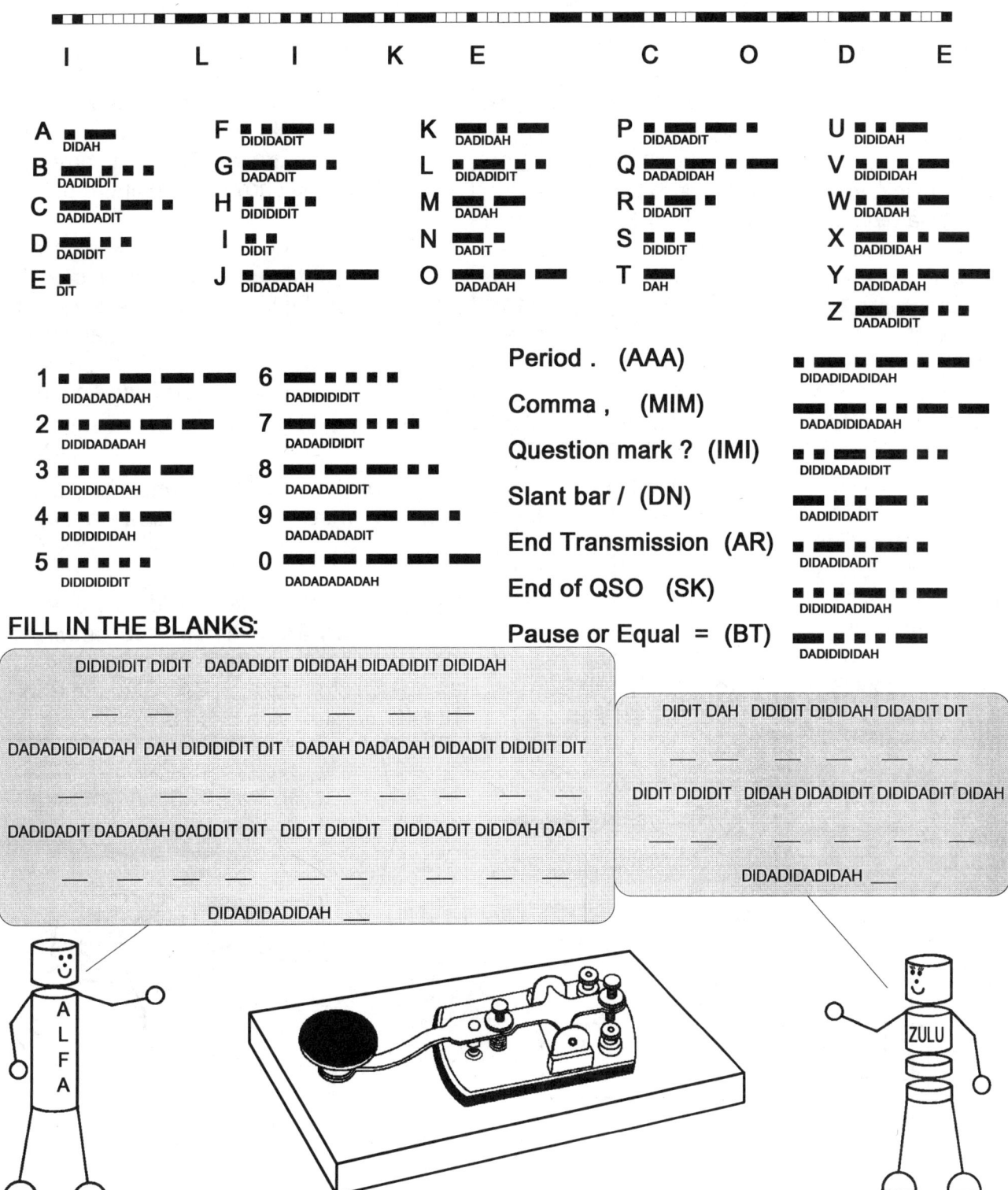

The Morse code can be learned in the normal letter sequence of the alphabet using Kawa Records "The Rhythm of the Code" tapes, <u>played repetitively</u>, or the conventional random letter method. If you are musically inclined, you will probably prefer the Kawa method, but if not, there is the "Spacecode Cassette", available from Carole Perry, WB2MGP, at Media Mentors Inc. (See page "iv" for addresses). A combination of both methods may be the answer for you!

It is very important that you obtain a code practice oscillator (CPO). The Element 1A, 5 word per minute (WPM), Morse code examination, does not require the ability to send the Morse code, but it is much easier to learn to receive if you have the ability to send. The average word is 5 letters long, so 5 WPM is 25 Morse code characters per minute.

An inexpensive CPO can be built using the following list of parts. It is a good beginner's project.

```
Key.........................AMECO* #K-1 - $9.95
Buzzer................Radio Shack #273-055 - $2.59
Battery Clip..........Radio Shack #270-325 - $0.28
Battery Holder..... Radio Shack #270-326 - $0.50
9-Volt Battery.........Radio Shack #23-553 - $2.39
Solder Lugs............Local Hardware Store - $0.25
Mounting Screws....Local Hardware Store - $0.10
Particle Board.........Local Hardware Store - $0.25
4"x6"x3/4"                         TOTAL: $16.31

*AMECO, 224 E. Second St., Mineola, NY 11501
Telephone: 516-741-5030 (Shipping - $2.75)
```

The parts are mounted on the heavy particle board, and it will keep the unit on the table when you are sending. The arrangement of parts is shown in the figure below.

When sending the code, only the elbow should be <u>on</u> the table, with the wrist arched <u>above</u> the table. The index and center finger should be on the top front, and the thumb on the side of the key knob. The other two fingers should be folded out of the way.

Never tap the key. It is impossible to send Morse code rapidly or correctly by tapping. The fingers should lightly grasp the key knob at all times, and the wrist should move in a smooth rhythm, much like playing a guitar.

Just as it is easier to learn a language by listening to it in use, Morse code should be listened to on the air. At first you will pick out only a few letters, but slowly words and sentences will become recognizable. Inexpensive "ham receiver" radio kits are available, such as the HR-40, 40 meter receiver, for approximately $30.00, from Ramsey Electronics Inc., 793 Canning Parkway, Victor, NY 14564, Telephone: 716-924-4560. The 40 meter novice band is active both day and night, and will provide good Morse code practice.

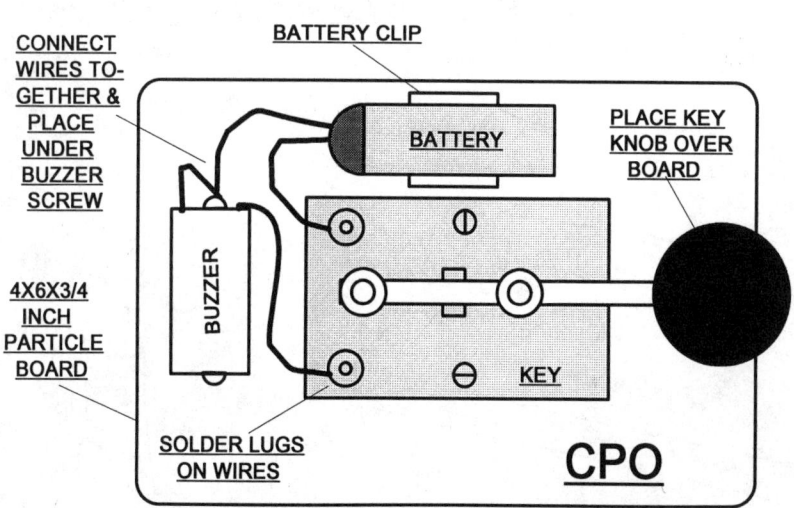

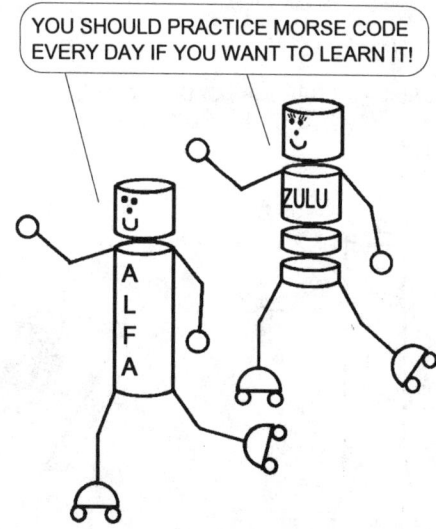

MORSE CODE LESSONS

LESSON 1
Letters: T H E S O

Words: HOT ETHOS TOES TO THESE SHOT SHOE HE THOSE THEO SO TEST HOST

Sentences: SHE SETS THE TEST SO HE SHOOTS THE HOST

LESSON 2
Letters: R W G P I

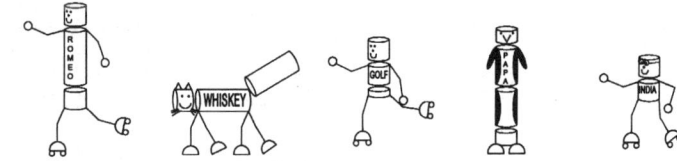

Words: WIPE PIT TWIG SOOTHE WRIST WIT TIRE HIGH HIRE SET THE WIG TO THE

Sentences: STRIPE OR WIPE THOSE EGGS WITH WIGS

LESSON 3
Letters: M N A L F

Words: NIGHT MAN FLOW FATHER LATHE TWO EAGLES HOT POWER FLAMES GREEN TREES MOTHER FATHER LARGE MAIL SEAS RIGHT ANSWER

Sentences: FLAMES AT NIGHT ARE IN THE LAME AIR LANES
THREE FLAMINGOS FLEW HOME TO THE GREEN TREES PLAIN

LESSON 4
Letters: C Q U D K

Words: ELF DEAR QUIET POWER DECK NAME CLOUD WAIT FLAME MATCH DECK QUEEN CALLED KING MELLOW MUSIC IS NICE FLOWING GREAT PINK ROSES LAME DUCK CUTE GIRL RICK AND SUE TAME TIGER WHITE

Sentences: THE QUICK CLUCK OF THE DUCK IS FUN TO HEAR
LETS PICK RED AND WHITE FLOWERS TOGETHER QUICK

LESSON 5 - Letters: Y Z B J X V

LESSON 6 - Numbers: 1, 2, 3, 4, 5, 6, 7, 8, 9, 0

LESSON 7 - Punctuation: Period (.), Comma (,), Question Mark (?), Slant Bar (/), End of Transmission (AR), End of Contact (SK), Pause or Equal (=)

HAM CROSSWORD PUZZLE

Across

1. EMERGENCY CALL FOR HELP
4. PROTECT EQUIPMENT ELECTRICALLY
7. MEASURE OF CAPACITANCE
9. USED FOR TUNE-UP IN PLACE OF ANTENNA
10. DIRECT QSO WITHOUT REPEATER
11. THOUSANDS OF HERTZ
16. COMBINED TRANSMITTER-RECEIVER
18. USED TO CONTROL CURRENT IN A CIRCUIT
19. MEASURE OF CURRENT IN A CIRCUIT
21. OPERATION USING A MICROPHONE
22. A CONTACT ON THE AIR
23. HAS A VACUUM AND A FILAMENT
25. CABLE USED TO CONNECT EQUIPMENT AND ANTENNA
26. BASIC TYPE OF ANTENNA
27. FEDERAL COMMUNICATIONS COMMISSION
29. HIGH FREQUENCY RADIO
30. MORSE CODE OPERATION
31. TERMINAL NODE CONTROLLER FOR PACKET
34. MILLION HERTZ
35. USED TO POWER CIRCUITS
36. VERY HIGH FREQUENCY RADIO
38. THE LENGTH OF A RADIO WAVE
40. REBROADCASTS RECEIVED RADIO SIGNALS
42. A VARIABLE RESISTOR

Down

2. JAPANESE BEAM ANTENNA INVENTOR
3. ALTERNATING CURRENT
5. DISCOVERED LAW FOR ELECTRICAL CIRCUITS
6. REBROADCASTS RECEIVED DIGITAL SIGNAL
7. PROTECTS CIRCUITS FROM HIGH CURRENT
8. MORSE CODE FOR 'FROM'
10. ENERGIZES THE EARTH'S IONOSPHERE
12. EXACT MULTIPLE OF OPERATING FREQUENCY
13. DIRECT CURRENT
14. RADIO WAVE RATE OF CHANGE
15. VERIFICATION OF CONTACT OR 'QSO'
16. SILICON SIGNAL AMPLIFIER
17. RADIO WAVE REFLECTING LAYER ABOVE THE EARTH
20. COMPUTER RADIO COMMUNICATION MODE
24. ULTRA HIGH FREQUENCY RADIO
28. COMPUTER PACKET RADIO MODE
32. COMPUTER RADIO OPERATION MODE
33. RADIO TELETYPE OPERATION
34. CHANGES HUMAN VOICE TO ELECTRICAL SIGNAL
35. SHARPLY DIRECTIONAL ANTENNA
36. MEASURE OF ELECTROMOTIVE FORCE
37. FREQUENCY MODULATION MODE
38. MEASURE OF POWER
39. MEASURE OF FREQUENCY IN CYCLES PER SECOND
41. READABILITY, STRENGTH, AND TONE

Word List

AC
AMPERE
BATTERY
BEAM
COAX
CONNECTED
CW
DATA
DC
DE
DIGIPEATER
DIPOLE
DUMMY
FARAD
FCC
FM
FREQUENCY
FUSE
GROUNDS
HARMONIC
HERTZ
HF
IONOSPHERE
KILOHERTZ
MAYDAY
MEGAHERTZ
MICROPHONE
OHM
PACKET
POTENTIOMETER
QSL
QSO
REPEATER
RESISTOR
RST
RTTY
SIMPLEX
SUNSPOT
TNC
TRANSCEIVER
TRANSISTOR
TUBE
UHF
VHF
VOICE
VOLTS
WATT
WAVELENGTH
YAGI

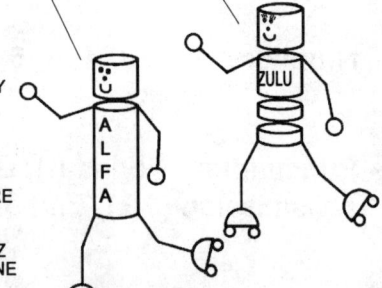

PREVIOUS *QUIZ* ANSWERS

N4A04 - D

N4A05 - C

N4A06 - D

TECHNICIAN AMATEUR RADIO LICENSE
FCC ELEMENT 3

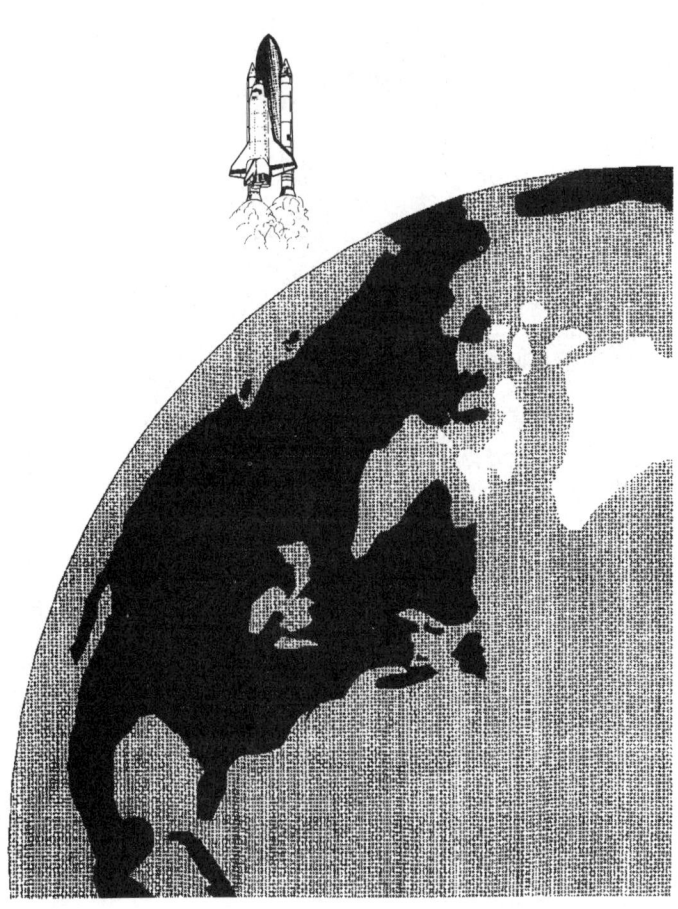

HAM CROSSWORD PUZZLE

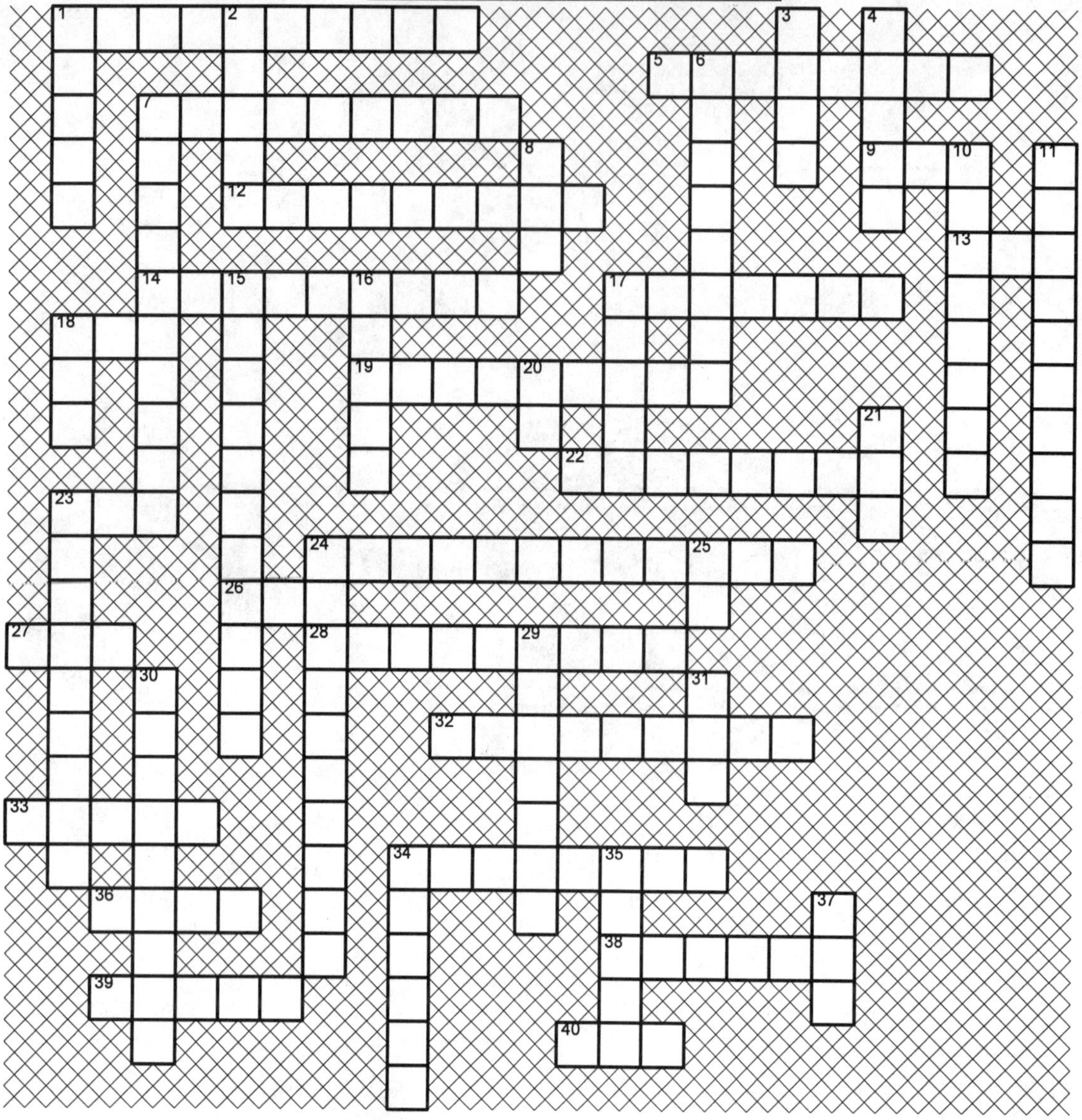

150

Across

1. LISTENING TO OTHER STATIONS WITHOUT TRANSMITTING
5. TUNED TO A SINGLE FREQUENCY
7. CARRIES ELECTRICAL CURRENT WELL
9. UPPER SIDEBAND
12. UNSEEN ELECTROMAGNETIC WAVES
13. LOWER SIDEBAND
14. RATIO OF VOLTAGE TO CURRENT IN OHMS
17. THE FLOW OF ELECTRONS IN A CONDUCTOR
18. INTERFERENCE ON THE AIR
19. VOICE LEVEL SETTING FOR AN FM TRANSMITTER
22. UNWANTED VOICE INTERFERENCE CAUSED BY A NEARBY STATION
23. STANDING WAVE RATIO
24. THOUSANDTHS OF AN AMPERE
26. TELEVISION INTERFERENCE
27. PEAK ENVELOPE POWER
28. ELECTRICAL DISCHARGE BETWEEN CLOUDS AND EARTH
32. CONNECTS REPEATER TO TELEPHONE LINE
33. TERMINAL WHERE SIGNALS ENTER
34. INPUT SIGNAL IS TOO LARGE
36. RANGE OF FREQUENCIES OF NEARLY THE SAME WAVELENGTH
38. RADIO INTERFERENCE CAUSED BY UNFILTERED CW KEYING
39. CONNECTS COMPUTERS TO RADIOS OR TELEPHONE LINES
40. WHO IS CALLING

Down

1. MEASURE OF WAVELENGTH
2. MATCHES ANTENNA AND TRANSCEIVER IMPEDANCES
3. SHORT FOR MORSE CODE OR CW
4. MATCHES BALANCED ANTENNAS TO UNBALANCED FEED LINES
6. ELEMENTARY NEGATIVELY CHARGED PARTICLE IN ALL MATTER
7. ONE HUNDREDTH OF A METER
8. MORSE CODE EMERGENCY CALL
10. BOTH TERMINALS OF A DEVICE ARE UNGROUNDED
11. ONE TERMINAL OF A DEVICE IS GROUNDED
15. A RADIO WAVE THROUGH SPACE
16. WAVES THAT CAN BE HEARD
17. CW SIGNAL THAT SHIFTS IN FREQUENCY AS IT IS KEYED
18. SEND SLOWER
20. AMPLITUDE MODULATION
21. DECREASE POWER
23. PREVENTS RF RADIATION
24. THOUSANDTHS OF A WATT
25. RADIO FREQUENCY
29. CONNECTION OF STATIONS TOGETHER
30. A POOR CONDUCTOR OF ELECTRONS
31. LOCATION
34. THE TERMINALS WHERE A SIGNAL EMERGES FROM A DEVICE
35. ORBITING SATELLITE CARRYING AMATEUR RADIO
37. SINGLE SIDEBAND

Word List

AM
AUDIO
AUTOPATCH
BALANCED
BALUN
BAND
CENTIMETER
CHIRP
CLICKS
CODE
CONDUCTOR
CURRENT
DEVIATION
ELECTRON
IMPEDANCE
INPUT
INSULATOR
LIGHTNING
LSB
METER
MILLIAMPERES
MILLIWATTS
MODEM
MONITORING
NETWORK
OSCAR
OUTPUT
OVERLOAD
PEP
PROPAGATION
QRM
QRP
QRS
QRZ
QTH
RADIATION
RESONANT
RF
SHIELDING
SOS
SPLATTER
SSB
SWR
TUNER
TVI
UNBALANCED
USB

THIS PUZZLE WILL HELP YOU LEARN THE HAM LANGUAGE!

SIGNAL REPORTS & Q - SIGNALS
TECHNICIAN LESSON 1

ROMEO, SIERRA, & TANGO were discussing the **RST** signal report method for telling another amateur station how **R**eadable, how **S**trong, and how its **T**one sounds, if it is using Morse code, known as *CW*.

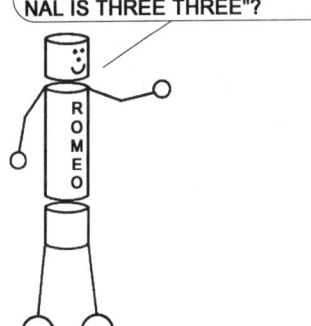

SIERRA, WHAT IS THE MEANING OF "YOUR SIGNAL REPORT IS FIVE SEVEN..."? TANGO, WHAT IS THE MEANING OF "YOUR SIGNAL IS THREE THREE"?

R - READABILITY	S - STRENGTH	T - TONE
1 - UNREADABLE	1 - FAINT	1 - VERY ROUGH & BROAD
2 - BARELY READABLE	2 - VERY WEAK	2 - VERY ROUGH AC
3 - DIFFICULTY READING	3 - WEAK	3 - ROUGH AC
4 - LITTLE DIFFICULTY READING	4 - FAIR	4 - ROUGH FILTERED AC
5 - PERFECTLY READABLE	5 - FAILY GOOD	5 - FILTERED ROUGH AC
	6 - GOOD	6 - FILTERED AC
	7 - MODERATE	7 - NEAR PURE TONE
	8 - STRONG	8 - NEAR PERFECT TONE
	9 - EXTREMELY STRONG	9 - PERFECT TONE

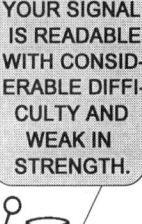

YOUR SIGNAL IS PERFECTLY READABLE AND MODERATELY STRONG.

YOUR SIGNAL IS READABLE WITH CONSIDERABLE DIFFICULTY AND WEAK IN STRENGTH.

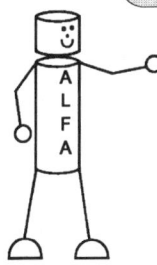

ZULU, WHAT IS THE MEANING OF "YOUR SIGNAL REPORT IS FIVE NINE PLUS 20 dB..."?

A RELATIVE SIGNAL-STRENGTH METER READING OF 20 DECIBELS GREATER THAN STRENGTH 9, ALFA. ONE DECIBEL IS THE SMALLEST CHANGE IN SOUND THAT THE HUMAN EAR CAN NOTICE!

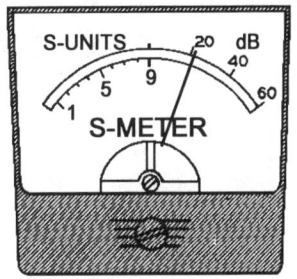

A MEOW CAN BE MANY DECIBELS, OR JUST A COUPLE!

WHAT IS USED TO MEASURE RELATIVE STRENGTH IN A RECEIVER, YANKEE?

AN S METER, QUEBEC. THIS ONE IS READING 20 dB OVER S-9.

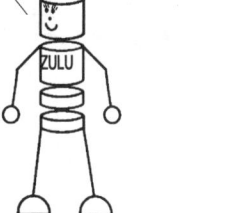

WHAT IS THE PROPER Q SIGNAL TO USE TO SEE IF A FREQUENCY IS IN USE BEFORE TRANSMITTING ON CW?

QRL?, VICTOR.

WHAT IS THE PROPER Q SIGNAL TO USE TO ASK IF SOMEONE IS CALLING YOU ON CW, LIMA?

QRZ?, VICTOR.

Q - SIGNALS

QRL - BUSY
QRM - INTERFERENCE
QRN - STATIC
QRO - INCREASE POWER
QRP - DECREASE POWER
QRQ - SEND FASTER
QRS - SEND SLOWER
QRT - STOP SENDING
QRX - STANDBY
QRZ - WHO IS CALLING
QSB - FADING
QSL - CONFIRMATION
QSO - CONTACT
QST - CALLING ALL HAMS
QSY - CHANGE FREQUENCY
QTH - LOCATION

WHAT IS ONE MEANING OF THE Q SIGNAL "QSY"?, KILO?

CHANGE FREQUENCY, GOLF.

WHAT IS ONE MEANING OF THE Q SIGNAL "QSO"?, KILO?

A CONVERSATION IS IN PROGRESS, GOLF.

NOW TRY THE QUIZ ON THE NEXT PAGE!

QUIZ

Answer the questions on a separate sheet. Look for the answers at the end of the next *QUIZ!*

SEE PAGE 7 FOR REVIEW.

T2B09
What is the meaning of: "Your signal report is five seven..."?
A. Your signal is perfectly readable and moderately strong
B. Your signal is perfectly readable, but weak
C. Your signal is readable with considerable difficulty
D. Your signal is perfectly readable with near pure tone

T2B10
What is the meaning of: "Your signal report is three three..."?
A. The contact is serial number thirty-three
B. The station is located at latitude 33 degrees
C. Your signal is readable with considerable difficulty and weak in strength
D. Your signal is unreadable, very weak in strength

T2B11
What is the meaning of: "Your signal report is five nine plus 20 dB..."?
A. Your signal strength has increased by a factor of 100
B. Repeat your transmission on a frequency 20 kHz higher
C. The bandwidth of your signal is 20 decibels above linearity
D. A relative signal-strength meter reading is 20 decibels greater than strength 9

T4D08
What is used to measure relative signal strength in a receiver?
A. An S meter
B. An RST meter
C. A signal deviation meter
D. An SSB meter

T2B05
What is the proper Q signal to use to see if a frequency is in use before transmitting on CW?
A. QRV?
B. QRU?
C. QRL?
D. QRZ?

T2B08
What is the proper Q signal to use to ask if someone is calling you on CW?
A. QSL?
B. QRZ?
C. QRL?
D. QRT?

T2B06
What is one meaning of the Q signal "QSY"?
A. Change frequency
B. Send more slowly
C. Send faster
D. Use more power

T2B07
What is one meaning of the Q signal "QSO"?
A. A contact is confirmed
B. A conversation is in progress
C. A contact is ending
D. A conversation is desired

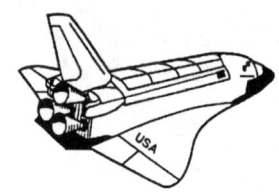

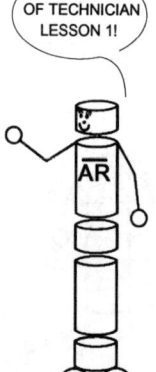

END OF TECHNICIAN LESSON 1!

IDENTIFICATION
TECHNICIAN LESSON 2

The Federal Communications Commission (FCC) permits CW operation, the basic form of communication, anywhere on any amateur band. CW is useful for voice station identification.

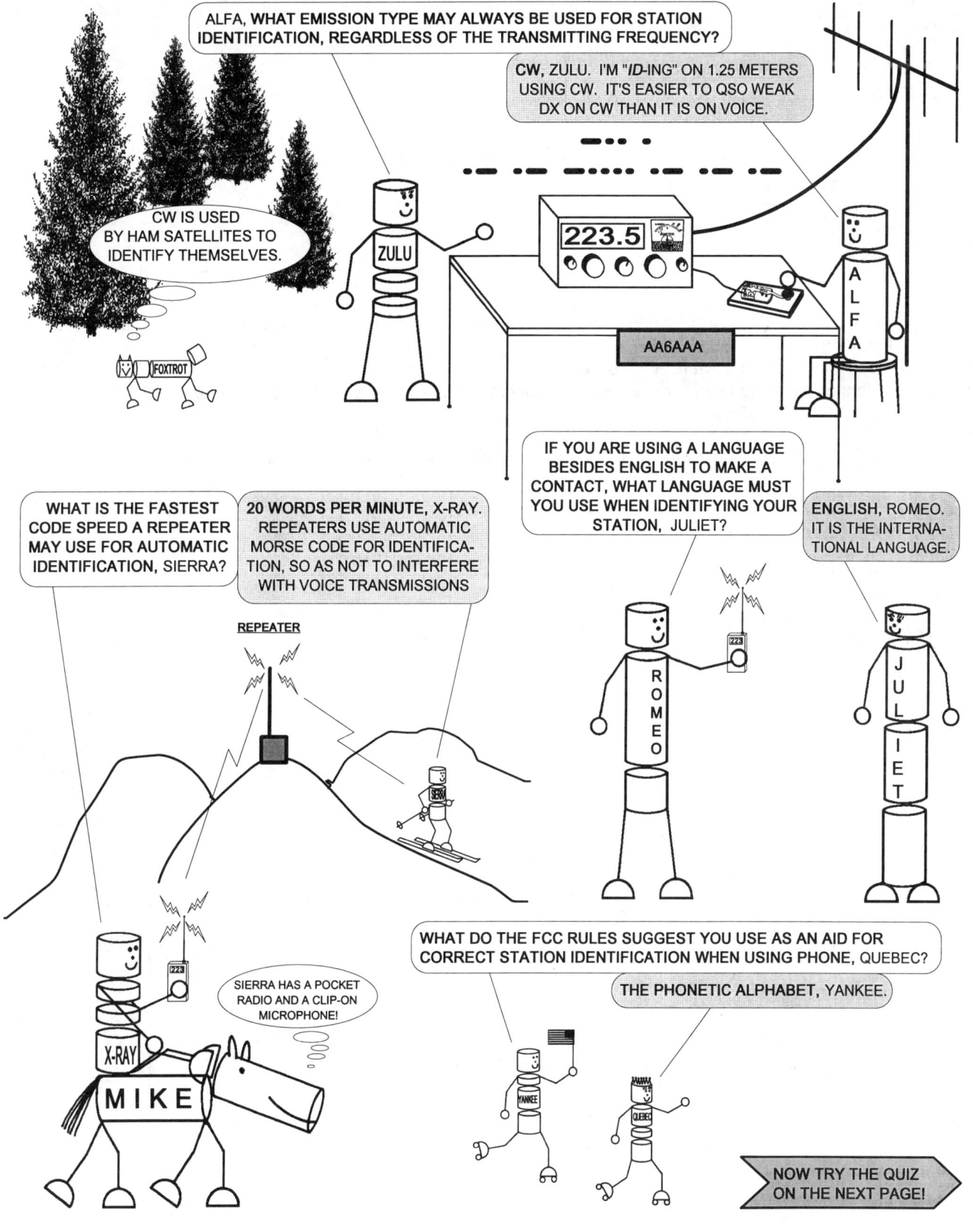

NOW TRY THE QUIZ ON THE NEXT PAGE!

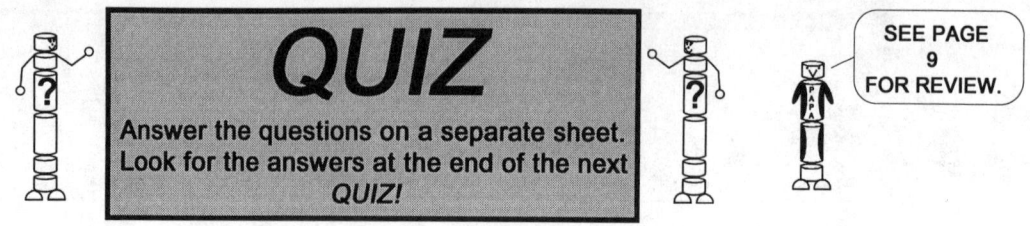

QUIZ

Answer the questions on a separate sheet. Look for the answers at the end of the next QUIZ!

SEE PAGE 9 FOR REVIEW.

T1B07
What emission type may always be used for station identification, regardless of the transmitting frequency?
A. CW
B. RTTY
C. MCW
D. Phone

T1D02
What is the fastest code speed a repeater may use for automatic identification?
A. 13 words per minute
B. 20 words per minute
C. 25 words per minute
D. There is no limitation

T1D03
If you are using a language besides English to make a contact, what language must you use when identifying your station?
A. The language being used for the contact
B. The language being used for the contact, providing the US has a third-party communications agreement with that country
C. English
D. Any language of a country which is a member of the International Telecommunication Union

T1D04
What do the FCC rules suggest you use as an aid for correct station identification when using phone?
A. A speech compressor
B. Q signals
C. A phonetic alphabet
D. Unique words of your choice

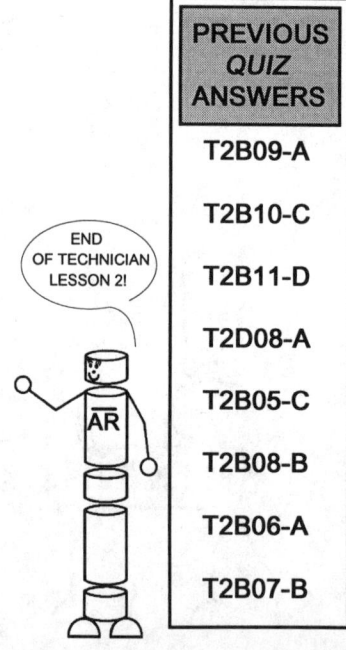

PREVIOUS QUIZ ANSWERS

T2B09-A

T2B10-C

T2B11-D

T2D08-A

T2B05-C

T2B08-B

T2B06-A

T2B07-B

EMERGENCY OPERATION
TECHNICIAN LESSON 3

One of the main purposes of amateur radio is emergency operation. It is the only reliable source of communications after every major disaster.

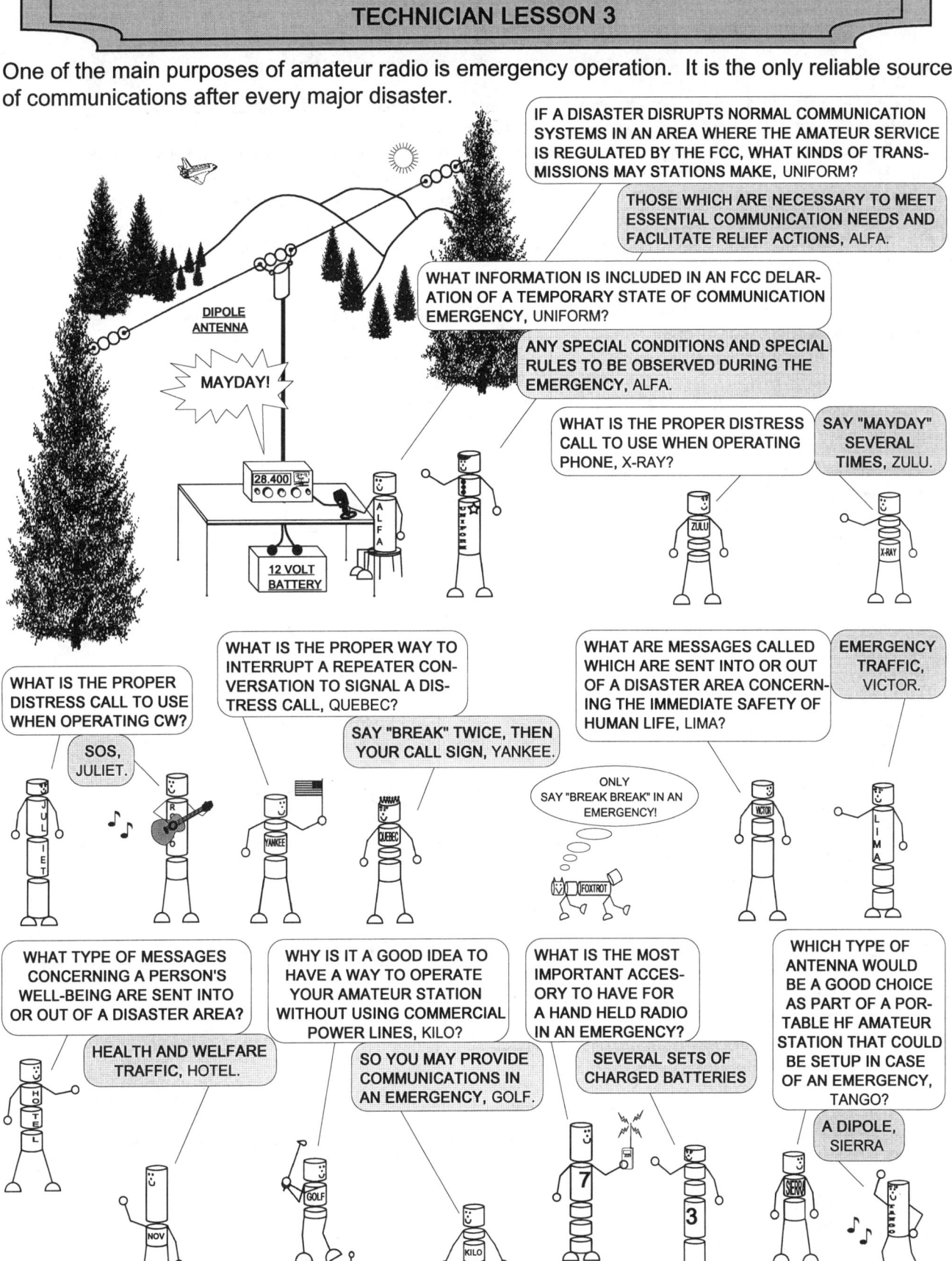

QUIZ

Answer the questions on a separate sheet. Look for the answers at the end of the next QUIZ!

SEE PAGE 23 FOR REVIEW.

T1E10
If a disaster disrupts normal communication systems in an area where the amateur service is regulated by the FCC, what kinds of transmissions may stations make?
A. Those which are necessary to meet essential communication needs and facilitate relief actions
B. Those which allow a commercial business to continue to operate in the affected area
C. Those for which material compensation has been paid to the amateur operator for delivery into the affected area
D. Those which are to be used for program production or newsgathering for broadcasting purposes

T1E11
What information is included in an FCC declaration of a temporary state of communication emergency?
A. A list of organizations authorized to use radio communications in the affected area
B. A list of amateur frequency bands to be used In the affected area
C. Any special conditions and special rules to be observed during the emergency
D. An operating schedule for authorized amateur emergency stations

T2C01
What is the proper distress call to use when operating phone?
A. Say "MAYDAY" several times
B. Say "HELP" several times
C. Say "EMERGENCY" several times
D. Say "SOS" several times

T2C02
What is the proper distress call to use when operating CW?
A. MAYDAY
B. QRRR
C. QRZ
D. SOS

T2C03
What is the proper way to interrupt a repeater conversation to signal a distress call?
A. Say "BREAK" twice, then your call sign
B. Say "HELP" as many times as it takes to get someone to answer
C. Say "SOS," then your call sign
D. Say "EMERGENCY" three times

T2C09
What are messages called which are sent into or out of a disaster area concerning the immediate safety of human life?
A. Tactical traffic
B. Emergency traffic
C. Formal message traffic
D. Health and Welfare traffic

T2C08
What type of messages concerning a person's well-being are sent into or out of a disaster area?
A. Routine traffic
B. Tactical traffic
C. Formal message traffic
D. Health and Welfare traffic

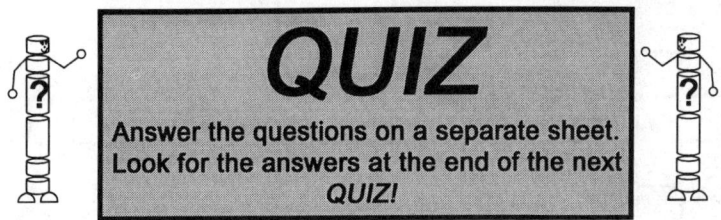

QUIZ
Answer the questions on a separate sheet. Look for the answers at the end of the next QUIZ!

T2C10
Why is it a good idea to have a way to operate your amateur station without using commercial AC power lines?
A. So you may use your station while mobile
B. So you may provide communications in an emergency
C. So you may operate in contests where AC power is not allowed
D. So you will comply with the FCC rules

T2C11
What is the most important accessory to have for a hand held radio in an emergency?
A. An extra antenna
B. A portable amplifier
C. Several sets of charged batteries
D. A microphone headset for hands-free operation

T2C12
Which type of antenna would be a good choice as part of a portable HF amateur station that could be set up in case of an emergency?
A. A three-element quad
B. A three-element Yagi
C. A dipole
D. A parabolic dish

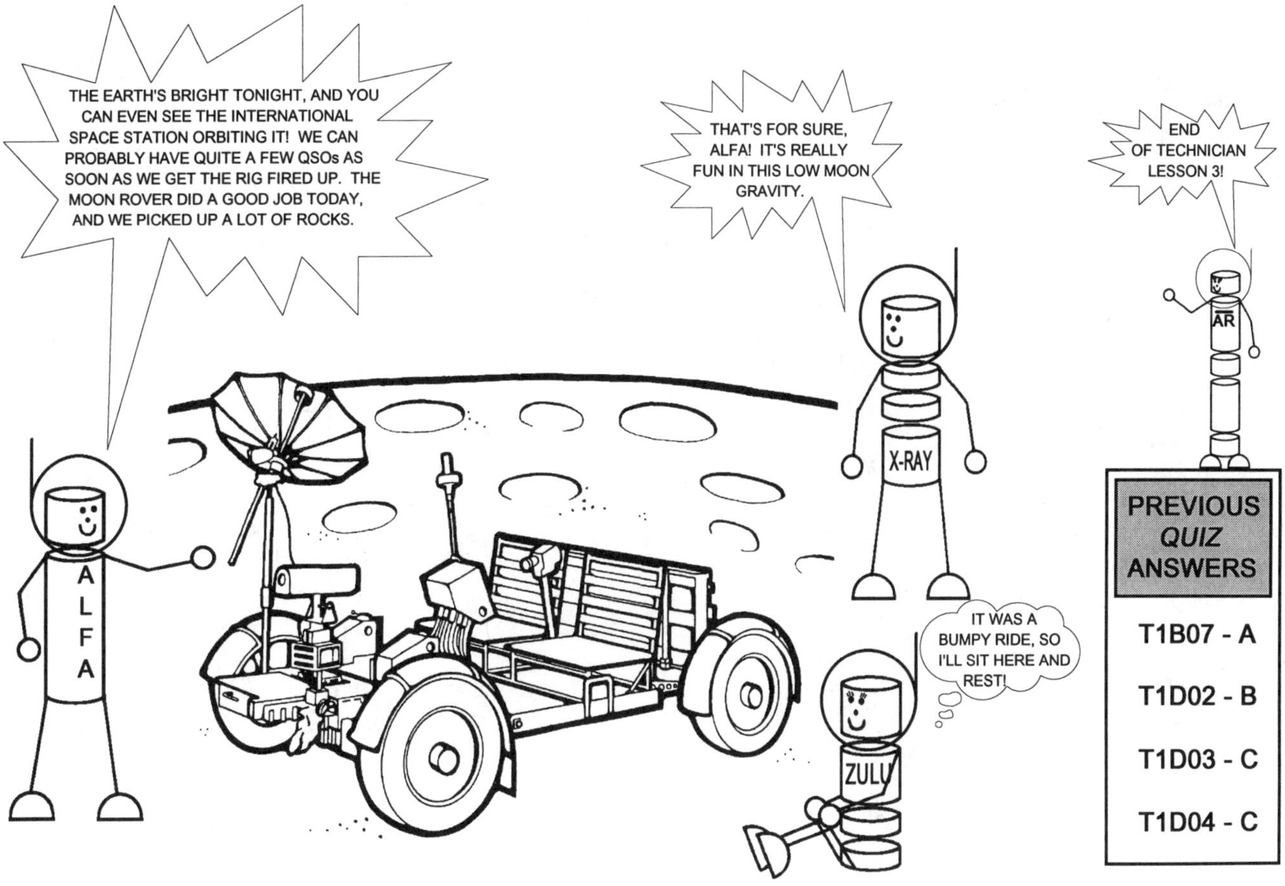

PREVIOUS QUIZ ANSWERS
T1B07 - A
T1D02 - B
T1D03 - C
T1D04 - C

HAM CROSSWORD PUZZLE

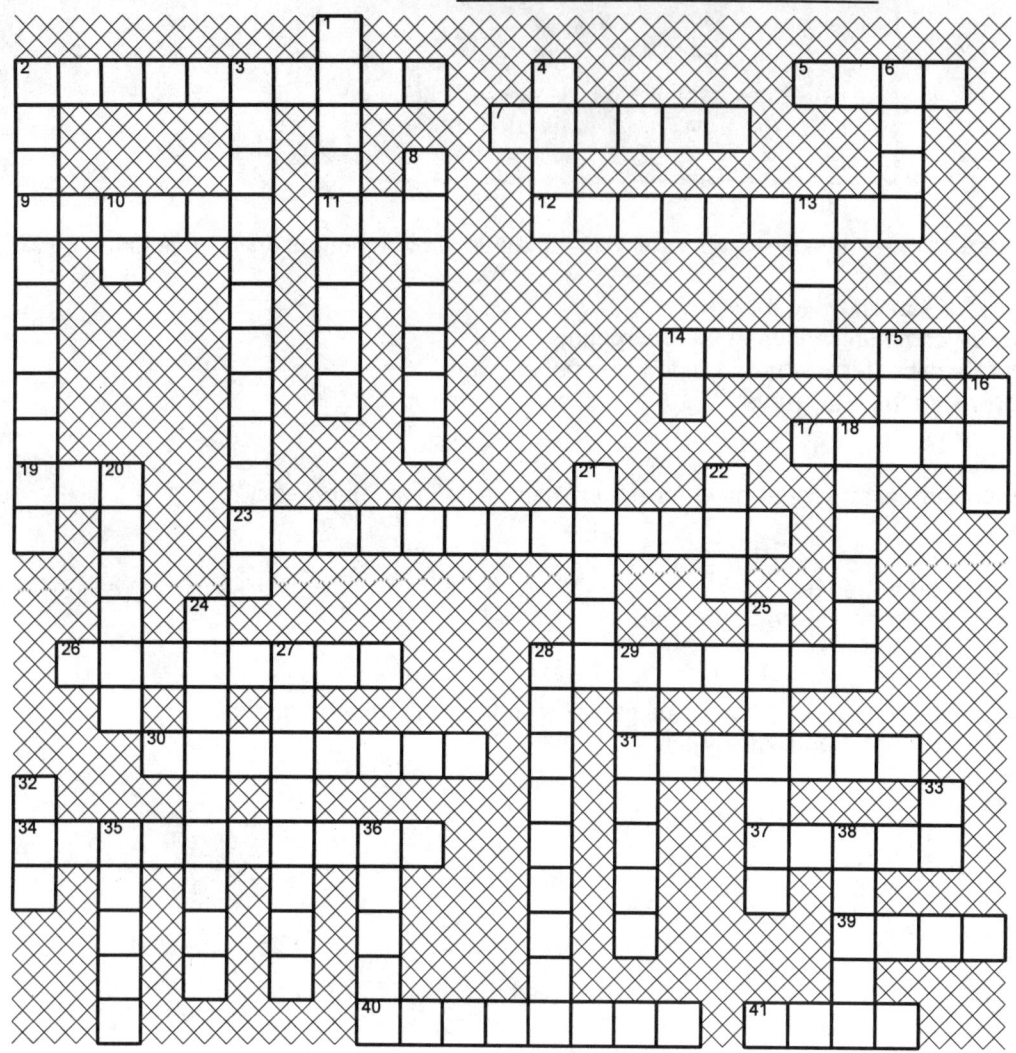

Across

2. FCC ELEMENT 2 & 3A LICENSE
5. SINGLE POLE DOUBLE THROW
7. COMMON ELECTRICAL WIRE CONDUCTOR
9. FCC ELEMENTS 2 & 1A LICENSE
11. SHORT FOR RADIO AMATEUR
12. MORSE CODE LETTER 'Z'
14. 2-WAY RADIO COMMUNICATION
17. VOICE OPERATION
19. ELECTROMOTIVE FORCE OR VOLTAGE
23. 2-WAY CONTACT BETWEEN STATIONS
26. TERMINAL FROM WHICH ELECTRONS FLOW
28. TERMINAL INTO WHICH ELECTRONS FLOW
30. DEVICE USED TO PICK UP RADIO SIGNALS
31. USED TO RADIATE RADIO SIGNALS INTO SPACE
34. PLACES INFORMATION ON A RADIO WAVE
37. SHUTTLE AMATEUR RADIO EXPERIMENT
39. IDENTIFYING LETTERS ISSUED BY FCC
40. SEND RADIO WAVES INTO SPACE
41. SINGLE POLE SINGLE THROW

Down

1. ONE THOUSAND HERTZ
2. DEVICE USED TO GENERATE RADIO WAVES
3. TWO STATIONS ON AT THE SAME TIME (QRM)
4. THE BEST CONDUCTOR OF ELECTRICITY
6. DOUBLE POLE DOUBLE THROW
8. AN UNPAID RADIO OPERATOR
10. VOLUNTEER EXAMINER
13. DOUBLE POLE SINGLE THROW
14. 'SEEKING YOU' GENERAL CALL
15. CODE PRACTICE OSCILLATOR
16. DEVICE USED TO SEND MORSE CODE
18. YOUR NAME ON THE AIR
20. USED TO ELIMINATE UNWANTED SIGNALS
21. NAME USED FOR ALL WIRELESS COMMUNICATIONS
22. MORSE CODE DISTRESS CALL
24. UNMANNED SPACE VEHICLE
25. ISSUED BY FCC FOR RADIO OPERATION
27. MUST BE DONE EVERY 10 MINUTES ON THE AIR
28. USED TO CLARIFY VOICE COMMUNICATIONS
29. EQUIPMENT USED AT ONE LOCATION FOR RADIO CONTACTS
32. EARTH-MOON-EARTH COMMUNICATIONS
33. DISTANT STATION
35. MORSE CODE LETTER 'A'
36. PATHWAY OF ONE BODY AROUND ANOTHER
38. RADIO AMATEUR CIVIL EMERGENCY SERVICE

Word List

AMATEUR
ANTENNA
CALL
COMMUNICATION
CONTACT
COPPER
CPO
CQ
DADADIDIT
DIDAH
DPDT
DPST
DX
EME
EMF
FILTER
GOLD
HAM
HANDLE
IDENTIFY
INTERFERENCE
KEY
KILOHERTZ
LICENSE
MODULATION
NEGATIVE
NOVICE
ORBIT
PHONE
PHONETICS
POSITIVE
RACES
RADIO
RECEIVER
SAREX
SATELLITE
SOS
SPDT
SPST
STATION
TECHNICIAN
TRANSMIT
TRANSMITTER
VE

HAM RADIO WORDS ARE USED IN ALL COMMUNICATIONS. THIS PUZZLE HAS SOME OF THEM!

RADIO AMATEUR CIVIL EMERGENCY SERVICE
TECHNICIAN LESSON 4

The Radio Amateur Civil Emergency Service (RACES) is a group of amateurs who volunteer for emergency operator training. This is done by having "drills" on the air, using special call letters.

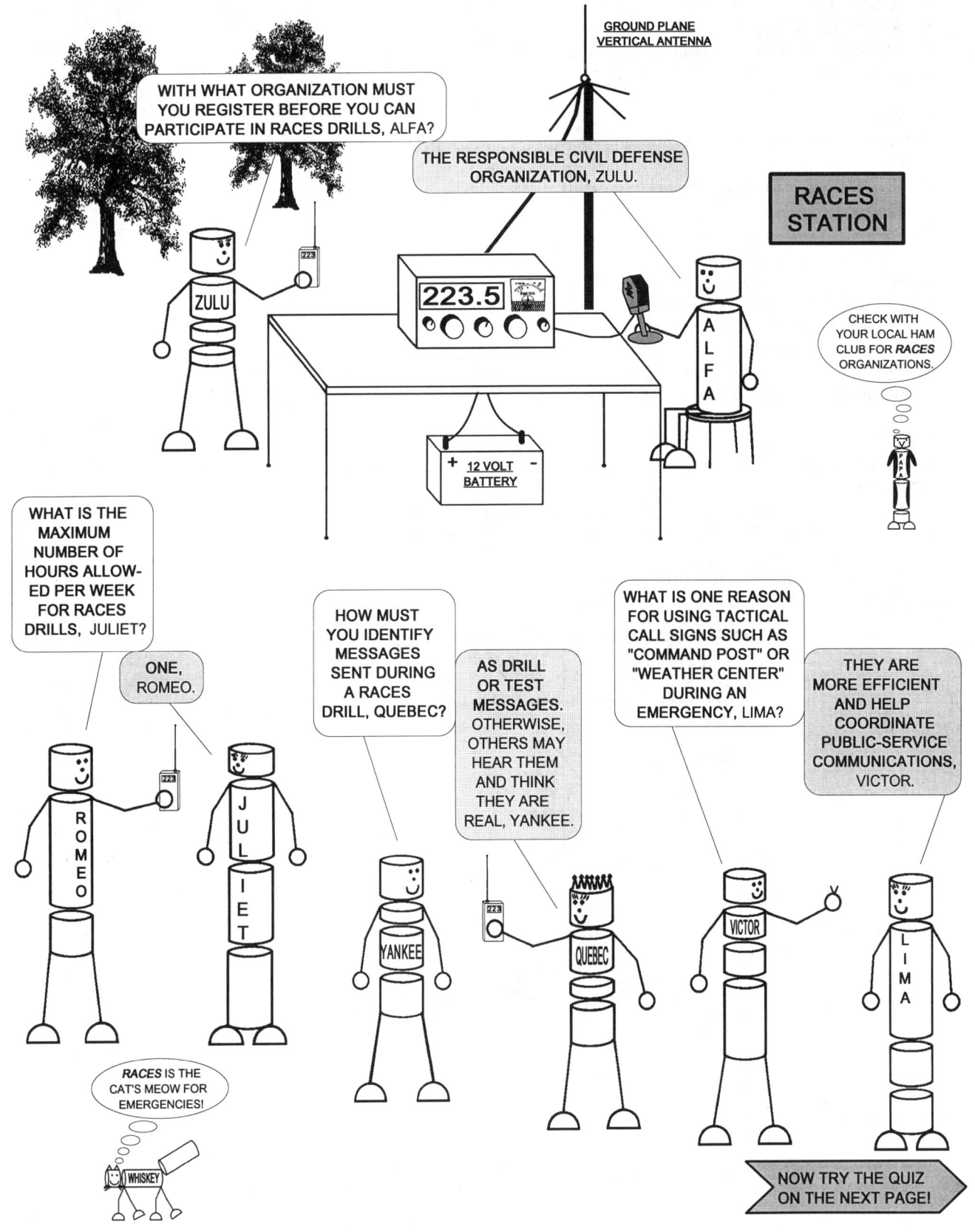

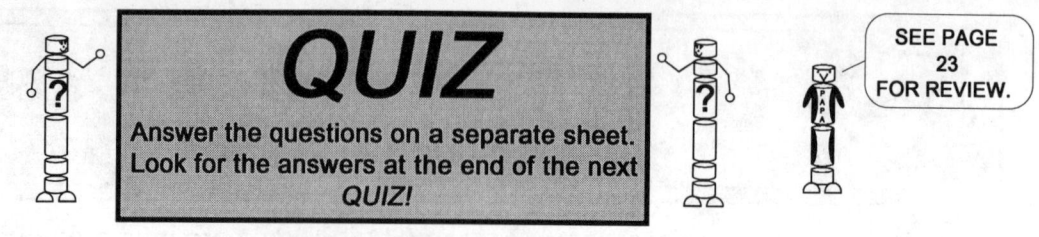

QUIZ

Answer the questions on a separate sheet. Look for the answers at the end of the next QUIZ!

SEE PAGE 23 FOR REVIEW.

T2C04
With what organization must you register before you can participate in RACES drills?
A. A local Amateur Radio club
B. A local racing organization
C. The responsible civil defense organization
D. The Federal Communications Commission

T2C05
What is the maximum number of hours allowed per week for RACES drills?
A. One
B. Six, but not more than one hour per day
C. Eight
D. As many hours as you want

T2C06
How must you identify messages sent during a RACES drill?
A. As emergency messages
B. As amateur traffic
C. As official government messages
D. As drill or test messages

T2C07
What is one reason for using tactical call signs such as "command post" or "weather center" during an emergency?
A. They keep the general public informed about what is going on
B. They are more efficient and help coordinate public-service communications
C. They are required by the FCC
D. They increase goodwill between amateurs

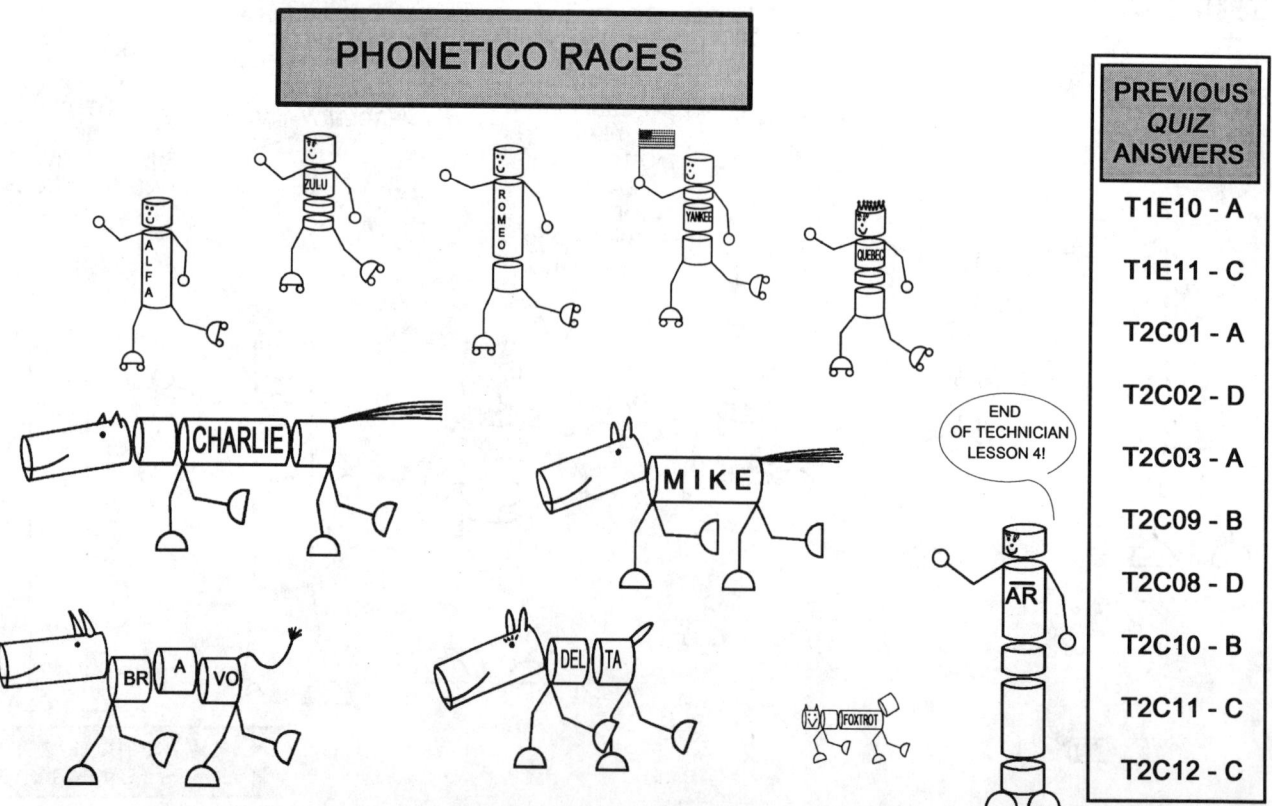

PHONETICO RACES

END OF TECHNICIAN LESSON 4!

PREVIOUS QUIZ ANSWERS
T1E10 - A
T1E11 - C
T2C01 - A
T2C02 - D
T2C03 - A
T2C09 - B
T2C08 - D
T2C10 - B
T2C11 - C
T2C12 - C

CONTROL POINT & LICENSE RENEWAL
TECHNICIAN LESSON 5

The control point of an amateur station is very important. The licensee must always make sure that the station is operated according to all Federal Communications Commission (FCC) rules.

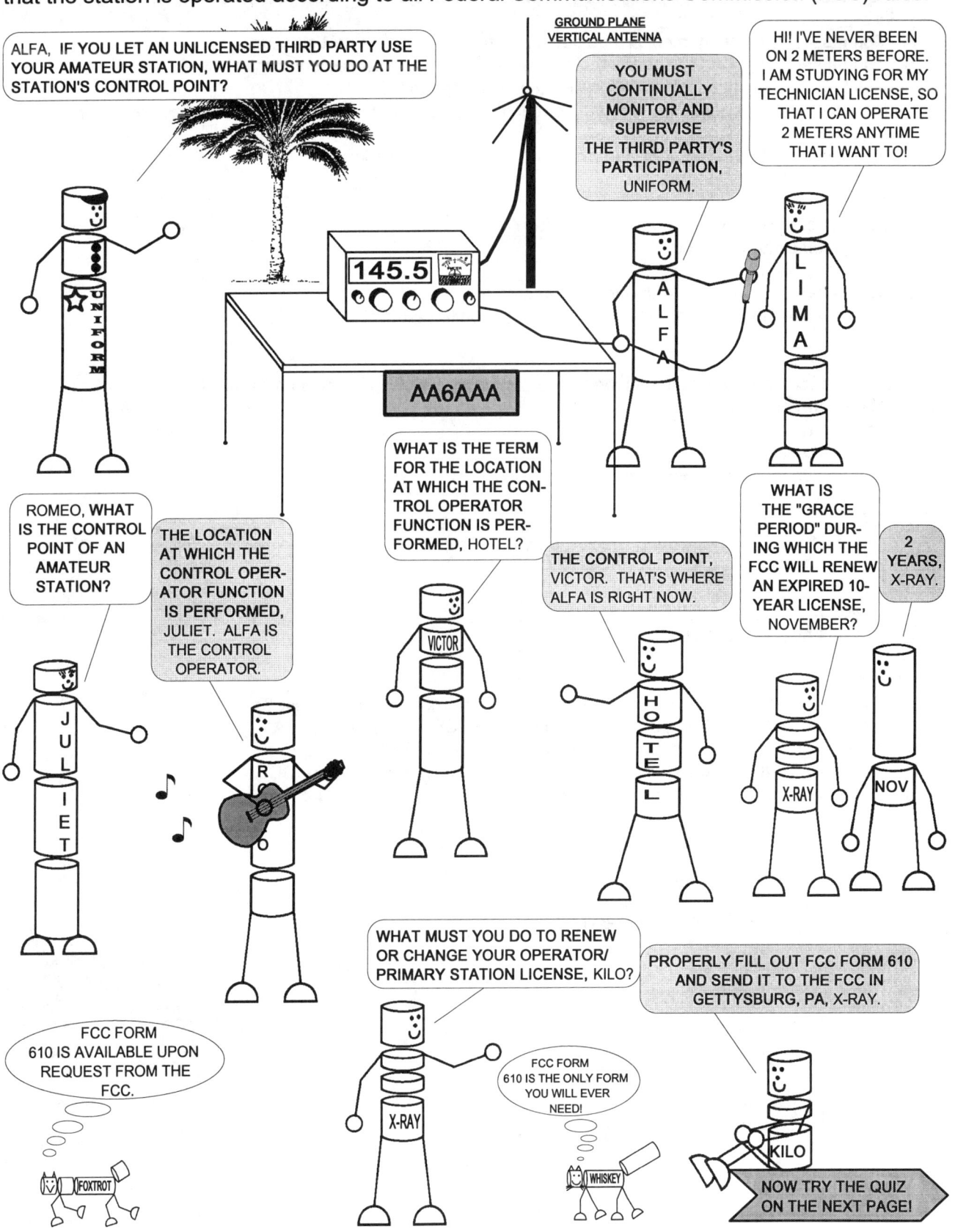

QUIZ

Answer the questions on a separate sheet. Look for the answers at the end of the next QUIZ!

SEE PAGES 25 & 27 FOR REVIEW.

T1E09
If you let an unlicensed third party use your amateur station, what must you do at your station's control point?
A. You must continuously monitor and supervise the third party's participation
B. You must monitor and supervise the communication only if contacts are made in countries which have no third-party communications agreement with the US
C. You must monitor and supervise the communication only if contacts are made on frequencies below 30 MHz
D. You must key the transmitter and make the station identification

T1A01
What is the control point of an amateur station?
A. The on/off switch of the transmitter
B. The input/output port of a packet controller
C. The variable frequency oscillator of a transmitter
D. The location at which the control operator function is performed

T1A02
What is the term for the location at which the control operator function is performed?
A. The operating desk
B. The control point
C. The station location
D. The manual control location

T1A04
What is the "grace period" during which the FCC will renew an expired 10-year license?
A. 2 years
B. 5 years
C. 10 years
D. There is no grace period

T1A03
What must you do to renew or change your operator/primary station license?
A. Properly fill out FCC Form 610 and send it to the FCC in Gettysburg, PA
B. Properly fill out FCC Form 610 and send it to the nearest FCC field office
C. Properly fill out FCC form 610 and send it to the FCC in Washington, DC
D. An amateur license never needs changing or renewing

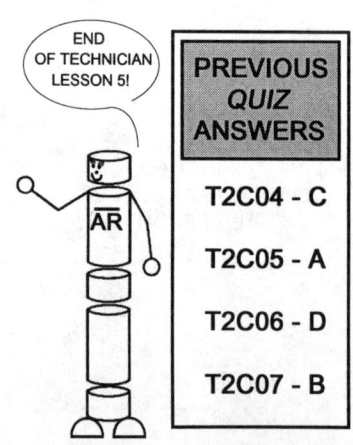

PREVIOUS QUIZ ANSWERS

T2C04 - C

T2C05 - A

T2C06 - D

T2C07 - B

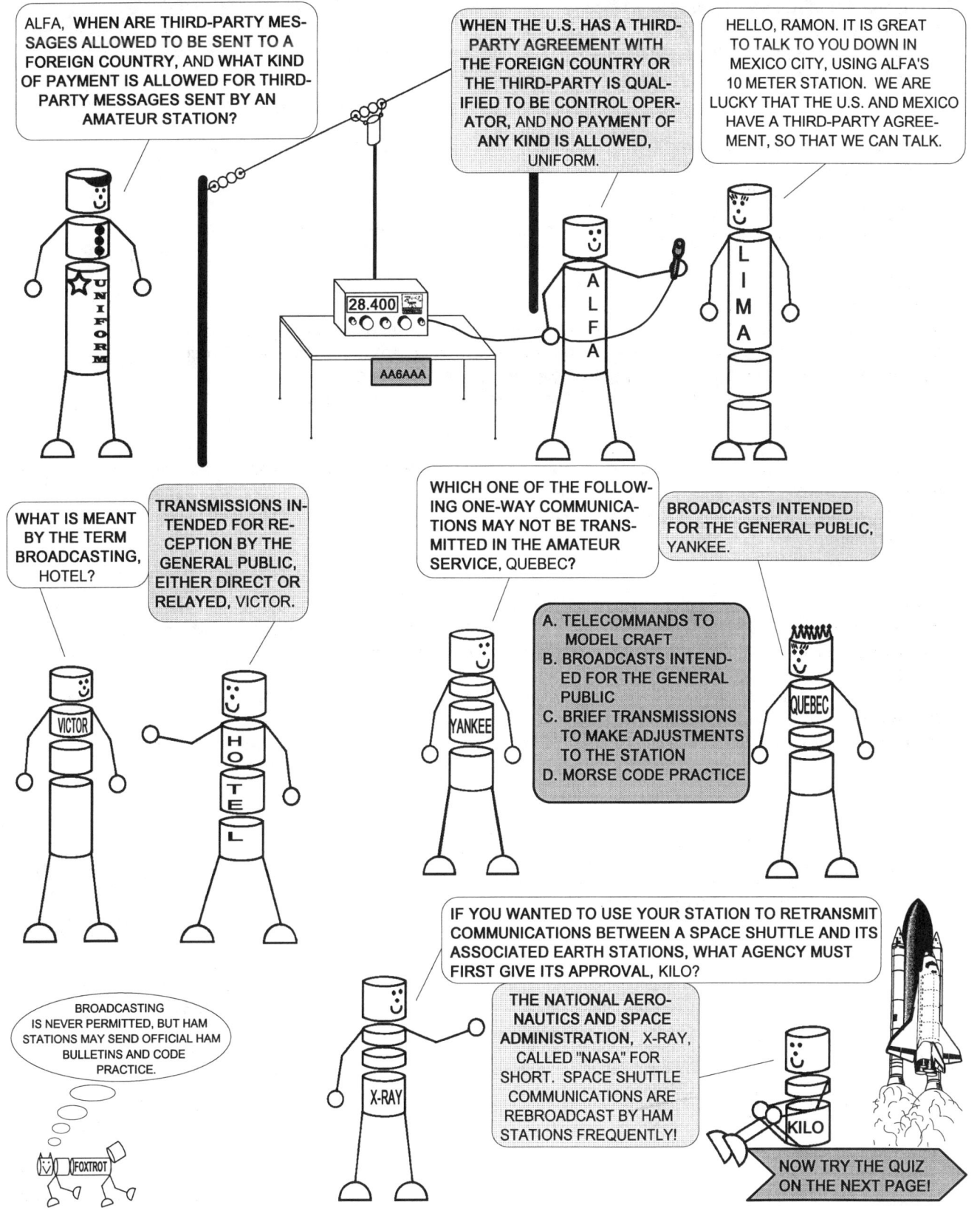

QUIZ

Answer the questions on a separate sheet. Look for the answers at the end of the next QUIZ!

SEE PAGES 35 & 37 FOR REVIEW.

T1E08
When are third-party messages allowed to be sent to a foreign country?
A. When sent by agreement of both control operators
B. When the third party speaks to a relative
C. They are not allowed under any circumstances
D. When the US has a third-party agreement with the foreign country or the third party is qualified to be a control operator

T1E03
What kind of payment is allowed for third-party messages sent by an amateur station?
A. Any amount agreed upon in advance
B. Donation of equipment repairs
C. Donation of amateur equipment
D. No payment of any kind is allowed

T1E01
What is meant by the term broadcasting?
A. Transmissions intended for reception by the general public, either direct or relayed
B. Retransmission by automatic means of programs or signals from non-amateur stations
C. One-way radio communications, regardless of purpose or content
D. One-way or two-way radio communications between two or more stations

T1E02
Which of the following one-way communications may not be transmitted in the amateur service?
A. Telecommands to model craft
B. Broadcasts intended for the general public
C. Brief transmissions to make adjustments to the station
D. Morse code practice

T1E07
If you wanted to use your amateur station to retransmit communications between a space shuttle and its associated Earth stations, what agency must first give its approval?
A. The FCC in Washington, DC
B. The office of your local FCC Engineer In Charge (EIC)
C. The National Aeronautics and Space Administration
D. The Department of Defense

THE U.S. HAS A THIRD PARTY AGREEMENT WITH MANY COUNTRIES, MOSTLY IN THE SOUTHERN HEMISPHERE. FORTUNATELY, WE HAVE AGREEMENTS WITH OUR NEIGHBORS, CANADA AND MEXICO!

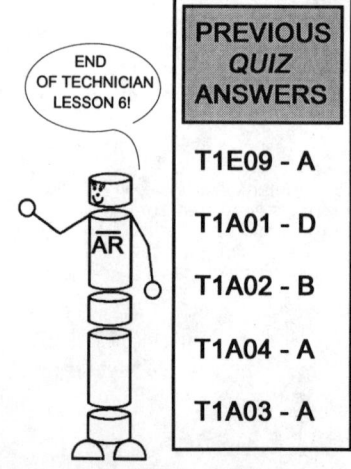

END OF TECHNICIAN LESSON 6!

PREVIOUS QUIZ ANSWERS

T1E09 - A
T1A01 - D
T1A02 - B
T1A04 - A
T1A03 - A

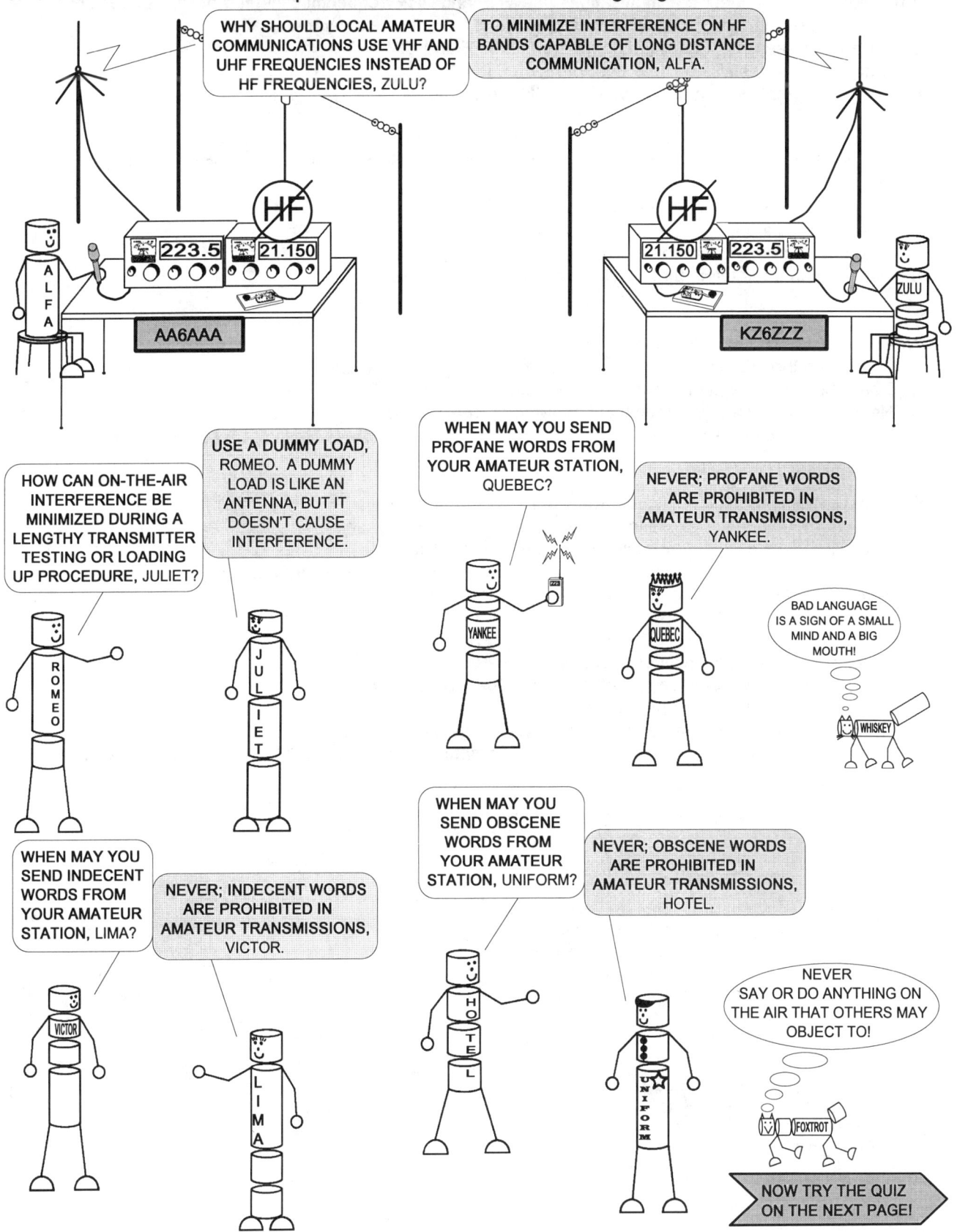

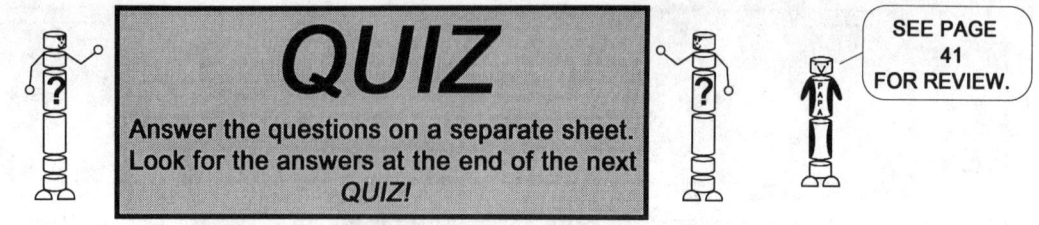

T2A15
Why should local amateur communications use VHF and UHF frequencies instead of HF frequencies?
A. To minimize interference on HF bands capable of long distance communication
B. Because greater output power is permitted on VHF and UHF
C. Because HF transmissions are not propagated locally
D. Because signals are louder on VHF and UHF frequencies

T2A17
How can on-the-air interference be minimized during a lengthy transmitter testing or loading up procedure?
A. Choose an unoccupied frequency
B. Use a dummy load
C. Use a non-resonant antenna
D. Use a resonant antenna that requires no loading-up procedure

T1E06
When may you send profane words from your amateur station?
A. Only when they do not cause interference to other communications
B. Only when they are not retransmitted through a repeater
C. Never; profane words are prohibited in amateur transmissions
D. Any time, but there is an unwritten rule among amateurs that they should not be used on the air

T1E05
When may you send indecent words from your amateur station?
A. Only when they do not cause interference to other communications
B. Only when they are not retransmitted through a repeater
C. Any time, but there is an unwritten rule among amateurs that they should not be used on the air
D. Never; indecent words are prohibited in amateur transmissions

T1E04
When may you send obscene words from your amateur station?
A. Only when they do not cause interference to other communications
B. Never; obscene words are prohibited in amateur transmissions
C. Only when they are not retransmitted through a repeater
D. Any time, but there is an unwritten rule among amateurs that they should not be used on the air

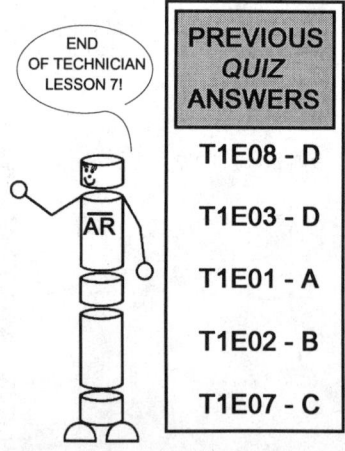

PREVIOUS QUIZ ANSWERS
T1E08 - D
T1E03 - D
T1E01 - A
T1E02 - B
T1E07 - C

DUMMY ANTENNAS
TECHNICIAN LESSON 8

Dummy antennas are used to test the transmitters in transceivers, so that on-the-air interference is eliminated. A dummy antenna consists of a 50 ohm "non-inductive" resistor in a box or can.

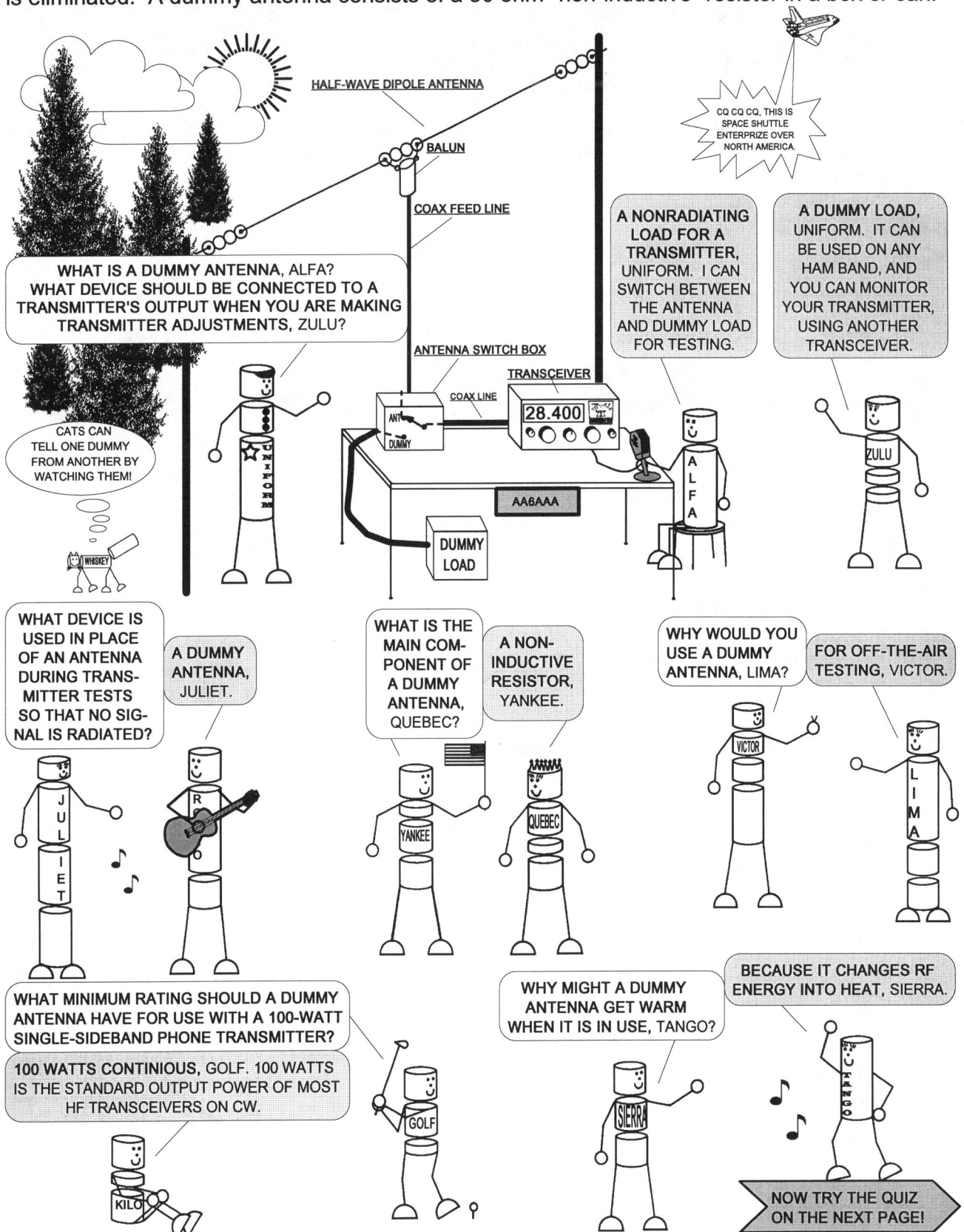

QUIZ

Answer the questions on a separate sheet. Look for the answers at the end of the next QUIZ!

SEE PAGE 41 FOR REVIEW.

T4D02
What is a dummy antenna?
A. An nondirectional transmitting antenna
B. A nonradiating load for a transmitter
C. An antenna used as a reference for gain measurements
D. A flexible antenna usually used on hand held transceivers

T4D01
What device should be connected to a transmitter's output when you are making transmitter adjustments?
A. A multimeter
B. A reflectometer
C. A receiver
D. A dummy antenna

T4D04
What device is used in place of an antenna during transmitter tests so that no signal is radiated?
A. An antenna matcher
B. A dummy antenna
C. A low-pass filter
D. A decoupling resistor

T4D03
What is the main component of a dummy antenna?
A. A wire-wound resistor
B. An iron-core coil
C. A noninductive resistor
D. An air-core coil

T4D05
Why would you use a dummy antenna?
A. For off-the-air transmitter testing
B. To reduce output power
C. To give comparative signal reports
D. To allow antenna tuning without causing interference

T4D06
What minimum rating should a dummy antenna have for use with a 100-watt single-sideband phone transmitter?
A. 100 watts continuous
B. 141 watts continuous
C. 175 watts continuous
D. 200 watts continuous

T4D07
Why might a dummy antenna get warm when in use?
A. Because it stores electric current
B. Because it stores radio waves
C. Because it absorbs static electricity
D. Because it changes RF energy into heat

END OF TECHNICIAN LESSON 8!

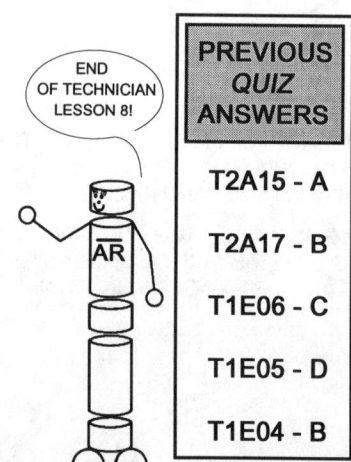

PREVIOUS QUIZ ANSWERS

T2A15 - A

T2A17 - B

T1E06 - C

T1E05 - D

T1E04 - B

FM REPEATER OPERATION

TECHNICIAN LESSON 9

FM Repeaters are usually located on mountain tops, and increase the range of handheld radios up to one hundred miles or more. Repeaters are located all over the world, and are maintained by dedicated individuals.

TIME-OUT TIMER REPEATER

- **WHAT IS THE PURPOSE OF REPEATER OPERATION, ALFA?** — TO HELP MOBILE AND LOW POWER STATIONS EXTEND THEIR USABLE RANGE, ZULU.
- **WHY SHOULD YOU PAUSE BRIEFLY BETWEEN TRANSMISSIONS WHEN USING A REPEATER, QUEBEC?** — TO LISTEN FOR ANYONE WANTING TO BREAK IN, YANKEE.
- **HOW DO YOU CALL ANOTHER STATION ON A REPEATER IF YOU KNOW THE STATION'S CALL SIGN?** — SAY THE STATION'S CALL SIGN, THEN IDENTIFY YOUR OWN STATION, ROMEO.
- **WHY SHOULD YOU KEEP TRANSMISSIONS SHORT WHEN USING A REPEATER, LIMA?** — A LONG TRANSMISSION MAY PREVENT SOMEONE WITH AN EMERGENCY FROM USING THE REPEATER, VICTOR.
- **WHAT IS THE PROPER WAY TO BREAK INTO A CONVERSATION ON A REPEATER, HOTEL?** — SAY YOUR CALL SIGN DURING A BREAK BETWEEN TRANSMISSIONS, UNIFORM.
- **WHAT CAUSES A REPEATER TO TIME OUT, KILO?** — SOMEONE'S TRANSMISSION GOES ON LONGER THAN THE REPEATER ALLOWS, GOLF.
- **DURING COMMUTING RUSH HOURS, WHAT TYPE OF REPEATER OPERATION SHOULD BE DISCOURAGED, X-RAY?** — THIRD-PARTY COMMUNICATIONS NETS, NOVEMBER.
- **WHAT IS A COURTESY TONE (USED IN REPEATER OPERATIONS), THREE?** — A SOUND USED TO INDICATE WHEN A TRANSMISSION IS COMPLETE, SEVEN.
- **WHAT IS THE MEANING OF: "YOUR SIGNAL IS FULL QUIETING....", TWO?** — YOUR SIGNAL IS STRONG ENOUGH TO OVERCOME ALL RECEIVER NOISE, EIGHT.
- **HOW SHOULD YOU GIVE A SIGNAL REPORT OVER A REPEATER, FIVE?** — SAY THE AMOUNT OF SIGNAL QUIETING INTO THE REPEATER, ZERO.
- **WHAT IS THE PROPER WAY TO ASK SOMEONE THEIR LOCATION WHEN USING A REPEATER, FOUR?** — WHERE ARE YOU, SIX.

USE SIMPLEX WHENEVER YOU CAN TALK DIRECTLY TO THE STATION YOU ARE LOOKING FOR. IT'S GOOD OPERATING!

NOW TRY THE QUIZ ON THE NEXT PAGE!

QUIZ

Answer the questions on a separate sheet. Look for the answers at the end of the next QUIZ!

SEE PAGES 43 & 45 FOR REVIEW.

T2A05
What is the purpose of repeater operation?
A. To cut your power bill by using someone else's higher power system
B. To help mobile and low-power stations extend their usable range
C. To transmit signals for observing propagation and reception
D. To make calls to stores more than 50 miles away

T2A01
How do you call another station on a repeater if you know the station's call sign?
A. Say "break, break 79," then say the station's call sign
B. Say the station's call sign, then identify your own station
C. Say "CQ" three times, then say the station's call sign
D. Wait for the station to call "CQ," then answer it

T2A02
Why should you pause briefly between transmissions when using a repeater?
A. To check the SWR of the repeater
B. To reach for pencil and paper for third-party communications
C. To listen for anyone wanting to break in
D. To dial up the repeater's autopatch

T2A03
Why should you keep transmissions short when using a repeater?
A. A long transmission may prevent someone with an emergency from using the repeater
B. To see if the receiving station operator is still awake
C. To give any listening non-hams a chance to respond
D. To keep long distance charges down

T2A04
What is the proper way to break into a conversation on a repeater?
A. Wait for the end of a transmission and start calling the desired party
B. Shout, "break, break!" to show that you're eager to join the conversation
C. Turn on an amplifier and override whoever is talking
D. Say your call sign during a break between transmissions

T2A06
What causes a repeater to "time out"?
A. The repeater's battery supply runs out
B. Someone's transmission goes on longer than the repeater allows
C. The repeater gets too hot and stops transmitting until its circuitry cools off
D. Something is wrong with the repeater

T2A07
During commuting rush hours, which type of repeater operation should be discouraged?
A. Mobile stations
B. Low-power stations
C. Highway traffic information nets
D. Third-party communications nets

T2A08
What is a courtesy tone (used in repeater operations)?
A. A sound used to identify the repeater
B. A sound used to indicate when a transmission is complete
C. A sound used to indicate that a message is waiting for someone
D. A sound used to activate a receiver in case of severe weather

T2A09
What is the meaning of: "Your signal is full quieting..."?
A. Your signal is strong enough to overcome all receiver noise
B. Your signal has no spurious sounds
C. Your signal is not strong enough to be received
D. Your signal is being received, but no audio is being heard

T2A10
How should you give a signal report over a repeater?
A. Say what your receiver's S-meter reads
B. Always say: "Your signal report is five five..."
C. Say the amount of signal quieting into the repeater
D. Try to imitate the sound quality you are receiving

T2A18
What is the proper way to ask someone their location when using a repeater?
A. What is your QTH
B. What is your 20
C. Where are you
D. Locations are not normally told by radio

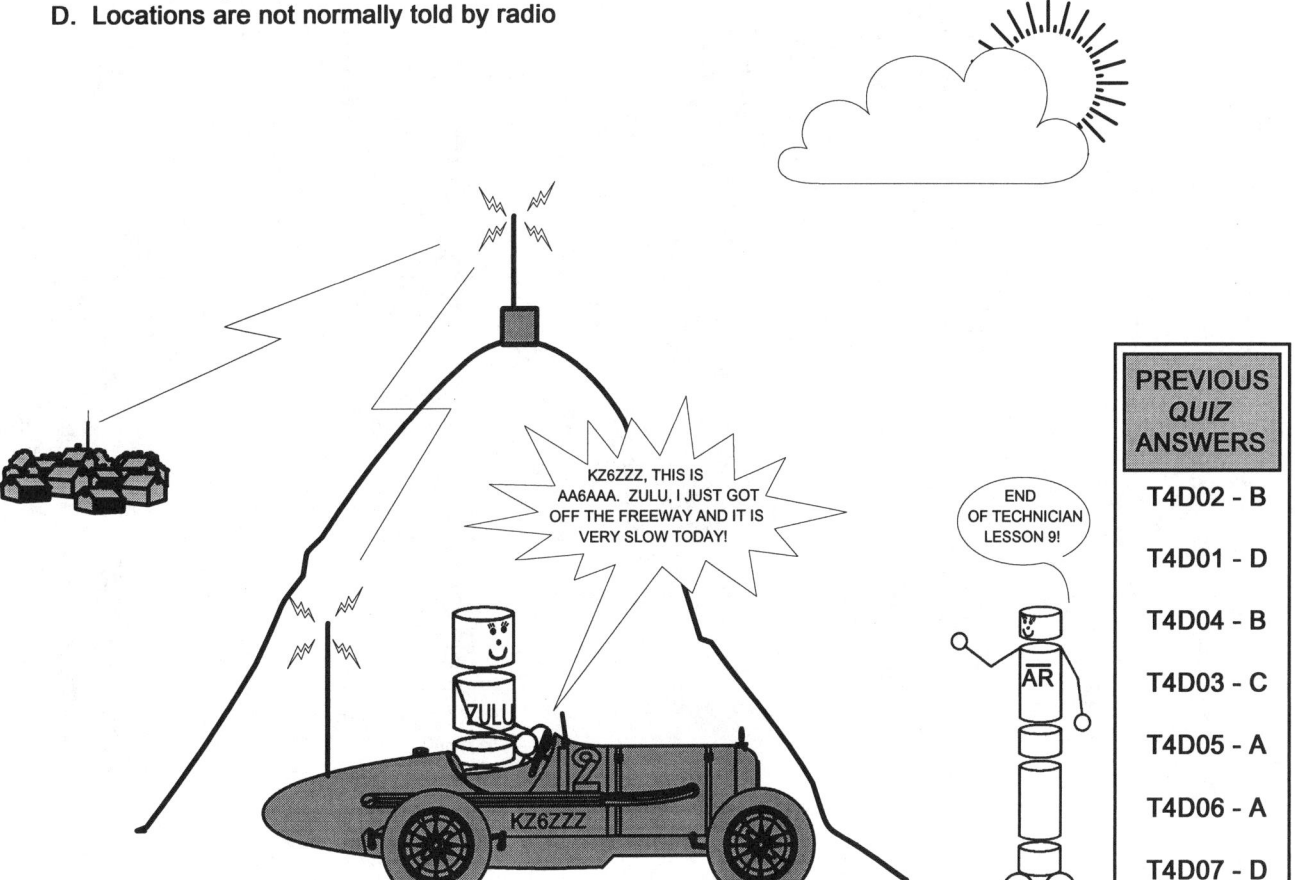

PREVIOUS QUIZ ANSWERS
T4D02 - B
T4D01 - D
T4D04 - B
T4D03 - C
T4D05 - A
T4D06 - A
T4D07 - D

HAM CROSSWORD PUZZLE

Across
1. USED TO ELIMINATE UNWANTED SIGNALS
3. A POOR CONDUCTOR OF ELECTRONS
4. SHARPLY DIRECTIONAL ANTENNA
5. TUNED TO A SINGLE FREQUENCY
7. VOICE LEVEL SETTING FOR AN FM TRANSMITTER
9. DISTANT STATION
11. MEASURES POWER OUTPUT OF TRANSMITTER
13. MEASURE OF CAPACITANCE
14. A VARIABLE RESISTOR
16. AMPLITUDE MODULATION
17. THOUSANDTHS OF AN AMPERE
20. CABLE USED TO CONNECT EQUIPMENT AND ANTENNA
22. ELECTROMOTIVE FORCE OR VOLTAGE
23. 2-WAY CONTACT BETWEEN STATIONS
24. INTERFERENCE ON THE AIR
27. ONE THOUSAND METERS
29. UPPER SIDEBAND
30. WAVES THAT CAN BE HEARD
33. INPUT SIGNAL IS TOO LARGE
34. MORSE CODE OPERATION
36. ELEMENTARY NEGATIVELY CHARGED PARTICLE IN ALL MATTER
38. READABILITY, STRENGTH, AND TONE
39. THE FLOW OF ELECTRONS IN A CONDUCTOR
41. RATIO OF VOLTAGE TO CURRENT IN OHMS
44. VERIFICATION OF CONTACT OR 'QSO'

Down
1. PROTECTS CIRCUITS FROM HIGH CURRENTS
2. EMERGENCY CALL FOR HELP
4. RANGE OF FREQUENCIES OF NEARLY THE SAME WAVELENGTH
6. CONNECTION OF STATIONS TOGETHER
7. REBROADCASTS RECEIVED DIGITAL SIGNALS
8. VERY HIGH FREQUENCY
10. MEASURE OF WAVELENGTH
12. MEASURE OF CURRENT IN A CIRCUIT
15. TELEVISION INTERFERENCE
17. CHANGES HUMAN VOICE TO ELECTRICAL SIGNAL
18. COMPUTER RADIO COMMUNICATION MODE
19. ALTERNATING CURRENT
21. DISCOVERED LAW FOR ELECTRICAL CIRCUITS
25. UNSEEN ELECTROMAGNETIC WAVES
26. LOWER SIDEBAND
28. RADIO WAVE REFLECTING LAYER ABOVE THE EARTH
31. ORBITING SATELLITE CARRYING AMATEUR RADIO
32. REBROADCASTS RECEIVED RADIO SIGNALS
35. SHORT FOR MORSE CODE OR CW
37. RADIO INTERFERENCE CAUSED BY UNFILTERED CW KEYING
40. ULTRA HIGH FREQUENCY
42. PEAK ENVELOPE POWER
43. DIRECT CURRENT

Word List
AC
AM
AMPERE
AUDIO
BAND
BEAM
CLICKS
COAX
CODE
COMMUNICATION
CURRENT
CW
DC
DEVIATION
DIGIPEATER
DX
ELECTRON
EMF
FARAD
FILTER
FUSE
IMPEDANCE
INSULATOR
IONOSPHERE
KILOMETER
LSB
MAYDAY
METER
MICROPHONE
MILLIAMPERES
NETWORK
OHM
OSCAR
OVERLOAD
PACKET
PEP
POTENTIOMETER
QRM
QSL
RADIATION
REPEATER
RESONANT
RST
TVI
UHF
USB
VHF
WATTMETER

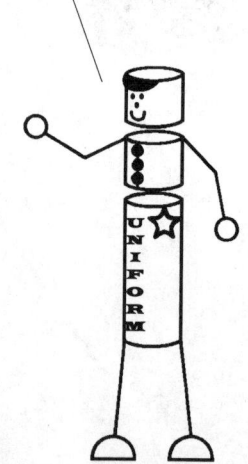

THIS PUZZLE HAS SOME INTERESTING WORDS THAT YOU SHOULD KNOW!

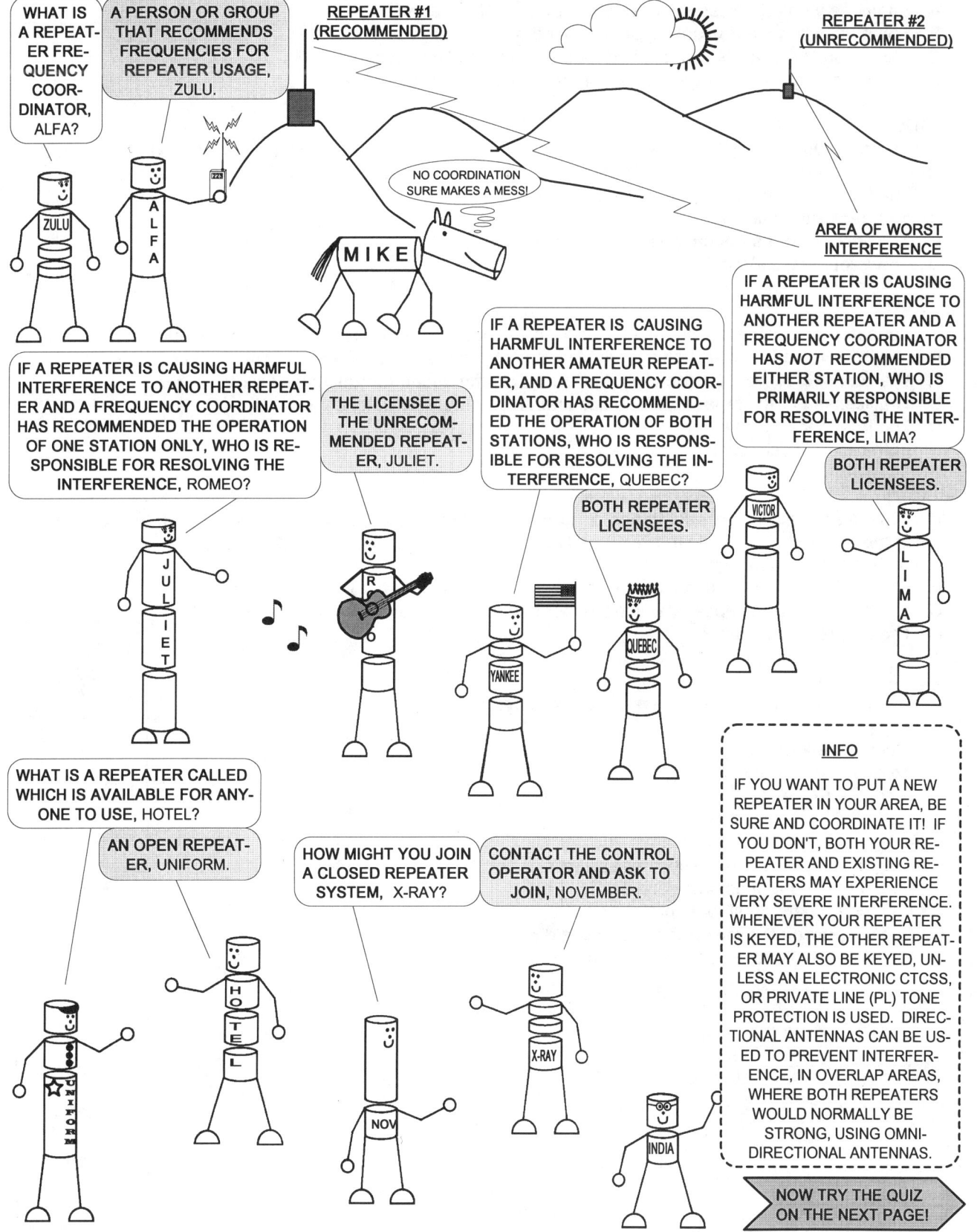

QUIZ

Answer the questions on a separate sheet. Look for the answers at the end of the next QUIZ!

SEE PAGES 43 & 45 FOR REVIEW.

T2B04
What is a repeater frequency coordinator?
A. Someone who organizes the assembly of a repeater station
B. Someone who provides advice on what kind of repeater to buy
C. The person whose call sign is used for a repeater's identification
D. A person or group that recommends frequencies for repeater usage

T1D06
If a repeater is causing harmful interference to another repeater and a frequency coordinator has recommended the operation of one station only, who is responsible for resolving the interference?
A. The licensee of the unrecommended repeater
B. Both repeater licensees
C. The licensee of the recommended repeater
D. The frequency coordinator

T1D07
If a repeater is causing harmful interference to another amateur repeater and a frequency coordinator has recommended the operation of both stations, who is responsible for resolving the interference?
A. The licensee of the repeater which has been recommended for the longest period of time
B. The licensee of the repeater which has been recommended the most recently
C. The frequency coordinator
D. Both repeater licensees

T1D08
If a repeater is causing harmful interference to another repeater and a frequency coordinator has NOT recommended either station, who is primarily responsible for resolving the interference?
A. Both repeater licensees
B. The licensee of the repeater which has been in operation for the longest period of time
C. The licensee of the repeater which has been in operation for the shortest period of time
D. The frequency coordinator

T2A11
What is a repeater called which is available for anyone to use?
A. An open repeater
B. A closed repeater
C. An autopatch repeater
D. A private repeater

T2A16
How might you join a closed repeater system?
A. Contact the control operator and ask to join
B. Use the repeater until told not to
C. Use simplex on the repeater input until told not to
D. Write the FCC and report the closed condition

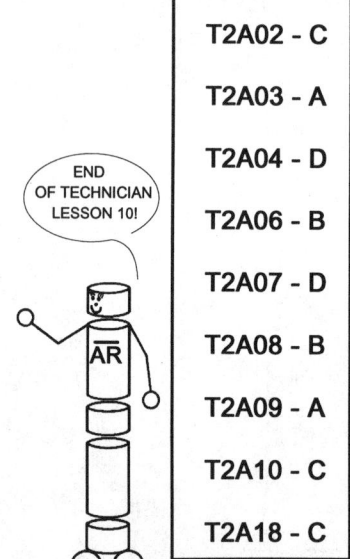

END OF TECHNICIAN LESSON 10!

PREVIOUS QUIZ ANSWERS

T2A05 - B
T2A01 - B
T2A02 - C
T2A03 - A
T2A04 - D
T2A06 - B
T2A07 - D
T2A08 - B
T2A09 - A
T2A10 - C
T2A18 - C

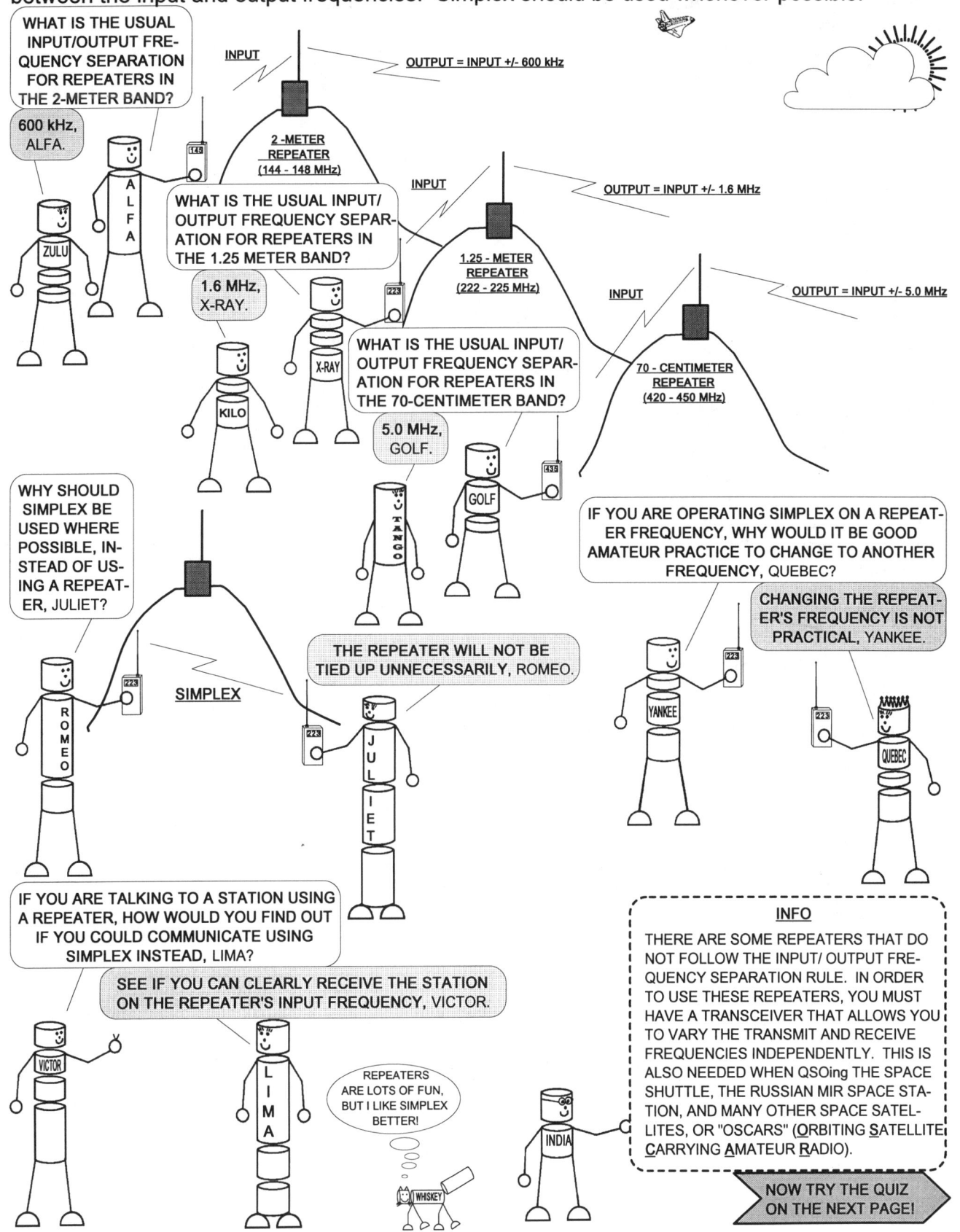

QUIZ

Answer the questions on a separate sheet. Look for the answers at the end of the next QUIZ!

SEE PAGES 43 & 45 FOR REVIEW.

T2A12
What is the usual input/output frequency separation for repeaters in the 2-meter band?
A. 600 kHz
B. 1.0 MHz
C. 1.6 MHz
D. 5.0 MHz

T2A13
What is the usual input/output frequency separation for repeaters in the 1.25-meter band?
A. 600 kHz
B. 1.0 MHz
C. 1.6 MHz
D. 5.0 MHz

T2A14
What is the usual input/output frequency separation for repeaters in the 70-centimeter band?
A. 600 kHz
B. 1.0 MHz
C. 1.6 MHz
D. 5.0 MHz

T2B01
Why should simplex be used where possible, instead of using a repeater?
A. Signal range will be increased
B. Long distance toll charges will be avoided
C. The repeater will not be tied up unnecessarily
D. Your antenna's effectiveness will be better tested

T2B02
If you are talking to a station using a repeater, how would you find out if you could communicate using simplex instead?
A. See if you can clearly receive the station on the repeater's input frequency
B. See if you can clearly receive the station on a lower frequency band
C. See if you can clearly receive a more distant repeater
D. See if a third station can clearly receive both of you

T2B03
If you are operating simplex on a repeater frequency, why would it be good amateur practice to change to another frequency?
A. The repeater's output power may ruin your station's receiver
B. There are more repeater operators than simplex operators
C. Changing the repeater's frequency is not practical
D. Changing the repeater's frequency requires the authorization of the FCC

PREVIOUS QUIZ ANSWERS

T2A12 - A
T2A13 - C
T2A14 - D
T1B01 - C
T1B03 - B
T1B02 - D

END OF TECHNICIAN LESSON 11!

CW & DATA MODULATION & EMISSIONS
TECHNICIAN LESSON 12

A radio wave can be varied in several different ways, called "modulation", to transmit information.

WHAT IS THE NAME FOR UNMODULATED CARRIER WAVE EMISSIONS, ZULU?

CW, ALFA. THIS MEANS "CONTINOUS WAVE".

UNMODULATED CARRIER WAVE

WHAT IS ANOTHER NAME FOR A CONSTANT-AMPLITUDE RADIO-FREQUENCY SIGNAL, KILO?

AN RF CARRIER, X-RAY. IT HAS NO INFORMATION!

WHAT IS MODULATION, JULIET?

VARYING A RADIO WAVE IN SOME WAY TO SEND INFORMATION.

WHAT IS THE NAME FOR MORSE CODE EMISSIONS PRODUCED BY SWITCHING A TRANSMITTER'S OUTPUT ON AND OFF, QUEBEC?

CW, YANKEE.

DIT   DAH = "A"
CW MORSE CODE LETTER "A"

WHAT IS THE NAME FOR EMISSIONS PRODUCED BY AN ON/OFF KEYED TONE INTO A TRANSMITTER?

MCW, VICTOR.

MCW ALSO STANDS FOR "MEOW CW", WHEN I MEOW IN THE MICROPHONE!

HOW IS TONE-MODULATED MORSE CODE PRODUCED, NOVEMBER?

BY FEEDING AN ON/OFF KEYED AUDIO TONE INTO A TRANSMITTER, GOLF.

AUDIO OSCILLATOR   223.5

MCW
(MIKE DISCONNECTED)

FREQUENCY SHIFT KEYING

WHAT IS RTTY, TWO?

0 1 0 0 1 0 0 1 0
DIGITAL WORD

FREQUENCY SHIFT KEYING HAS 2 DIFFERENT FREQUENCIES FOR "1'S" & "0'S".

FREQUENCY-SHIFT KEYED TELEGRAPHY, NINE. THIS IS WHAT IT LOOKS LIKE.

WHAT IS THE NAME FOR PACKET-RADIO EMISSIONS, THREE?

DATA, SEVEN.

HOW WOULD YOU MODULATE A 2-METER FM TRANSCEIVER TO PRODUCE PACKET-RADIO EMISSIONS, TANGO

CONNECT A TERMINAL-NODE-CONTROLLER TO THE TRANSCEIVER'S MICROPHONE INPUT, SIERRA.

NOW TRY THE QUIZ ON THE NEXT PAGE!

QUIZ

SEE PAGES 47, 49, 53, & 55 FOR REVIEW.

Answer the questions on a separate sheet. Look for the answers at the end of the next QUIZ!

T8A01
What is the name for unmodulated carrier wave emissions?
A. Phone
B. Test
C. CW
D. RTTY

T8B01
What is another name for a constant-amplitude radio-frequency signal?
A. An RF carrier
B. An AF carrier
C. A sideband carrier
D. A subcarrier

T8B02
What is modulation?
A. Varying a radio wave in some way to send information
B. Receiving audio information from a signal
C. Increasing the power of a transmitter
D. Suppressing the carrier in a single-sideband transmitter

T8A02
What is the name for Morse code emissions produced by switching a transmitter's output on and off?
A. Phone
B. Test
C. CW
D. RTTY

T8A05
How is tone-modulated Morse code produced?
A. By feeding a microphone's audio signal into an FM transmitter
B. By feeding an on/off keyed audio tone into a CW transmitter
C. By on/off keying of a carrier
D. By feeding an on/off keyed audio tone into a transmitter

T8A11
What is the name for emissions produced by an on/off keyed audio tone?
A. RTTY
B. MCW
C. CW
D. Phone

T8A03
What is RTTY?
A. Amplitude-keyed telegraphy
B. Frequency-shift-keyed telegraphy
C. Frequency-modulated telephony
D. Phase-modulated telephony

T8A04
What is the name for packet-radio emissions?
A. CW
B. Data
C. Phone
D. RTTY

T8B04
How would you modulate a 2-meter FM transceiver to produce packet-radio emissions?
A. Connect a terminal-node-controller to interrupt the transceiver's carrier wave
B. Connect a terminal-node-controller to the transceiver's microphone input
C. Connect a keyboard to the transceiver's microphone input
D. Connect a DTMF key pad to the transceiver's microphone input

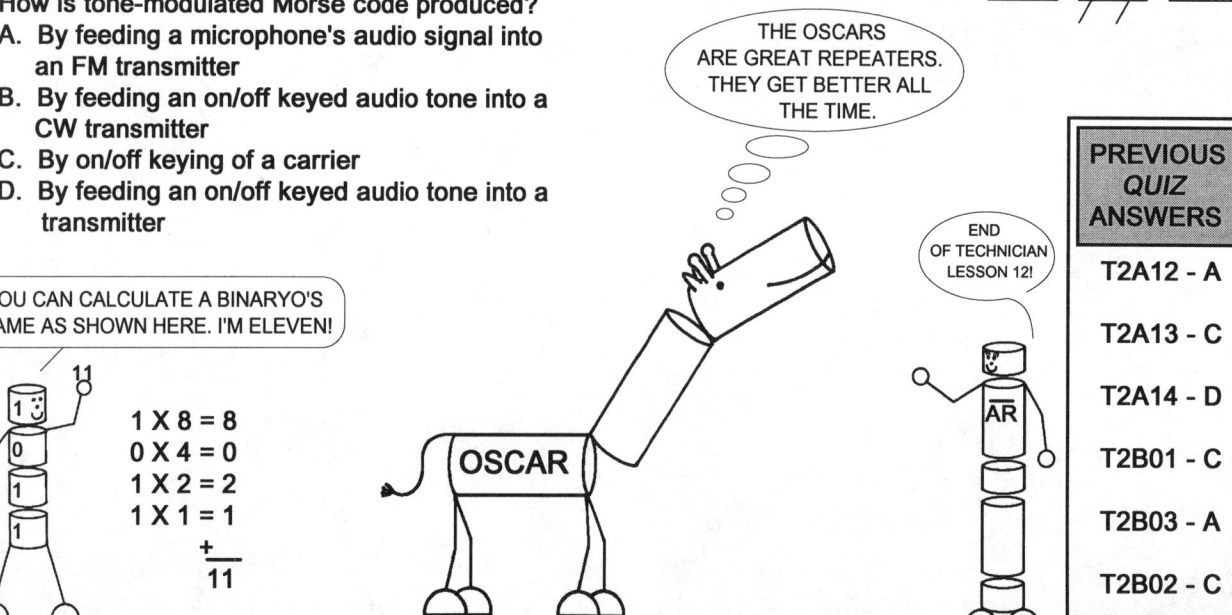

THE OSCARS ARE GREAT REPEATERS. THEY GET BETTER ALL THE TIME.

END OF TECHNICIAN LESSON 12!

YOU CAN CALCULATE A BINARYO'S NAME AS SHOWN HERE. I'M ELEVEN!

1 X 8 = 8
0 X 4 = 0
1 X 2 = 2
1 X 1 = 1
+
11

PREVIOUS QUIZ ANSWERS

T2A12 - A
T2A13 - C
T2A14 - D
T2B01 - C
T2B03 - A
T2B02 - C

VOICE MODULATION & EMISSIONS
TECHNICIAN LESSON 13

Frequency modulation (FM), phase modulation (PM), and single-sideband (SSB) voice operation are used by amateurs for different purposes. They are three different ways of putting the human voice on a radio wave, which has a "frequency", a "phase", and an "amplitude" (SSB) that can be varied.

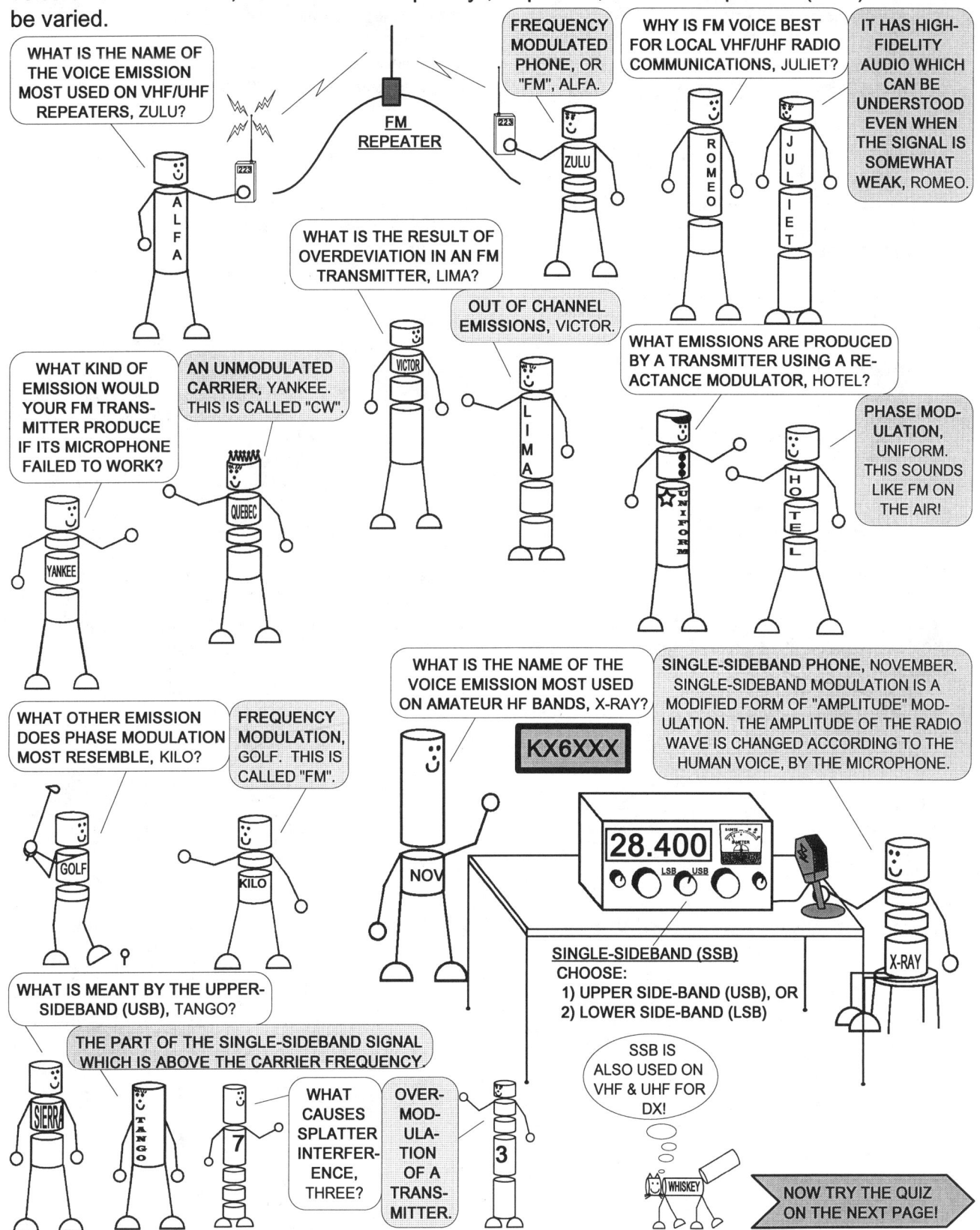

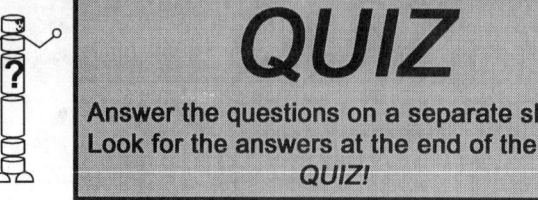

QUIZ

Answer the questions on a separate sheet. Look for the answers at the end of the next QUIZ!

SEE PAGE 51 FOR REVIEW.

T8A06
What is the name of the voice emission most used on VHF/UHF repeaters?
A. Single-sideband phone
B. Pulse-modulated phone
C. Slow-scan phone
D. Frequency modulated phone

T8B05
Why is FM voice best for local VHF/UHF radio communications?
A. The carrier is not detectable
B. It is more resistant to distortion caused by reflected signals
C. It has high-fidelity audio which can be understood even when the signal is somewhat weak
D. Its RF carrier stays on frequency better than the AM modes

T8B03
What kind of emission would your FM transmitter produce if its microphone failed to work?
A. An unmodulated carrier
B. A phase-modulated carrier
C. An amplitude-modulated carrier
D. A frequency-modulated carrier

T8B10
What is the result of overdeviation in an FM transmitter?
A. Increased transmitter power
B. Out-of-channel emissions
C. Increased transmitter range
D. Poor carrier suppression

T8A09
What emissions are produced by a transmitter using a reactance modulator?
A. CW
B. Test
C. Single-sideband, suppressed-carrier phone
D. Phase-modulated phone

T8A10
What other emission does phase modulation most resemble?
A. Amplitude modulation
B. Pulse modulation
C. Frequency modulation
D. Single-sideband modulation

T8A07
What is the name of the voice emission most used on amateur HF bands?
A. Single-sideband phone
B. Pulse-modulated phone
C. Slow-scan phone
D. Frequency modulated phone

T8A08
What is meant by the upper-sideband (USB)?
A. The part of a single-sideband signal which is above the carrier frequency
B. The part of a single-sideband signal which is below the carrier frequency
C. Any frequency above 10 MHz
D. The carrier frequency of a single-sideband signal

T8B11
What causes splatter interference?
A. Keying a transmitter too fast
B. Signals from a transmitter's output circuit are being sent back to its input circuit
C. Overmodulation of a transmitter
D. The transmitting antenna is the wrong length

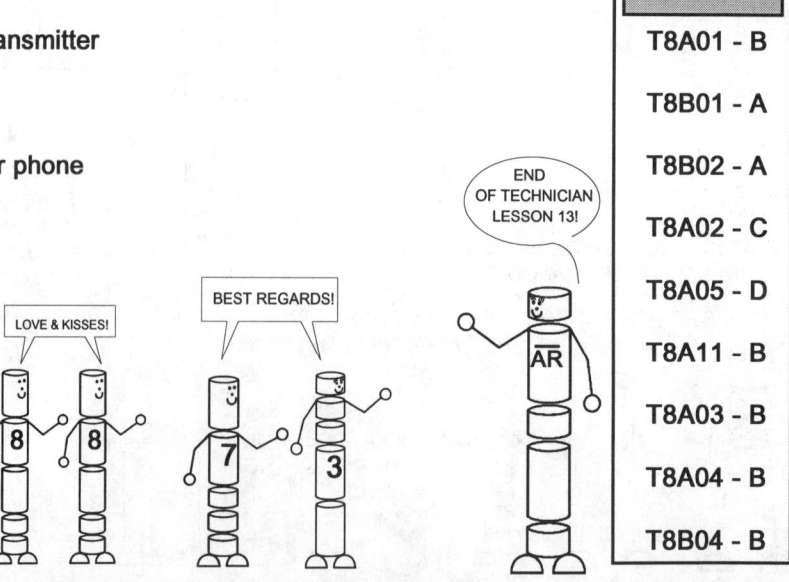

PREVIOUS QUIZ ANSWERS
T8A01 - B
T8B01 - A
T8B02 - A
T8A02 - C
T8A05 - D
T8A11 - B
T8A03 - B
T8A04 - B
T8B04 - B

END OF TECHNICIAN LESSON 13!

DIGITAL SYMBOL RATE
TECHNICIAN LESSON 14

Data can be sent at different speeds, depending on the amateur band that you operate on. The higher the frequency, the greater the data rate, in "bauds"!

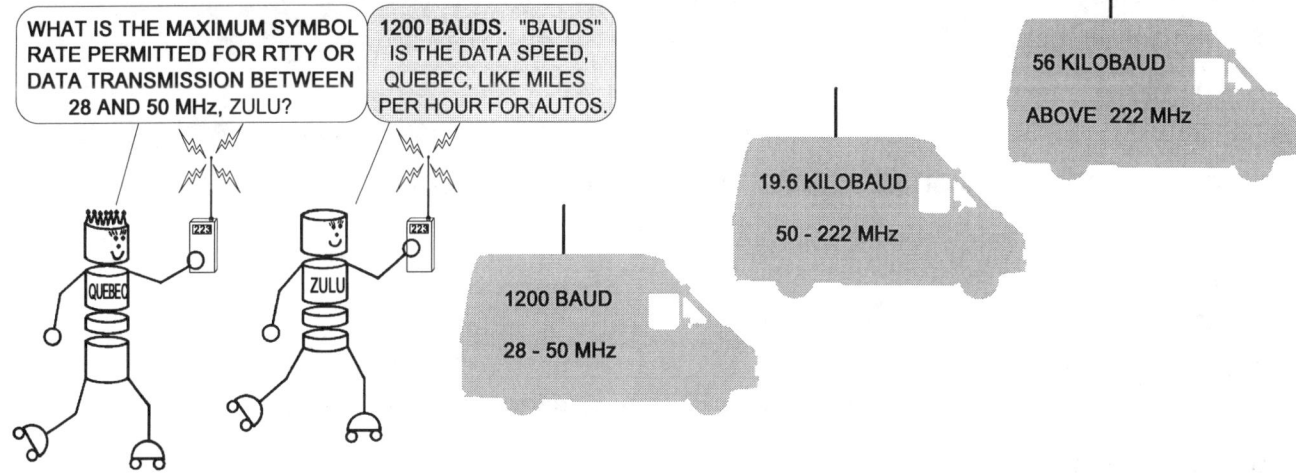

WHAT IS THE MAXIMUM SYMBOL RATE PERMITTED FOR PACKET TRANSMISSIONS ON THE 10-METER BAND, ALFA?

1200 BAUDS. 10 METERS IS 28.0 TO 28.5 MHz, X-RAY.

WHAT IS THE MAXIMUM SYMBOL RATE PERMITTED FOR RTTY OR DATA TRANSMISSIONS BETWEEN 50 AND 222 MHz?

19.6 KILOBAUDS. THIS IS THE SAME AS 19,600 BAUDS, X-RAY.

WHAT IS THE MAXIMUM SYMBOL RATE PERMITTED FOR PACKET TRANSMISSIONS ON THE 2-METER BAND, ALFA?

19.6 KILOBAUDS. 2 METERS IS 144 TO 148 MHz, X-RAY.

WHAT IS THE MAXIMUM SYMBOL RATE PERMITTED FOR RTTY OR DATA TRANSMISSIONS ABOVE 222 MHz, ALFA?

56 KILOBAUDS. THIS IS THE SAME AS 56,000 BAUDS.

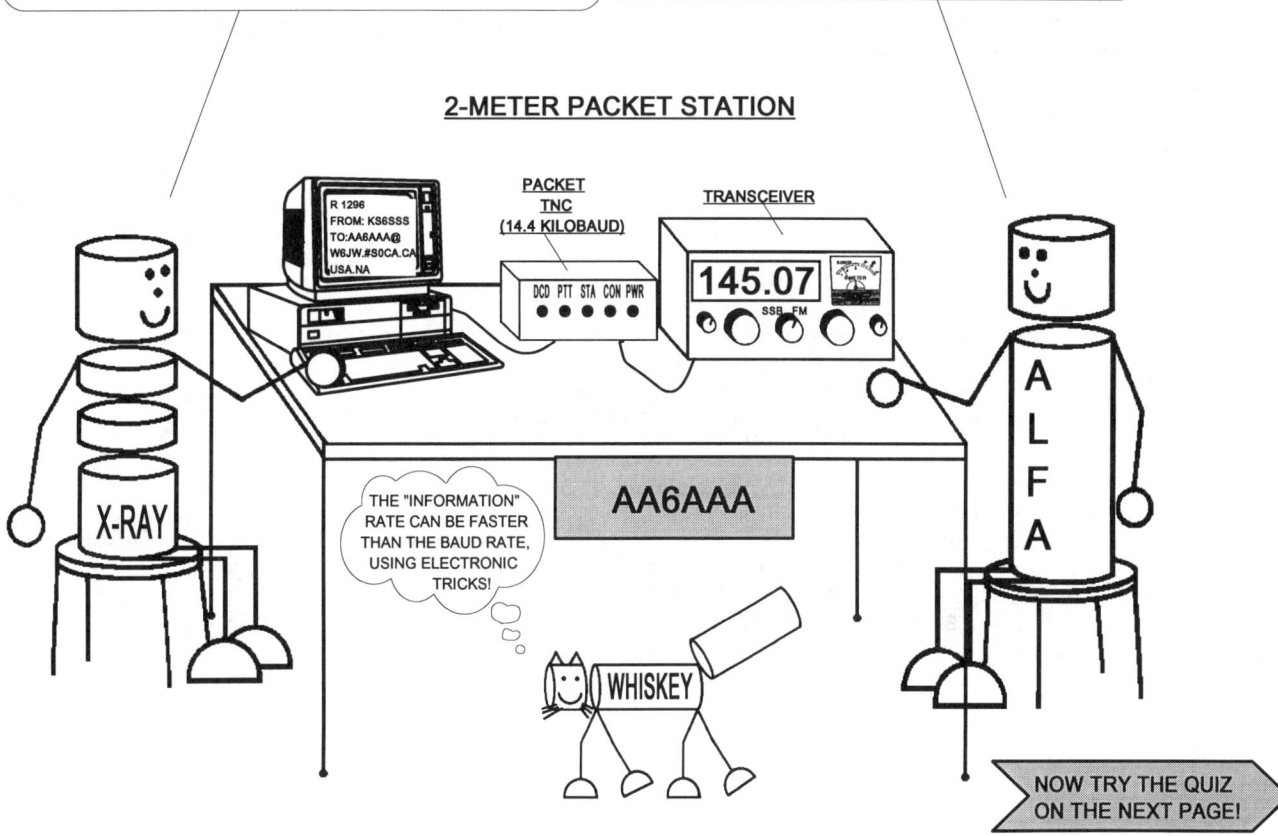

NOW TRY THE QUIZ ON THE NEXT PAGE!

QUIZ

Answer the questions on a separate sheet. Look for the answers at the end of the next QUIZ!

SEE PAGES 53, 55, & 57 FOR REVIEW.

T1C06
What is the maximum symbol rate permitted for RTTY or data transmissions between 28 and 50 MHz?
A. 56 kilobauds
B. 19.6 kilobauds
C. 1200 bauds
D. 300 bauds

T1C04
What is the maximum symbol rate permitted for packet transmissions on the 10-meter band?
A. 300 bauds
B. 1200 bauds
C. 19.6 kilobauds
D. 56 kilobauds

T1C07
What is the maximum symbol rate permitted for RTTY or data transmissions between 50 and 222 MHz?
A. 56 kilobauds
B. 19.6 kilobauds
C. 1200 bauds
D. 300 bauds

T1C05
What is the maximum symbol rate permitted for packet transmissions on the 2-meter band?
A. 300 bauds
B. 1200 bauds
C. 19.6 kilobauds
D. 56 kilobauds

T1C09
What is the maximum symbol rate permitted for RTTY or data transmissions above 222 MHz?
A. 300 bauds
B. 1200 bauds
C. 19.6 kilobauds
D. 56 kilobauds

INFO

PACKET, AND RTTY "DIGITAL" OPERATION, ARE VERY POPULAR, & PACKET IS SIMILAR TO THE INTERNET. ONE DIFFERENCE IS THAT PACKET USES RADIO FREQUENCIES, INSTEAD OF TELEPHONE LINES. PACKET IS USED EXCLUSIVELY FOR PERSONAL, NON-BUSINESS, COMMUNICAITONS, AND IS MORE "FRIENDLY" THAN THE INTERNET. IT IS ALSO MORE PORTABLE. YOU CAN COMMUNICATE WITH YOUR HAND HELD RADIO, A SMALL "TNC", AND A PORTABLE NOTEBOOK COMPUTER, NO MATTER WHERE YOU GO IN THE USA AND THROUGHOUT THE WORLD. MESSAGES ARE RELAYED WORLDWIDE BY DEDICATED "SYSOPS", WHO MAINTAIN A HIGH STANDARD ON THEIR SYSTEMS. PACKET IS USED PRIMARILY ON VHF & UHF. A VARIATION OF IT, CALLED "PACTOR", IS BECOMING VERY POPULAR ON THE HF BANDS, WHERE FADING AND INTERFERENCE MAKE PACKET LESS ERROR FREE THAN ON VHF & UHF. RTTY IS PRIMARILY USED ON THE HF BANDS, AND BEFORE COMPUTERS, CONSISTED OF NOISY MECHANICAL TELEPRINTERS OPERATED BY RADIO CONTROL. TODAY, RTTY OPERATION IS USUALLY DONE USING A COMPUTER AND ITS PRINTER. THERE ARE MANY RTTY STATIONS ON 10 METERS, AND USING A NOVICE OR TECHNICIAN PLUS LICENSE, YOU CAN COMMUNICATE WORLDWIDE WITH RTTY IN "REAL TIME", WHEN THAT BAND IS OPEN.

END OF TECHNICIAN LESSON 14!

PREVIOUS QUIZ ANSWERS

T8A06 - D
T8B05 - C
T8B03 - A
T8B10 - B
T8A09 - D
T8A10 - C
T8A07 - A
T8A08 - A
T8B11 - C

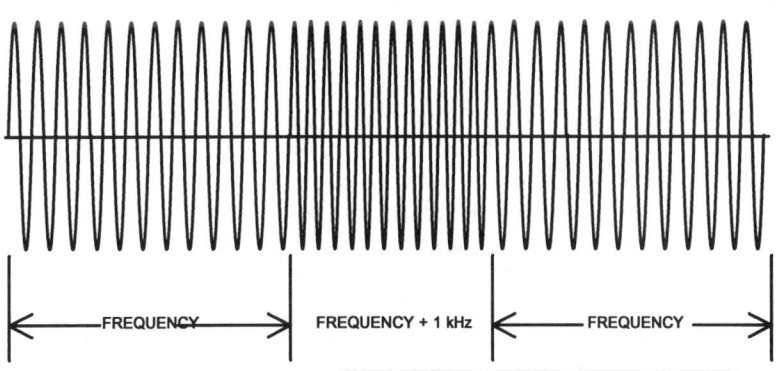

QUIZ

Answer the questions on a separate sheet. Look for the answers at the end of the next QUIZ!

SEE PAGES 53, 55, & 57 FOR REVIEW.

T1C02
What is the maximum frequency shift permitted for RTTY or data transmissions below 50 MHz?
A. 0.1 kHz
B. 0.5 kHz
C. 1 kHz
D. 5 kHz

T1C03
What is the maximum frequency shift permitted for RTTY or data transmissions above 50 MHz?
A. 0.1 kHz or the sending speed, in bauds, whichever is greater
B. 0.5 kHz or the sending speed, in bauds, whichever is greater
C. 5 kHz or the sending speed, in bauds, whichever is greater
D. The FCC rules do not specify a maximum frequency shift above 50 MHz

T1C08
What is the maximum authorized bandwidth of RTTY, data or multiplexed emissions using an unspecified digital code within the frequency range of 50 to 222 MHz?
A. 20 kHz
B. 50 kHz
C. The total bandwidth shall not exceed that of a single-sideband phone emission
D. The total bandwidth shall not exceed 10 times that of a CW emission

T1C10
What is the maximum authorized bandwidth of RTTY, data or multiplexed emissions using an unspecified digital code within the frequency range of 222 to 450 MHz?
A. 50 kHz
B. 100 kHz
C. 150 kHz
D. 200 kHz

T1C11
What is the maximum authorized bandwidth of RTTY, data or multiplexed emissions using an unspecified digital code within the 70 cm amateur band?
A. 300 kHz
B. 200 kHz
C. 100 kHz
D. 50 kHz

THE HIGHER THE FREQUENCY, THE GREATER THE BANDWIDTH ALLOWED BY THE FCC. THAT'S BECAUSE THE VHF AND UHF BANDS ARE BIG!

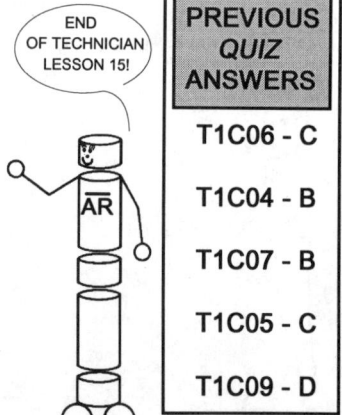

END OF TECHNICIAN LESSON 15!

PREVIOUS QUIZ ANSWERS

T1C06 - C
T1C04 - B
T1C07 - B
T1C05 - C
T1C09 - D

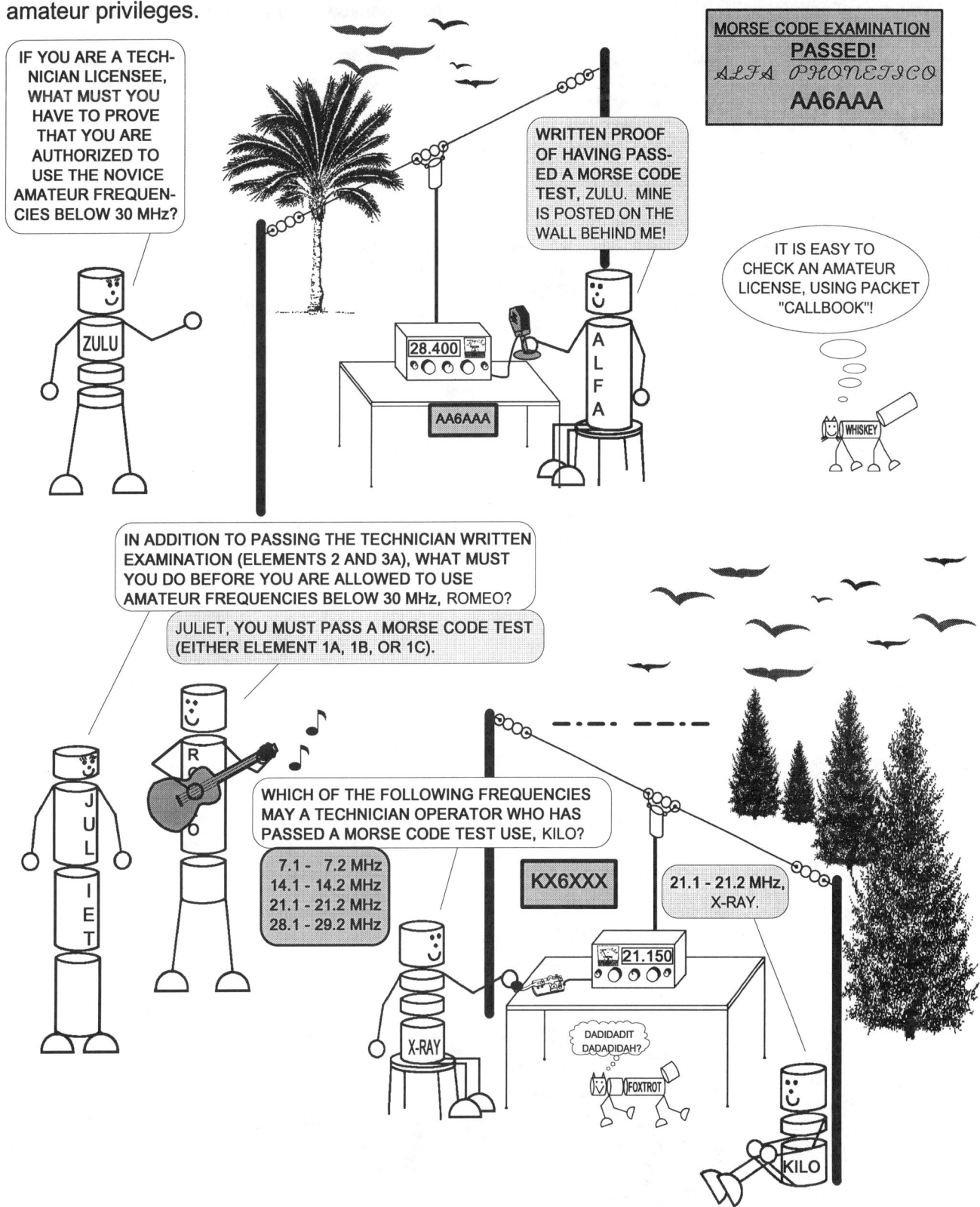

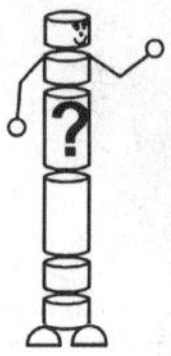

QUIZ

Answer the questions on a separate sheet. Look for the answers at the end of the next QUIZ!

SEE PAGES 67 & 71 FOR REVIEW.

T1A11
If you are a Technician licensee, what must you have to prove that you are authorized to use the Novice amateur frequencies below 30 MHz?
A. A certificate from the FCC showing that you have notified them that you will be using the HF bands
B. A certificate from an instructor showing that you have attended a class in HF communications
C. Written proof of having passed a Morse code test
D. No special proof is required before using the HF bands

T1A10
In addition to passing the Technician written examination (Elements 2 and 3A), what must you do before you are allowed to use amateur frequencies below 30 MHz?
A. Nothing special is needed; all Technicians may use the HF bands at any time
B. You must notify the FCC that you intend to operate on the HF bands
C. You must attend a class to learn about HF communications
D. You must pass a Morse code test (either Element 1A, 1B or 1C)

T1A05
Which of the following frequencies may a Technician operator who has passed a Morse code test use?
A. 7.1 - 7.2 MHz
B. 14.1 - 14.2 MHz
C. 21.1 - 21.2 MHz
D. 28.1 - 29.2 MHz

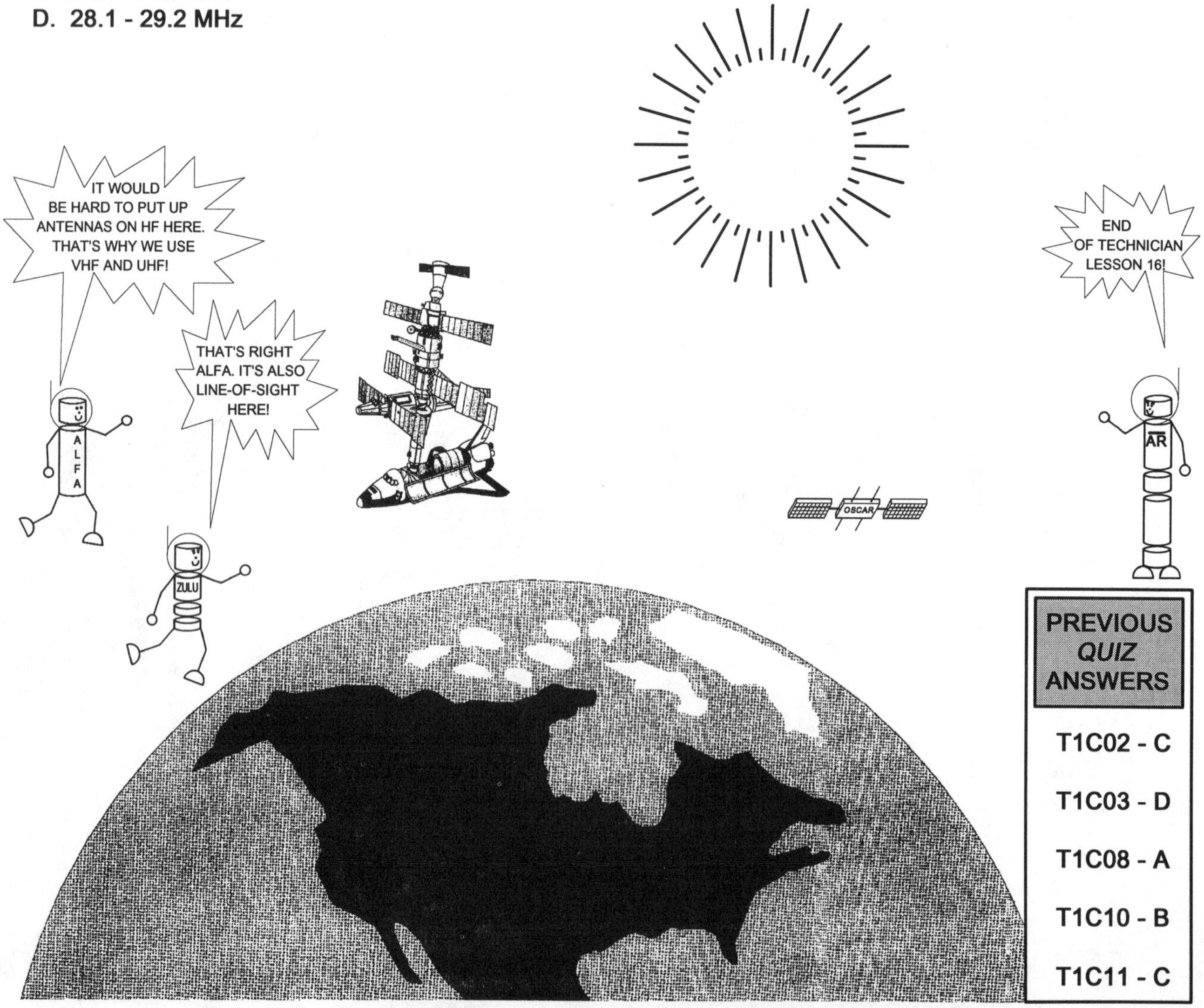

END OF TECHNICIAN LESSON 16!

PREVIOUS QUIZ ANSWERS

T1C02 - C

T1C03 - D

T1C08 - A

T1C10 - B

T1C11 - C

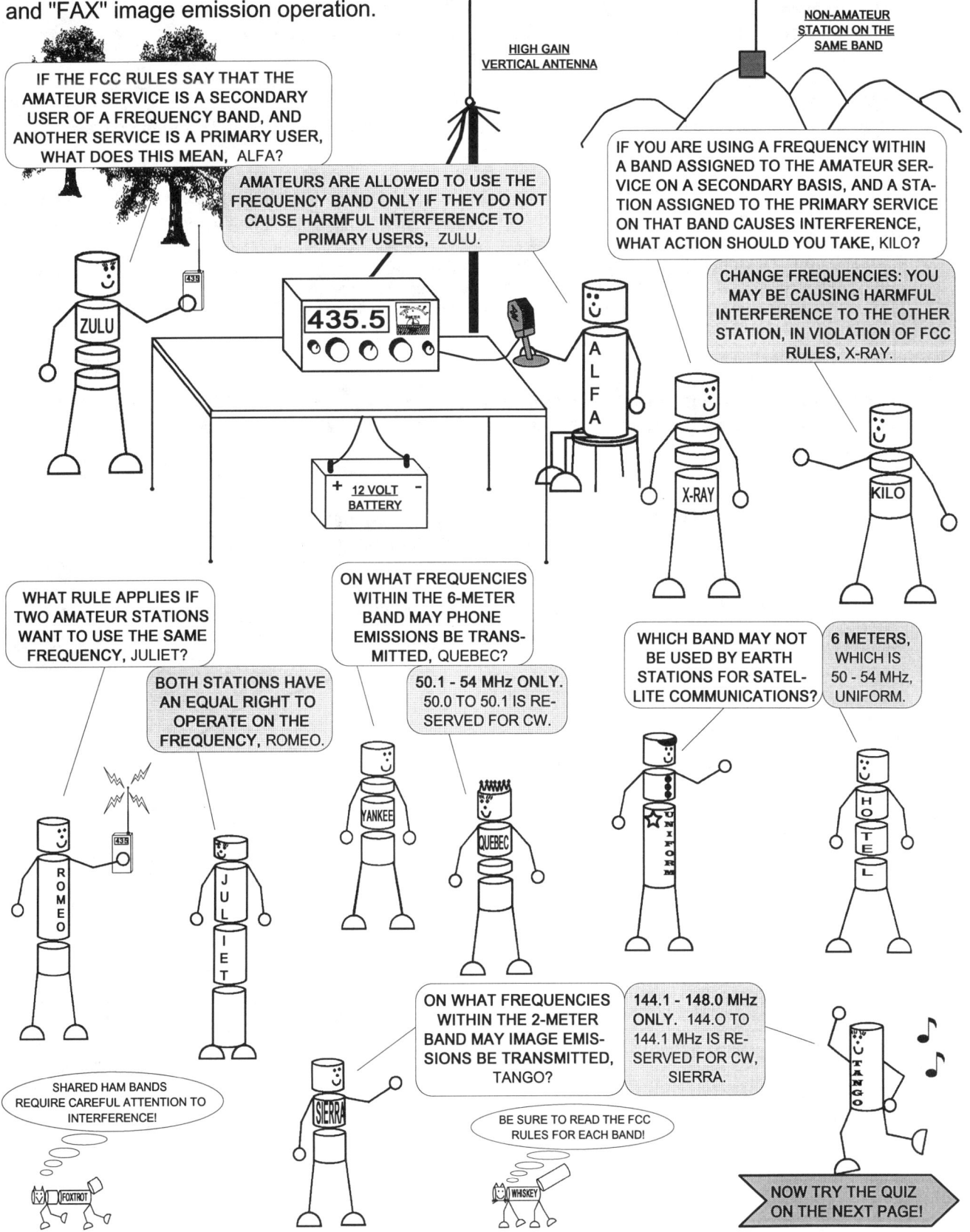

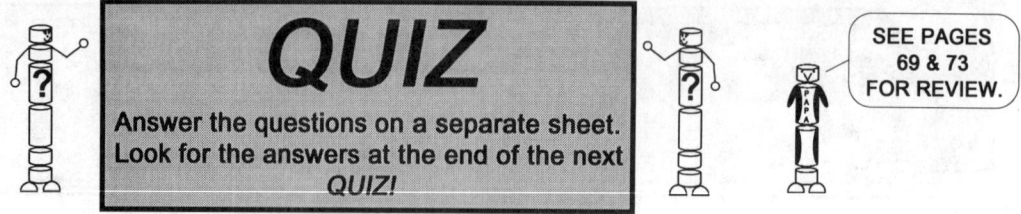

QUIZ

Answer the questions on a separate sheet. Look for the answers at the end of the next QUIZ!

SEE PAGES 69 & 73 FOR REVIEW.

T1B04
If the FCC rules say that the amateur service is a secondary user of a frequency band, and another service is a primary user, what does this mean?
A. Nothing special; all users of a frequency band have equal rights to operate
B. Amateurs are only allowed to use the frequency band during emergencies
C. Amateurs are allowed to use the frequency band only if they do not cause harmful interference to primary users
D. Amateurs must increase transmitter power to overcome any interference caused by primary users

T1B05
If you are using a frequency within a band assigned to the amateur service on a secondary basis, and a station assigned to the primary service on that band causes interference, what action should you take?
A. Notify the FCC's regional Engineer in Charge of the interference
B. Increase your transmitter's power to overcome the interference
C. Attempt to contact the station and request that it stop the interference
D. Change frequencies; you may be causing harmful interference to the other station, in violation of FCC rules

T1B06
What rule applies if two amateur stations want to use the same frequency?
A. The station operator with a lesser class of license must yield the frequency to a higher class licensee
B. The station operator with a lower power output must yield the frequency to the station with a higher power output
C. Both station operators have an equal right to operate on the frequency
D. Station operators in ITU Regions 1 and 3 must yield the frequency to stations in ITU Region 2

T1B08
On what frequencies within the 6-meter band may phone emissions be transmitted?
A. 50.0 - 54.0 MHz only
B. 50.1 - 54.0 MHz only
C. 51.0 - 54.0 MHz only
D. 52.0 - 54.0 MHz only

T1B11
Which band may NOT be used by Earth stations for satellite communications?
A. 6 meters
B. 2 meters
C. 70 centimeters
D. 23 centimeters

T1B09
On what frequencies within the 2-meter band may image emissions be transmitted?
A. 144.1 - 148.0 MHz only
B. 146.0 - 148.0 MHz only
C. 144.0 - 148.0 MHz only
D. 146.0 - 147.0 MHz only

END OF TECHNICIAN LESSON 17!

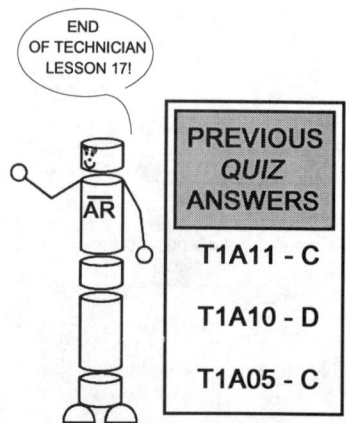

PREVIOUS QUIZ ANSWERS

T1A11 - C

T1A10 - D

T1A05 - C

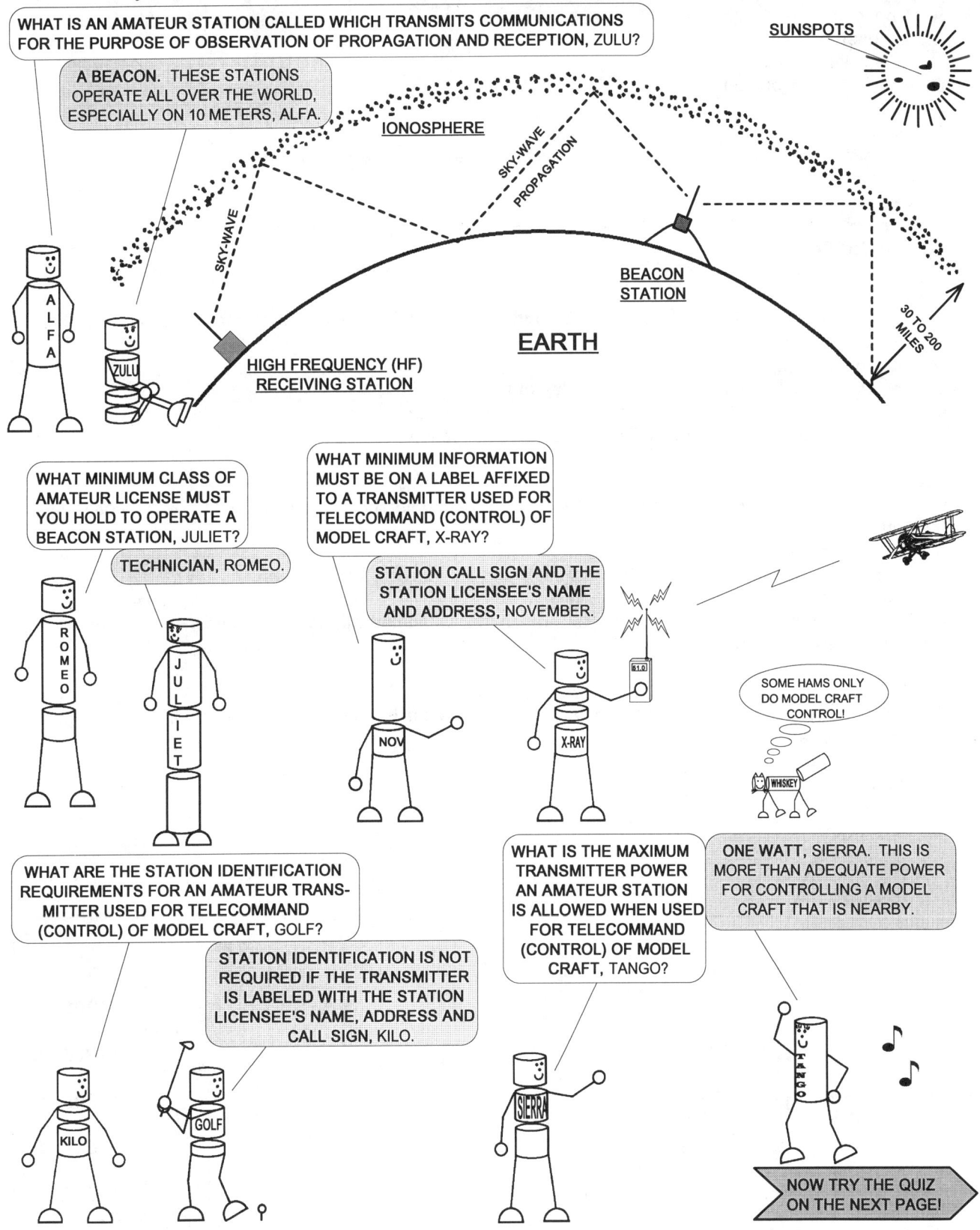

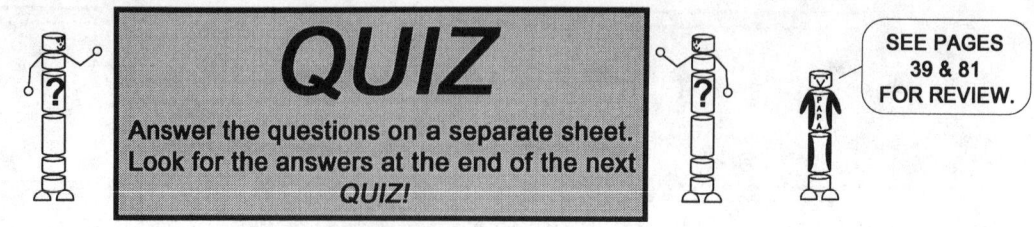

QUIZ

Answer the questions on a separate sheet. Look for the answers at the end of the next QUIZ!

SEE PAGES 39 & 81 FOR REVIEW.

T1D01
What is an amateur station called which transmits communications for the purpose of observation of propagation and reception?
A. A beacon
B. A repeater
C. An auxiliary station
D. A radio control station

T1D05
What minimum class of amateur license must you hold to operate a beacon station?
A. Novice
B. Technician
C. General
D. Amateur Extra

T1D09
What minimum information must be on a label affixed to a transmitter used for telecommand (control) of model craft?
A. Station call sign
B. Station call sign and the station licensee's name
C. Station call sign and the station licensee's name and address
D. Station call sign and the station licensee's class of license

T1D10
What are the station identification requirements for an amateur transmitter used for telecommand (control) of model craft?
A. Once every ten minutes
B. Once every ten minutes, and at the beginning and end of each transmission
C. At the beginning and end of each transmission
D. Station identification is not required if the transmitter is labeled with the station licensee's name, address and call sign

T1D11
What is the maximum transmitter power an amateur station is allowed when used for telecommand (control) of model craft?
A. One milliwatt
B. One watt
C. Two watts
D. Three watts

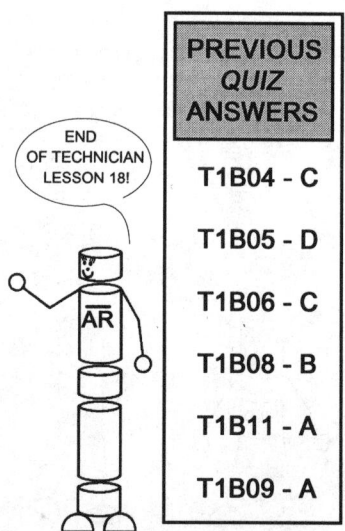

END OF TECHNICIAN LESSON 18!

PREVIOUS QUIZ ANSWERS

T1B04 - C
T1B05 - D
T1B06 - C
T1B08 - B
T1B11 - A
T1B09 - A

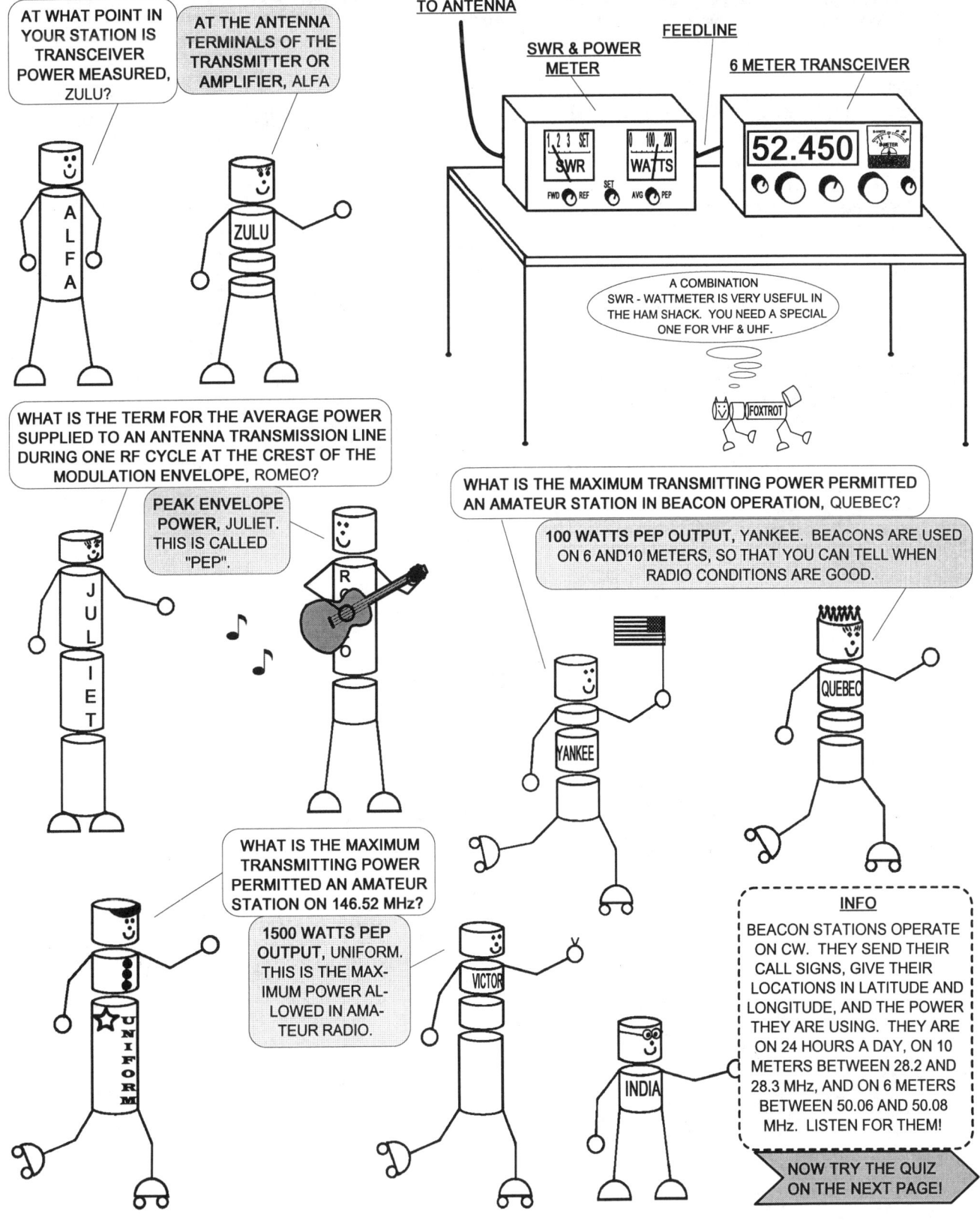

QUIZ

Answer the questions on a separate sheet. Look for the answers at the end of the next QUIZ!

SEE PAGES 75, 77, 79, & 115 FOR REVIEW.

T1B01
At what point in your station is transceiver power measured?
A. At the power supply terminals inside the transmitter or amplifier
B. At the final amplifier input terminals inside the transmitter or amplifier
C. At the antenna terminals of the transmitter or amplifier
D. On the antenna itself, after the feed line

T1B02
What is the term for the average power supplied to an antenna transmission line during one RF cycle at the crest of the modulation envelope?
A. Peak transmitter power
B. Peak output power
C. Average radio-frequency power
D. Peak envelope power

T1B03
What is the maximum transmitting power permitted an amateur station in beacon operation?
A. 10 watts PEP output
B. 100 watts PEP output
C. 500 watts PEP output
D. 1500 watts PEP output

T1B10
What is the maximum transmitting power permitted an amateur station on 146.52 MHz?
A. 200 watts PEP output
B. 500 watts ERP
C. 1000 watts DC input
D. 1500 watts PEP output

YOU CAN REMEMBER THAT POWER IS MEASURED IN "PEP" WATTS, BECAUSE POWER GIVES YOU LOTS OF PEP! PEP, OR "PEAK ENVELOPE POWER", IS USED, BECAUSE THE HUMAN VOICE VARIES IN POWER LEVEL. IT HAS CERTAIN PEAKS, AND THAT IS WHAT LIMITS THE POWER. ELECTRONIC TRICKS, CALLED "COMPRESSION", CAN BE DONE, THAT REDUCE THE PEAKS, AND FILL IN THE DIPS, FOR GREATER SPEECH POWER!

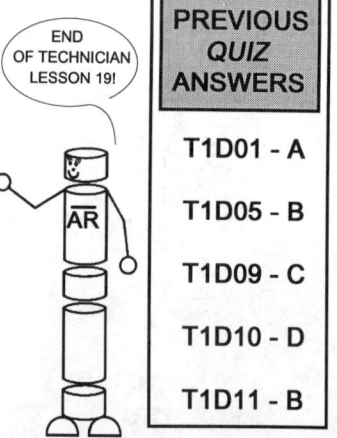

END OF TECHNICIAN LESSON 19!

PREVIOUS QUIZ ANSWERS

T1D01 - A
T1D05 - B
T1D09 - C
T1D10 - D
T1D11 - B

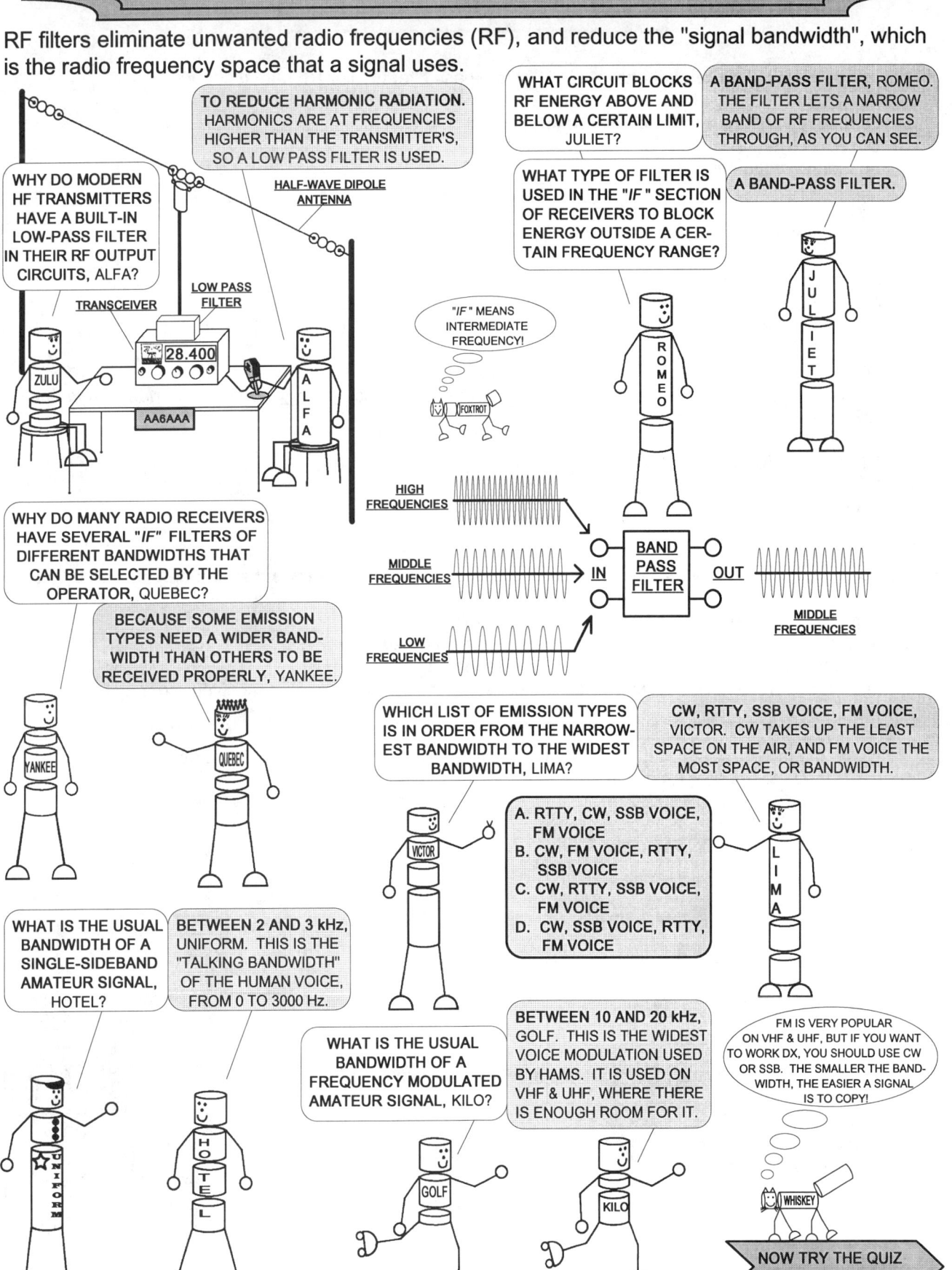

QUIZ

Answer the questions on a separate sheet. Look for the answers at the end of the next QUIZ!

SEE PAGES 105 & 107 FOR REVIEW.

T7A01
Why do modern HF transmitters have a built-in low-pass filter in their RF output circuits?
A. To reduce RF energy below a cutoff point
B. To reduce low-frequency interference to other amateurs
C. To reduce harmonic radiation
D. To reduce fundamental radiation

T7A02
What circuit blocks RF energy above and below a certain limit?
A. A band-pass filter
B. A high-pass filter
C. An input filter
D. A low-pass filter

T7A03
What type of filter is used in the IF section of receivers to block energy outside a certain frequency range?
A. A band-pass filter
B. A high-pass filter
C. An input filter
D. A low-pass filter

T8B06
Why do many radio receivers have several IF filters of different bandwidths that can be selected by the operator?
A. Because some frequency bands are wider than others
B. Because different bandwidths help increase the receiver sensitivity
C. Because different bandwidths improve S-meter readings
D. Because some emission types need a wider bandwidth than others to be received properly

T8B07
Which list of emission types is in order from the narrowest bandwidth to the widest bandwidth?
A. RTTY, CW, SSB voice, FM voice
B. CW, FM voice, RTTY, SSB voice
C. CW, RTTY, SSB voice, FM voice
D. CW, SSB voice, RTTY, FM voice

T8B08
What is the usual bandwidth of a single-sideband amateur signal?
A. 1 kHz
B. 2 kHz
C. Between 3 and 6 kHz
D. Between 2 and 3 kHz

T8B09
What is the usual bandwidth of a frequency-modulated amateur signal?
A. Less than 5 kHz
B. Between 5 and 10 kHz
C. Between 10 and 20 kHz
D. Greater than 20 kHz

END OF TECHNICIAN LESSON 20!

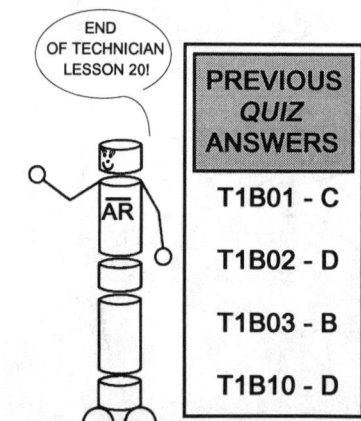

PREVIOUS QUIZ ANSWERS

T1B01 - C

T1B02 - D

T1B03 - B

T1B10 - D

DETECTORS, VFO'S, & FM CIRCUITS
TECHNICIAN LESSON 21

Every radio receiver has a "detector", to "detect" the incoming signal. Variable frequency oscillators (VFO's), are controlled by the dial on every radio, so that you can listen, or transmit, on different frequencies. Frequency modulation (FM) circuits always use "limiters" and "frequency discriminators" in receivers, and "reactance modulators" in transmitters.

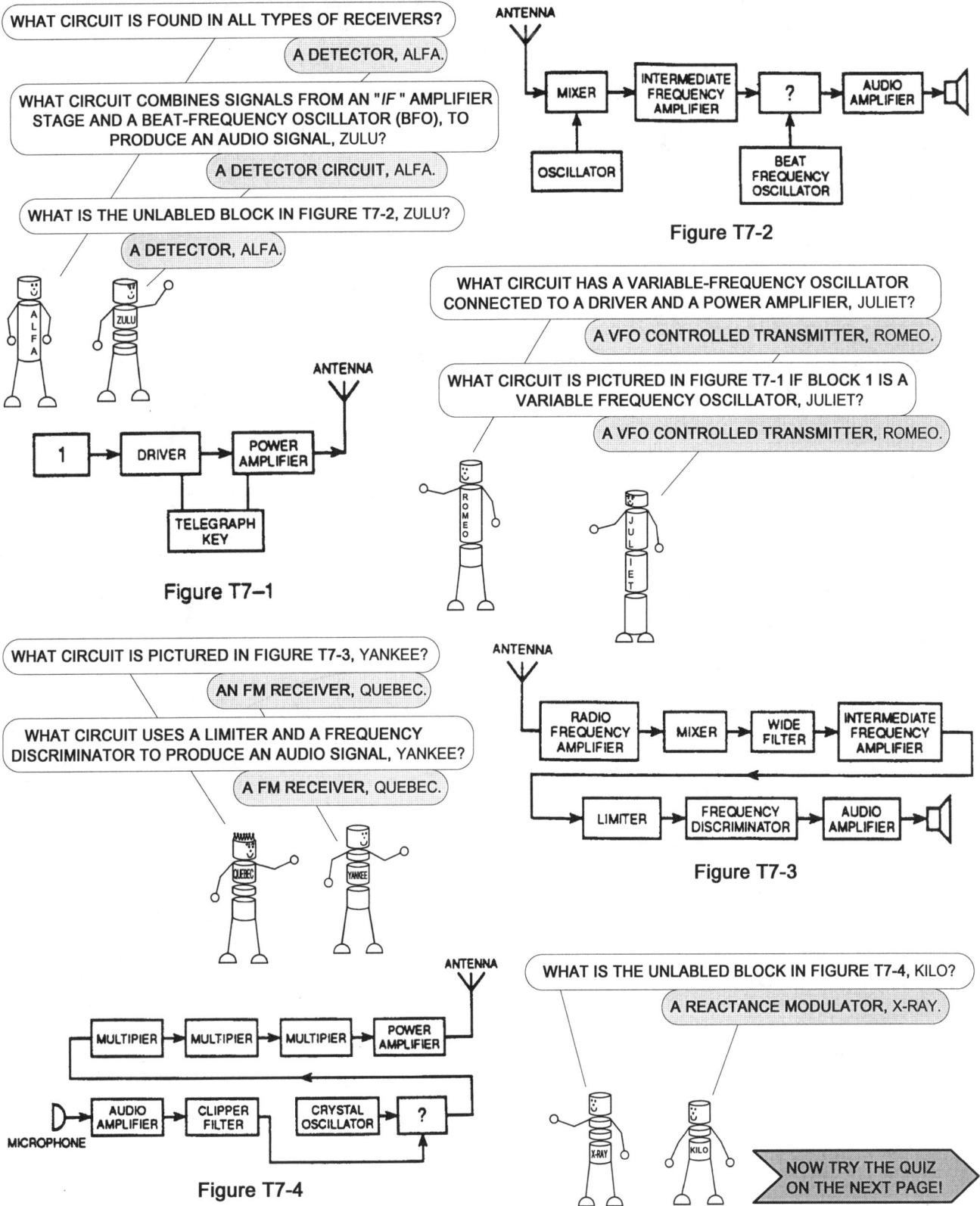

Figure T7-1

Figure T7-2

Figure T7-3

Figure T7-4

NOW TRY THE QUIZ ON THE NEXT PAGE!

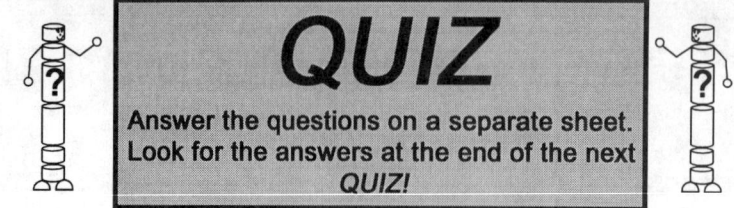

QUIZ
Answer the questions on a separate sheet. Look for the answers at the end of the next QUIZ!

T7A04
What circuit is found in all types of receivers?
A. An audio filter
B. A beat-frequency oscillator
C. A detector
D. An RF amplifier

T7A06
What circuit combines signals from an IF amplifier stage and a beat-frequency oscillator (BFO), to produce an audio signal?
A. An AGC circuit
B. A detector circuit
C. A power supply circuit
D. A VFO circuit

T7A09
What is the unlabeled block in Figure T7-2?
A. An AGC circuit
B. A detector
C. A power supply
D. A VFO circuit

T7A05
What circuit has a variable-frequency oscillator connected to a driver and a power amplifier?
A. A packet-radio transmitter
B. A crystal-controlled transmitter
C. A single-sideband transmitter
D. A VFO-controlled transmitter

T7A08
What circuit is pictured in Figure T7-1 if block 1 is a variable-frequency oscillator?
A. A packet-radio transmitter
B. A crystal-controlled transmitter
C. A single-sideband transmitter
D. A VFO-controlled transmitter

T7A10
What circuit is pictured in Figure T7-3?
A. A double-conversion receiver
B. A variable-frequency oscillator
C. A superheterodyne receiver
D. An FM receiver

T7A07
What circuit uses a limiter and a frequency discriminator to produce an audio signal?
A. A double-conversion receiver
B. A variable-frequency oscillator
C. A superheterodyne receiver
D. A FM receiver

T7A11
What is the unlabeled block in Figure T7-4?
A. A band-pass filter
B. A crystal oscillator
C. A reactance modulator
D. A rectifier modulator

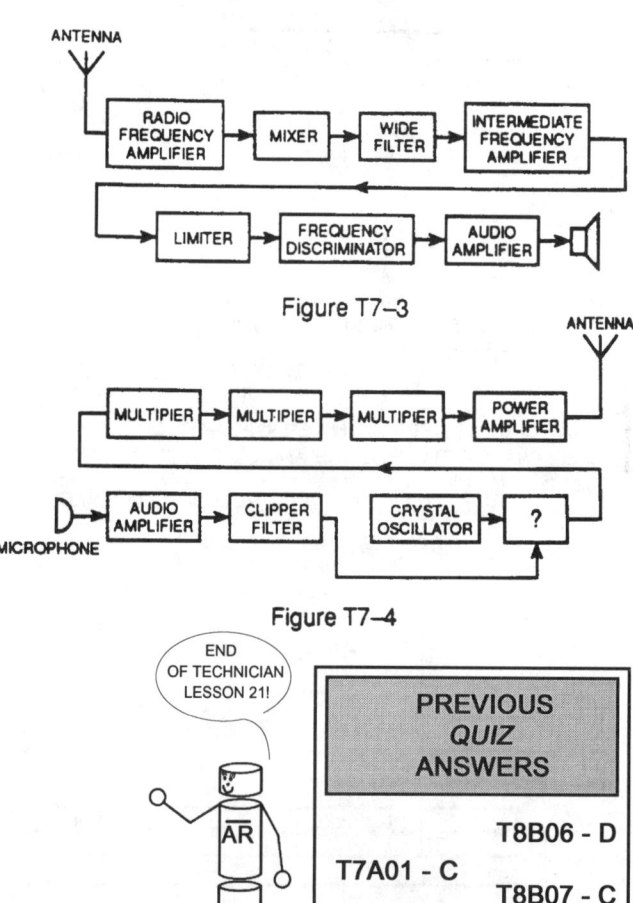

Figure T7-3

Figure T7-4

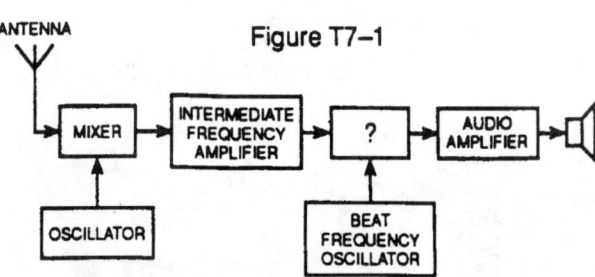

Figure T7-1

Figure T7-2

END OF TECHNICIAN LESSON 21!

PREVIOUS QUIZ ANSWERS
T7A01 - C
T7A02 - A
T7A03 - A
T8B06 - D
T8B07 - C
T8B08 - D
T8B09 - C

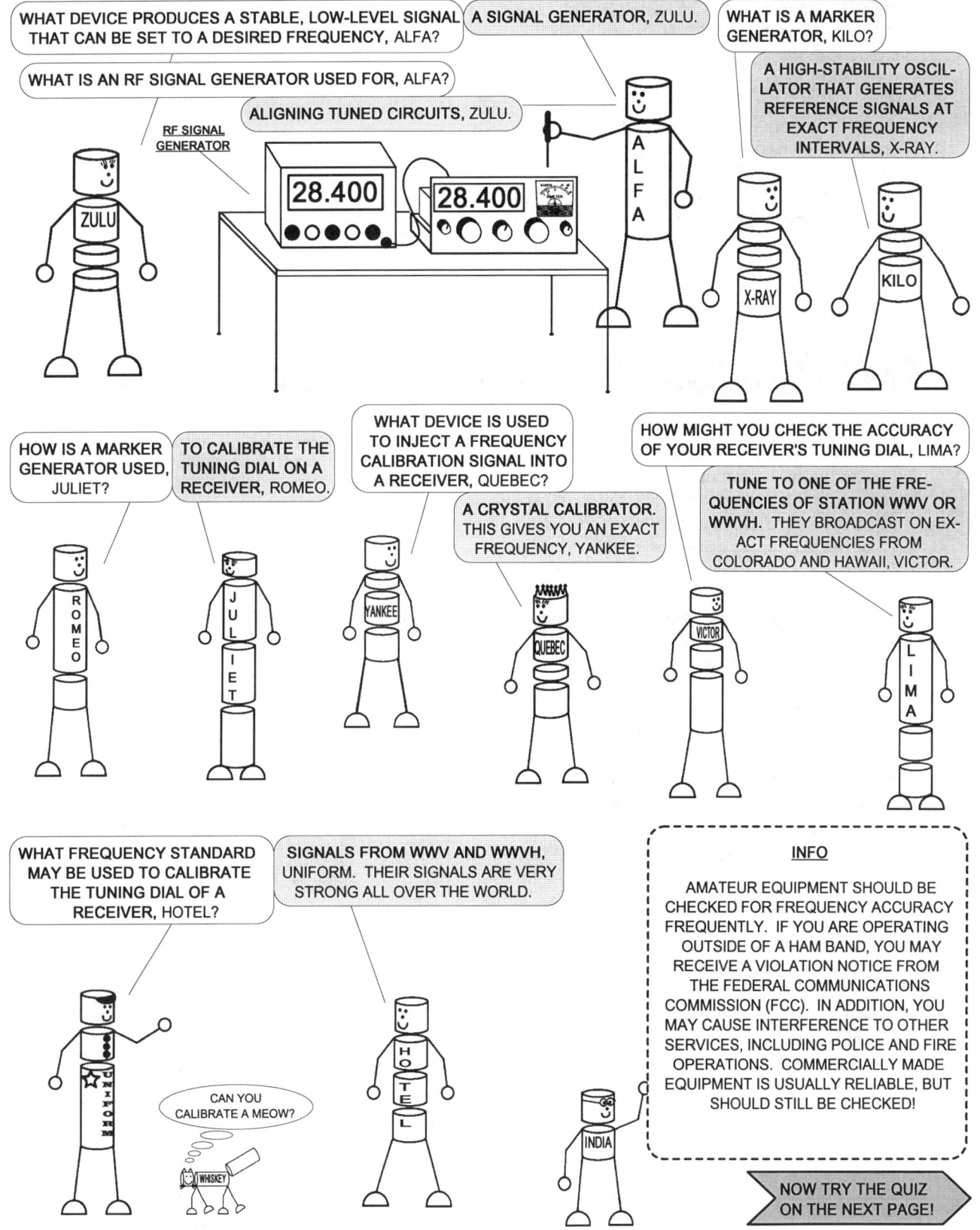

198

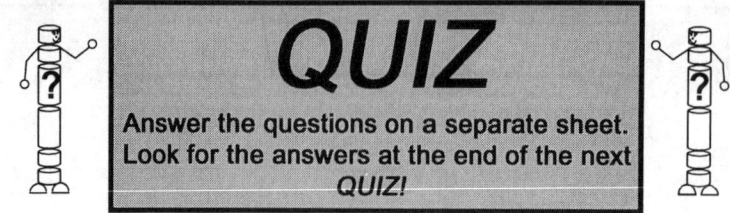

QUIZ
Answer the questions on a separate sheet. Look for the answers at the end of the next QUIZ!

T4C06
What device produces a stable, low-level signal that can be set to a desired frequency?
A. A wavemeter
B. A reflectometer
C. A signal generator
D. An oscilloscope

T4C07
What is an RF signal generator used for?
A. Measuring RF signal amplitudes
B. Aligning tuned circuits
C. Adjusting transmitter impedance-matching networks
D. Measuring transmission line impedances

T4C01
What is a marker generator?
A. A high-stability oscillator that generates reference signals at exact frequency intervals
B. A low-stability oscillator that "sweeps" through a range of frequencies
C. A low-stability oscillator used to inject a signal into a circuit under test
D. A high-stability oscillator which can produce a wide range of frequencies and amplitudes

T4C02
How is a marker generator used?
A. To calibrate the tuning dial on a receiver
B. To calibrate the volume control on a receiver
C. To test the amplitude linearity of a transmitter
D. To test the frequency deviation of a transmitter

T4C03
What device is used to inject a frequency calibration signal into a receiver?
A. A calibrated voltmeter
B. A calibrated oscilloscope
C. A calibrated wavemeter
D. A crystal calibrator

T4C05
How might you check the accuracy of your receiver's tuning dial?
A. Tune to the frequency of a shortwave broadcasting station
B. Tune to a popular amateur net frequency
C. Tune to one of the frequencies of station WWV or WWVH
D. Tune to another amateur station and ask what frequency the operator is using

T4C04
What frequency standard may be used to calibrate the tuning dial of a receiver?
A. A calibrated voltmeter
B. Signals from WWV and WWVH
C. A deviation meter
D. A sweep generator

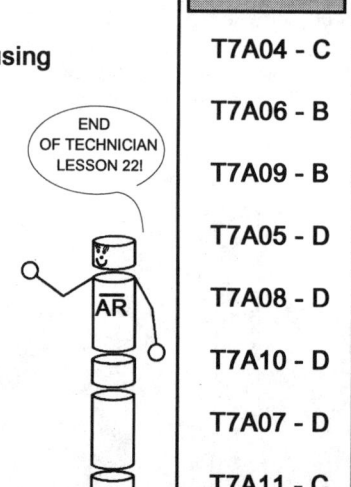

END OF TECHNICIAN LESSON 22!

PREVIOUS QUIZ ANSWERS

T7A04 - C
T7A06 - B
T7A09 - B
T7A05 - D
T7A08 - D
T7A10 - D
T7A07 - D
T7A11 - C

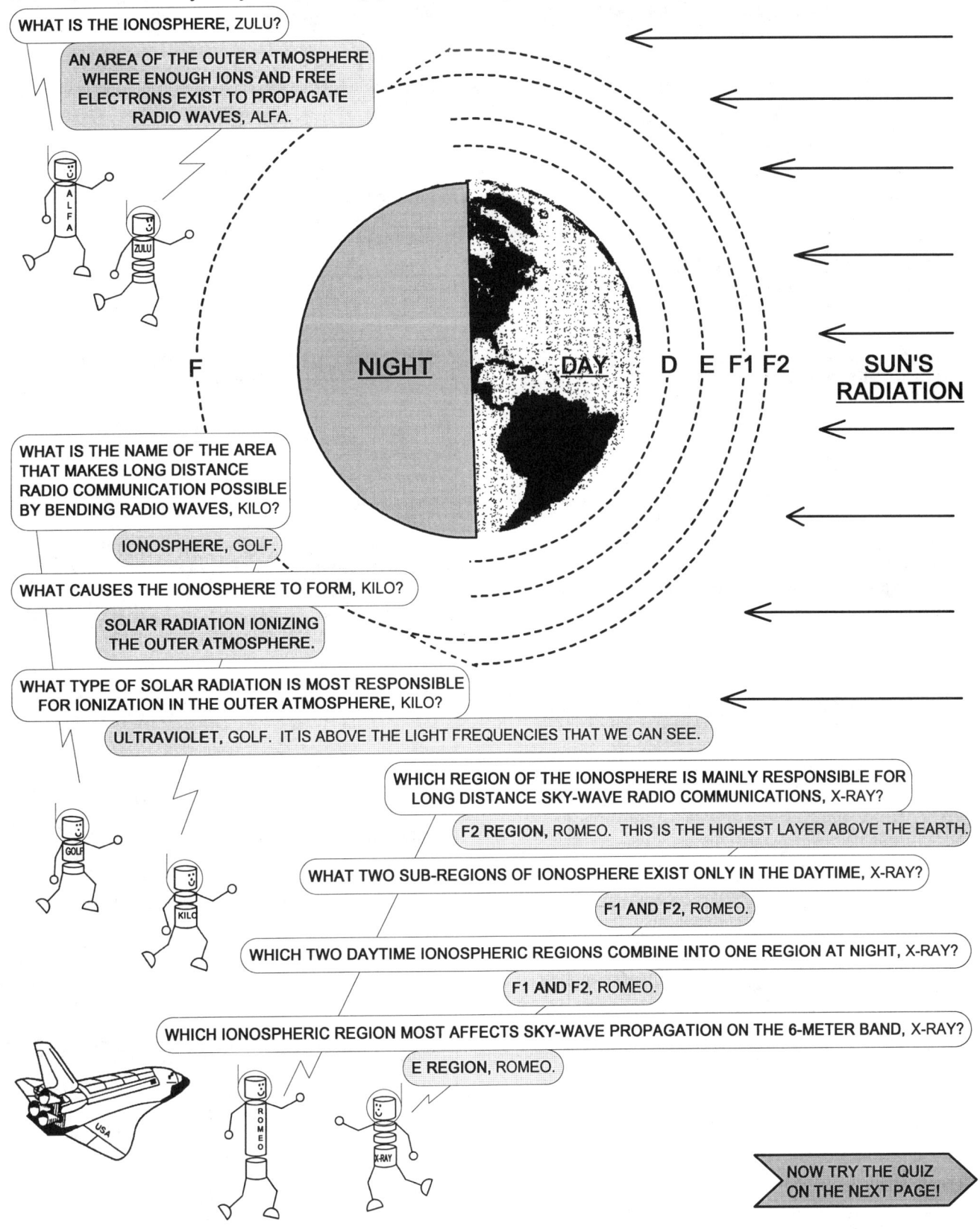

QUIZ

Answer the questions on a separate sheet. Look for the answers at the end of the next QUIZ!

SEE PAGE 81 FOR REVIEW.

T3A01
What is the ionosphere?
A. A area of the outer atmosphere where enough ions and free electrons exist to propagate radio waves
B. A area between two air masses of different temperature and humidity, along which radio waves can travel
C. An ionized path in the atmosphere where lightning has struck
D. An area of the atmosphere where weather takes place

T3A02
What is the name of the area that makes long-distance radio communications possible by bending radio waves?
A. Troposphere
B. Stratosphere
C. Magnetosphere
D. Ionosphere

T3A03
What causes the ionosphere to form?
A. Solar radiation ionizing the outer atmosphere
B. Temperature changes ionizing the outer atmosphere
C. Lightning ionizing the outer atmosphere
D. Release of fluorocarbons into the atmosphere

T3A04
What type of solar radiation is most responsible for ionization in the outer atmosphere?
A. Thermal
B. Ionized particle
C. Ultraviolet
D. Microwave

T3A09
Which region of the ionosphere is mainly responsible for long-distance sky-wave radio communications?
A. D region
B. E region
C. F1 region
D. F2 region

T3A10
What two sub-regions of ionosphere exist only in the daytime?
A. Troposphere and stratosphere
B. F1 and F2
C. Electrostatic and electromagnetic
D. D and E

T3A11
Which two daytime ionospheric regions combine into one region at night?
A. E and F1
B. D and E
C. F1 and F2
D. E1 and E2

T3A07
Which ionospheric region most affects sky-wave propagation on the 6-meter band?
A. The D region
B. The E region
C. The F1 region
D. The F2 region

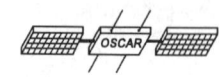

OSCARS SOMETIMES ORBIT ABOVE THE IONOSPHERE. VHF AND UHF CAN PENETRATE THE IONOSPHERE, SO THAT THERE IS NO PROBLEM COMMUNICATING WITH SATELLITES.

END OF TECHNICIAN LESSON 23!

PREVIOUS QUIZ ANSWERS

T4C06 - C
T4C07 - B
T4C01 - A
T4C02 - A
T4C03 - D
T4C05 - C
T4C04 - B

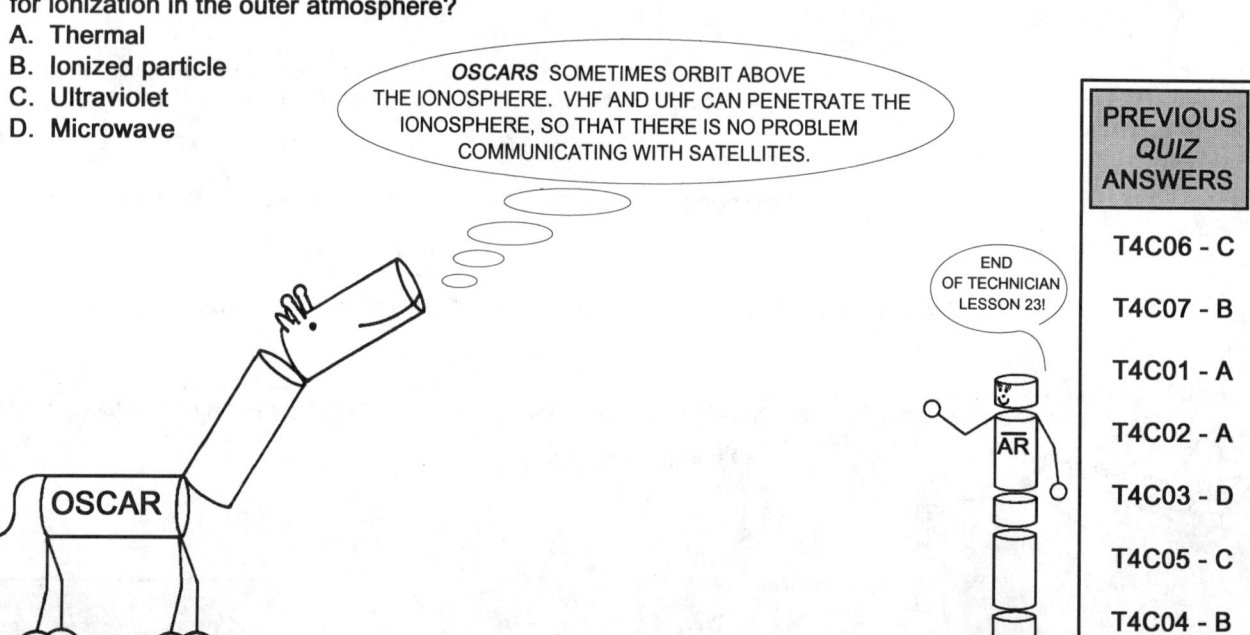

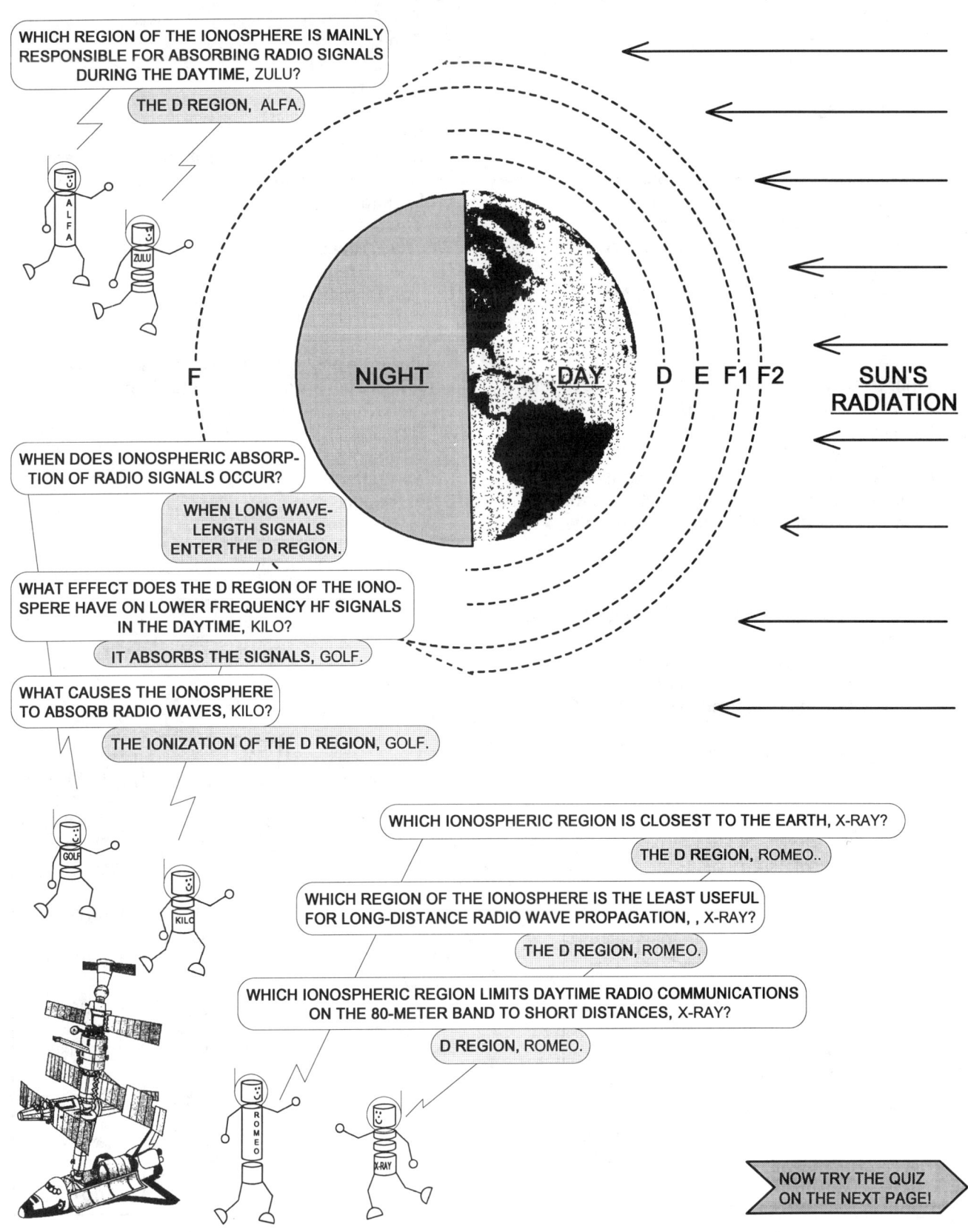

QUIZ

Answer the questions on a separate sheet. Look for the answers at the end of the next QUIZ!

SEE PAGE 81 FOR REVIEW.

T3B01
Which region of the ionosphere is mainly responsible for absorbing radio signals during the daytime?
A. The F2 region
B. The F1 region
C. The E region
D. The D region

T3B02
When does ionospheric absorption of radio signals occur?
A. When tropospheric ducting occurs
B. When long wavelength signals enter the D region
C. When signals travel to the F region
D. When a temperature inversion occurs

T3B03
What effect does the D region of the ionosphere have on lower-frequency HF signals in the daytime?
A. It absorbs the signals
B. It bends the radio waves out into space
C. It refracts the radio waves back to earth
D. It has little or no effect on 80-meter radio waves

T3B04
What causes the ionosphere to absorb radio waves?
A. The weather below the ionosphere
B. The ionization of the D region
C. The presence of ionized clouds in the E region
D. The splitting of the F region

T3A06
Which ionospheric region is closest to the earth?
A. The A region
B. The D region
C. The E region
D. The F region

T3A08
Which region of the ionosphere is the least useful for long-distance radio wave propagation?
A. The D region
B. The E region
C. The F1 region
D. The F2 region

T3A05
Which ionospheric region limits daytime radio communications on the 80-meter band to short distances?
A. D region
B. E region
C. F1 region
D. F2 region

PREVIOUS QUIZ ANSWERS
T3A01 - A
T3A02 - D
T3A03 - A
T3A04 - C
T3A09 - D
T3A10 - B
T3A11 - C
T3A07 - B

IONOSPHERIC CHANGES

TECHNICIAN LESSON 25

The ionosphere changes with the time of day, and the highest usable frequency for long distance, or DX, varies all the time.

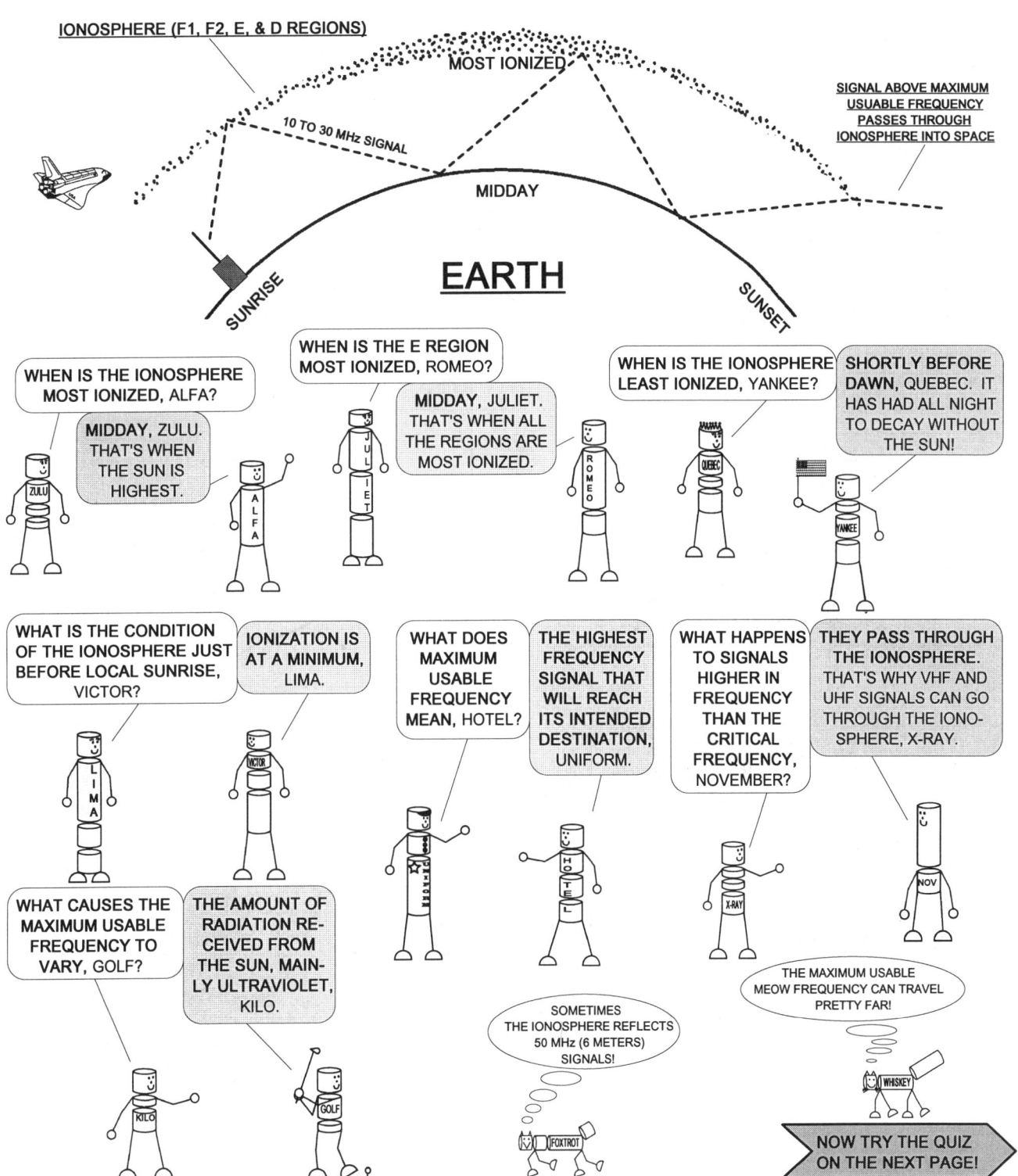

QUIZ

Answer the questions on a separate sheet. Look for the answers at the end of the next QUIZ!

SEE PAGE 81 FOR REVIEW.

T3B06
When is the ionosphere most ionized?
A. Dusk
B. Midnight
C. Midday
D. Dawn

T3B08
When is the E region most ionized?
A. Dawn
B. Midday
C. Dusk
D. Midnight

T3B07
When is the ionosphere least ionized?
A. Shortly before dawn
B. Just after noon
C. Just after dusk
D. Shortly before midnight

T3B05
What is the condition of the ionosphere just before local sunrise?
A. Atmospheric attenuation is at a maximum
B. The D region is above the E region
C. The E region is above the F region
D. Ionization is at a minimum

T3B11
What does maximum usable frequency mean?
A. The highest frequency signal that will reach its intended destination
B. The lowest frequency signal that will reach its intended destination
C. The highest frequency signal that is most absorbed by the ionosphere
D. The lowest frequency signal that is most absorbed by the ionosphere

T3B09
What happens to signals higher in frequency than the critical frequency?
A. They pass through the ionosphere
B. They are absorbed by the ionosphere
C. Their frequency is changed by the ionosphere to be below the maximum usable frequency
D. They are reflected back to their source

T3B10
What causes the maximum usable frequency to vary?
A. The temperature of the ionosphere
B. The speed of the winds in the upper atmosphere
C. The amount of radiation received from the sun, mainly ultraviolet
D. The type of weather just below the ionosphere

END OF TECHNICIAN LESSON 25!

PREVIOUS QUIZ ANSWERS

T3B01 - D
T3B02 - B
T3B03 - A
T3B04 - B
T3A06 - B
T3A08 - A
T3A05 - A

TROPOSPHERE VHF COMMUNICATIONS
TECHNICIAN LESSON 26

In the summertime, a warm air mass sometimes traps a cold air mass below it, in an area of the earth's atmosphere called the "troposphere". The troposphere is the area where clouds form, below the ionosphere, about 7 to 10 miles above the earth. It's the area where "ducting" can occur, that lets VHF, and sometimes UHF, signals travel hundreds of miles.

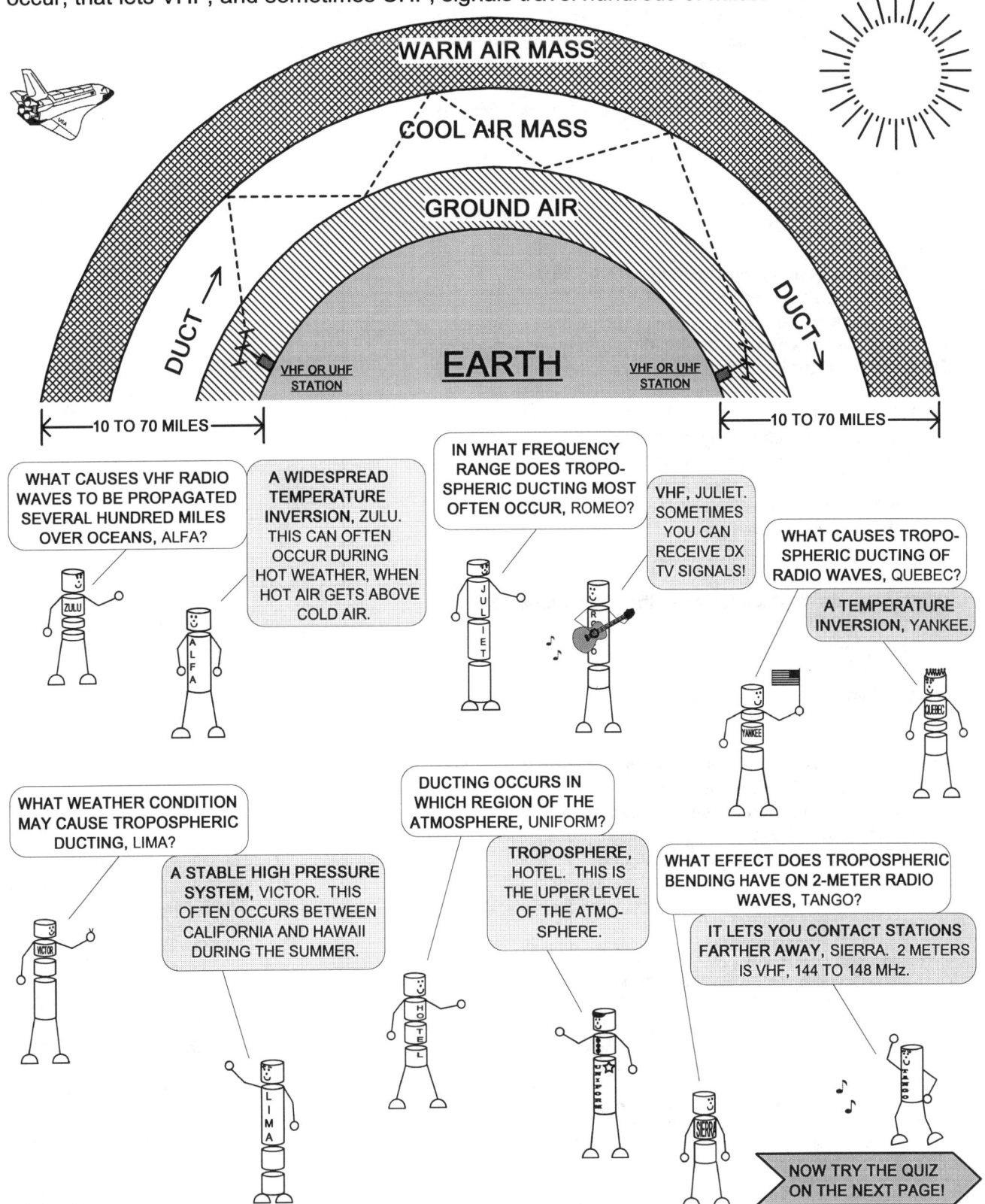

Now try the quiz on the next page!

QUIZ

Answer the questions on a separate sheet. Look for the answers at the end of the next QUIZ!

SEE PAGE 81 FOR REVIEW.

T3C07
What causes VHF radio waves to be propagated several hundred miles over oceans?
A. A polar air mass
B. A widespread temperature inversion
C. An overcast of cirriform clouds
D. A high-pressure zone

T3C08
In what frequency range does tropospheric ducting most often occur?
A. SW
B. MF
C. HF
D. VHF

T3C06
What causes tropospheric ducting of radio waves?
A. A very low pressure area
B. An aurora to the north
C. Lightning between the transmitting and receiving stations
D. A temperature inversion

T3C10
What weather condition may cause tropospheric ducting?
A. A stable high-pressure system
B. An unstable low-pressure system
C. A series of low-pressure waves
D. Periods of heavy rainfall

T3C04
Ducting occurs in which region of the atmosphere?
A. F2
B. Ectosphere
C. Troposphere
D. Stratosphere

T3C05
What effect does tropospheric bending have on 2-meter radio waves?
A. It lets you contact stations farther away
B. It causes them to travel shorter distances
C. It garbles the signal
D. It reverses the sideband of the signal

SUMMERTIME IS A LOT OF FUN ON 2 METERS, WHEN YOU CAN WORK TROPOSPHERIC DX!

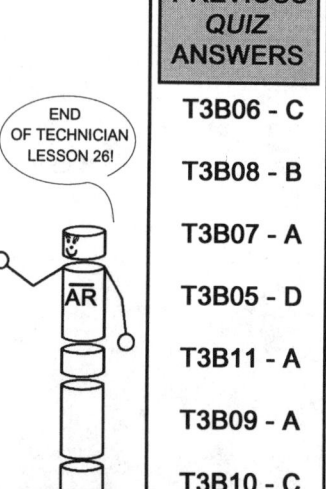

END OF TECHNICIAN LESSON 26!

PREVIOUS QUIZ ANSWERS
T3B06 - C
T3B08 - B
T3B07 - A
T3B05 - D
T3B11 - A
T3B09 - A
T3B10 - C

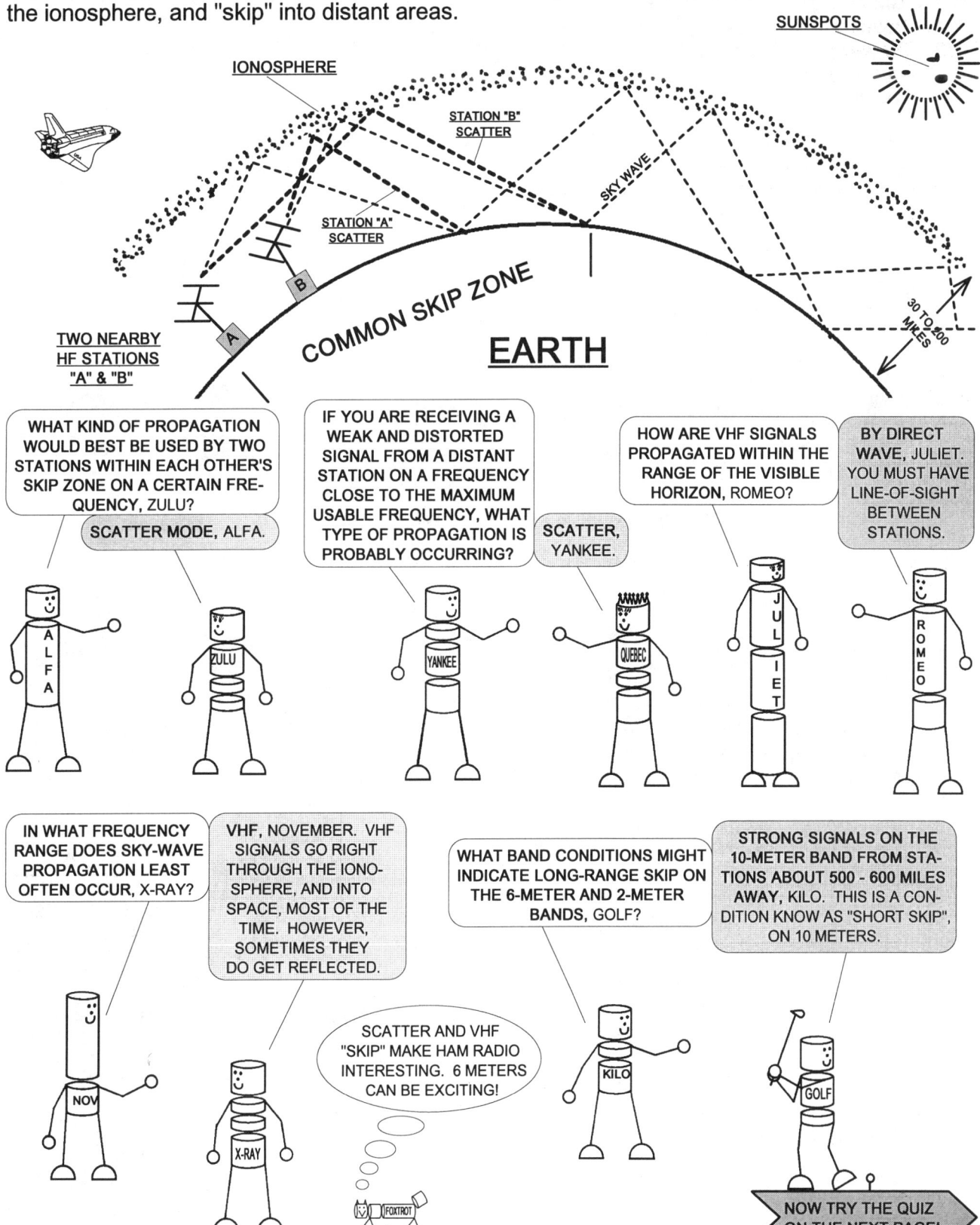

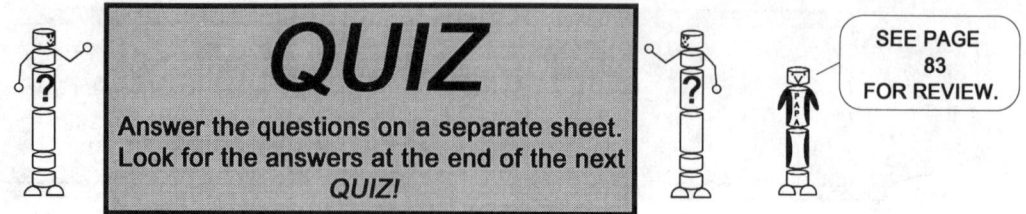

T3C01
What kind of propagation would best be used by two stations within each other's skip zone on a certain frequency?
A. Ground-wave
B. Sky-wave
C. Scatter-mode
D. Ducting

T3C02
If you are receiving a weak and distorted signal from a distant station on a frequency close to the maximum usable frequency, what type of propagation is probably occurring?
A. Ducting
B. Line-of-sight
C. Scatter
D. Ground-wave

T3C03
How are VHF signals propagated within the range of the visible horizon?
A. By sky wave
B. By direct wave
C. By plane wave
D. By geometric wave

T3C09
In what frequency range does sky-wave propagation least often occur?
A. LF
B. MF
C. HF
D. VHF

T3C11
What band conditions might indicate long-range skip on the 6-meter and 2-meter bands?
A. Noise on the 80-meter band
B. The absence of signals on the 10-meter band
C. Very long-range skip on the 10-meter band
D. Strong signals on the 10-meter band from stations about 500-600 miles away

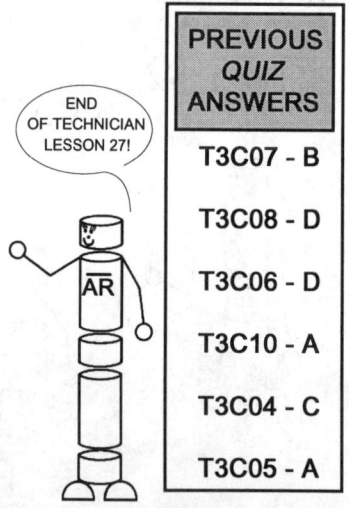

PREVIOUS QUIZ ANSWERS

T3C07 - B
T3C08 - D
T3C06 - D
T3C10 - A
T3C04 - C
T3C05 - A

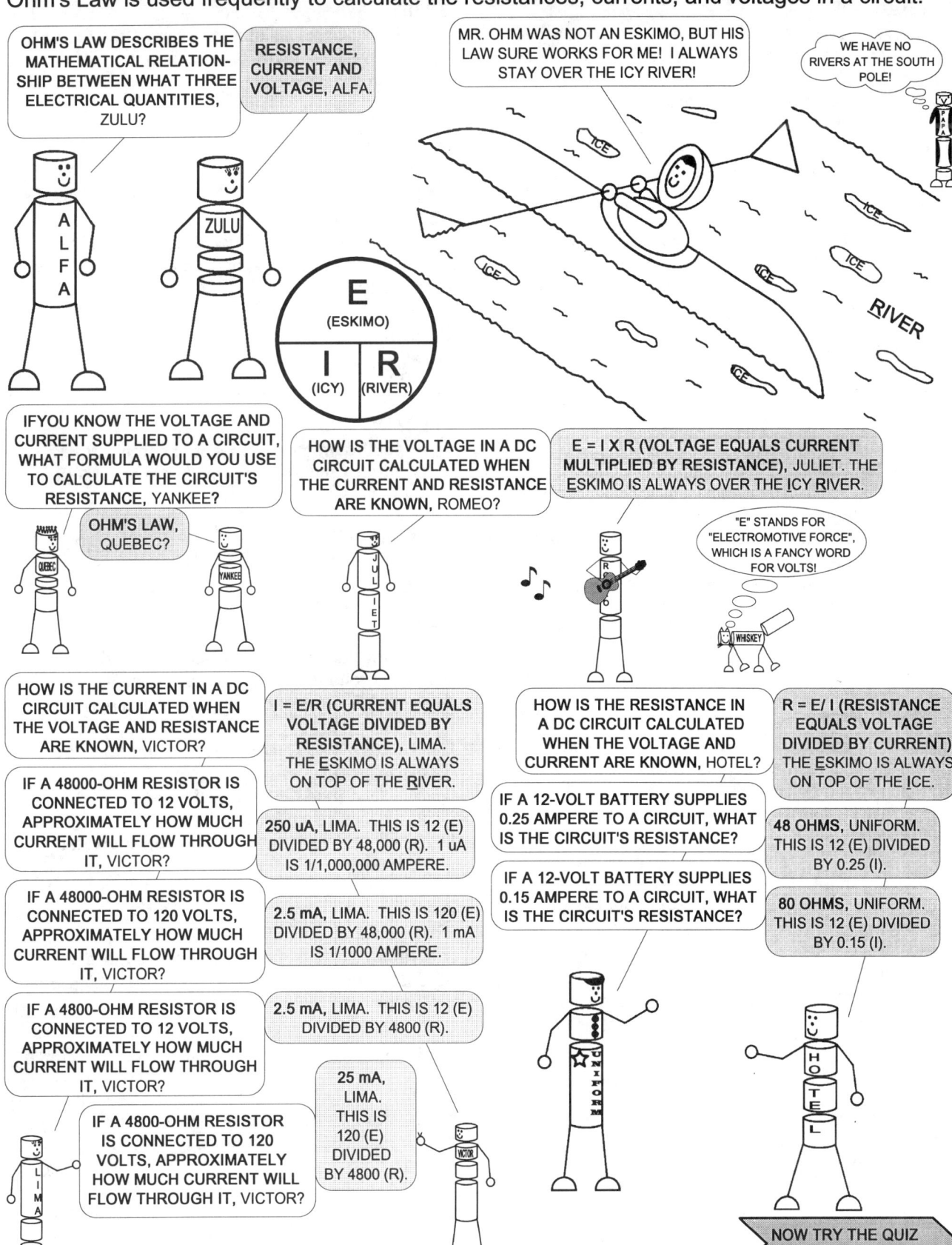

QUIZ

Answer the questions on a separate sheet. Look for the answers at the end of the next QUIZ!

SEE PAGE 89 FOR REVIEW.

T5B01
Ohm's Law describes the mathematical relationship between what three electrical quantities?
A. Resistance, voltage and power
B. Current, resistance and power
C. Current, voltage and power
D. Resistance, current and voltage

T5B11
If you know the voltage and current supplied to a circuit, what formula would you use to calculate the circuit's resistance?
A. Ohm's law
B. Tesla's law
C. Ampere's law
D. Kirchhoff's law

T5B04
How is the voltage in a DC circuit calculated when the current and resistance are known?
A. E = I / R [voltage equals current divided by resistance]
B. E = R / I [voltage equals resistance divided by current]
C. E = I x R [voltage equals current multiplied by resistance]
D. E = P / I [voltage equals power divided by current]

T5B02
How is the current in a DC circuit calculated when the voltage and resistance are known?
A. I = R x E [current equals resistance multiplied by voltage]
B. I = R / E [current equals resistance divided by voltage]
C. I = E / R [current equals voltage divided by resistance]
D. I = P / E [current equals power divided by voltage]

T5B10
If a 48000-ohm resistor is connected to 12 volts, approximately how much current will flow through it?
A. 250 uA
B. 250 mA
C. 4000 mA
D. 4000 A

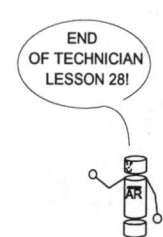

END OF TECHNICIAN LESSON 28!

T5B08
If a 48000-ohm resistor is connected to 120 volts, approximately how much current will flow through it?
A. 400 A
B. 40 A
C. 25 mA
D. 2.5 mA

T5B09
If a 4800-ohm resistor is connected to 12 volts, approximately how much current will flow through it?
A. 2.5 mA
B. 25 mA
C. 40 A
D. 400 A

T5B07
If a 4800-ohm resistor is connected to 120 volts, approximately how much current will flow through it?
A. 4 A
B. 25 mA
C. 25 A
D. 40 MA

T5B03
How is the resistance in a DC circuit calculated when the voltage and current are known?
A. R = I / E [resistance equals current divided by voltage]
B. R = E / I [resistance equals voltage divided by current]
C. R = I x E [resistance equals current multiplied by voltage]
D. R = P / E [resistance equals power divided by voltage]

T5B05
If a 12-volt battery supplies 0.25 ampere to a circuit, what is the circuit's resistance?
A. 0.25 ohm
B. 3 ohm
C. 12 ohms
D. 48 ohms

T5B06
If a 12-volt battery supplies 0.15 ampere to a circuit, what is the circuit's resistance?
A. 0.15 ohm
B. 1.8 ohm
C. 12 ohms
D. 80 ohms

PREVIOUS QUIZ ANSWERS
T3C01 - C
T3C02 - C
T3C03 - B
T3C09 - D
T1C11 - D

RESISTORS
TECHNICIAN LESSON 29

Resistors are used in circuits to limit the flow of electrons to desired values. Resistors come in all sizes and shapes, with different values and wattage ratings.

RESISTOR COLOR BANDS — VALUE IN OHMS / TOLERANCE IN %

WHAT DOES RESISTANCE DO IN AN ELECTRIC CIRCUIT, ALFA?
IT OPPOSES THE FLOW OF ELECTRONS, ZULU.

WHAT ARE THE MOST COMMON RESISTOR TYPES, ALFA?
FILM AND WIRE-WOUND, ZULU. WIRE-WOUND RESISTORS ARE NOT USED AT HIGH FREQUENCIES.

HOW DO YOU FIND A RESISTOR'S VALUE, ALFA?
BY USING THE RESISTOR'S COLOR CODE, ZULU. EACH NUMBER IS REPRESENTED BY A DIFFERENT COLOR.

WHAT DO THE FIRST THREE COLOR BANDS ON A RESISTOR INDICATE?
THE VALUE OF THE RESISTOR IN OHMS, ZULU. A RED-VIOLET-ORANGE COMBINATION IS 27,000 OHMS. RED IS "2", VIOLET IS "7", AND "3" IS ORANGE, MEANING 3 - ZEROS.

WHAT DOES THE FOURTH COLOR BAND ON A RESISTOR INDICATE?
THE RESISTORS TOLERANCE IN PERCENT, ZULU. IT CAN BE 0.1 %, 5%, 10%, OR 20%.

HOW DO YOU FIND A RESISTOR'S TOLERANCE RATING, ALFA?
BY READING THE RESISTOR'S COLOR CODE, ZULU. GOLD IS 5%, SILVER IS 10%, AND NO COLOR IS 20%. 0.1% IS A PRECISION RESISTOR, AND NOT COMMON.

WHICH TOLERANCE RATING WOULD A HIGH-QUALITY RESISTOR HAVE?
0.1 %, ZULU. THE RESISTOR MAY NOT BE OF HIGH QUALITY ITSELF, ONLY ITS TOLERANCE!

WHICH TOLERANCE RATING WOULD A LOW-QUALITY RESISTOR HAVE?
20%, ZULU. THE RESISTOR MAY NOT BE OF LOW-QUALITY, ONLY ITS TOLERANCE!

WHAT ARE THE POSSIBLE VALUES OF A 100-OHM RESISTOR WITH A 10% TOLERANCE, ALFA?
90 TO 100 OHMS, ZULU. THIS IS CALCULATED AS 100 X 0.10 = 10 OHMS, UP OR DOWN, AROUND 100 OHMS.

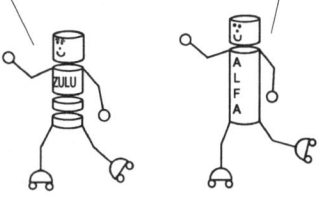

WHY DO RESISTORS SOMETIMES GET HOT WHEN IN USE, ROMEO?
SOME ELECTRICAL ENERGY PASSING THROUGH THEM IS LOST AS HEAT, JULIET.

WHY WOULD A LARGE SIZE RESISTOR BE USED INSTEAD OF A SMALLER ONE OF THE SAME RESISTANCE, YANKEE?
FOR GREATER POWER DISSIPATION, QUEBEC. LARGE RESISTORS CAN TAKE MORE WATTS OF HEAT.

A WARM RESISTOR IS 'OHMY!

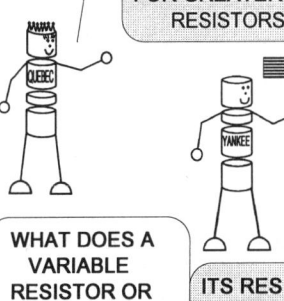

WHAT DOES A VARIABLE RESISTOR OR POTENTIOMETER DO, X-RAY?
ITS RESISTANCE CHANGES WHEN ITS SLIDE OR CONTACT IS MOVED, KILO, ADJUSTING THE CURRENT.

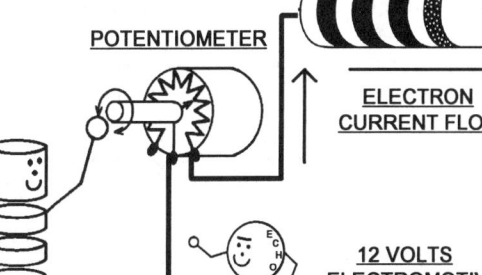

HEAT — POTENTIOMETER — ELECTRON CURRENT FLOW — LIGHT — 12 VOLTS ELECTROMOTIVE FORCE — 12 V BATTERY

NOW TRY THE QUIZ ON THE NEXT PAGE!

QUIZ

Answer the questions on a separate sheet. Look for the answers at the end of the next QUIZ!

SEE PAGE 87 FOR REVIEW.

T5A01
What does resistance do in an electric circuit?
A. It stores energy in a magnetic field
B. It stores energy in an electric field
C. It provides electrons by a chemical reaction
D. It opposes the flow of electrons

T6A01
What are the most common resistor types?
A. Plastic and porcelain
B. Film and wire-wound
C. Electrolytic and metal-film
D. Iron core and brass core

T6A09
How do you find a resistor's value?
A. By using a voltmeter
B. By using the resistor's color code
C. By using Thevenin's theorem for resistors
D. By using the Baudot code

T6A04
What do the first three color bands on a resistor indicate?
A. The value of the resistor in ohms
B. The resistance tolerance in percent
C. The power rating in watts
D. The resistance material

T6A05
What does the fourth color band on a resistor indicate?
A. The value of the resistor in ohms
B. The resistance tolerance in percent
C. The power rating in watts
D. The resistance material

T6A03
How do you find a resistor's tolerance rating?
A. By using a voltmeter
B. By reading the resistor's color code
C. By using Thevenin's theorem for resistors
D. By reading its Baudot code

T6A10
Which tolerance rating would a high-quality resistor have?
A. 0.1%
B. 5%
C. 10%
D. 20%

T6A11
Which tolerance rating would a low-quality resistor have?
A. 0.1%
B. 5%
C. 10%
D. 20%

T6A08
What are the possible values of a 100-ohm resistor with a 10% tolerance?
A. 90 to 100 ohms
B. 10 to 100 ohms
C. 90 to 110 ohms
D. 80 to 120 ohms

T6A06
Why do resistors sometimes get hot when in use?
A. Some electrical energy passing through them is lost as heat
B. Their reactance makes them heat up
C. Hotter circuit components nearby heat them up
D. They absorb magnetic energy which makes them hot

T6A07
Why would a large size resistor be used instead of a smaller one of the same resistance?
A. For better response time
B. For a higher current gain
C. For greater power dissipation
D. For less impedance in the circuit

T6A02
What does a variable resistor or potentiometer do?
A. Its resistance changes when AC is applied to it
B. It transforms a variable voltage into a constant voltage
C. Its resistance changes when its slide or contact is moved
D. Its resistance changes when it is heated

END OF TECHNICIAN LESSON 29!

PREVIOUS QUIZ ANSWERS
T5B01 - D
T5B11 - A
T5B04 - C
T5B02 - C
T5B10 - A
T5B08 - D
T5B09 - A
T5B07 - B
T5B03 - B
T5B05 - D
T5B06 - D

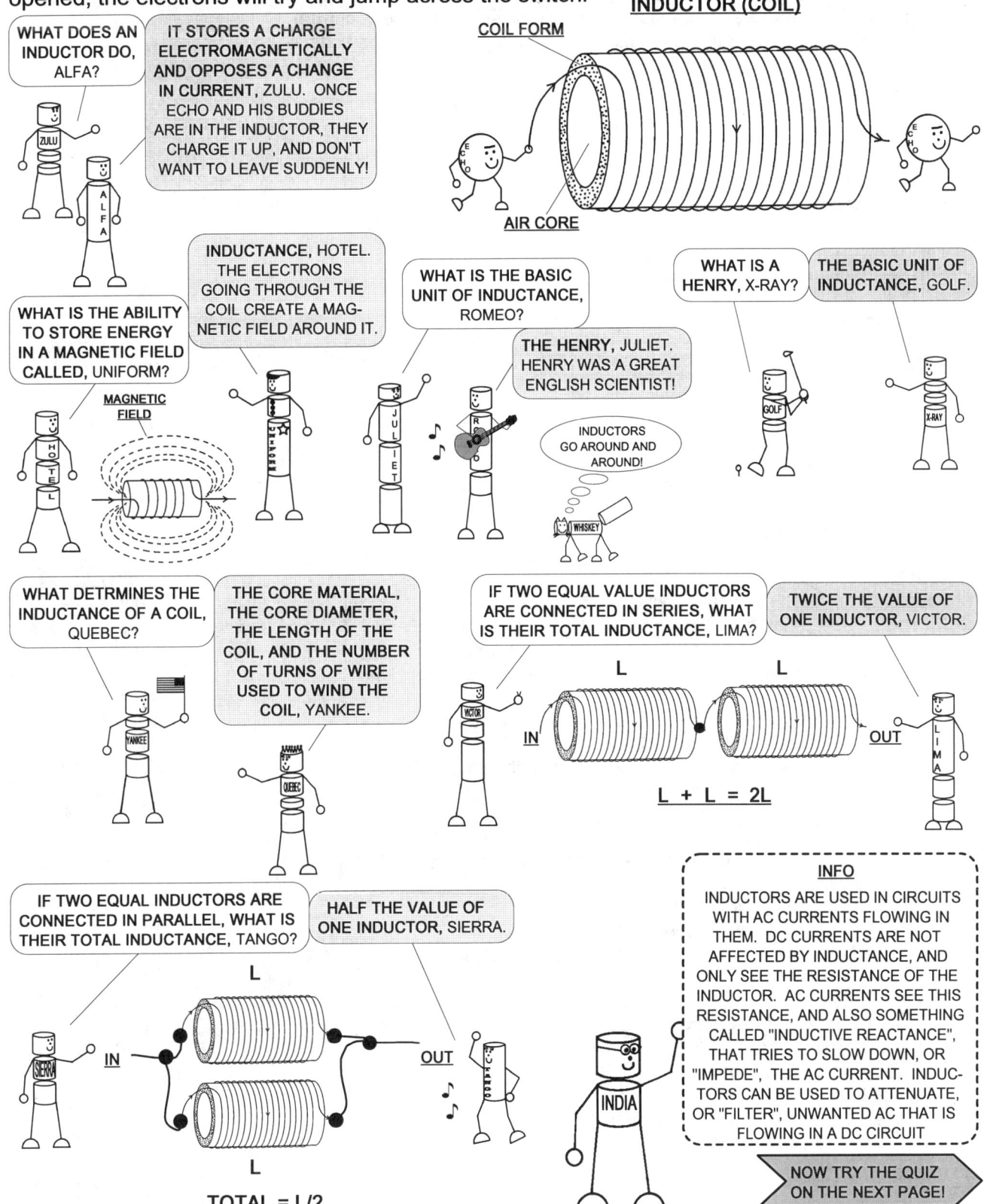

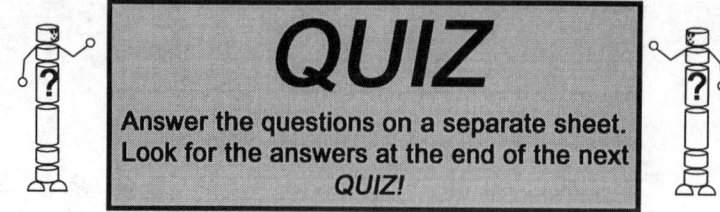

T6B02
What does an inductor do?
A. It stores a charge electrostatically and opposes a change in voltage
B. It stores a charge electrochemically and opposes a change in current
C. It stores a charge electromagnetically and opposes a change in current
D. It stores a charge electromechanically and opposes a change in voltage

T5A02
What is the ability to store energy in a magnetic field called?
A. Admittance
B. Capacitance
C. Resistance
D. Inductance

T5A03
What is the basic unit of inductance?
A. The coulomb
B. The farad
C. The henry
D. The ohm

T5A04
What is a henry?
A. The basic unit of admittance
B. The basic unit of capacitance
C. The basic unit of inductance
D. The basic unit of resistance

T6B03
What determines the inductance of a coil?
A. The core material, the core diameter, the length of the coil and whether the coil is mounted horizontally or vertically
B. The core diameter, the number of turns of wire used to wind the coil and the type of metal used for the wire
C. The core material, the number of turns used to wind the core and the frequency of the current through the coil
D. The core material, the core diameter, the length of the coil and the number of turns of wire used to wind the coil

T5A08
If two equal-value inductors are connected in series, what is their total inductance?
A. Half the value of one inductor
B. Twice the value of one inductor
C. The same as the value of either inductor
D. The value of one inductor times the value of the other

T5A09
If two equal-value inductors are connected in parallel, what is their total inductance?
A. Half the value of one inductor
B. Twice the value of one inductor
C. The same as the value of either inductor
D. The value of one inductor times the value of the other

PREVIOUS QUIZ ANSWERS
T5A01 - D
T6A01 - B
T6A09 - B
T6A04 - A
T6A05 - B
T6A03 - B
T6A10 - A
T6A11 - D
T6A08 - C
T6A08 - A
T6A07 - C
T6A02 - C

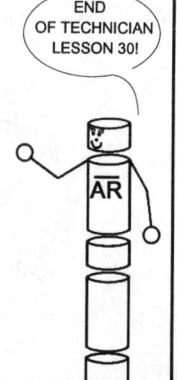

END OF TECHNICIAN LESSON 30!

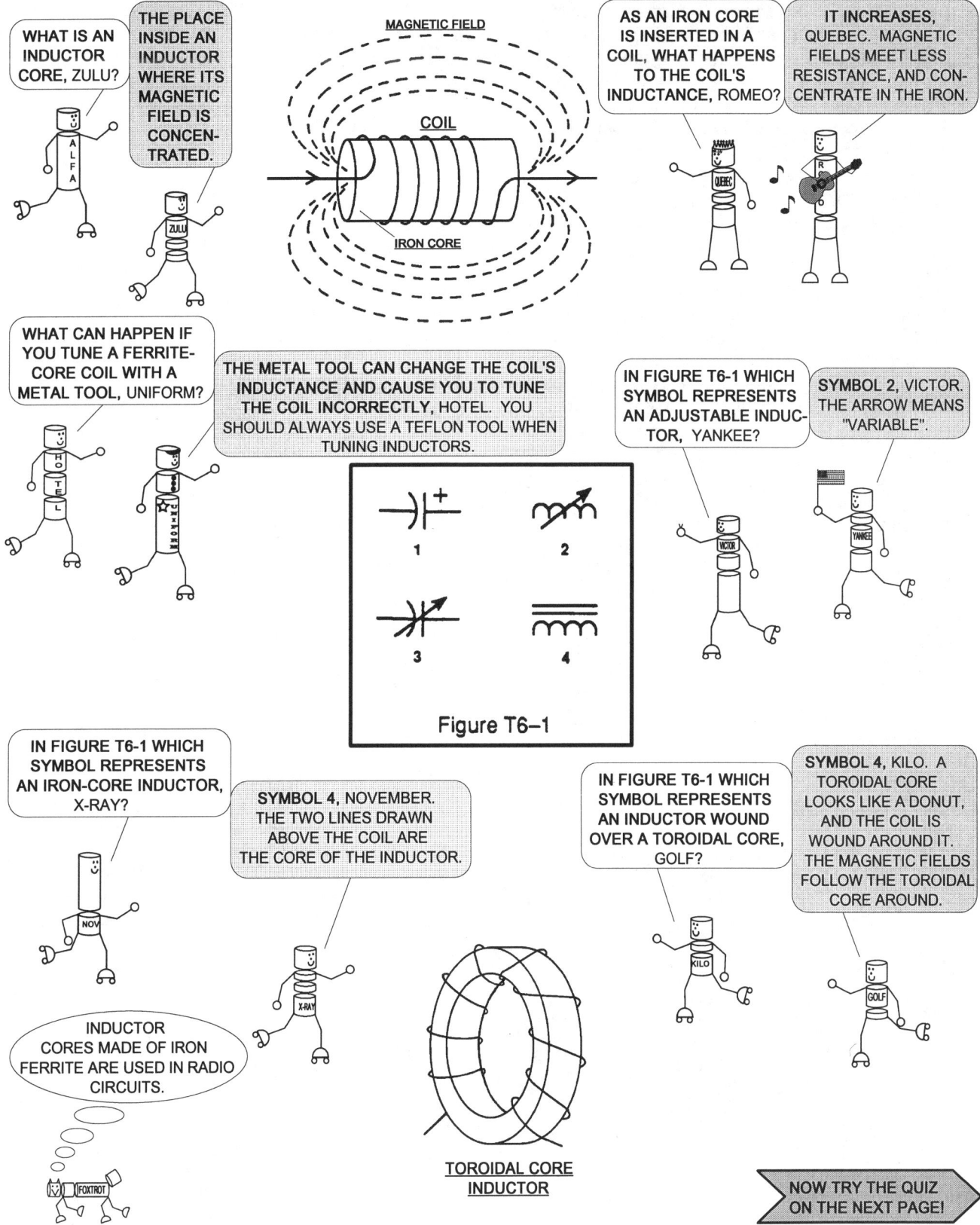

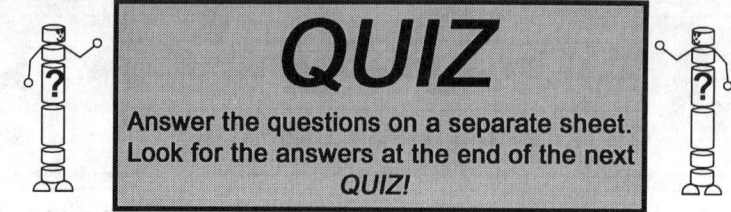

QUIZ
Answer the questions on a separate sheet. Look for the answers at the end of the next QUIZ!

T6B01
What is an inductor core?
A. The place where a coil is tapped for resonance
B. A tight coil of wire used in a transformer
C. Insulating material placed between the wires of a transformer
D. The place inside an inductor where its magnetic field is concentrated

T6B04
As an iron core is inserted in a coil, what happens to the coil's inductance?
A. It increases
B. It decreases
C. It stays the same
D. It disappears

T6B05
What can happen if you tune a ferrite-core coil with a metal tool?
A. The metal tool can change the coil's inductance and cause you to tune the coil incorrectly
B. The metal tool can become magnetized so much that you might not be able to remove it from the coil
C. The metal tool can pick up enough magnetic energy to become very hot
D. The metal tool can pick up enough magnetic energy to become a shock hazard

T6B06
In Figure T6-1 which symbol represents an adjustable inductor?
A. Symbol 1
B. Symbol 2
C. Symbol 3
D. Symbol 4

T6B07
In Figure T6-1 which symbol represents an iron-core inductor?
A. Symbol 1
B. Symbol 2
C. Symbol 3
D. Symbol 4

T6B08
In Figure T6-1 which symbol represents an inductor wound over a toroidal core?
A. Symbol 1
B. Symbol 2
C. Symbol 3
D. Symbol 4

Figure T6-1

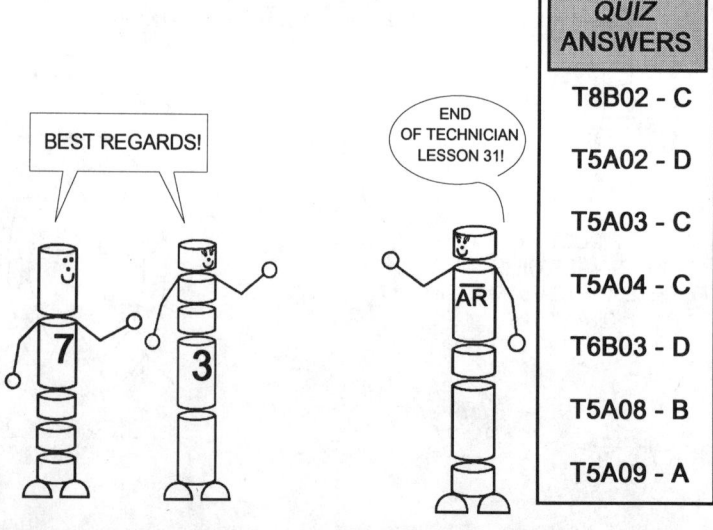

PREVIOUS QUIZ ANSWERS
T8B02 - C
T5A02 - D
T5A03 - C
T5A04 - C
T6B03 - D
T5A08 - B
T5A09 - A

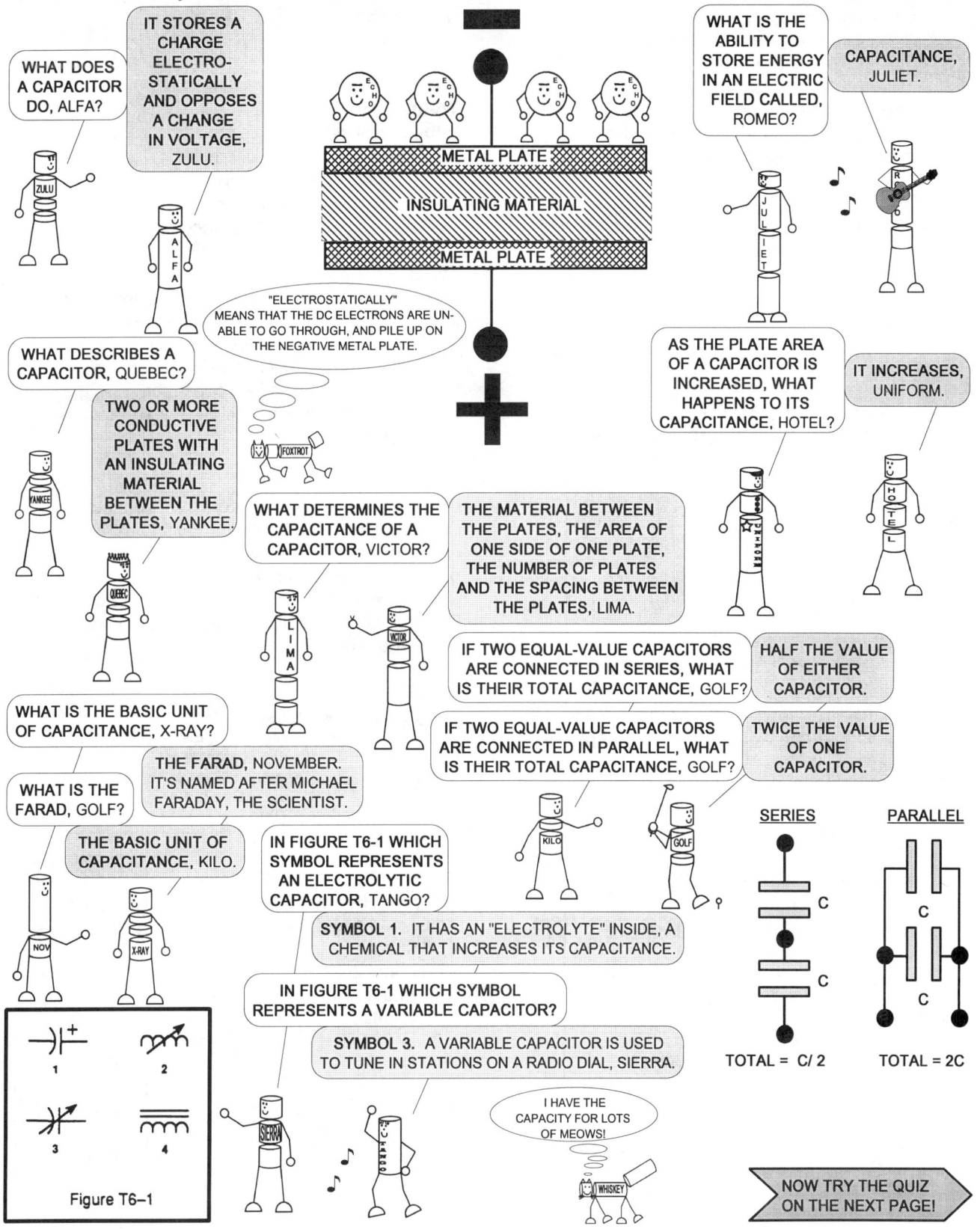

QUIZ

Answer the questions on a separate sheet. Look for the answers at the end of the next QUIZ!

T6B12
What does a capacitor do?
A. It stores a charge electrochemically and opposes a change in current
B. It stores a charge electrostatically and opposes a change in voltage
C. It stores a charge electromagnetically and opposes a change in current
D. It stores a charge electromechanically and opposes a change in voltage

T5A05
What is the ability to store energy in an electric field called?
A. Inductance
B. Resistance
C. Tolerance
D. Capacitance

T6B11
What describes a capacitor?
A. Two or more layers of silicon material with an insulating material between them
B. The wire used in the winding and the core material
C. Two or more conductive plates with an insulating material between them
D. Two or more insulating plates with a conductive material between them

T6B13
What determines the capacitance of a capacitor?
A. The material between the plates, the area of one side of one plate, the number of plates and the spacing between the plates
B. The material between the plates, the number of plates and the size of the wires connected to the plates
C. The number of plates, the spacing between the plates and whether the dielectric material is N type or P type
D. The material between the plates, the area of one plate, the number of plates and the material used for the protective coating

T6B14
As the plate area of a capacitor is increased, what happens to its capacitance?
A. It decreases
B. It increases
C. It stays the same
D. It disappears

T5A06
What is the basic unit of capacitance?
A. The farad
B. The ohm
C. The volt
D. The henry

T5A07
What is a farad?
A. The basic unit of resistance
B. The basic unit of capacitance
C. The basic unit of inductance
D. The basic unit of admittance

T5A10
If two equal-value capacitors are connected in series, what is their total capacitance?
A. Twice the value of one capacitor
B. The same as the value of either capacitor
C. Half the value of either capacitor
D. The value of one capacitor times the value of the other

T5A11
If two equal-value capacitors are connected in parallel, what is their total capacitance?
A. Twice the value of one capacitor
B. Half the value of one capacitor
C. The same as the value of either capacitor
D. The value of one capacitor times the value of the other

T6B09
In Figure T6-1 which symbol represents an electrolytic capacitor?
A. Symbol 1
B. Symbol 2
C. Symbol 3
D. Symbol 4

T6B10
In Figure T6-1 which symbol represents a variable capacitor?
A. Symbol 1
B. Symbol 2
C. Symbol 3
D. Symbol 4

END OF TECHNICIAN LESSON 32!

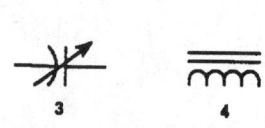

Figure T6-1

PREVIOUS QUIZ ANSWERS
T6B01 - D
T6B04 - A
T6B05 - A
T6B06 - B
T6B07 - D
T6B08 - D

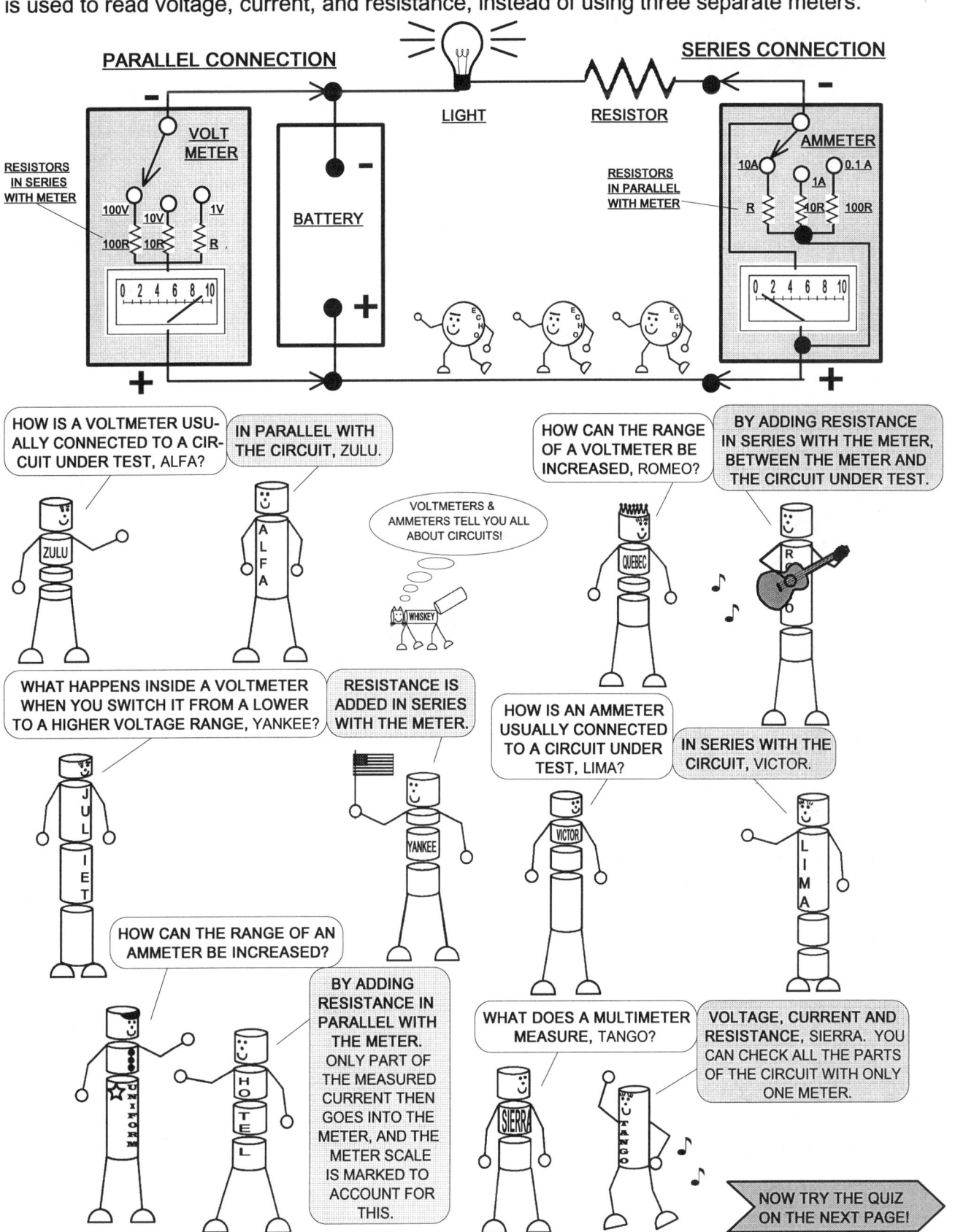

QUIZ

Answer the questions on a separate sheet. Look for the answers at the end of the next QUIZ!

SEE PAGE 91 FOR REVIEW.

T4B01
How is a voltmeter usually connected to a circuit under test?
A. In series with the circuit
B. In parallel with the circuit
C. In quadrature with the circuit
D. In phase with the circuit

T4B02
How can the range of a voltmeter be increased?
A. By adding resistance in series with the circuit under test
B. By adding resistance in parallel with the circuit under test
C. By adding resistance in series with the meter, between the meter and the circuit under test
D. By adding resistance in parallel with the meter, between the meter and the circuit under test

T4B03
What happens inside a voltmeter when you switch it from a lower to a higher voltage range?
A. Resistance is added in series with the meter
B. Resistance is added in parallel with the meter
C. Resistance is reduced in series with the meter
D. Resistance is reduced in parallel with the meter

T4B04
How is an ammeter usually connected to a circuit under test?
A. In series with the circuit
B. In parallel with the circuit
C. In quadrature with the circuit
D. In phase with the circuit

T4B05
How can the range of an ammeter be increased?
A. By adding resistance in series with the circuit under test
B. By adding resistance in parallel with the circuit under test
C. By adding resistance in series with the meter
D. By adding resistance in parallel with the meter

T4B06
What does a multimeter measure?
A. SWR and power
B. Resistance, capacitance and inductance
C. Resistance and reactance
D. Voltage, current and resistance

METERS ARE VERY USEFUL IN TELLING YOU HOW YOUR EQUIPMENT IS OPERATING. A MULTIMETER IS HANDY AROUND THE SHACK!

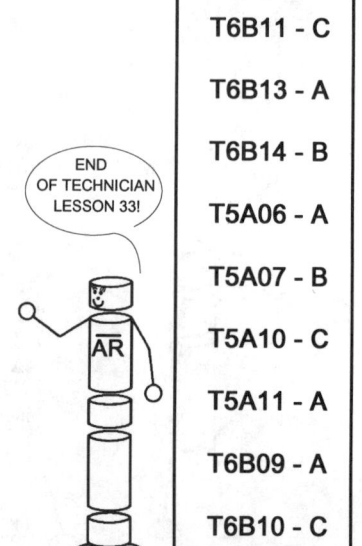

END OF TECHNICIAN LESSON 33!

PREVIOUS QUIZ ANSWERS

T6B12 - B
T5A05 - D
T6B11 - C
T6B13 - A
T6B14 - B
T5A06 - A
T5A07 - B
T5A10 - C
T5A11 - A
T6B09 - A
T6B10 - C

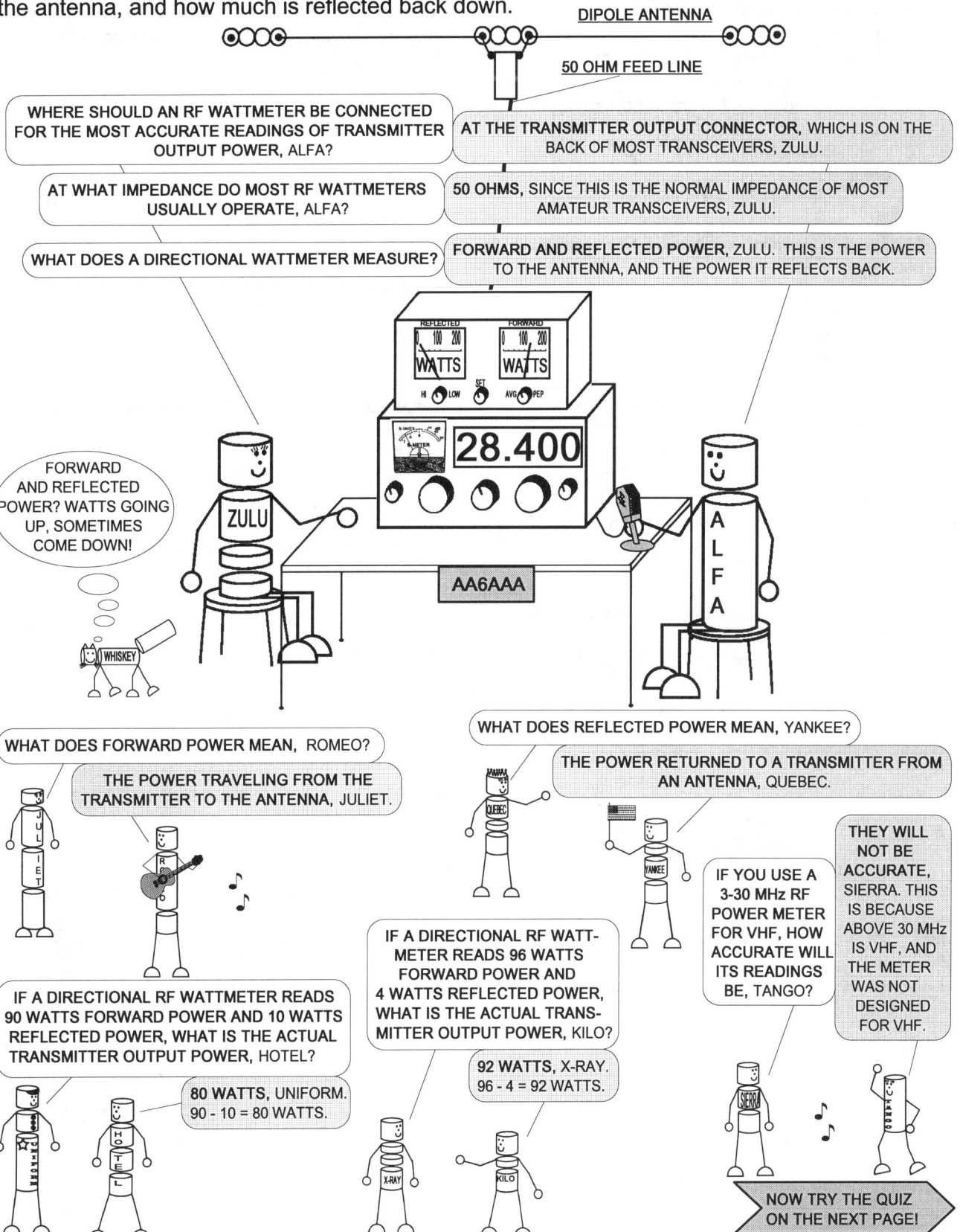

QUIZ

Answer the questions on a separate sheet. Look for the answers at the end of the next QUIZ!

SEE PAGES 91 & 115 FOR REVIEW.

T4B07
Where should an RF wattmeter be connected for the most accurate readings of transmitter output power?
A. At the transmitter output connector
B. At the antenna feed point
C. One-half wavelength from the transmitter output
D. One-half wavelength from the antenna feed point

T4B08
At what line impedance do most RF wattmeters usually operate?
A. 25 ohms
B. 50 ohms
C. 100 ohms
D. 300 ohms

T4B09
What does a directional wattmeter measure?
A. Forward and reflected power
B. The directional pattern of an antenna
C. The energy used by a transmitter
D. Thermal heating in a load resistor

T9B07
What does forward power mean?
A. The power traveling from the transmitter to the antenna
B. The power radiated from the top of an antenna system
C. The power produced during the positive half of an RF cycle
D. The power used to drive a linear amplifier

T9B08
What does reflected power mean?
A. The power radiated down to the ground from an antenna
B. The power returned to a transmitter from an antenna
C. The power produced during the negative half of an RF cycle
D. The power returned to an antenna by buildings and trees

T4B10
If a directional RF wattmeter reads 90 watts forward power and 10 watts reflected power, what is the actual transmitter output power?
A. 10 watts
B. 80 watts
C. 90 watts
D. 100 watts

T4B11
If a directional RF wattmeter reads 96 watts forward power and 4 watts reflected power, what is the actual transmitter output power?
A. 80 watts
B. 88 watts
C. 92 watts
D. 100 watts

T4C10
If you use a 3-30 MHz RF power meter for VHF, how accurate will its readings be?
A. They will not be accurate
B. They will be accurate enough to get by
C. If it properly calibrates to full scale in the set position, they may be accurate
D. They will be accurate providing the readings are multiplied by 4.5

END OF TECHNICIAN LESSON 34!

BEST REGARDS!

PREVIOUS QUIZ ANSWERS

T4B01 - B
T4B02 - C
T4B03 - A
T4B04 - A
T4B05 - D
T4B06 - D

STANDING WAVE RATIO & REFLECTOMETERS
TECHNICIAN LESSON 35

Standing wave ratio (SWR) is a simple measurement that tells you if your antenna is matched to the frequency your transceiver is operating on. Another meter, called a "reflectometer", is more complicated, and can tell you exact detail about the "impedance" match to your antenna.

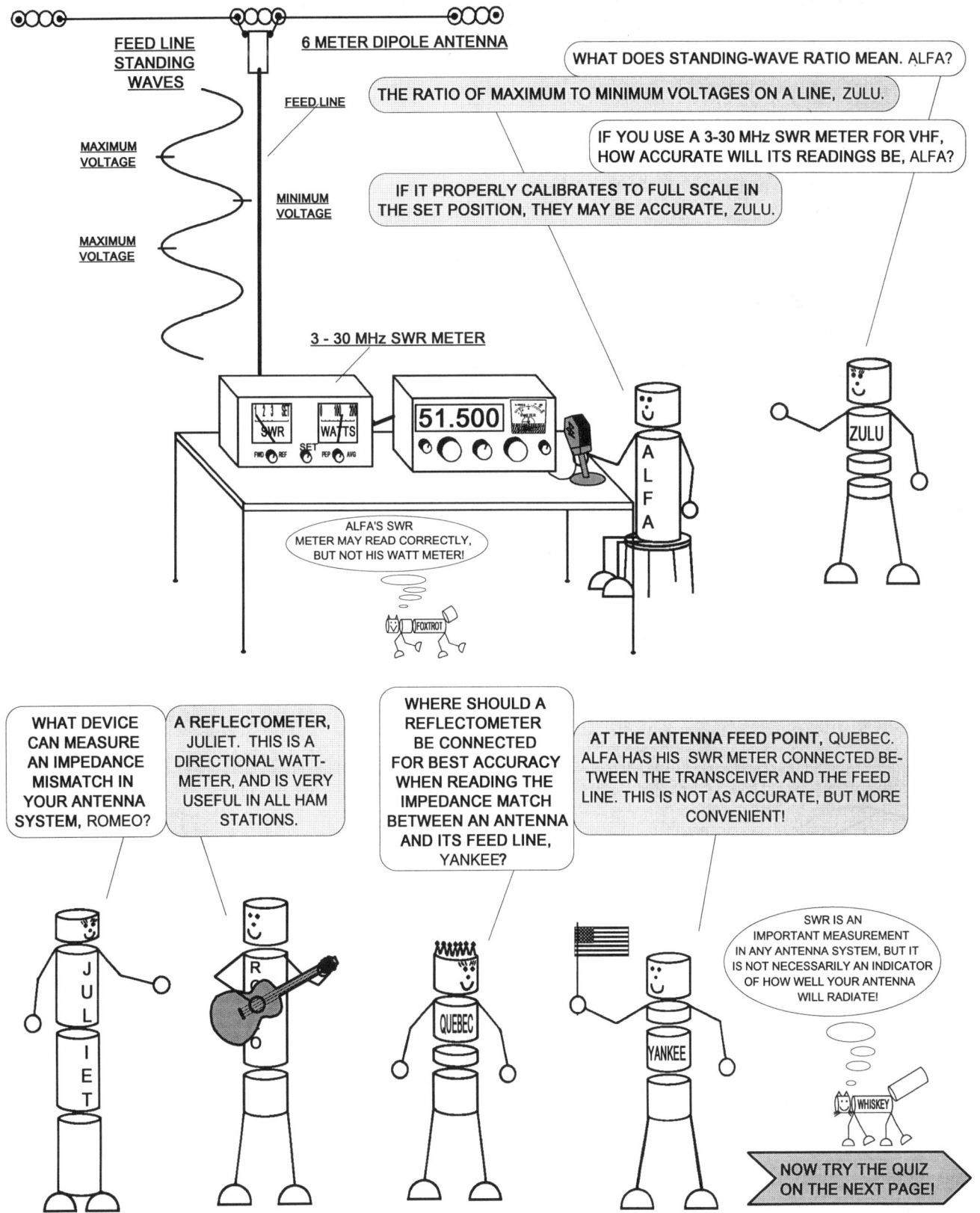

QUIZ

Answer the questions on a separate sheet. Look for the answers at the end of the next QUIZ!

SEE PAGES 113 & 115 FOR REVIEW.

T9B06
What does standing-wave ratio mean?
A. The ratio of maximum to minimum inductances on a feed line
B. The ratio of maximum to minimum resistances on a feed line
C. The ratio of maximum to minimum impedances on a feed line
D. The ratio of maximum to minimum voltages on a feed line

T4C11
If you use a 3-30 MHz SWR meter for VHF, how accurate will its readings be?
A. They will not be accurate
B. They will be accurate enough to get by
C. If it properly calibrates to full scale in the set position, they may be accurate
D. They will be accurate providing the readings are multiplied by 4.5

T4C08
What device can measure an impedance mismatch in your antenna system?
A. A field-strength meter
B. An ammeter
C. A wavemeter
D. A reflectometer

T4C09
Where should a reflectometer be connected for best accuracy when reading the impedance match between an antenna and its feed line?
A. At the antenna feed point
B. At the transmitter output connector
C. At the midpoint of the feed line
D. Anywhere along the feed line

PREVIOUS QUIZ ANSWERS

T4B07 - A
T4B08 - B
T4B09 - A
T9B07 - A
T9B08 - B
T4B10 - B
T4B11 - C
T4C10 - A

END OF TECHNICIAN LESSON 35!

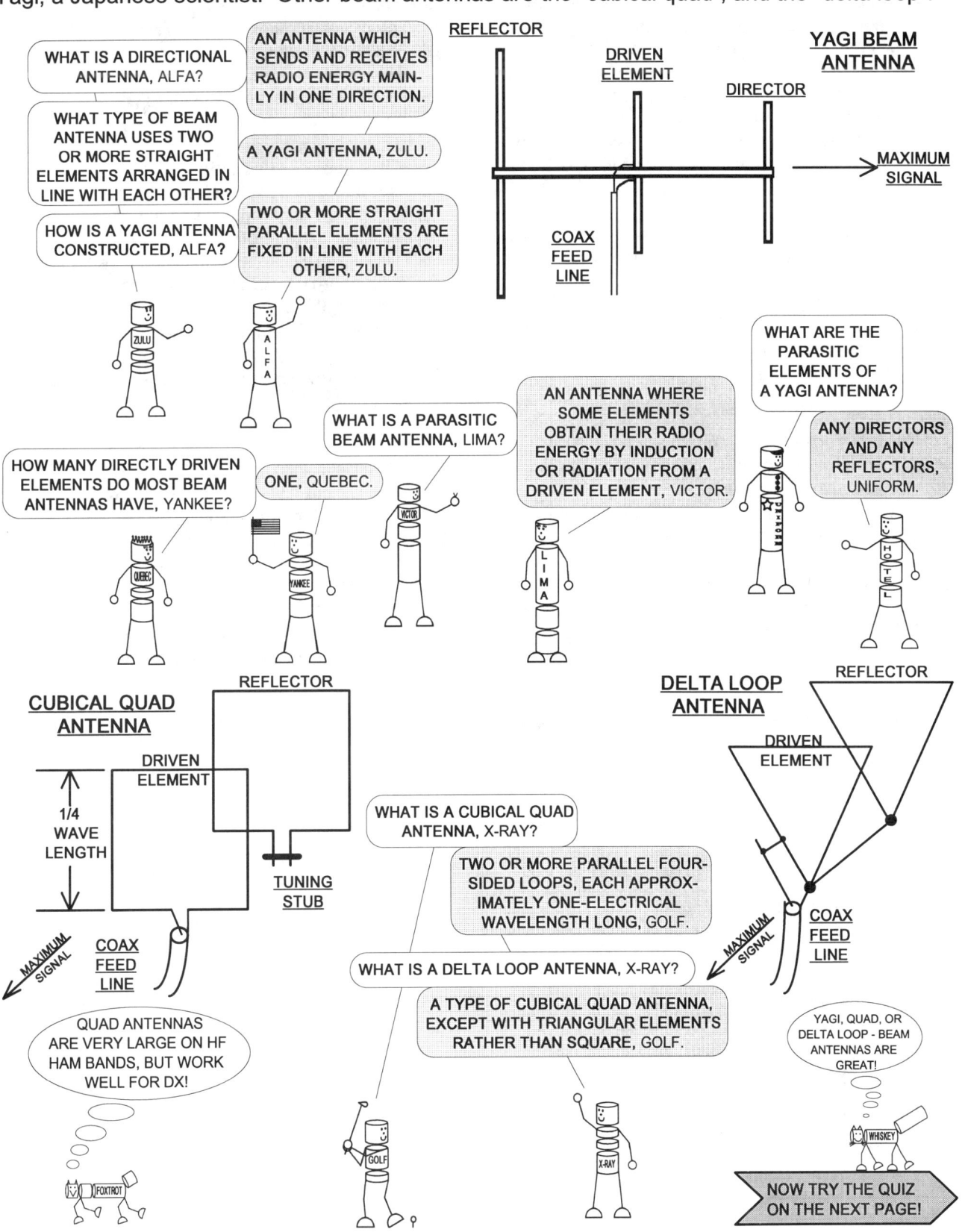

QUIZ

Answer the questions on a separate sheet. Look for the answers at the end of the next QUIZ!

SEE PAGE 127 FOR REVIEW.

T9A01
What is a directional antenna?
A. An antenna which sends and receives radio energy equally well in all directions
B. An antenna that cannot send and receive radio energy by skywave or skip propagation
C. An antenna which sends and receives radio energy mainly in one direction
D. An antenna which sends and receives radio energy equally well in two opposite directions

T9A03
What type of beam antenna uses two or more straight elements arranged in line with each other?
A. A delta loop antenna
B. A quad antenna
C. A Yagi antenna
D. A Zepp antenna

T9A02
How is a Yagi antenna constructed?
A. Two or more straight, parallel elements are fixed in line with each other
B. Two or more square or circular loops are fixed in line with each other
C. Two or more square or circular loops are stacked inside each other
D. A straight element is fixed in the center of three or more elements which angle toward the ground

T9A04
How many directly driven elements do most beam antennas have?
A. None
B. One
C. Two
D. Three

T9A05
What is a parasitic beam antenna?
A. An antenna where some elements obtain their radio energy by induction or radiation from a driven element
B. An antenna where wave traps are used to magnetically couple the elements
C. An antenna where all elements are driven by direct connection to the feed line
D. An antenna where the driven element obtains its radio energy by induction or radiation from director elements

T9A06
What are the parasitic elements of a Yagi antenna?
A. The driven element and any reflectors
B. The director and the driven element
C. Only the reflectors (if any)
D. Any directors or any reflectors

T9A07
What is a cubical quad antenna?
A. Four straight, parallel elements in line with each other, each approximately 1/2-electrical wavelength long
B. Two or more parallel four-sided wire loops, each approximately one-electricaL wavelength long
C. A vertical conductor 1/4-electrical wavelength high, fed at the bottom
D. A center-fed wire 1/2-electrical wavelength long

T9A08
What is a delta loop antenna?
A. A type of cubical quad antenna, except with triangular elements rather than square
B. A large copper ring or wire loop, used in direction finding
C. An antenna system made of three vertical antennas, arranged in a triangular shape
D. An antenna made from several triangular coils of wire on an insulating form

END OF TECHNICIAN LESSON 36!

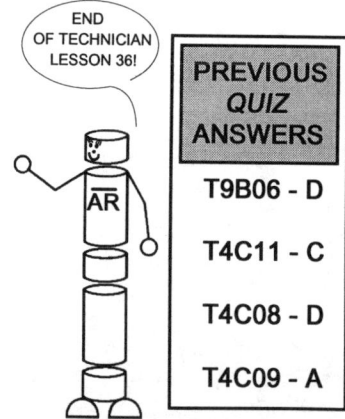

PREVIOUS QUIZ ANSWERS

T9B06 - D

T4C11 - C

T4C08 - D

T4C09 - A

NON-DIRECTIONAL ANTENNAS & POLARIZATION
TECHNICIAN LESSON 37

Non-directional antennas let you contact stations in any direction. They are usually vertically mounted, instead of horizontally. Vertical "polarization" picks up more noise than horizontal polarization, but has many advantages.

GROUND PLANE VERTICAL ANTENNA (with coaxial feed line)

- **WHAT TYPE OF NON-DIRECTIONAL ANTENNA IS EASY TO MAKE AT HOME AND WORKS WELL OUTDOORS, ALFA?**
  - A GROUND PLANE, ZULU. THIS IS A VERTICAL ANTENNA WITH ITS OWN GROUND SYSTEM UNDERNEATH IT.

- **WHAT TYPE OF ANTENNA IS MADE WHEN A MAGNETIC-BASE WHIP ANTENNA IS PLACED ON THE ROOF OF A CAR, ALFA?**
  - A GROUND PLANE, ZULU. THE ROOF ACTS AS A GROUND SYSTEM.

- **IF A MAGNETIC-BASE WHIP ANTENNA IS PLACED ON THE ROOF OF A CAR, IN WHAT DIRECTION DOES IT SEND OUT RADIO ENERGY, ALFA?**
  - IT GOES OUT EQUALLY WELL IN ALL HORIZONTAL DIRECTIONS, ZULU.

MAGNET-BASE MOUNTED VERTICAL

- **WHAT DOES VERTICAL WAVE POLARIZATION MEAN, ROMEO?**
  - THE ELECTRIC LINES OF FORCE OF A RADIO WAVE ARE PERPENDICULAR TO THE EARTH'S SURFACE.

- **WHAT ELECTROMAGNETIC-WAVE POLARIZATION DOES A HALF-WAVELENGTH ANTENNA HAVE WHEN IT IS PERPENDICULAR TO THE EARTHS SURFACE, LIMA?**
  - VERTICAL, VICTOR.

- **WHAT ELECTROMAGNETIC-WAVE POLARIZATION DOES MOST MAN-MADE ELECTRICAL NOISE HAVE IN THE HF AND VHF SPECTRUM, HOTEL?**
  - VERTICAL, UNIFORM.

- **WHAT ELECTROMAGNETIC-WAVE POLARIZATION DOES A YAGI ANTENNA HAVE WHEN ITS ELEMENTS ARE PARALLEL TO THE EARTH'S SURFACE, GOLF?**
  - HORIZONTAL, KILO.

HORIZONTAL YAGI BEAM ANTENNA

- **WHAT DOES HORIZONTAL WAVE POLARIZATION MEAN, X-RAY?**
  - THE ELECTRIC LINES OF FORCE OF A RADIO WAVE ARE PARALLEL TO THE EARTH'S SURFACE, NOVEMBER.

- HORIZONTAL POLARIZATION IS USED ON VHF & UHF CW AND SSB. VERTICAL POLARIZATION IS USED ON VHF & UHF FM. (FOXTROT)

- HORIZONTAL OR VERTICAL, RADIO WAVES GO ON FOREVER! (WHISKEY)

NOW TRY THE QUIZ ON THE NEXT PAGE!

QUIZ

Answer the questions on a separate sheet. Look for the answers at the end of the next QUIZ!

SEE PAGE 129 FOR REVIEW.

T9A09
What type of non-directional antenna is easy to make at home and works well outdoors?
A. A Yagi
B. A delta loop
C. A cubical quad
D. A ground plane

T9A10
What type of antenna is made when a magnetic-base whip antenna is placed on the roof of a car?
A. A Yagi
B. A delta loop
C. A cubical quad
D. A ground plane

T9A11
If a magnetic-base whip antenna is placed on the roof of a car, in what direction does it send out radio energy?
A. It goes out equally well in all horizontal directions
B. Most of it goes in one direction
C. Most of it goes equally in two opposite directions
D. Most of it is aimed high into the air

T9B02
What does vertical wave polarization mean?
A. The electric lines of force of a radio wave are parallel to the earth's surface
B. The magnetic lines of force of a radio wave are perpendicular to the earth's surface
C. The electric lines of force of a radio wave are perpendicular to the earth's surface
D. The electric and magnetic lines of force of a radio wave are parallel to the earth's surface

T9B04
What electromagnetic-wave polarization does a half-wavelength antenna have when it is perpendicular to the earth's surface?
A. Circular
B. Horizontal
C. Parabolical
D. Vertical

T9B05
What electromagnetic-wave polarization does most man-made electrical noise have in the HF and VHF spectrum?
A. Horizontal
B. Left-hand circular
C. Right-hand circular
D. Vertical

T9B03
What electromagnetic-wave polarization does a Yagi antenna have when its elements are parallel to the earth's surface?
A. Circular
B. Helical
C. Horizontal
D. Vertical

T9B01
What does horizontal wave polarization mean?
A. The magnetic lines of force of a radio wave are parallel to the earth's surface
B. The electric lines of force of a radio wave are parallel to the earth's surface
C. The electric lines of force of a radio wave are perpendicular to the earth's surface
D. The electric and magnetic lines of force of a radio wave are perpendicular to the earth's surface

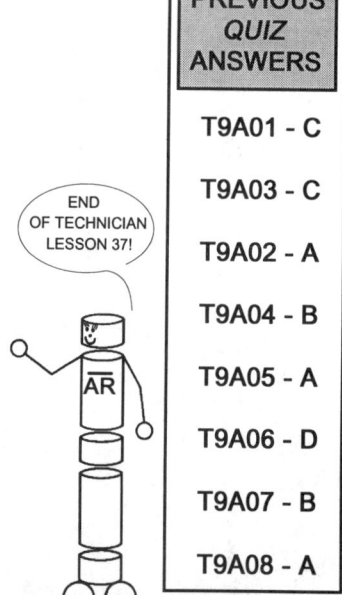

END OF TECHNICIAN LESSON 37!

PREVIOUS QUIZ ANSWERS
T9A01 - C
T9A03 - C
T9A02 - A
T9A04 - B
T9A05 - A
T9A06 - D
T9A07 - B
T9A08 - A

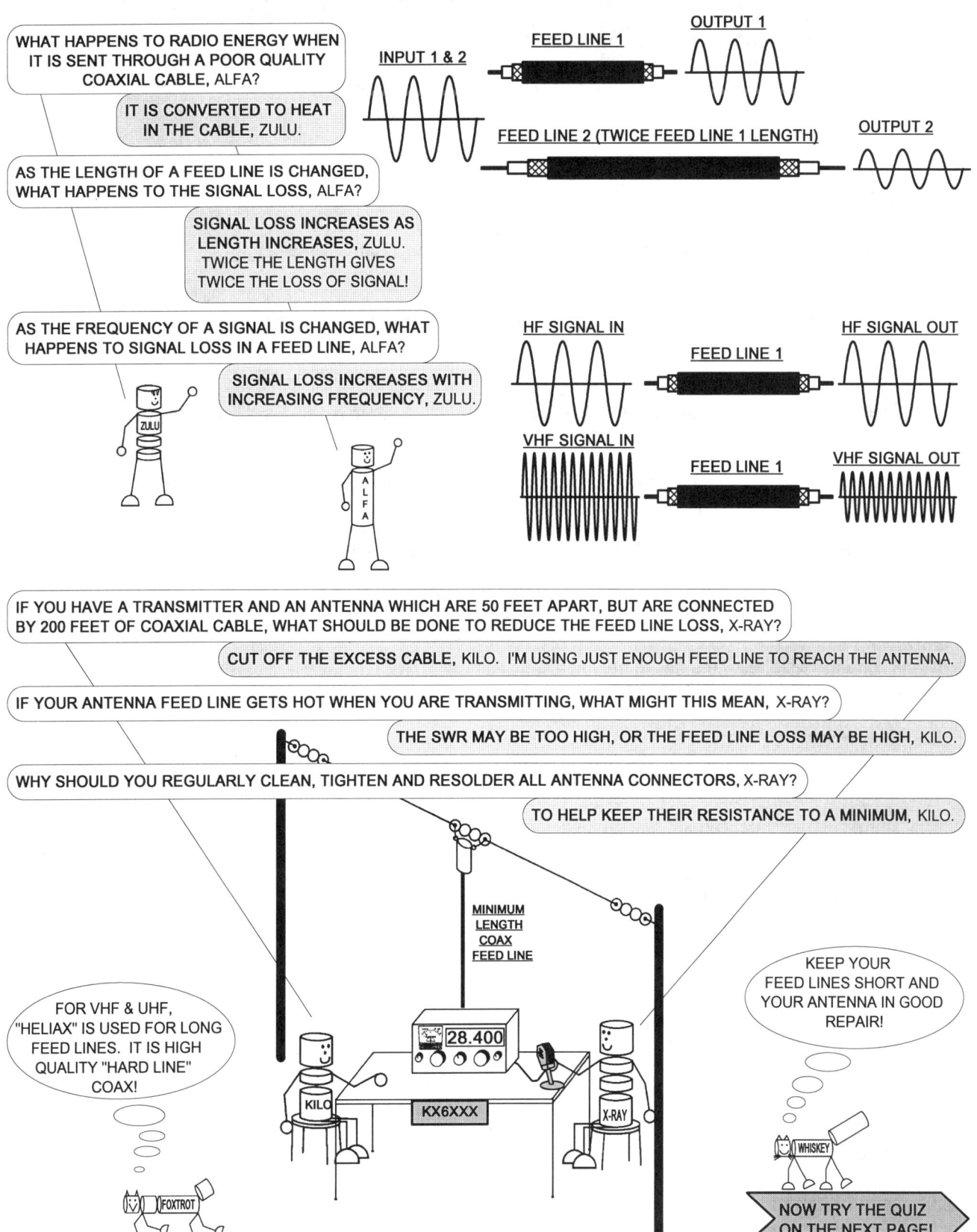

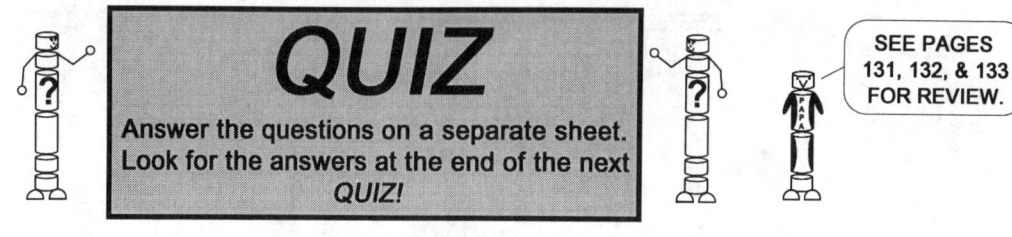

QUIZ
Answer the questions on a separate sheet.
Look for the answers at the end of the next QUIZ!

SEE PAGES 131, 132, & 133 FOR REVIEW.

T9B09
What happens to radio energy when it is sent through a poor quality coaxial cable?
A. It causes spurious emissions
B. It is returned to the transmitter's chassis ground
C. It is converted to heat in the cable
D. It causes interference to other stations near the transmitting frequency

T9C06
As the length of a feed line is changed, what happens to signal loss?
A. Signal loss is the same for any length of feed line
B. Signal loss increases as length increases
C. Signal loss decreases as length increases
D. Signal loss is the least when the length is the same as the signal's wavelength

T9C07
As the frequency of a signal is changed, what happens to signal loss in a feed line?
A. Signal loss is the same for any frequency
B. Signal loss increases with increasing frequency
C. Signal loss increases with decreasing frequency
D. Signal loss is the least when the signal's wavelength is the same as the feed line's length

T9C05
If you have a transmitter and an antenna which are 50 feet apart, but are connected by 200 feet of RG-58 coaxial cable, what should be done to reduce feed line loss?
A. Cut off the excess cable so the feed line is an even number of wavelengths long
B. Cut off the excess cable so the feed line is an odd number of wavelengths long
C. Cut off the excess cable
D. Roll the excess cable into a coil which is as small as possible

T9C08
If your antenna feed line gets hot when you are transmitting, what might this mean?
A. You should transmit using less power
B. The conductors in the feed line are not insulated very well
C. The feed line is too long
D. The SWR may be too high, or the feed line loss may be high

T9C11
Why should you regularly clean, tighten and re-solder all antenna connectors?
A. To help keep their resistance at a minimum
B. To keep them looking nice
C. To keep them from getting stuck in place
D. To increase their capacitance

PREVIOUS QUIZ ANSWERS
T9A09 - D
T9A10 - D
T9A11 - A
T9B02 - C
T9B04 - D
T9B05 - D
T9B03 - C
T9B01 - B

COAX FEED LINE IS LIKE GARDEN HOSE. THE SMALLER THE DIAMETER AND THE LONGER THE LENGTH, THE LOWER THE AMOUNT OF WATER AT THE END OF THE HOSE. HOLES IN THE HOSE MAKE IT "LOSSY", LIKE COAX FEED LINE!

END OF TECHNICIAN LESSON 38!

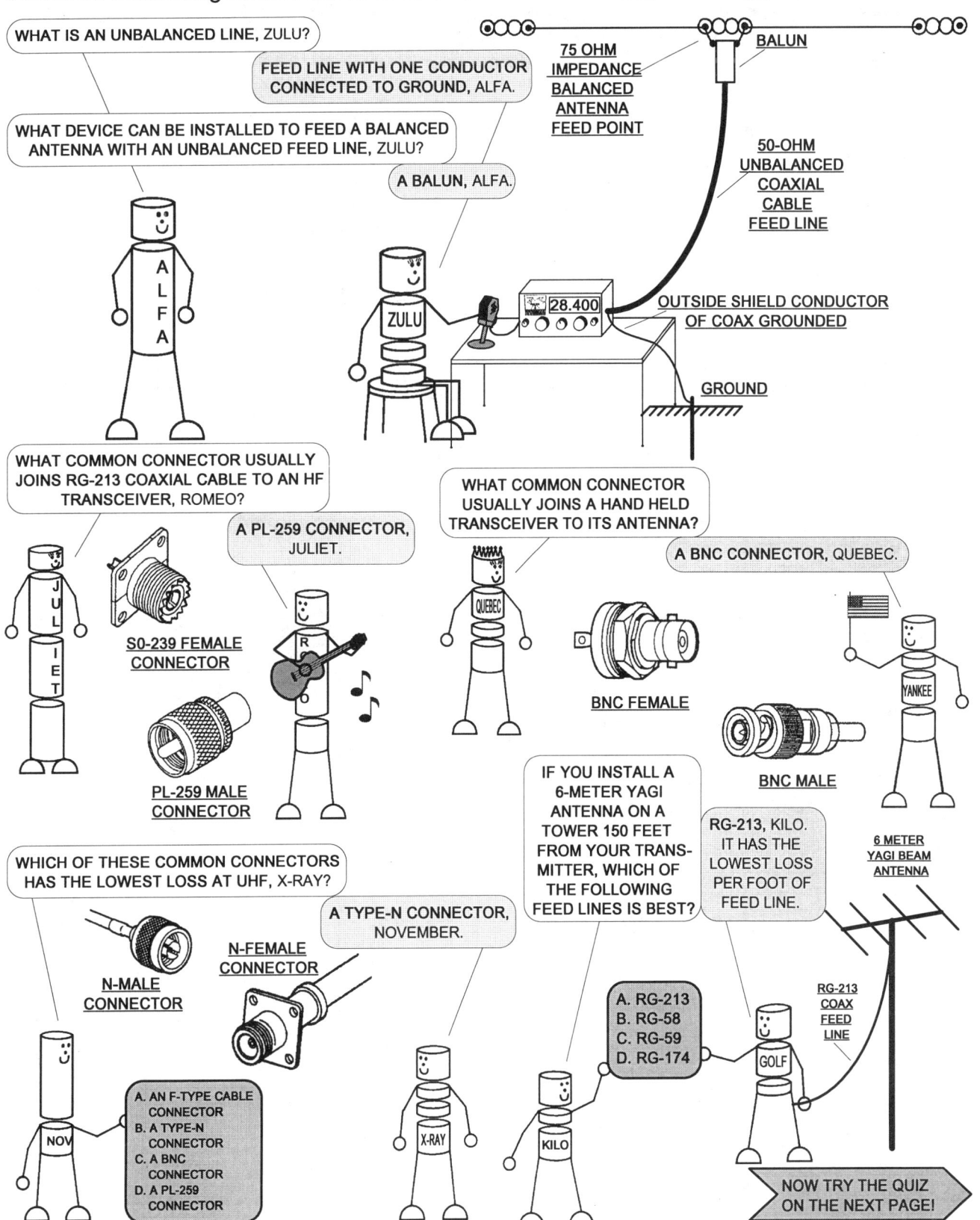

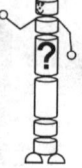

QUIZ

Answer the questions on a separate sheet. Look for the answers at the end of the next QUIZ!

SEE PAGES 131, 132, & 133 FOR REVIEW.

T9B10
What is an unbalanced line?
A. Feed line with neither conductor connected to ground
B. Feed line with both conductors connected to ground
C. Feed line with one conductor connected to ground
D. Feed line with both conductors connected to each other

T9B11
What device can be installed to feed a balanced antenna with an unbalanced feed line?
A. A balun
B. A loading coil
C. A triaxial transformer
D. A wavetrap

T9C01
What common connector usually joins RG-213 coaxial cable to an HF transceiver?
A. An F-type cable connector
B. A PL-259 connector
C. A banana plug connector
D. A binding post connector

T9C02
What common connector usually joins a hand held transceiver to its antenna?
A. A BNC connector
B. A PL-259 connector
C. An F-type cable connector
D. A binding post connector

T9C03
Which of these common connectors has the lowest loss at UHF?
A. An F-type cable connector
B. A type-N connector
C. A BNC connector
D. A PL-259 connector

T9C04
If you install a 6-meter Yagi antenna on a tower 150 feet from your transmitter, which of the following feed lines is best?
A. RG-213
B. RG-58
C. RG-59
D. RG-174

RG-213 COAX HAS A LOSS OF 2.2 dB PER HUNDRED FEET AT 100 MHz. HOWEVER, RG-8/U IS ANOTHER 50 OHM COAX THAT CAN BE PURCHASED, AS BELDEN #9913, THAT ONLY HAS 1.4 dB LOSS PER HUNDRED FEET AT 100 MHz!

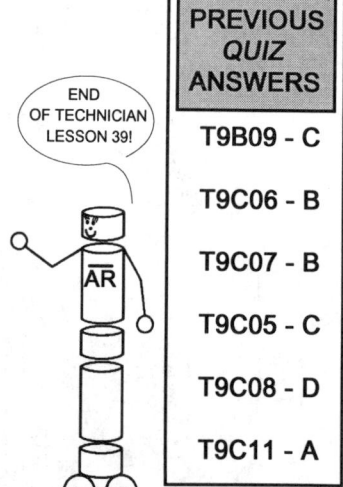

END OF TECHNICIAN LESSON 39!

PREVIOUS QUIZ ANSWERS

T9B09 - C

T9C06 - B

T9C07 - B

T9C05 - C

T9C08 - D

T9C11 - A

HEALTH RISK & ANTENNA LOCATION
TECHNICIAN LESSON 40

In order to avoid both RF radiation and possible skin burns, energized antennas and unshielded equipment should be kept at a safe distance.

HOW CAN EXPOSURE TO A LARGE AMOUNT OF RF ENERGY AFFECT BODY TISSUE, ZULU?

IT HEATS THE TISSUE, ALFA. THIS IS WHAT HAPPENS INSIDE A MICROWAVE OVEN.

WHICH BODY ORGAN IS THE MOST LIKELY TO BE DAMAGED FROM THE HEATING EFFECTS OF RF RADIATION, ZULU?

EYES, ALFA.

MICROWAVE OVEN — RADIATION — HEAVY SHIELDING

WHAT ORGANIZATION HAS PUBLISHED SAFETY GUIDELINES FOR THE MAXIMUM LIMITS OF RF ENERGY NEAR THE HUMAN BODY, ROMEO?

THE AMERICAN NATIONAL STANDARDS INSTITUTE (ANSI), JULIET.

WHAT IS THE PURPOSE OF THE ANSI RF PROTECTION GUIDE, YANKEE?

IT GIVES RF EXPOSURE LIMITS FOR THE HUMAN BODY, QUEBEC.

ACCORDING TO THE ANSI PROTECTION GUIDE, WHAT FREQUENCIES CAUSE US THE GREATEST RISK FROM RF ENERGY, LIMA?

30 TO 300 MHz, VICTOR. THIS IS THE VHF REGION.

WHY IS THE LIMIT OF EXPOSURE TO RF THE LOWEST IN THE FREQUENCY RANGE OF 30 MHz TO 300 MHz, ACCORDING TO THE ANSI RF PROTECTION GUIDE?

THE HUMAN BODY ABSORBS RF ENERGY THE MOST IN THIS RANGE, NOVEMBER.

ACCORDING TO THE ANSI RF PROTECTION GUIDE, WHAT IS THE MAXIMUM SAFE POWER OUTPUT TO THE ANTENNA OF A HAND HELD VHF OR UHF RADIO?

7 WATTS, SIERRA.

AFTER YOU HAVE OPENED A VHF POWER AMPLIFIER TO MAKE INTERNAL TUNING ADJUSTMENTS, WHAT SHOULD YOU DO BEFORE YOU TURN THE AMPLIFIER ON?

BE CERTAIN ALL AMPLIFIER SHIELDING IS FASTENED IN PLACE, GOLF.

RADIATION — 145.20 — UNSHIELDED VHF POWER AMPLIFIER

WHY SHOULD YOU MAKE SURE THAT NO ONE CAN TOUCH AN OPEN-WIRE FEED LINE WHILE YOU ARE TRANSMITTING WITH IT, HOTEL?

BECAUSE HIGH-VOLTAGE RADIO ENERGY MIGHT BURN THE PERSON, UNIFORM.

FOR RF SAFETY, WHAT IS THE BEST THING TO DO WITH YOUR TRANSMITTING ANTENNAS, HOTEL?

MOUNT THE ANTENNAS WHERE NO ONE CAN COME NEAR THEM, UNIFORM.

OPEN WIRE FEED LINE

MICROWAVE OVENS OPERATE ON UHF, NEAR 2000 MHz. BE VERY CAREFUL ON HAM BANDS ABOVE 1000 MHz!

NOW TRY THE QUIZ ON THE NEXT PAGE!

QUIZ

Answer the questions on a separate sheet. Look for the answers at the end of the next QUIZ!

SEE PAGES 137 & 139 FOR REVIEW.

T4D09
How can exposure to a large amount of RF energy affect body tissue?
A. It causes radiation poisoning
B. It heats the tissue
C. It paralyzes the tissue
D. It produces genetic changes in the tissue

T4D10
Which body organ is the most likely to be damaged from the heating effects of RF radiation?
A. Eyes
B. Hands
C. Heart
D. Liver

T4D11
What organization has published safety guidelines for the maximum limits of RF energy near the human body?
A. The Institute of Electrical and Electronics Engineers (IEEE)
B. The Federal Communications Commission (FCC)
C. The Environmental Protection Agency (EPA)
D. The American National Standards Institute (ANSI)

T4D12
What is the purpose of the ANSI RF protection guide?
A. It lists all RF frequency allocations for interference protection
B. It gives RF exposure limits for the human body
C. It sets transmitter power limits for interference protection
D. It sets antenna height limits for aircraft protection

T4D13
According to the ANSI RF protection guide, what frequencies cause us the greatest risk from RF energy?
A. 3 to 30 MHz
B. 300 to 3000 MHz
C. Above 1500 MHz
D. 30 to 300 MHz

T4D14
Why is the limit of exposure to RF the lowest in the frequency range of 30 MHz to 300 MHz, according to the ANSI RF protection guide?
A. There are more transmitters operating in this range
B. There are fewer transmitters operating in this range
C. Most transmissions in this range are for a longer time
D. The human body absorbs RF energy the most in this range

T4D15
According to the ANSI RF protection guide, what is the maximum safe power output to the antenna of a hand held VHF or UHF radio?
A. 125 milliwatts
B. 7 watts
C. 10 watts
D. 25 watts

T4D16
After you have opened a VHF power amplifier to make internal tuning adjustments, what should you do before you turn the amplifier on?
A. Remove all amplifier shielding to ensure maximum cooling
B. Make sure that the power interlock switch is bypassed so you can test the amplifier
C. Be certain all amplifier shielding is fastened in place
D. Be certain no antenna is attached so that you will not cause any interference

T9C09
Why should you make sure that no one can touch an open-wire feed line while you are transmitting with it?
A. Because contact might cause a short circuit and damage the transmitter
B. Because contact might break the feed line
C. Because contact might cause spurious emissions
D. Because high-voltage radio energy might burn the person

T9C10
For RF safety, what is the best thing to do with your transmitting antennas?
A. Use vertical polarization
B. Use horizontal polarization
C. Mount the antennas where no one can come near them
D. Mount the antenna close to the ground

END OF TECHNICIAN LESSON 40!

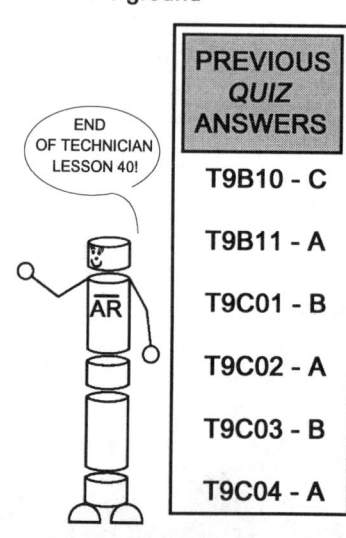

PREVIOUS QUIZ ANSWERS

T9B10 - C
T9B11 - A
T9C01 - B
T9C02 - A
T9C03 - B
T9C04 - A

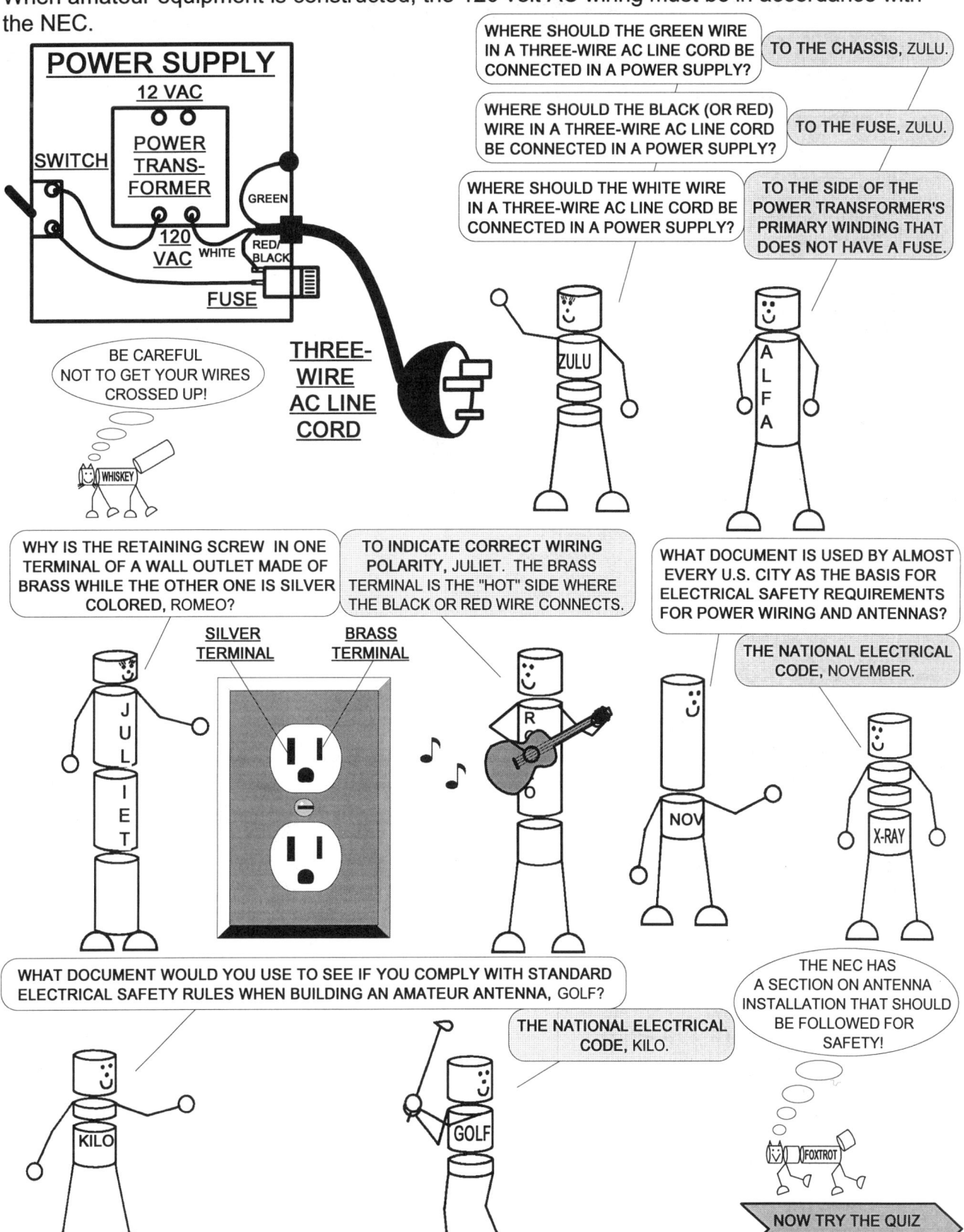

QUIZ

Answer the questions on a separate sheet. Look for the answers at the end of the next QUIZ!

SEE PAGES 139 & 140 FOR REVIEW.

T4A01
Where should the green wire in a three-wire AC line cord be connected in a power supply?
A. To the fuse
B. To the "hot" side of the power switch
C. To the chassis
D. To the white wire

T4A02
Where should the black (or red) wire in a three-wire AC line cord be connected in a power supply?
A. To the white wire
B. To the green wire
C. To the chassis
D. To the fuse

T4A03
Where should the white wire in a three-wire AC line cord be connected in a power supply?
A. To the side of the power transformer's primary winding that has a fuse
B. To the side of the power transformer's primary winding that does not have a fuse
C. To the chassis
D. To the black wire

T4A07
Why is the retaining screw in one terminal of a wall outlet made of brass while the other one is silver colored?
A. To prevent corrosion
B. To indicate correct wiring polarity
C. To better conduct current
D. To reduce skin effect

T4A04
What document is used by almost every US city as the basis for electrical safety requirements for power wiring and antennas?
A. The Code of Federal Regulations
B. The Proceedings of the IEEE
C. The ITU Radio Regulations
D. The National Electrical Code

T4A05
What document would you use to see if you comply with standard electrical safety rules when building an amateur antenna?
A. The Code of Federal Regulations
B. The Proceedings of the IEEE
C. The National Electrical Code
D. The ITU Radio Regulations

PREVIOUS QUIZ ANSWERS

T4D09 - B
T4D10 - A
T4D11 - D
T4D12 - B
T4D13 - D
T4D14 - D
T4D15 - B
T4D16 - C
T9C09 - D
T9C10 - C

END OF TECHNICIAN LESSON 41!

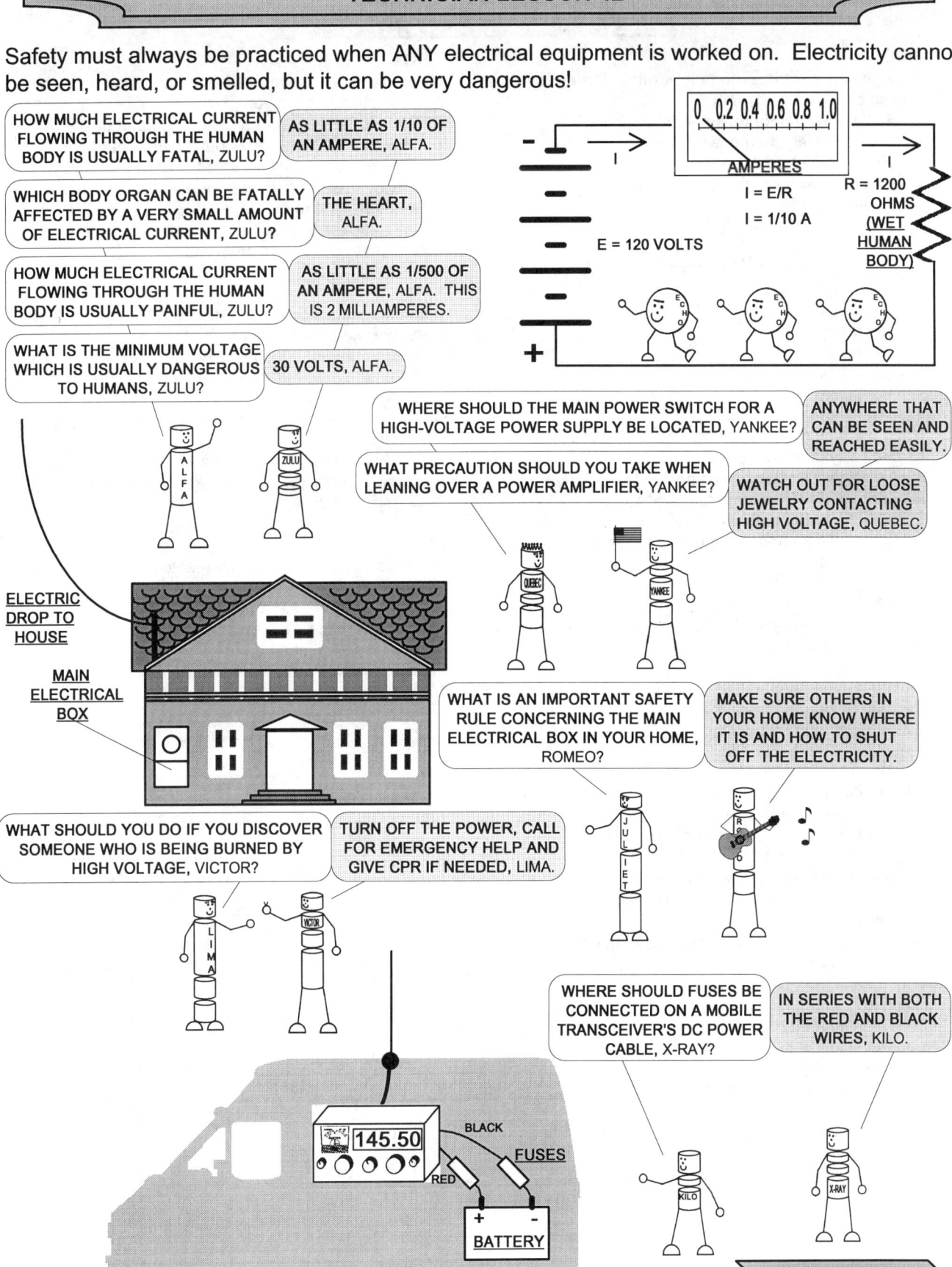

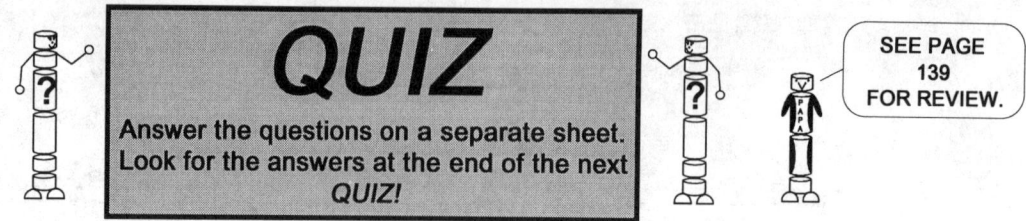

T4A08
How much electrical current flowing through the human body is usually fatal?
A. As little as 1/10 of an ampere
B. Approximately 10 amperes
C. More than 20 amperes
D. Current flow through the human body is never fatal

T4A09
Which body organ can be fatally affected by a very small amount of electrical current?
A. The heart
B. The brain
C. The liver
D. The lungs

T4A10
How much electrical current flowing through the human body is usually painful?
A. As little as 1/500 of an ampere
B. Approximately 10 amperes
C. More than 20 amperes
D. Current flow through the human body is never painful

T4A11
What is the minimum voltage which is usually dangerous to humans?
A. 30 volts
B. 100 volts
C. 1000 volts
D. 2000 volts

T4A12
Where should the main power switch for a high-voltage power supply be located?
A. Inside the cabinet, to kill the power if the cabinet is opened
B. On the back side of the cabinet, out of sight
C. Anywhere that can be seen and reached easily
D. A high voltage power supply should not be switch-operated

T4A13
What precaution should you take when leaning over a power amplifier?
A. Take your shoes off
B. Watch out for loose jewelry contacting high voltage
C. Shield your face from the heat produced by the power supply
D. Watch out for sharp edges which may snag your clothing

T4A14
What is an important safety rule concerning the main electrical box in your home?
A. Make sure the door cannot be opened easily
B. Make sure something is placed in front of the door so no one will be able to get to it easily
C. Make sure others in your home know where it is and how to shut off the electricity
D. Warn others in your home never to touch the switches, even in an emergency

T4A15
What should you do if you discover someone who is being burned by high voltage?
A. Run from the area so you won't be burned too
B. Turn off the power, call for emergency help and give CPR if needed
C. Immediately drag the person away from the high voltage
D. Wait for a few minutes to see if the person can get away from the high voltage on their own, then try to help

T4A06
Where should fuses be connected on a mobile transceiver's DC power cable?
A. Between the red and black wires
B. In series with just the black wire
C. In series with just the red wire
D. In series with both the red and black wires

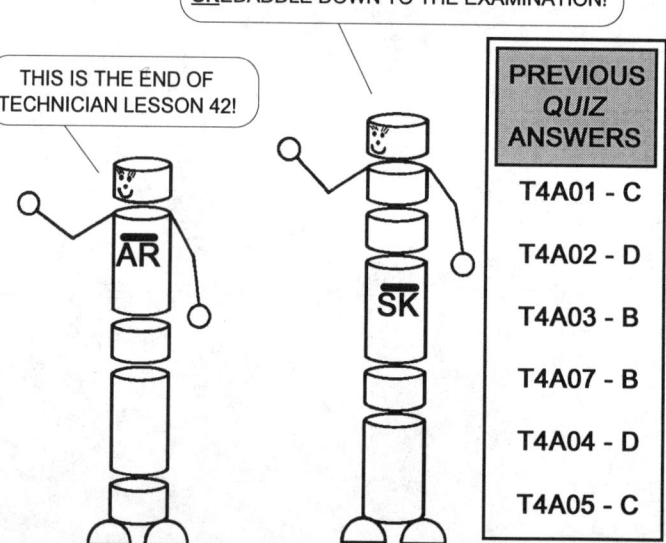

PREVIOUS QUIZ ANSWERS

T4A01 - C
T4A02 - D
T4A03 - B
T4A07 - B
T4A04 - D
T4A05 - C

III. BINARY NUMBERS & QUESTION INDEX
BINARY NUMBERS

Computers operate using millions of transistors, switching "off" and "on", at very high frequency. "Off" and "on" are represented by "0" and "1" in the computer, and a combination of these 0's and 1's becomes a computer "word". Each word represents a number, but in order to represent all numbers, beginning with "0", powers of "2" are assigned to each 0 or 1 in the computer word. This is where the word "binary" comes from, since binary means "something made of **2** things".

$1 \times 2^3 = 1 \times 2 \times 2 \times 2 = 8$

$1 \times 2^2 = 1 \times 2 \times 2 = 4$

$1 \times 2^1 = 1 \times 2 = 2$

$1 \times 2^0 = 1 \times 1 = \underline{1}$

15

$1 \times 2^3 = 1 \times 2 \times 2 \times 2 = 8$

$0 \times 2^2 = 0 \times 2 \times 2 = 0$

$1 \times 2^1 = 1 \times 2 = 2$

$0 \times 2^0 = 0 \times 1 = \underline{0}$

10

FILL IN THE BLANKS FOR THE BINARYOS BELOW!

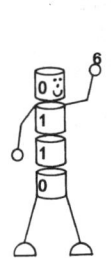

$\_ \times 2^3 = \_ \times 2 \times 2 \times 2 = \_$

$\_ \times 2^2 = \_ \times 2 \times 2 = \_$

$\_ \times 2^1 = \_ \times 2 = \_$

$\_ \times 2^0 = \_ \times 1 = \_\_$

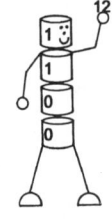

$\_ \times 2^3 = \_ \times 2 \times 2 \times 2 = \_$

$\_ \times 2^2 = \_ \times 2 \times 2 = \_$

$\_ \times 2^1 = \_ \times 2 = \_$

$\_ \times 2^0 = \_ \times 1 = \_\_$

$\_ \times 2^3 = \_ \times 2 \times 2 \times 2 = \_$

$\_ \times 2^2 = \_ \times 2 \times 2 = \_$

$\_ \times 2^1 = \_ \times 2 = \_$

$\_ \times 2^0 = \_ \times 1 = \_\_$

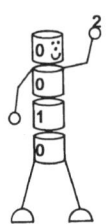

$\_ \times 2^3 = \_ \times 2 \times 2 \times 2 = \_$

$\_ \times 2^2 = \_ \times 2 \times 2 = \_$

$\_ \times 2^1 = \_ \times 2 = \_$

$\_ \times 2^0 = \_ \times 1 = \_\_$

CREATE YOUR OWN TESTS!

Using the Question Index on pages 241 through 243, select 30 Novice, or 25 Technician questions, which begin with the following letter/number prefixes. The number next to the question letter/number prefix, is the number of questions from this group that should be selected:

NOVICE	TECHNICIAN
N1 - 10	T1 - 5
N2 - 2	T2 - 3
N3 - 1	T3 - 3
N4 - 4	T4 - 4
N5 - 4	T5 - 2
N6 - 2	T6 - 2
N7 - 2	T7 - 1
N8 - 2	T8 - 2
N9 - 3	T9 - 3
30	25

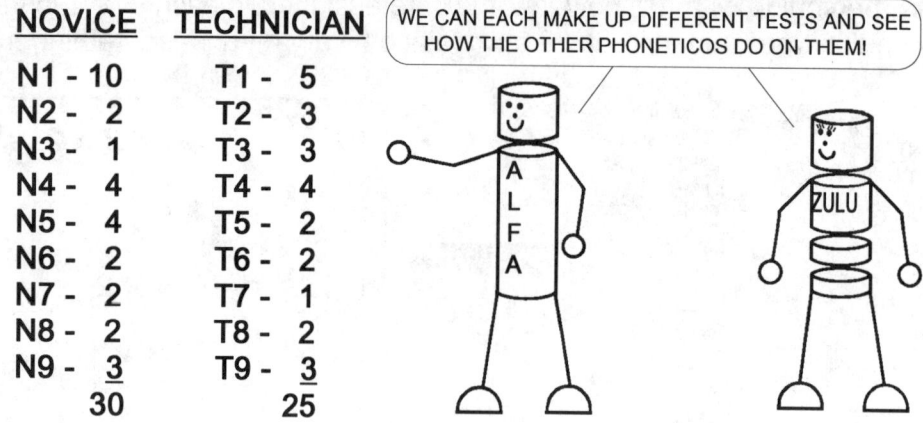

WE CAN EACH MAKE UP DIFFERENT TESTS AND SEE HOW THE OTHER PHONETICOS DO ON THEM!

Example: For the Novice Element 2 examination, select ten N1 questions, two N2 questions, one N3 question, etc., for a total of 30 questions. On a separate piece of paper, write down the question numbers, and the number of the page that the questions are on. <u>Do not write the answers!</u> Go to the page number in the book, of each question you have selected, and write down your answer letter. When you have finished, check your answer letters against the answers in the Question Index. If you miss a question, read the lesson for that question again. Create more tests, and watch how your scores improve! Passing is 74%, which means 23 out of 30 Novice questions, and 19 out of 25 Technician questions, correct.

SAMPLE NOVICE EXAMINATION

N1A03 - 12	N2A07 - 50	N6A07 - 94
N1B04 - 16	N2B12 - 44	N6B04 - 100
N1C11 - 72	N3A03 - 84	N7A03 - 118
N1D10 - 22	N4A03 - 32	N7B07 - 54
N1E11 - 74	N4B10 - 138	N8A05 - 56
N1F07 - 80	N4C07 - 116	N8B08 - 112
N1G05 - 26	N4D03 - 104	N9A08 - 126
N1H08 - 10	N5A04 - 92	N9B03 - 128
N1I04 - 30	N5B06 - 86	N9C09 - 134
N1J08 - 24	N5C09 - 90	
	N5D11 - 60	

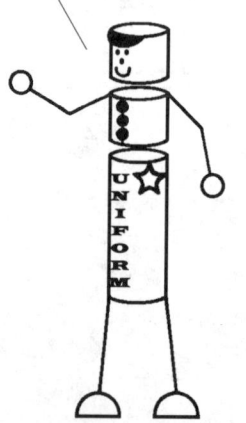

NOTICE THAT EACH LETTER/PREFIX GROUP, HAS THE SAME NUMBER OF SUB-GROUPS, THAT THERE ARE QUESTIONS FROM THAT GROUP. THERE ARE 10 QUESTIONS FROM LETTER/PREFIX GROUP N1, AND THERE ARE 10 SUB-GROUPS, A. B. C. D. E. F. G. H. I, & J. <u>YOU MUST PICK ONE QUESTION FROM EACH QUESTION INDEX SUB-GROUP!</u>

PREVIOUS QUIZ ANSWERS

T4A08 - A
T4A09 - A
T4A10 - A
T4A11 - A
T4A12 - C
T4A13 - B
T4A14 - C
T4A15 - B
T4A06 - D

QUESTION INDEX

Question Number-Answer-Page Number

N1A	N1D	N1G	N2A	N3A	N4D
01-A-12	07-C-20	10-A-26	03-C-42	09-C-82	01-C-104
02-B-12	08-B-20	11-B-26	04-D-24	10-A-82	02-B-104
03-A-12	09-D-20		05-B-50	11-A-82	03-C-104
04-D-12	10-C-22	N1H	06-B-50	12-C-82	04-D-106
05-A-12	11-A-22	01-D-30	07-C-50		05-B-104
06-D-12		02-C-30	08-D-5	N4A	06-B-106
07-B-14	N1E	-	09-A-50	01-B-32	07-A-106
08-C-14	01-A-70	-	10-A-50	02-A-32	08-A-106
09-D-14	02-A-70	-	11-B-5	03-A-32	09-A-106
10-C-14	03-A-70	06-C-10	12-B-5	04-D-144	10-C-110
11-C-14	04-D-70	07-B-10	13-C-8	05-C-144	11-A-106
	05-D-70	08-A-10	14-D-8	06-D-144	
N1B	06-D-70	09-C-10	15-B-8	07-B-142	N5A
01-D-16	07-C-74	10-B-36	16-D-8	08-A-142	01-B-64
02-B-16	08-C-74	11-B-10	17-C-8	09-C-142	02-C-64
03-C-16	09-D-74		18-C-5	10-B-142	03-D-64
04-B-16	10-D-74	N1I	19-D-5	11-C-142	04-B-92
05-C-16	11-D-74	01-A-36	20-A-5		05-C-92
-	-	02-D-36		N4B	06-B-92
07-C-18	13-B-74	03-C-30	N2B	01-B-138	07-B-92
-	14-B-74	04-B-30	01-B-54	02-A-138	08-B-92
09-A-18		05-D-34	02-B-54	03-C-140	09-C-64
-	N1F	06-A-38	03-C-58	04-A-132	10-C-64
11-D-18	01-D-78	07-A-38	04-D-58	05-B-138	11-B-92
	02-C-78	08-C-38	05-A-58	06-D-138	
N1C	03-C-78	09-B-36	06-B-58	07-D-140	N5B
01-B-68	04-C-78	10-A-36	07-A-46	08-D-140	01-D-88
02-C-68	05-C-78	11-D-36	08-B-46	09-D-140	02-C-88
03-A-68	06-C-78		09-C-44	10-A-138	03-B-86
04-C-72	07-B-80	N1J	10-A-44	11-C-140	04-A-86
-	08-A-80	01-B-38	11-D-44		05-A-86
06-C-72	09-A-78	02-B-38	12-A-44	N4C	06-C-86
07-A-68	10-C-80	03-C-38	13-C-46	01-C-114	07-C-88
08-B-68	11-D-80	04-A-40	14-D-46	02-D-114	08-A-88
09-C-68		05-C-40	15-B-46	03-A-114	09-B-88
10-D-72	N1G	06-C-40		04-B-114	10-D-88
11-D-72	01-D-28	07-A-40	N3A	05-C-114	11-D-88
	02-C-26	08-D-24	01-A-84	06-D-114	
N1D	03-A-28	-	02-C-84	07-A-116	N5C
01-A-20	04-D-26		03-B-84	08-A-116	01-A-90
02-D-20	05-C-26	10-C-24	04-C-84	09-B-116	02-C-90
03-C-20	06-B-28	11-B-24	05-D-82	10-C-116	03-B-90
04-B-22	07-A-28		06-B-82	11-A-116	04-A-90
05-D-22	08-B-28	N2A	07-A-82		05-C-76
06-B-22	09-C-26	01-A-42	08-C-82		06-C-76
		02-D-42			07-B-76

241

QUESTION INDEX

Question Number-Answer-Page Number

N5C	N7A	N8B	T1A	T1D	T2B
08-C-90	01-B-120	06-A-110	01-D-162	08-A-174	08-B-152
09-D-90	02-C-118	07-B-112	02-B-162	09-C-190	09-A-152
10-B-60	03-D-118	08-B-112	03-A-162	10-D-190	10-C-152
11-A-60	04-B-118	09-B-112	04-A-162	11-B-190	11-D-152
	05-D-118	10-B-112	05-C-186		
N5D	06-D-118	11-D-112		**T1E**	**T2C**
01-D-60	07-A-102			01-A-164	01-A-156
02-A-60	08-A-120	**N9A**		02-B-164	02-D-156
03-B-62	09-B-120	01-D-122		03-D-164	03-A-156
04-B-62	10-A-120	02-B-124	10-D-186	04-B-166	04-C-160
05-C-62	11-B-120	03-A-122	11-C-186	05-D-166	05-A-160
06-B-62	12-C-102	04-C-122		06-C-166	06-D-160
07-C-62	13-C-102	05-D-124	**T1B**	07-C-164	07-B-160
08-C-66		06-B-124	01-C-192	08-D-164	08-D-156
09-A-66	**N7B**	07-C-122	02-D-192	09-A-162	09-B-156
10-A-66	01-B-48	08-A-126	03-B-192	10-A-156	10-B-157
11-B-60	02-C-48	09-B-126	04-C-188	11-C-156	11-C-157
	03-B-48	10-A-126	05-D-188		12-C-157
N6A	04-C-52	11-B-126	06-C-188	**T2A**	
01-B-96	05-D-52		07-A-154	01-B-170	**T3A**
02-D-96	06-A-54	**N9B**	08-B-188	02-C-170	01-A-200
03-A-94	07-C-54	01-B-128	09-A-188	03-A-170	02-D-200
04-B-94	08-A-56	02-C-128	10-D-192	04-D-170	03-A-200
05-B-94	09-C-56	03-D-128	11-A-188	05-B-170	04-C-200
06-C-94	10-D-54	04-A-128		06-B-170	05-A-202
07-A-94	11-B-56	05-B-128	**T1C**	07-D-170	06-B-202
08-D-94		06-B-128		08-B-171	07-B-200
09-A-96	**N8A**	07-B-130	02-C-184	09-A-171	08-A-202
10-D-96	01-B-48	08-C-130	03-D-184	10-C-171	09-D-200
11-C-96	02-A-54	09-C-130	04-B-182	11-A-174	10-B-200
12-B-96	03-C-48	10-A-138	05-C-182	12-A-176	11-C-200
	04-A-54	11-B-138	06-C-182	13-C-176	
N6B	05-B-56		07-B-182	14-D-176	**T3B**
01-A-98	06-D-52	**N9C**	08-A-184	15-A-166	01-D-202
02-B-98	07-D-48	01-D-132	09-D-182	16-A-174	02-B-202
03-A-100	08-C-48	02-B-132	10-B-184	17-B-166	03-A-202
04-D-100	09-D-48	03-B-132	11-C-184	18-C-171	04-B-202
05-A-100	10-D-102	04-A-132			05-D-204
06-C-100	11-A-52	05-B-136	**T1D**	**T2B**	06-C-204
07-D-98		06-D-136	01-A-190	01-C-176	07-A-204
08-A-98	**N8B**	07-A-136	02-B-154	02-A-176	08-B-204
09-B-98	01-C-108	08-B-136	03-C-154	03-C-176	09-A-204
10-A-98	02-A-108	09-C-134	04-C-154	04-D-174	10-C-204
11-C-98	03-C-108	10-D-134	05-B-190	05-C-152	11-A-204
	04-D-110	11-A-134	06-A-174	06-A-152	
	05-D-110		07-D-174	07-B-152	

QUESTION INDEX

Question Number-Answer-Page Number

T3C	T4C	T5B	T8A	T9B
01-C-208	05-C-198	08-D-210	01-B-178	09-C-230
02-C-208	06-C-198	09-A-210	02-C-178	10-C-232
03-B-208	07-B-198	10-A-210	03-B-178	11-A-232
04-C-206	08-D-224	11-A-210	04-B-178	
05-A-206	09-A-224		05-D-178	T9C
06-D-206	10-A-222	T6A	06-D-180	01-B-232
07-B-206	11-C-224	01-B-212	07-A-180	02-A-232
08-D-206		02-C-212	08-A-180	03-B-232
09-D-208	T4D	03-B-212	09-D-180	04-A-232
10-A-206	01-D-168	04-A-212	10-C-180	05-C-230
11-D-208	02-B-168	05-B-212	11-B-178	06-B-230
	03-C-168	06-A-212		07-B-230
T4A	04-B-168	07-C-212	T8B	08-D-230
01-C-236	05-A-168	08-C-212	01-A-178	09-D-234
02-D-236	06-A-168	09-B-212	02-A-178	10-C-234
03-B-236	07-D-168	10-A-212	03-A-180	11-A-230
04-D-236	08-A-152	11-D-212	04-B-178	
05-C-236	09-B-234		05-C-180	
06-D-238	10-A-234	T6B	06-D-194	
07-B-236	11-D-234	01-D-216	07-C-194	
08-A-238	12-B-234	02-C-214	08-D-194	
09-A-238	13-D-234	03-D-214	09-C-194	
10-A-238	14-D-234	04-A-216	10-B-180	
11-A-238	15-B-234	05-A-216	11-C-180	
12-C-238	16-C-234	06-B-216		
13-B-238		07-D-216	T9A	
14-C-238	T5A	08-D-216	01-C-226	
15-B-238	01-D-212	09-A-218	02-A-226	
	02-D-214	10-C-218	03-C-226	
T4B	03-C-214	11-C-218	04-B-226	
01-B-220	04-C-214	12-B-218	05-A-226	
02-C-220	05-D-218	13-A-218	06-D-226	
03-A-220	06-A-218	14-B-218	07-B-226	
04-A-220	07-B-218		08-A-226	
05-D-220	08-B-214	T7A	09-D-228	
06-D-220	09-A-214	01-C-194	10-D-228	
07-A-222	10-C-218	02-A-194	11-A-228	
08-B-222	11-A-218	03-A-194		
09-A-222		04-C-196	T9B	
10-B-222	T5B	05-D-196	01-B-228	
11-C-222	01-D-210	06-B-196	02-C-228	
	02-C-210	07-D-196	03-C-228	
T4C	03-B-210	08-D-196	04-D-228	
01-A-198	04-C-210	09-B-196	05-D-228	
02-A-198	05-D-210	10-D-196	06-D-224	
03-D-198	06-D-210	11-C-196	07-A-222	
04-B-198	07-B-210		08-B-222	

HAM CROSSWORD PUZZLE

Across

1. A DEVICE FOR STORING STATIC ELECTRIC CHARGE
3. VHF SIGNALS TRAVEL BETWEEN LAYERS OF AIR IN THE TROPOSPHERE
5. SETS STANDARDS FOR RADIATION
6. UNMANNED REMOTE STATION
7. CUBICAL BEAM ANTENNA
9. REFLECTS HF RADIO WAVES
13. 30 TO 300 MHz
14. HF SIGNALS WITH SAME SKIP ZONE
16. MEASURES VOLTS, AMPS, AND OHMS
18. SENDS TIME AND FREQUENCY INFO ON 2.5, 5, 10, 15 & 20 MHz
20. CONNECTS COMPUTERS TO TELEPHONE LINES
22. CONNECTS HAM TRANSCEIVERS TO A COMPUTER
24. FREQUENCY MODULAITON
25. HORIZONTAL OR VERTICAL
27. ATTENUATES HF RADIO WAVES DURING THE DAY
29. SMALLEST DIGITAL QUANTITY
30. MATERIAL USED IN THE CENTER OF AN INDUCTOR
31. OCCURS FROM ANTENNAS
34. MODULATED CW
35. RELAYS PACKET RADIO SIGNALS
38. THE AMOUNT OF SPACE A RADIO SIGNAL TAKES UP
39. EVERY RADIO USES ONE FOR CONVERTING RADIO WAVES
40. CAUSED BY OVER MODULATION
43. FEDERAL COMMUNICATIONS COMMISSION
44. BEAM ANTENNA INVENTED IN JAPAN

Down

2. WAVES ABOVE 20 kHz
3. USES '1'S' & '0'S' TO TRANSMIT DATA
4. A BURST OF DATA SENT OVER THE AIR
8. 300 TO 3000 MHz
10. COMPUTERS CONNECTED TOGETHER
11. RADIO BELOW 30 MHz
12. TUNED TO ONE FREQUENCY
15. MEASURES CURRENT
16. READING COMPUTER DATA NOT DIRECTED TO YOUR STATION
17. THE EARTH'S ATMOSPHERE BELOW THE IONOSPHERE
19. MEASURES VOLTS
21. MILLIONS OF HERTZ
23. TWO DIGITAL STATIONS IN CONTACT
26. SENDING ONE-WAY COMMUNICATIONS
28. STANDING WAVE RATIO
29. SENDS RADIO WAVE STRONGEST IN ONE DIRECTION
32. DIGITAL COMMUNICATION
33. NUMBER OF CYCLES OF A WAVE
36. WIRE WOUND AROND A CORE OR FORM
37. NUMBERS BASED ON 2 INSTEAD OF 10
38. WORD USED TO ENTER A CONTACT OR QSO
41. RADIO TELETYPE
42. RATE OF DATA FLOW

Word List

ABSORPTION
AMMETER
ANSI
BANDWIDTH
BAUD
BEACON
BEAM
BINARY
BIT
BREAK
BROADCASTING
CAPACITOR
CONNECTED
CORE
DATA
DETECTOR
DIGIPEATER
DIGITAL
DUCTING
FCC
FM
HERTZ
HF
INDUCTOR
IONOSPHERE
MCW
MEGAHERTZ
MODEM
MONITORING
MULTIMETER
NETWORK
PACKET
POLARIZATION
QUAD
RADIATION
RADIO
RESONANT
RTTY
SCATTER
SPLATTER
SWR
TNC
TROPOSPHERE
UHF
VHF
VOLTMETER
WWV
YAGI

HERE ARE SOME ADDITIONAL WORDS THAT ARE USED IN HAM RADIO. BY DOING THE PUZZLES IN THIS BOOK, YOU WILL LEARN WHAT THE WORDS THAT HAMS USE ON THE AIR MEAN!

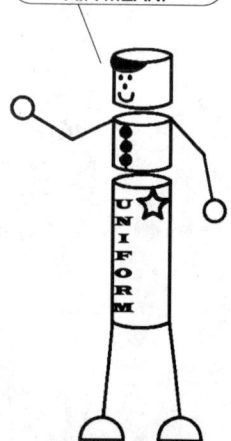